THE DULCE PROT

By

Robert K. Teske

Robert K Teske

THE DULCE PROTOCOL

FOREWORD

(NOTE: The Prophesies of Revelation, Daniel, and Ezekiel are playing out before our eyes today, before the eyes of THIS generation TODAY! In view of the current environmental, social, political, and economical atmosphere that permeates every culture of this world, you must be able to see the BIGGER picture; the entire spectrum, if you will, not just one color. And that spectrum goes far beyond what anyone could have ever perceived possible. It goes beyond science fiction. Hollywood couldn't even have conceived the reality of Hell ON, BENEATH, or ABOVE Earth. But rest assured, they will damned sure try to convince you otherwise. With that said, don't even try to imagine what is between the covers of this manuscript. You have to read it for yourself. There will be many who will discard any and all notion that any of this could remotely be true. Are the words between these cover true? I don't know. I pray to God that they're NOT. But I will tell you this much, I have definitely gone through an Attitude Adjustment, and I have seriously begun to question my concepts of reality. We are living in very dangerous and very treacherous times. So read on and see if any of this makes as much sense to you as it does to me. Open your hearts, open your minds, and question EVERYTHING! – Bob Teske – April, 2012)

NOTE: Sections of THE DULCE PROTOCOL were "Originally published on the Internet as THE DULCE BOOK".

For many years now I have tried to find the original author(s) of the majority of the following material contained within this mindboggling journey that you are about to embark on. But my attempts to locate even just this mysterious "Branton", a.k.a. Bruce Alan DeWalton, or Walton (if that is even his real name), so I could either verify or disprove the majority of this compilation has proven to be a mission in futility. I can understand "Branton's" caution in coming out into the open; too many good people have been martyred trying to bring the truth out into the light. It has only been just recently that I have come out of the shadows. I am an unknown "commodity" in this field, no credentials to speak of, just a rekindled burning desire to shed light on a subject that should have been brought out into the open long ago.

If any of this material is even remotely true, then God help us. Our little tiny blue-green oasis in space is on the verge of a very rude, if not horrifying, awakening as the Prophesies of the Book of Revelation begin unfolding before the eyes of ***this*** generation.

For the most part, some sections of this manuscript can be found scattered throughout the Internet. There is no known copyright information or documentation that I can find. With that being said upfront, I can only assume that the material found within these pages is in the realm of the Public Domain. It is my sincere hope that one day **Branton** and I will finally meet as I believe that he and I may have more in common than what we may believe.

One of the hardest parts of researching this particular field is disseminating the facts from fiction. I have found, though, that when it comes to conspiracy theories, myths and legends, and ufology, if you dig deep enough, you will always find at least one tiny shred of truth that started the whole ball of wax rolling. *ALWAYS!* No matter where you go, or how far back you go, you will always find something that triggers everything else. And when that happens, ***"Hang on to your pantyhose, Dorothy! Kansas is going bye-bye!"***

As I compile and edit this manuscript, I will leave ***Branton's*** commentaries in place while, at the same time, I will be interjecting my own. There will also be a few others under various pseudonyms, to protect their identities.

THE DULCE PROTOCOL

And now, in the words of *John Creighton* ("Farscape: The Peacekeeper Wars" Mini-Series):

> **"We're catching the 7:15 to enlightenment! So, zip up your diaper, Big Boy, the first time is always the roughest!"**

Robert K. "Bob" Teske – April, 2012

# # #

> *"HAVE RESPECT UNTO THE COVENANT, FOR THE DARK PLACES OF THE EARTH ARE FULL OF THE HABITATIONS OF CRUELTY." -- Psalms 74:20*

- What's going on near Dulce, New Mexico?
- Above Top Secret Military-Industrial Black Projects?
- Headquarters for a Bavarian-backed New World Order?
- Vanguard for Alien Infiltration and Invasion?
- Massive Intelligence Agency Disinformation?
- Collective Mind Control or Mass Hallucination?
- All of or a Combination of the Above?

For several decades, researchers of "paranormal phenomena" have devoted themselves to specialized fields of "fringe scientific" investigation. Some of these various fields of 'borderline' research -- which have surfaced in order to document or attempt to explain a wide divergence of phenomena -- have included:

- Aerial or UFO phenomena
- Psychic or Psychotronic investigation
- Cattle and Animal Mutilations
- Vampirism

- Men In Black
- Conspiracies and Assassinations
- Secret Societies
- Underground Anomalies
- Quantum Mechanics
- Legends and Mythology
- Ancient Civilizations
- the 'Mothmen' and other 'Crypto-Zoological' encounters
- Energy Grids and other Geo-Magnetic anomalies
- Biogenetics and Cloning
- Cybernetics and Artificial Intelligence
- Abductions and Missing Time
- Hypnotherapy and Mind Control
- Missing Persons...

There is no doubt many others that I have not mentioned.

In the 1950's, experts in some of these areas of investigation began hearing the first faint hints that 'something' was going on in the American southwest, near the "Four Corners" region of the United States. First these hints and rumors were brief, vague and confusing, yet they sparked enough interest to provoke further investigations as the years passed.

At first these fringe scientists who concerned themselves with the mysteries and anomalies of this region began raising more questions than answers, as they continued to probe into an 'enigma' which seemed to eventually focus itself in and around a small desert town lost amidst the mesas of northwestern New Mexico.

In the late 1970's and early 1980's, the mystery -- and subsequently the interest -- deepened as reports began to slowly emanate from the area suggesting that something significant and horrifying had taken place there, near the small town of Dulce [pronounced "dul-see"], New Mexico. The many different 'phenomena', those previously mentioned, seemed for some strange reason to converge and coagulate into one vast enigmatic scenario of high strangeness in and around this seemingly insignificant and small New Mexican town.

Researchers commenced to analyze and categorize their respective phenomena, looking for patterns and concentrations, and came to the realization that several of these phenomena apparently converged in the American southwest... the charts showed the largest concentrations of UFO sightings -- Northwestern New Mexico; the epicenter of Cattle Mutilation Phenomena - Northwestern New Mexico. Other experts in their fields began to find similar patterns merging and linking with other 'phenomena' at underlying levels.

Researchers into Conspiracies, Secret Societies, Underground Anomalies, Legends and Mythology, Ancient Civilizations, Energy Grids, Geo-Magnetic anomalies, Biogenetics, Abductions and Missing Time, Missing Persons and investigators of other specialized 'vanguard' fields of research began looking toward this small desert town. These unusual convergences of phenomena in a singular locale sparked even more interest and investigation.

From that point on, it was as if some ancient seal had been broken, as if an ancient cloud of darkness had begun imploding in upon itself, broken apart by the piercing light of human perception and the relentless probing's and scrutiny of brave and daring souls.

Sensing that something very wrong and unnatural was going on here, something ancient and evil, some of these brave souls -- who by choice or chance found themselves battling-it-out on the front lines against ancient forces that were determined to keep themselves from being exposed -- continued to wage their all-too-often personal battles against the enigma... some of these inevitably losing their minds if not their very lives in the process.

As these brave souls were worn down by the intensity of this psychic warfare in their efforts to expose and defeat this 'mystery of iniquity' [to coin a Biblical phrase], they sent out desperate calls for 'reinforcements'. Many answered the call, and the ancient and formerly invisible 'beast' that had managed to hide itself below the deserts of the southwest like a dragon in its lair, began to stir in rage and terror at these new exposures, and to lash back at its new-found enemies. The repercussions began to be felt throughout the whole country, through which the beast had reached out its deadly tentacles -- which were also in the process of being exposed along with the black 'heart' of the beast itself.

The walls of the ancient fortress concealing the 'beast' or the 'enigma' began to crumble and fall with increasing intensity. From the murky blackness within, a faint collective cry was 'heard' as if from another world -- the voices of multitudes who were desperately calling out for help to the only ones who could hear them, those who were beginning to 'see' yet had not yet become the slaves of the 'enigma' itself.

Many of 'us' who have continued the battle have sacrificed our comfort, our social and economic welfare, and in some cases even our very lives to fight the Enigma, because we have caught a brief glimpse of the potential threat that "the enemy within" poses to the future of Liberty and to this great Independent nation of America.

What you will see throughout these pages is the collective results of our efforts and -- I'm not ashamed to say -- the results of more than a little Divine Intervention as well. Many of us, such as yours truly, have been 'victimized' by the enigma for the greater part of our lives, and have decided that the only way to be 'free' from its grasp is to practice the old military rule: "The best Defense is a good Offense..."

THE DULCE PROTOCOL

So there you have it. Like those before us, we send this work forth as a warning and a call to arms, to others who value truth and freedom. For those who may not believe everything that follows, I challenge you to become personally involved [however using caution in the event that these collective reports DO turn out to be true] and PROVE the claims made herein point-by-point, one way or another.

This is the challenge that those of us who have contributed to this work leave with you. I remain...

'Branton' – October 1996

Bob Teske – April, 2012

DEDICATION:

To the woman of my 'dreams', whose distant cries have reached me in the night, whoever you are, wherever you are, this 'book' is for you.

THE DULCE PROTOCOL

INTRODUCTION

NOTE:
(Branton – 1996)

I must confess that I have thought very long and hard about the possibility of publishing this text in book format in order to relieve the financial burden upon myself that has resulted from a lifetime of mental and emotional suffering due to my own personal involvement with the 'enigma'.

Angry at the personal loss, I justified to myself that if I can make a profit by selling the innermost secrets of those hidden and insidious powers working behind the enigma, as its overlords, then there would be nothing wrong with benefiting at their expense.

I still believe this to be so. However, realizing that events in this world are quickly leading to a final apocalyptic crisis, understanding the pain that millions of 'abductees' around the world have felt and are feeling, and hearing the 'distant cries' of those who are lost deep within the labyrinthine depths of the Enigma itself, I have decided that the right thing to do would be to send this information forth at no cost, other than the heavy price that all those who have brought this information to you have paid.

Consider it my 'patriotic' duty. All I ask in Return would be for your prayers: for the many abductees who have been rejected by an unbelieving and cynical world; for myself and those who have contributed to this work so that our sacrifices will not have been in vain; and especially for those who are the most desperate of all... those who have become lost within the cruel dungeons of the Enigma itself.

Pray that they might be protected and preserved even in the midst of the fearful hopelessness and despair which they face, so that they might once again see the light of day. *(Branton – 1996.)*

NOTE 2:
(Bob Teske – 2012)

In 1996, the screenplay CONSPIRACY OF SILENCE was written and created, that first introduced what Branton and Thomas C. termed "Nightmare Hall" and the Dulce underground facility, as well as two members of an alien Studies and Observation Group based on Earth in a remote region of Glacier National Park in Northwestern Montana; this Studies and Observation Group (or SOG) was the frontline defense for Earth and Humanity established in the late 1940's and early 1950's. At the time of the creation of this screenplay little did the screenwriter (Bob Teske) know that there was indeed a place called "Dulce, New Mexico" or an actual person named "Tal". "Tal" was a fictional character created by this screenwriter to be the second-in-command of a fictional alien outpost. Tal and his superior – the outpost commander, a female named "Chrysalaas" were "blue-skinned" humanoids (homo-sapiens-sapiens) from the star system of Altair Much of what the screenwriter placed in the script has later been revealed in the writings of Branton, Thomas C.; the lectures of Bill Cooper, Phil Schneider, and John Lear – just to mention five – that the writer has only just learned about in the course of the last 10 or 15 years.

THE DULCE PROTOCOL

The writer has had to ask himself, "How is this possible?" "Did he somehow ACTUALLY live the experiences?" "Was he actually PART of a program that was involved with tracking alien activities on Earth, and somehow got too close to the truth and had a memory block placed in his mind so he wouldn't remember?" The screenwriter of CONSPIRACY OF SILENCE, like so many others who have had encounters with extraterrestrial intelligences and the enigmatic UFOs, also suffers from periods of "missing" and "lost time" that cannot be accounted for since the early 1970's, perhaps even longer. Lost and missing time in Louisiana, lost and missing time in Vietnam, and lost and missing time in the *Southwestern United States* between 1971 and 1976. Something happened, and something IS happening.

The world is asleep and needs so very desperately to be woken up. We are, indeed, a species with amnesia. Everything that we have ever been told and taught is a LIE. The truth needs to be known, and the LIES EXPOSED for what they are.

I don't know if the majority content of this manuscript has ever been edited and brought up to date since the original creator(s) first compiled it, and judging by the commentaries interjected by Branton, I would have to believe that it was somehow passed down to him, just by the date of Branton's signature, as a reminder, that was *16 years ago*; but this writer will attempt to edit, verify, and compile this, and other information, into a salable manuscript that needs a wider distribution network. I have not been able to find any copyright notices anywhere in regards to the material within these pages. It is this writer's hope that this material will reach the sleepers and that they will finally wake up to the horrific realities that we, as a species, face in our everyday lives – if any of this is even remotely true. Any profits from the sale of this manuscript will be used for the development, production, and distribution of a major motion picture that has a much wider range of distribution capabilities.

It is also the hope of this writer that, by the release of this manuscript, more and more people will awaken from their slumber in this MATRIX-like world and begin to openly question this reality that we find ourselves trapped in.

There's an old saying that *"What you don't know can't hurt you,"* but let me assure you that *"What you don't know CAN and WILL kill you."*

The stakes are high in this game. What are the stakes, you may ask? The stakes are nothing short than your very souls. It's time to FIX THAT! "It's time to ride…" (Bob Teske – 2012.)

THE DULCE PROTOCOL

DISCLAIMER

Much of the information in this volume is of an incredible and, some might say, an unbelievable nature.

I have decided NOT to hold back ANY information or claims regarding the Dulce enigma and related scenarios, the reason for this being that underground or earth-based anomalies are always there for anyone who is interested or daring enough to probe and investigate.

UFO events often appear and disappear [along with the evidence] when the object or objects depart. Underground or earth-based anomalies on the other hand cannot and do not 'disappear' at will, and because of this they are far more vulnerable to being exposed -- as legitimate or not.

Throughout this volume I have nevertheless offered my own 'opinions' and 'perspectives' based on circumstantial evidence [two or more reports from different sources which relay identical themes, and so on]. These admittedly are my own opinions and can be received or discarded according to the readers own perceptions in regards to the nature of reality. I have formed these opinions based on my own perceptions of the overall data, and since these are my perceptions, they are not infallible but are subject to change or revision with the revelation of new information. The reader is free to form his or her own conclusions and opinions based on the accumulated data, just as I have done.

Whether you consider the information which follows science fact, science fiction or perhaps a little of both ["science faction", you might say], this should not detract from the fact that these reports -- which have arrived from HUNDREDS of different sources and have been condensed within this one volume -- make for fascinating reading, either way one looks at it.

So with this there is nothing else to share in the way of introductions, other than to say...

Sit back and enjoy the ride!

Branton
October, 1996

In Agreement:

Bob Teske
April, 2012

THE DULCE PROTOCOL

Chapter 1

The Octopus, Black Projects and the Dulce Facility

"Those conspiracies that are too incredible to be believed are by the same right those which most often succeed."

The following article comes from the 'TC TECHNICAL CONSULTANT', Nov.-Dec., 1991 issue:

"The death of a journalist in West Virginia, plus the jailing of an alleged CIA computer consultant in Washington State may be elements of a much wider scandal that could have serious implications...

"What started out as an investigation of an apparent case of pirated software has grown to be a project involving hundreds of journalists all over the world.

"The dead journalist, Joseph Daniel 'Danny' Casolaro was found dead August 10th in a motel room in West Virginia. His wrists were slashed seven times on each wrist and a suicide note was found nearby. The only manuscript of his book, with accompanying notes, WAS MISSING.

"The book, provisionally titled 'The Octopus', was meant to be an explosive expose of misdeeds by the Justice Department under the Reagan Administration. Time Magazine also reported that Casolaro's research centered on gambling and attempted arms deals at the Cabazon reservation near Indio [California].

"Indeed, the scope of Casolaro's investigation was so large that any one of a large number of areas of research could have been the trigger for a possible hit.

"While authorities declared his death a suicide, his relatives definitely stated that Casolaro's mental state was sound, indeed upbeat, after the completion of his book.

"Casolaro started his work nearly two years before, investigating the bankrupting of a small computer software company called Inslaw, allegedly by the U.S. Justice Department. INSLAW, a company headed by Bill and Nancy Hamilton of Washington D.C., (no connection to researcher Bill Hamilton, whose writings on the Dulce enigma appear later in this volume. - Branton) had developed a package known as PROMIS -- short for Prosecutor's Management Information System -- to act as a case management tool for the Justice Department's unwieldy work load.

"Inslaw President Bill Hamilton has claimed that Ed Meese associate EARL BRIAN was given control of pirated versions of the PROMIS software by Meese to sell back to different U.S. government agencies for great profit. Two courts have so far agreed with Hamilton, awarding an 8 million dollar judgment, but a higher ('Justice Dept.'? - Branton) court of appeal has quashed the award and the verdict, declaring that it was not the jurisdiction of the lower courts. As of October 9, the case has moved into the realm of the Supreme Court.

"EARL BRIAN OWNS UNITED PRESS INTERNATIONAL [UPI] and FINANCIAL NEWS NETWORK [FNN]

THE DULCE PROTOCOL

"According to a Washington man, who claims to have modified the Cobol-based software for the CIA and other intelligence agencies, the software was a reward for Earl Brian's role in arranging the so-called 'October Surprise' gambit, the alleged conspiracy to withhold the American hostages in Iran until after the 1980 election which saw Carter removed from power. The 'October Surprise' scandal has taken some time to emerge.

"In a Paris meeting, President Bush is alleged to have met with Ali Akabar Hashemi Rafsanjani, the speaker of the Iranian Parliament, Mohammed Ali Rajai, the future President of Iran and Manucher Ghorbanifar, an Iranian arms dealer with connections to Mossad, according to Navy Captain Gunther Russbacher who claims to have flown Bush, William Casey -- the CIA chief -- and Donald Gregg, a CIA operative to that location. Russbacher, who made these allegations in May is now in jail on Terminal Island, convicted on the charge of impersonating a U.S. Attorney.

(Note: Russbacher 'defected' from the CIA with 12 Navy Seals under his command, and was on at least two occasions the target of attempted CIA hits. The would-be assassins attempted to drive Gunther and his wife off of roads and down the side-cliffs to their deaths, however according to Russbacher his SEAL-team agents who were watching over him unbeknownst to the intended assassins, moved up quickly from behind and sent the CIA "hit men" to THEIR deaths instead. - Branton)

"The Washington man is MICHAEL RICONOSCIUTO who is now waiting for a trial in a Washington jail on conspiracy to sell drugs charges, charges which Riconosciuto claims are manufactured. Indeed, the charges made against Riconosciuto were made one week after Riconosciuto authored and signed an affidavit describing his role in modifying the pirated software.

(Note: It is interesting what connections we can find here. Michael Riconosciuto was a Wackenhut-CIA employee who told researcher Michael Lindemann that he had attempted to get a whole helicopter full of documents and evidence detailing illegal biogenetic activities and non-Congressionally sanctioned projects involving 'illegal aliens' out of the Nevada Test Site. The chopper was blown out of the sky, killing all five personnel on board. Michael's father happened to be Marshall Riconosciuto, a fascist and a supporter of Adolph Hitler who was a very close friend of Fred L. Crisman. Crisman was involved in the Maurey Island 'UFO' sighting incident in 1947 near Tacoma, Washington, which researcher Anthony Kimory believes involved the test-flight of hybrid CIA - PROJECT PAPERCLIP - NAZI aerial disks.

There are several sources which claim that by the early 1940's the Nazi's had succeeded in test-flying wingless lenticular craft powered by rotary devices, rocket power, and DONUT CONFIGURATION jet turbine engines -- rather than cylindrical -- with the cabin stabilized by gyro, the compressors rotating in one direction and the expansion chambers and vectored exhausts rotating in the opposite direction. In fact the movie "THE BATTLE OF THE BULGE" correctly implies that this, one of the largest military battles during World War II between American and German forces, was an attempt by the Germans to buy time and prolong the war just a little while longer, for within a few more months the Germans would have been mass-producing jet fighters, bombers and other super-weapons that would have been invincible to the turbo-prop fleets of the Allies.

With the Allied invasion of Germany just before mass-production began, many of the prototypes and plans of the Nazi military machine were captured. However most of the most sophisticated prototypes, plans and even scientists mysteriously turned up missing following the war. We will reserve further discussion on this subject until later in this volume. After the war had ended several of the Nazi scientists who WERE captured -- and who had helped to develop the revolutionary aircraft -- were recruited by the CIA as a result of a secret deal that had been made between Allen Dulles, a member of the Bavarian Illuminati; and Nazi S.S. General Reinhardt Gehlen, a member of the Bavarian Thule Society.

The deep connections between the Bavarian Illuminati which sponsored the CIA and the Bavarian Thule society which sponsored the Nazi's allowed for the upper covert-ops levels of the CIA to be manned by nothing less than the core of the Nazi S.S. itself, with the help of fascist sympathizers and fifth column double-agents working within American intelligence, although some leading Nazi's were 'sacrificed' to the Nuremberg trials to appease the Allies and establish the illusion that Europe had been de-Nazified. Fred L. Crisman incidentally was a 'witness' to the Maurey Island event and had helped two Army G-2 agents acquire 'slag samples' which fell from one of the six DONUT-SHAPED ships observed. On their way to deliver the samples to Wright-Patterson AFB in Ohio, their plane crashed and both G-2 agents were killed.

Some people at the time insisted that the plane had been sabotaged. Two of the reporters who investigated the incident lost their lives, and Kenneth Arnold who investigated the incident after being commissioned by AMAZING STORIES editor Ray Palmer, claimed that his conversations with a high Air Force official concerning the subject were electronically monitored. Also, strange government agents in dark suits were seen in the area. Shortly after his investigation Kenneth Arnold, during an air-search for a crashed plane over Mt. Rainier, saw 9 crescent-shaped discs which he called 'flying saucers'. The news media publicized the incident and the term stuck and became a media catch word ever since.

Also around this same time -- 1947 -- Arnold escaped a near-fatal crash when his airplane mysteriously lost power. The connections do not end here. Fred L. Crisman was a close friend to Clay Shaw, whom Louisiana District Attorney James Garrison -- see the movie 'JFK' -- accused of being the CIA-Mafia go-between in the John F. Kennedy murder. Garrison arrested Shaw in an effort to charge him and the CIA with the JFK assassination, however only a few days before the hearing Garrison's star witness David Ferry was killed, and Garrison's remaining evidence was not enough to bring about a conviction.

Fred Crisman was the first man Clay Shaw called when he heard that Garrison intended to implicate him. Garrison also believed that Clay Shaw himself was involved with PROJECT PAPERCLIP, the secret operation to bring Nazi war criminals into the

United States by the hundreds -- some say thousands -- and give them immunity and new identities in such institutions as U.S. Intelligence, the Military-Industrial complex, the Space agencies, and the various Rockefeller-connected oil cartels such as ARCO, STANDARD [EXXON], ZAPATA, etc., corporations that were supported by the Bavarian-based secret-society lodges, corporations that had actually sold oil to the Nazi's during World War II and helped keep the Nazi "war machine" operating.

According to Garrison, Crisman worked as a middle-man between the fascist policy makers and the lower echelons of the Military-Industrial Complex. "Oh what a tangled web... (we weave...)" These American mega-bankers and traitors to freedom had supported the Nazi's in an effort to initiate a Bavarian-backed "New World Order", under the cover of the "Third Reich".

(Read the book NONE DARE CALL IT CONSPIRACY, by the late Gary Allen for more on the Rockefeller connection, and also the various works by Dr. Antony Sutton. - Branton)

"The affidavit also claimed that he [Michael Riconosciuto], had been contacted by phone and threatened by PETER VIDENIEKS -- a Justice Department employee and Customs official who Riconosciuto alleged had intelligence ties -- as to the possible consequences of his going public with certain information.

"According to Riconosciuto, Videnieks was a frequent visitor to the Cabazon Indian reservation near Palm Springs and visited with tribal manager, John P. Nichols. Nichols was in essence Riconosciuto's boss in a number of enterprises conducted on reservation land and the PROMIS modification was just one of these projects.

According to Riconosciuto, in an interview with T.C. conducted from jail, the PROMIS software was modified to install a backdoor access for use by American intelligence services. The software was then sold to 88 different countries as a sort of

THE DULCE PROTOCOL

'Trojan horse' package enabling us to access their intelligence systems. According to Riconosciuto these countries included Iraq and Libya.

"Correspondence between Nichols and other companies, if authentic, indicates that Riconosciuto's claims of his expertise in the area of electronics and armaments appear to be true. Marshall Riconoscuito, Michael's father, is a reputed former business partner of Richard Nixon.

"According to Riconosciuto, the fuzzy status of reservation land as 'sovereign' allowed elements of the CIA and organized crime to conduct business uniquely.

"Among the projects worked on during this time were joint projects with WACKENHUT, a company loaded with former CIA and NSA personnel and business ventures with the Saudi Arabian royal family and other unusual projects.

"A joint venture with Southern California Edison will soon be generating power for bio-mass drawn from local waste outlets. Biological warfare projects were investigated with Stormont laboratories looking into the creation of 'pathogenic viruses' and enhanced fuel-air explosive weapons were created and tested in league with Meridian Arms at the NEVADA TESTING RANGE which matched the explosive power of nuclear devices.

"These enhanced weapons gained their power from polarizing the molecules in the gas cloud by modification of the electric field, a technology developed from exploring Thomas Townsend Brown's suppressed work, a knowledge which Riconosciuto claims he gained from working at LEAR in Reno, Nevada.

"Riconosciuto is said to have worked on the enhanced fuel-air explosive weapons with Gerald Bull of Space Research Corporation. Bull, now deceased, later became an arms advisor to Saddam Hussein. It is said that HUSSEIN POSSESSES THE FAE TECHNOLOGY.

"In July, Anson Ng, a reporter for the Financial Times of London was shot and killed in Guatemala. He had reportedly been trying to interview an American there named Jimmy Hughes, a one-time director of security for the Cabazon Indian Reservation secret projects.

"In April, a Philadelphia attorney named Dennis Eisman was found dead, killed by a single bullet in his chest. According to a former federal official who worked with Eisman, the attorney was found dead in the parking lot where he had been due to meet with a woman who had crucial evidence to share substantiating Riconosciuto's claims.

"Both Eisman's and Ng's deaths were declared suicides by authorities.

"Fred Alvarez, a Cabazon tribal leader who was in vocal opposition to the developments on the reservation, was found shot to death WITH two friends in 1981. Their murder remains unsolved.

"The leader of the House, Thomas Foley, announced last month that a formal inquiry will be initiated into the Inslaw case. Foley appointed Senator Terry Sanford as co-chairman of the joint congressional panel. Prior to his election, Senator Sanford was the attorney REPRESENTING Earl Brian in his 1985 takeover bid for United Press International and was instrumental in appointing Earl Brian, a medical doctor, to the board of Duke Medical School, of which Sanford is President.

"However, despite repeated requests from journalists to produce photographs showing Riconosciuto together with Brian, and requests to produce his passport showing his alleged trip to Iran, he has not yet done so. Also Riconosciuto failed to be able to describe Peter Videnieks to CNN's Moneyline program, claiming a medical condition prevented him from remembering clearly.

THE DULCE PROTOCOL

"This led one former intelligence operative to speculate that we may be witnessing a very sophisticated intelligence operation being played out in public.

"Former F.B.I. Special Agent, Ted Gunderson, speaks FOR Riconosciuto's credibility. Gunderson, who lives in Manhattan Beach, has worked with Riconosciuto for many years in his capacity as private investigator.

"Together, according to Gunderson, they were responsible for thwarting a terrorist operation during the Los Angeles Olympics. According to Gunderson, Riconosciuto was well known in certain circles as a genius in almost all sciences.

"The so-called drug operation broken up in Washington State was an electro hydrodynamic mining operation claimed Gunderson, using Townsend Brown technology. A videotape viewed by this journalist revealed metallic powders and apparent processes unrelated to drug manufacture. Indeed, a government analysis of soil samples revealed the absence of drug contamination, but a high concentration of barium. Barium is often found in high voltage related work.

"Unsubstantiated information from an intelligence source claims that the current situation is THE VISIBLE EFFECT OF A WAR CURRENTLY GOING ON IN THE INTELLIGENCE COMMUNITY between a group centered in the CIA called AQUARIUS [around a powerful center known as MJ-12] and a group known as COM-12 centered around Naval Intelligence. COM-12 is reputedly trying to sustain a rearguard action to sustain and preserve constitutional government and is deliberately LEAKING INFORMATION damaging to the former group."

In the same publication, same issue, there appeared a follow-up article just following the one given above. Written by Thomas Zed, the article, titled "WACKENHUT'S CONNECTION WITH THE BLACK PROJECT WORLD" stated:

"The Wackenhut Company has a very close connection to the world of BLACK BUDGET PROJECTS. Besides being connected with the Cabazon venture mentioned in this issue it is also responsible, according to jailed computer consultant Michael Riconosciuto, FOR THE SECRET PROJECTS BEING UNDERTAKEN IN DULCE, NEW MEXICO where the JICARILLA INDIAN RESERVATION IS BEING SIMILARLY USED.

"After sending two of my colleagues there recently AND RECEIVING CONFIRMATION THAT THERE WAS A TOP SECRET MILITARY TYPE INSTALLATION, I decided to call the newspaper office and make an educated bluff.

"I identified myself as a freelance reporter from Los Angeles -- and told the newspaper that I was doing a story on the Cabazon reservation biological warfare projects that had been undertaken there on behalf of the CIA. I told her that I had heard that there were similar things being done in Dulce and would like to know what was going on.

"The official I spoke to BECAME FRIGHTENED and said, 'I can't talk to you about that! It would be very unprofessional of me to talk to you about that. You'll have to speak to the President of the tribe.' She then hung up.

"I have yet to call back and ask the President of the tribe, but will report on that in the next issue.

"Wackenhut is also responsible for security of a lot of UNDERGROUND FACILITIES in California and Nevada, including the notorious S-4 or AREA 51 in Nevada where Townsend Brown flying disk technology [written about in a T.C. recent issue] has been flying and developing for decades.

"A recent helicopter crash at the area, where two pilots and three security guards from Wackenhut flying in a Messerschmitt BO-105 helicopter were killed was not at all accidental claimed Riconosciuto, who said that the individuals aboard the helicopter were traveling with sensitive documents.

"Groups are now investigating Riconosciuto's claims..."

THE DULCE PROTOCOL

Chapter 2
High Strangeness on the Archuleta Plateau

In the spring of 1990 researcher 'Jason Bishop' sent copies of the following report to a select few investigators, and later gave permission for the report to be distributed among a wider readership.

- Is the object described within the report the product of secret technology being developed by the Military-Industrial Complex as part of some covert or deep-cover space project?
- Or does it involve something a bit more 'alien' than mere top secret black-project research and top-of-the-line vanguard aircraft designs - the Stealth series, the Aurora, etc. - which are being developed at the Nevada Test Site?
- Or, could it be a combination of both?

The transcript, titled: 'RECOLLECTIONS AND IMPRESSIONS OF VISIT TO DULCE, NEW MEXICO - OCTOBER 23, 24, 1988', is reproduced in its entirety below.

"Upon arrival I was introduced to Dr. John F. Gille, a French National. Dr. Gille has a PhD in Math/Physics from the University of Paris. He had worked very closely with the French Government on the UFO phenomena in that country.

(Side Note: Dr. Gille had also released a report on another "Dulce-like" base near Pine Gap - Alice Springs, Australia. This base is a massive multi-leveled facility run by the "Club of Rome" which, like the 'Bilderberger' organization, is reputedly a cover for the Bavarian Illuminati. The article spoke of antigravity disk research, and plans to make Pine Gap a major "control center" for a "New World Order". Pine Gap is equipped with whole levels of computer terminals tied-in to the major computer mainframes of the world which contain the intimate details of most of the inhabitants of industrialized nations. The article also spoke of the infiltration of several major religious denominations, the media, international governments, the economy, education, and other levels of society by the Bavarian Illuminati, in order to prepare the way for a New World Order dictatorship. The report also stated that the workers at Pine Gap are highly indoctrinated and programmed so that they do not threaten or sabotage the security of the Illuminati projects being carried out there. - Branton).

"He told me," Bishop continues, "that he has not worked in his chosen field for fifteen years, having devoted all of his time to research on UFOs. Dr. Gille is an amiable, forthright man. He has no reservations about expressing his own views on the subject. He does hold several beliefs that border on the paranormal. Dr. Gille had his wife, Elaine, with him. My personal view of him is one of caution. Until I get to know him better, I feel that I should be very careful.

"Edmound Gomez is a rancher. His ranch is 13 miles west of Dulce.

(Note: Accounts given by others state that the ranch is 13 miles east of Dulce, however whatever the case may be it's safe to say that the ranch is 13 miles FROM Dulce. -Branton).

THE DULCE PROTOCOL

"From 1975 until 1983 the Gomez ranch was the scene [epicenter] of most of the cattle mutilations that took place in the northern New Mexico / southern Colorado area. He told me that his family homesteaded the Dulce area 111 years ago and that as a result of these mutilations; they lost $100,000 in cattle over an eight year period. One of these cases occurred only 200 yards behind his home. He showed me the area.

"Edmound was very open and discussed with me the various mutilation cases that had occurred on his ranch and on those of others. Upon our Return from the mountain trip, he invited me to his home where he shared with me various photographs, clippings, letters etc. relating to the cases. He loaned me several overhead photographs of the Mt. Archuleta area. I hope to be able to have them examined through image intensification techniques.

"Edmound also told me about the many times that combat ready troops had been spotted in the area. Some of these troops were found in areas that are only gotten to through four-wheel drive trucks or on foot. [This is VERY rugged country]. The troops were also spotted in areas that only the Apache has permission to go. When the reported 'experimental aircraft' went down in 1983, there were 'hundreds of troops, armed to the teeth' reported in the area. When approached, the troops would run and disappear.

"Participants in the Mt. Archuleta expedition were:

- Gabe Valdez
- Edmound Gomez
- Dr. John Gille
- [name deleted]
- Manuel Gomez [Edmound's brother]
- Jeff and Matt Valdez [Gabe's sons]

Robert K Teske

Because of Gabe's position as head of the State Police in Dulce and Edmound being a part of the community, we were given permission to go onto the mountain. It is located on the Apache Reservation.

"We left about 1430 hrs, Sunday, 23 October 1988. We used Gabe's four wheel drive pickup truck to get up the mountain. The road was incredibly difficult. At one time we had to dig out the side of the mountain in order to allow the truck to pass. At about 17:30 hrs we arrived at the proposed campsite. It was on a relatively flat area about 300 yards from the peak of Mt. Archuleta.

(**Note:** The "Time" in the previous paragraph, as well as the next several paragraphs are given in a military 24-hour format; whereas 14:30 hours is 2:30 PM. – Robert K. Teske.)

"Gabe and Edmound both told me that in 1978 there was an agreement between the Ute Indians [Colorado] and the Federal Government. This agreement consisted of the Ute Nation receiving all the territory now occupied along the New Mexico/Colorado border with the explicit agreement that they would strictly enforce a 'NO TRESPASSING' regulation along the border of their territory.

Therefore, it is not possible to even cross the Ute Reservation without special permission from the Tribal Headquarters. If caught without this permission you are liable for a fine and/or jail and expulsion. There is now a road leading to the Archuleta area through the reservation. It is patrolled by the Indian Forest Service

(Note: the Colorado border is only a relatively few miles away from and to the north of the Archuleta plateau. -Branton)

"At 19:51 hrs, all seven of us spotted a very bright light coming from the northwest at a very high rate of speed. The object appeared to be boomerang shaped with a very bright light just below its center

THE DULCE PROTOCOL

(Some have alleged that these 'boomerang' shaped vehicles may have some connection with a super-secret black budget space operation called Alternative-3. - Branton).

The light was a bright white, blue and green. As it approached, it slowed down [obviously under intelligent control], seemed to reverse direction, finally stopping. When it stopped, a shower of what appeared to be sparks were emitted from each end of the boomerang, and then it began moving forward again and disappeared from sight at a very high rate of speed. All this took place in approximately 10 to 15 seconds. We attempted to take a picture of the object but were unsuccessful.

"About 22:00 hours we climbed to the summit of Mt. Archuleta and watched for about an hour and a half. We could see across the canyon in the moonlight. This canyon wall is where Paul Bennewitz [prominent and well known physicist and UFO investigator] claimed an 'alien' base is located and that during the night their ships are seen entering and leaving cave openings in the cliff wall.

(Note: It has been reported that Paul Bennewitz died on June 23rd, 2003, believed to be under mysterious circumstances – Bob Teske.)

During our stay on the peak, we saw two very bright lights on the cliff walls in the exact location where Paul said the base openings were. There are no roads on this cliff. The lights would appear suddenly and then fade over a period of time until you could not see them. At this time we also heard voices that sounded like radio transmissions.

The voices were not understandable but they were there none the less. The same light pattern was seen by myself and Edmound Gomez as we sat on the cliff...at about 01:00 hours. We also heard voices. At one time we thought we could hear trucks moving but we could not be sure about this. After 02:00 hours there were no more sightings or sounds.

"On Monday, 24 October 1988 the entire party climbed to the peak once again. We were looking for evidence that there had been a crash of an 'experimental aircraft' flown by an Air Force General in 1983. This crash was reported in the newspapers for two days as a small plane and then hushed up. The craft was rumored to be a captured UFO, flown by Americans. We were hoping to prove that there indeed had been a crash but also to find some physical evidence.

"Dr. Bennewitz reported that the craft had clipped off a large tree in it's descent, had hit another tree, regained altitude, skimmed over the peak of Archuleta, [and] hit a third tree in the valley north of the peak. It was then reported to have hit the ground, flipped over twice and came to rest. We found the trees as reported by Bennewitz.

They were all in line with each other and the final resting place. The first tree was about 40 inches in diameter. It was hit about 30 feet off the ground. There was no fire. I have taken samples of this tree for analysis. The other two trees were smaller [approximately 12 to 20 inches in diameter]. There was evidence of fire with these. Samples of [these] trees were also taken. Between the second tree and the third tree we found large pieces of what appeared to be part of the first tree.

One piece was burnt while next to it was one that had not been burned. Samples were taken. While searching for physical evidence, a standard issue style ball-point pen was found. This is of the same type used by the U.S. Government but can also be purchased by the general public. Strange to have been found in such a remote place as this canyon. The alleged crash area showed a large SEMI-CIRCULAR area with new vegetation. The area above the semi-circular area was covered with new vegetation also. Samples of the soil of this area were taken.

THE DULCE PROTOCOL

"My overall impressions of this trip are mixed. I believe that there is definitely something going on in the area. What it is, I do not know. Perhaps there is a base there. Perhaps it is jointly operated by 'aliens' and the government, as claimed by John Lear. Then again, it could be a US base so super secret that there are no fences around to arouse any suspicion... then again I cannot say for sure.

"I do know that the evidence that we found and saw definitely points to the fact that something is going on in this area."

In apparent confirmation of the above, Gabe Valdez - the former State Police officer in Dulce, New Mexico who was a part of the expedition described above - was contacted by researcher Alan deWalton in 1990, in an attempt to confirm some of the information concerning his involvement in the UFO-mutilation investigations.

During a telephone conversation with Valdez, the following was learned:

"-- He and others HAD seen strange flying objects in the area, however he himself was unsure whether these were 'UFO's' of alien origin, or some type of top secret aircraft being tested by some secret faction of the government.

"-- Something DID crash near Mt. Archuleta several years ago, but again, he did not find any evidence conclusively proving whether it was an object of human OR alien origin.

"-- There is another road leading to the Mt. Archuleta area [and mesa] aside from the one which goes through the Ute Indian reservation. As for the Ute Reservation road, much of it is in good condition [paved?]. Only the area around the Archuleta region itself requires four-wheel drive vehicles.

"-- He did investigate cattle mutilations, and at least in SOME cases a known nerve agent was discovered in the carcasses, and other indications suggesting that the cattle were being used for research in 'DNA' experiments."

Quite by accident, while scanning the Internet, I was surprised to discover yet another confirmation of the events described earlier by Jason Bishop. This THIRD confirmation of UFO activity near Dulce, New Mexico by members of the expedition team was given by none other than John Gille, one of the Mt. Archuleta expedition team members mentioned earlier.

Gille's own report follows:

SUBJECT: UFO REPORT FROM DULCE, NEW MEXICO - FILE: UFO749

SUMMARY: - Report of UFO sighting over Mt. Archuleta, NM on October 23, 1988 by John F. Gille et.al.

LOCATION AND TIME

-- Southern slopes of Mt. Archuleta, 5 miles NW of Dulce, NM.
-- Location of the phenomenon: South to North trajectory for about two miles stopping very close to Mt. Archuleta summit.
-- Estimated closest observers distance: 480 yards.
-- Distance from observers to spot where the UFO stopped: 510 yards.
-- Time: 7:51 pm Mountain time.
-- Duration: est. 5-6 seconds

WITNESSES:

-- Eliane Allegre, RN
-- Gabe Valdez

THE DULCE PROTOCOL

-- Edmund, friend of Valdez

-- "Jack" [pseudonym], PhD

-- Manuel, local kid

-- Greg, son of Valdez

-- Jeff, another son of Valdez

-- John Gille, PhD

(Note: "Jack" would probably be Jason Bishop, which is itself a pseudonym used by a researcher and a friend of mine who uses this pseudonym because of his deep-level research into some very dangerous areas of investigation. That is, IF one considers the revelations such as those contained within this volume to be 'dangerous' information under certain circumstances. - Branton)

CIRCUMSTANCES OF SIGHTING:

- I [John Gille] was interested in the Dulce area because of rumors related to a jointly [CIA-Alien] occupied underground facility under Mt. Archuleta, and to numerous UFO sightings, as reported by local residents.

- A night of observation in the mountains had been planned under the leadership of Valdez.

- Since about 7:30pm, we had been playing OUIJA at the instigation of Valdez. Just as we were processing the last person, one of Valdez's sons shouted: "Look! Here it comes!"

[NOTE: I {Gille} DO NOT make the statement that there was a causal correlation between what we had just been doing and what we saw next. I merely report two consecutive events which may or may not have been correlated.]

LOOK OF THE PHENOMENON:

- The object came from the south at great speed on a flat, straight, rectilinear, horizontal trajectory resulting in a perfectly straight luminous yellowish line. It was definitely not a plane or a shooting star.

- There was no sound coming from the object.

- The object stopped dead in its tracks near the top of the mountain.

- At the same time, it became extremely luminous, lighting at least half the sky. There was a display of various colors: yellow, pink, green, and a shower of sparks.

- Then the object folded on itself and disappeared.

ANNEXES [Maps]:

-- New Mexico maps

-- US Geological Survey maps [Wirt Canyon]

PHOTOS:

-- Group photo of witnesses

-- Campsite

-- Mt. Archuleta

The trajectory was about 2000 ft. above the lowest point under the estimated path of the object, which is the Navajo River, elevation 6600 ft.

Chapter 3
Dulce New Mexico and a Cosmic Conspiracy?

John Lear, a captain of a major U.S. Airline has flown over 160 different types of aircraft in over 50 different countries. He holds 17 world speed records in the Lear Jet and is the only pilot ever to hold every airman certificate issued by the Federal Aviation Administration.

Mr. Lear has flown missions worldwide for the CIA and other government agencies. He has flown clandestine missions in war-zones and hot-spots around the world, often engineering hairs'-breath escapes under dangerous conditions. A former Nevada State Senatorial candidate, he is the son of William P. Lear, designer of the Lear Jet executive airplane, the 8-track stereo, and founder of the LEAR Siegler Corporation.

John Lear became interested in the subject of UFO's 13 months prior to the date given below, after talking with a friend in the United States Air Force by the name of Greg Wilson who had witnessed a UFO landing at Bentwaters AFB, near London, England, during which three small 'gray' aliens walked up to the Wing Commander. Since then Lear has tapped his contacts in intelligence, investigating the allegations that the executive and military-industrial branches of the United States 'government' knows about, and colludes with, alien forces.

Lear no longer suggests the following scenario is a 'possibility', he emphatically states that the aliens are here, and that many of them bode us ill.

"It started after World War II," he begins. "We [the Allied forces] recovered some alien technology from Germany -- not all that they had; some of it disappeared. It appears that some time in the late '30s, Germany recovered a saucer. What happened to it we don't know. But what we did get was some kind of ray gun..."

The following is a "Public Statement" released by John Lear on December 29, 1987 and revised on March 25, 1988. It was originally sent to some of Lear's personal friends and research associates who in turn put pressure on the Ace Pilot to release this information publicly.

The first version of the statement was apparently meant for the 'inside' crowd of researchers with whom Lear associated, whereas the following revision contains the same information as the first edition, yet is directed towards the public in general:

NOTE TO THE PRESS:

"The government of the United States continues to rely on your personal and professional gullibility to suppress the information contained herein. Your cooperation over the past 40 years has exceeded OUR wildest expectations and we salute you.

"'The sun does not revolve around the Earth'.

"'The United States Government has been in business with little gray extraterrestrials for about 20 years'.

"The first truth stated here got Giordano Bruno (right) burned at the stake in AD 1600 for daring to propose that it was

real. THE SECOND TRUTH HAS GOTTEN FAR MORE PEOPLE KILLED TRYING TO STATE IT PUBLICLY THAN WILL EVER BE KNOWN.

(<u>Note</u>: emphasis here and throughout this section is ours. - Branton)

"But the truth must be told. The fact that the Earth revolves around the sun was <u>successfully suppressed</u> by the [Roman] church for over 200 years. It eventually caused a major upheaval in the church, government, and thought. A realignment of social and traditional values. That was in the 1600's.

"Now, about <u>400 years after the first truth was pronounced</u> we must again face the shocking facts. The 'horrible truth' the government has been hiding from us over 40 years. Unfortunately, the 'horrible truth' is far more horrible than the government ever imagined.

"In its effort to 'protect democracy', our government sold us to the aliens. And here is how it happened. But before I begin, I'd like to offer a word in defense of those who bargained us away. They had the best of intentions.

"Germany may have recovered a flying saucer as early as 1939. General James H. Doolittle went to Norway in 1952 to inspect a flying saucer that had crashed there in Spitzbergen.

"The 'horrible truth' was known by only a very few persons: They were indeed ugly little creatures, shaped like praying mantises... Of the original group that were the first to learn the 'horrible truth', SEVERAL COMMITTED SUICIDE, the most prominent of which was Defense Secretary [and Secretary of the NAVY] James V. Forrestal who jumped to his death from a 16th story hospital window.

(<u>Note</u>: William Cooper, a former member of a Navy Intelligence briefing team, insists that Forrestal was in fact murdered by CIA agents who made his death look like a suicide. Based on sensitive documents Cooper claims to have read, two CIA agents entered the hospital room, tied a bed sheet around Forrestal's neck and to a light fixture, and threw him out the window to hang. The bed sheet[s] broke and he fell to his death, screaming on his way down according to some witnesses "We're being invaded!" - Branton).

"Secretary Forrestal's medical records are sealed to this day.

"President Truman put a lid on the secret and turned the screws so tight that the general public still thinks that flying saucers <u>are a joke</u>. Have I ever got a surprise for them.

"In 1947, President Truman established a group of 12 of the top military scientific personnel of their time. They were known as MJ-12. Although the group exists today, none of the ORIGINAL members are still alive. The last one to die was Gordon Gray, former Secretary of the Army, in 1984.

"As each member passed away, the group itself appointed a new member to fill the position. There is some speculation that the group known as MJ-12 expanded to at least <u>seven more members</u>.

"There were several more saucer crashes in the late 1940's, one in Roswell, New Mexico; one in Aztec, New Mexico; and one near Laredo, Texas, about 30 miles inside the Mexican border.

"Consider, if you will, the position of the United States Government at that time. They proudly thought of themselves as the most powerful nation on Earth, having recently produced the atomic bomb, an achievement so stupendous, it would take Russia 4 years to catch up, and only with the help of traitors to Democracy. They had built a jet aircraft that had exceeded the speed of sound in flight. They had built jet bombers with inter-continental range that could carry weapons of enormous destruction.

THE DULCE PROTOCOL

"The post war era, and the future seemed bright. Now imagine what it was like for those same leaders, all of whom had witnessed the panic of Orson Wells' radio broadcast, "The War of the Worlds", in 1938. Thousands of Americans panicked at a realistically presented invasion of Earth by beings from another planet. Imagine their horror as they actually viewed THE DEAD BODIES OF THESE FRIGHTENING LITTLE CREATURES WITH ENORMOUS EYES, REPTILIAN SKIN AND CLAW LIKE FINGERS.

Imagine their shock as they attempted to determine how these strange 'saucers' were powered and could discover no part even remotely similar to components they were familiar with: no cylinders or pistons, no vacuum tubes or turbines or hydraulic actuators. It is only when you fully understand the overwhelming helplessness the government was faced with in the late 40's that you can comprehend their perceived need for a total, thorough and sweeping cover up, to include the use of 'deadly force'.

"The cover-up was so successful that as late as 1985 a senior scientist with the Jet Propulsion Laboratory in Pasadena, California, Dr. Al Hibbs, would look at a video tape of an enormous flying saucer and state the record, 'I'm not going to assign anything to that [UFO] phenomena without a lot more data.' Dr. Hibbs was looking at the naked emperor and saying, 'He certainly looks naked, but that doesn't prove he's naked.'

"In July 1952, a panicked government watched helplessly as a squadron of 'flying saucers' flew over Washington, D.C., and buzzed the White House, the Capitol Building, and the Pentagon. *It took all the imagination and intimidation the government could muster to force that incident out of the memory of the public.*

"Thousands of sightings occurred during the Korean War and several more saucers were retrieved by the Air Force. Some were stored at Wright-Patterson Air Force Base; some were stored at Air Force bases near the locations of the crash site.

"One saucer was so enormous and the logistic problem in transportation so enormous that it was buried at the crash site and remains there today. The stories are legendary on transporting crashed saucers over long distances, moving only at night, purchasing complete farms, slashing through forests, blocking major highways, sometimes driving 2 or 3 lo-boys in tandem with an extraterrestrial load a hundred feet in diameter.

(Note: It is alleged that ALPHA or BLUE Teams out of Wright-Patterson AFB were the ones who were most often mobilized to carry out "crash-retrieval" operations. - Branton)

"On April 30, 1964, the first communication [occurred] between these aliens and the 'U.S. Government'.

(Note: Others claim that there was an even earlier contact-communication in 1954 during the Eisenhower administration. - Branton)

"During the period of 1969-1971, MJ-12 representing the U.S. Government made a deal with these creatures, called EBE's [Extraterrestrial Biological Entities, named by Detley Bronk, original MJ-12 member and 6th President of John Hopkins University]. The 'deal' was that in exchange for 'technology' that they would provide to us, we agreed to 'ignore' the abductions that were going on and suppress information on the cattle mutilations. The EBE's assured MJ-12 that the abductions [usually lasting about 2 hours] were merely the ongoing monitoring of developing civilizations.

"In fact, the purposes for the abductions turned out to be:

"(1) The insertion of a 3mm spherical device through the nasal cavity of the abductee into the brain [optic and/or nerve center], the device is used for the biological monitoring, tracking, and control of the abductee.

THE DULCE PROTOCOL

"(2) Implementation of Posthypnotic Suggestion to carry out a specific activity during a specific time period, the actuation of which will occur within the next 2 to 5 years.

"(3) Termination of some people so that they could function as living sources for biological material and substances.

"(4) TERMINATION OF INDIVIDUALS WHO REPRESENT A THREAT TO THE CONTINUATION OF THEIR ACTIVITY.

"(5) Effect genetic engineering experiments.

"(6) Impregnation of human females and early termination of pregnancies to secure the crossbreed infant.

(Note: Or perhaps a better term for it would be a "genetically altered" infant, since there has been no evidence forthcoming that an actual 'hybrid' between humans and the 'EBE' or 'Grey' species has been successful. In other words, the offspring would tend to fall to one side or the other, a 'reptiloid' or 'grey' entity possessing no 'soul-energy-matrix', or a humanoid being possessing such a matrix or soul although somewhat altered genetically in it's outward physical appearance or characteristics. - Branton).

"The U.S. Government was NOT initially aware of the far reaching consequences of their 'deal'. They were LED to believe that the abductions were essentially benign AND SINCE THEY FIGURED THAT THE ABDUCTIONS WOULD PROBABLY GO ON ANYWAY WHETHER THEY AGREED OR NOT, they merely insisted on a current list of abductees be submitted, on a periodic basis, to MJ-12 and the National Security Council. Does this sound incredible? An actual list of abductees sent to the National Security Council? Read on, because I have news for you...

"The EBE's have a genetic disorder in that their digestive system is atrophied and not functional... In order to sustain themselves they use enzyme or hormonal secretions obtained from the tissues that they extract from humans and animals.

"The secretions obtained are then mixed with <u>hydrogen peroxide</u> [to kill germs, viruses, etc.] and applied on the skin by spreading or dipping parts of their bodies in the solution. The body absorbs the solution, and then excretes the waste back through the skin.

(<u>Note</u>: Urine is also excreted through the skin in this manner, which may explain the ammonia-like STENCH that many abductees or witnesses have reported during encounters with the grey-type 'aliens'. - Branton).

"The cattle mutilations that were prevalent throughout the period from 1973 to 1983 and publicly noted through newspaper and magazine stories and included a documentary produced by Linda Howe for a Denver CBS affiliate KMGH-TV, were for the collection of these tissues by the aliens. The mutilations included genitals taken, rectums cored out to the colon, eyes, tongue, and throat all surgically removed with extreme precision. In some cases the incisions were made by cutting between the cells, a process we are not yet capable of performing in the field.

In many of the mutilations there was no blood found at all in the carcass, yet there was no vascular collapse of the internal organs. THIS HAS ALSO BEEN NOTED IN THE HUMAN MUTILATIONS, one of the first of which was Sgt. Jonathan P. Lovette at the White Sands Missile Test Range in 1956, who was found three days after an Air Force Major had witnessed his abduction by a 'disk shaped' object at 0300 while on search for missile debris downrange.

His genitals had been removed, rectum cored out in a surgically precise 'plug' up to the colon, eyes removed and all blood removed with, again, no vascular collapse.

THE DULCE PROTOCOL

From some of the evidence it is apparent that this surgery is accomplished, in most cases, WHILE THE VICTIM, ANIMAL OR HUMAN, IS STILL ALIVE.

(Note: According to former Green Beret commander Bill English, THIS incident was also mentioned in the Above-Top-Secret "GRUDGE / BLUE BOOK REPORT NO. 13" which was never released with the rest of the innocuous and voluminous "Project Blue Book" reports.

The "Blue Teams" who were sent on crash-retrieval operations were reportedly working on behalf of the covert branch of the Blue Book operations, and Ufological legend has it that a secret warehouse with multiple underground levels exists at Wright Patterson AFB in Ohio, one which is literally packed with alien craft, hardware, and even alien bodies 'on ice'. Wright Patterson was -- and is? -- the headquarters of Project Blue Book. - Branton)

"THE VARIOUS PARTS OF THE BODY ARE TAKEN TO VARIOUS UNDERGROUND LABORATORIES, ONE OF WHICH IS KNOWN TO BE NEAR THE SMALL NEW MEXICO TOWN OF DULCE. THIS JOINTLY OCCUPIED [CIA-ALIEN] FACILITY HAS BEEN DESCRIBED AS ENORMOUS, WITH HUGE TILED WALLS THAT 'GO ON FOREVER'. WITNESSES HAVE REPORTED HUGE VATS FILLED WITH AMBER LIQUID WITH PARTS OF HUMAN BODIES BEING STIRRED INSIDE.

"After the initial agreement, Groom Lake, one of the nations most secret test centers, was closed for a period of about a year, sometime between about 1972 and 1974, AND A HUGE UNDERGROUND FACILITY WAS CONSTRUCTED FOR AND WITH THE HELP OF THE EBE'S. THE 'BARGAINED FOR' TECHNOLOGY WAS SET IN PLACE BUT COULD ONLY BE OPERATED BY THE EBE'S THEMSELVES. NEEDLESS TO SAY, THE ADVANCED TECHNOLOGY COULD NOT BE USED AGAINST THE EBE'S THEMSELVES, EVEN IF NEEDED.

"During the period between 1979 and 1983 it became increasingly obvious to MJ-12 that things were not going as planned. IT BECAME KNOWN THAT MANY MORE PEOPLE [IN THE THOUSANDS] WERE BEING ABDUCTED THAN WERE LISTED ON THE OFFICIAL ABDUCTION LISTS. IN ADDITION IT BECAME KNOWN THAT SOME, NOT ALL, BUT SOME OF THE NATION'S MISSING CHILDREN HAD BEEN USED FOR SECRETIONS AND OTHER PARTS REQUIRED BY THE ALIENS.

"IN 1979 THERE WAS AN ALTERCATION OF SORTS AT THE DULCE LABORATORY. A SPECIAL ARMED FORCES UNIT WAS CALLED IN TO TRY AND FREE A NUMBER OF OUR PEOPLE TRAPPED IN THE FACILITY, WHO HAD BECOME AWARE OF WHAT WAS REALLY GOING ON. ACCORDING TO ONE SOURCE 66 OF THE SOLDIERS WERE KILLED AND OUR PEOPLE WERE NOT FREED.

"By 1984, MJ-12 must have been in stark terror at the mistake they had made in dealing with the EBE's. They had subtly promoted 'Close Encounters of the Third Kind' and 'E.T.' to get the public used to 'odd looking' aliens that were compassionate, benevolent and very much our 'space brothers'. MJ-12 'sold' the EBE's to the public, and was now faced with the fact THAT QUITE THE OPPOSITE WAS TRUE. In addition, a plan was formulated in 1968 to make the public aware of the existence of aliens on earth over the next 20 years to be culminated with several documentaries to be released during 1985-1987 period of time. These documentaries would explain the history and intentions of the EBE's. The discovery of the 'GRAND DECEPTION' put the entire plans, hopes and dreams of MJ-12 into utter confusion and panic.

"Meeting at the 'Country Club', a remote lodge with private golf course, comfortable sleeping and working quarters, and its own private airstrip built by and exclusively for the members of MJ-12, it was a factional fight of what to do now. PART OF MJ-12 WANTED TO CONFESS THE WHOLE SCHEME AND SHAMBLES IT HAD BECOME TO THE PUBLIC, BEG THEIR FORGIVENESS AND ASK FOR THEIR SUPPORT. The other part [the majority] of MJ-12 argued that there was no way they could do that, that the situation was untenable and there was no use in exciting the public with the 'horrible truth' and that the best plan was to continue the development of a weapon that could be used against the EBE's under the guise of 'SDI', the Strategic Defense Initiative, which had nothing whatsoever to do with a defense for inbound Russian nuclear missiles.

As these words are being written, Dr. Edward Teller, 'father' of the H-Bomb is personally in the test tunnels of the Nevada Test Site, driving his workers and associates in the words of one, 'like a man possessed'. And well he should, for Dr. Teller is a member of MJ-12 along with Dr. Kissinger, Admiral Bobby Inman, and possibly Admiral Poindexter, to name a few of the current members of MJ-12.

"Before the 'Grand Deception' was discovered and according to a meticulous plan for metered release of information to the public, several documentaries and video tapes were made. William Moore, a Burbank, California, based UFO researcher who wrote 'The Roswell Incident' -- a book published in 1980 that detailed the crash, recovery and subsequent cover-up of a UFO with 4 alien bodies -- has a video tape of 2 newsmen interviewing a military officer associated with MJ-12.

This military officer answers questions relating to the history of MJ-12 and the cover-up, the recovery of a number of flying saucers and the existence of a live alien [one of 3 living aliens captured and designated, or named, EBE-1, EBE-2, and EBE-3, being held in a facility designated as YY-II at Los Alamos, New Mexico. The only other facility of this type, which is electromagnetically secure, is at Edwards Air Force Base in Mojave, California]. The officer names as previously mentioned plus a few others: Harold Brown, Richard Helms, Gen. Vernon Walters, JPL's Dr. Allen and Dr. Theodore van Karman, to name a few of the current and past members of MJ-12.

"The officer also relates the fact that the EBE's claim to have created Christ. The EBE's have a type of recording device that has recorded all of Earth's history and can display it in the form of a hologram. This hologram can be filmed but because of the way holograms work does not come out very clear on movie film or video tape. The crucifixion of Christ on the Mount of Olives **(this actually took place on the hill Calvary, not the Mt. of Olives - Branton)** has allegedly been put on film to show the public. The EBE's 'claim' to have created Christ, which, IN VIEW OF THE 'GRAND DECEPTION', COULD BE AN EFFORT TO DISRUPT TRADITIONAL VALUES FOR UNDETERMINED REASONS.

"Another video tape allegedly in existence is an interview with an EBE. Since EBE's communicate telepathically **(via psionic crystalline transceiver-like implants that link the Grays together into a mass collective-hive-mind - Branton)**, an Air Force Colonel serves as interpreter. Just before the recent stock market correction in October of 1987, several newsmen, including Bill Moore, had been invited to Washington D.C., to personally film the EBE in a similar type interview, and distribute the film to the public. Apparently, because of the correction in the market, it was felt the timing was not propitious. In any case, it certainly seems like an odd method to inform the public of extraterrestrials, but it would be in keeping with the actions of A PANICKED ORGANIZATION WHO AT THIS POINT IN TIME DOESN'T KNOW WHICH WAY TO TURN.

"Moore is also in possession of more Aquarius documents, a few pages of which leaked out several years ago and detailed the super secret NSA project which had been denied by them until just recently. In a letter to Senator John

THE DULCE PROTOCOL

Glenn, NSA's Director of Policy, Julia B. Wetzel, wrote, 'Apparently there is or was an Air Force project with the name [Aquarius] which dealt with UFO's.

Coincidentally, there is also an NSA project by that name.' NSA's project AQUARIUS deals specifically with 'communications with the aliens' [EBE's]. Within the Aquarius program was project 'Snowbird', a project to test-fly a recovered alien aircraft at Groom Lake, Nevada. This project continues today at that location. In the words of an individual who works at Groom Lake, 'Our people are much better at taking things apart than they are at putting them back together.'

"Moore, who claims he has a contact with MJ-12, feels that they have been stringing him along, slipping him documents and providing him with leads, promising to go public with some of the information on extraterrestrials by the end of 1987.

"Certain of Moore's statements lead one to believe that Moore himself is a government agent working for MJ-12, not to be strung along, but to string along ever hopeful Ufologists that the truth is just around the corner. Consider.

"1. Moore states emphatically that he is not a government agent, although when Lee Graham [a Southern California based Ufologist] was investigated by DIS [Defense Investigative Service] for possession of classified documents received from Moore, Moore himself was not.

"2. Moore states emphatically that the cattle mutilations of 1973-1983 were a hoax by Linda Howe [producer of 'A Strange Harvest'] to create publicity for herself. He cites the book 'Mute Evidence' as the bottom line of the hoax. 'Mute Evidence' was a government sponsored book to explain the mutilations in conventional terms.

"3. Moore states that the U.S.A.F. Academy physics book, 'Introductory Space Science', vol. II chapter 13, entitled 'Unidentified Flying Objects', which describes four of the most commonly seen aliens [one of which is the EBE] was written by Lt. Col. Edward R. Therkelson and Major Donald B. Carpenter. Air Force personnel who did not know what they were talking about and were merely citing 'crackpot' references. He, Moore, states that the book was withdrawn to excise the chapter.

"If the government felt they were being forced to acknowledge the existence of aliens on Earth because of the overwhelming evidence such as the October and November sightings in Wytheville, Va., and recently released books such as 'Night Siege' [Hynek, J. Allen; Imbrogno, Phillip J.; Pratt, Bob: NIGHT SIEGE, Ballantine Books, Random House, New York], and taking into consideration the 'grand deception' AND OBVIOUSLY HOSTILE INTENT OF THE EBE'S, it might be expedient for MJ-12 to admit the EBE's but conceal the information on the mutilations and abductions.

If MJ-12 and Moore were in some kind of agreement then it would be beneficial to Moore to tow the party line. For example, MJ-12 would say... 'here are some more genuine documents... but remember... no talking about the mutilations or abductions'. This would be beneficial to Moore as it would supply the evidence to support his theory that ET's exist but deny the truths about the ET's. However, if Moore was indeed working for MJ-12, he would follow the party line anyway, admitting the ET's but pooh poohing the mutilations and abductions. If working alone, Moore might not even be aware of the 'grand deception'.

"Time will tell. It is possible that Moore will go ahead and release the video interview with the military officer around the first of the year, as he has promised. From MJ-12's point of view, the public would be exposed to the information without really having to believe it because Moore is essentially not as credible a source as, say, the President of the United States. After a few months of digestion and discussion, a more credible source could emerge with a statement that yes in fact the interview was essentially factual.

This scenario would cushion somewhat the blow to the public. If, however, Moore does not release the tape by, say, February 1 of 1988, but comes instead with a story similar to: 'MJ-12 has informed me that they are definitely planning a release of all information by October of 88... I have seen the plan and have seen the guarantee that this will happen, so I have decided to withhold the release of my video tape at this time as it may cause some problems with MJ-12's plans.' This would in effect buy more time for MJ-12 and time is what they desperately need.

"Now you ask, 'Why haven't I heard any of this?' Who do you think you would hear it from? Dan Rather? Tom Brokaw? Sam Donaldson? Wrong. These people just read the news, they don't find it. They have ladies who call and interview witnesses and verify statements on stories coming over the wire [either AP or UPI]. It's not like Dan Rather would go down to Wytheville, Virginia, and dig into why there were FOUR THOUSAND reported sightings in October and November of 1987.

Better Tom Brokaw or someone else should risk their credibility on this type of story. Tom Brokaw? Tom wants Sam Donaldson to risk his credibility. No one, <u>but no one, is going to risk their neck</u> on such outlandish ideas, regardless of how many people report sightings of 900 foot objects running them off the road. In the case of the Wytheville sightings, dozens of vans with NASA lettered on the side failed to interest newsmen. And those that asked questions were informed that NASA was doing a weather survey.

"Well then, you ask, what about our scientists? What about Carl Sagan? Isaac Asimov? Arthur C. Clarke? Wouldn't they have known? If Carl Sagan knows then he is committing a great fraud through the solicitation of memberships in the Planetary Society, 'to search for extraterrestrial intelligence'. Another charade into which the U.S. Government dumps millions of dollars every year is the radio-telescope in Arecibo, Puerto Rico, operated by Cornell University with - guess who? - Carl Sagan. Cornell is ostensibly searching for signals from Outer Space, a sign maybe, that somebody is out there. It is hard to believe that relatively intelligent astronomers like Sagan could be so ignorant.

(Note: Also, even if 'they' did find evidence of extraterrestrial life, do you think that SETI and similar government-sponsored projects would tell US about it? Let's just take a look at some actual statements from those involved with these projects.

The following is a quote from Matt Spetalnick's article "IS ANYBODY OUT THERE? NASA LOOKS FOR REAL ET'S", in REUTERS Magazine, Oct. 5, 1992:

"At least 70 times scientists have picked up radio waves that bore the marks of communication by beings from other worlds, but they were never verified, [Frank] Drake said."

And researcher John Spencer, in a reference to Dr. Otto Strove, tells how this astrophysicist assisted Frank Drake in establishing Project OZMA, and it's very mysterious conclusion: "...the project began its search by focusing on the star TAU CETI.

According to claims made at the time, AS SOON AS the project got underway STRONG INTELLIGENT SIGNALS were picked up, leaving all the scientists stunned. Abruptly, Dr. Strove then declared Project OZMA had been shut down, and commented that there was no sensible purpose for listening to messages from another world." [THE UFO ENCYCLOPEDIA]. So then, these 'insiders' will accept ALL of our hard-earned tax dollars to finance their radio projects -- if not their underground bases and covert space operations. Yet cursed be any 'mere mortal' for having the audacity to actually insist on having access to the products of their 'financial investments'! - Branton)

"What about Isaac Asimov? Surely the most prolific science fiction writer of all time would have guessed by now that there must be an enormous cover-up? Maybe, but if he knows he's not saying. Perhaps he's afraid that Foundation and Empire will turn out to be inaccurate.

"What about Arthur C. Clarke? Surely the most technically accurate of Science Fiction writers with very close ties to NASA would have at least a hint of what's really going on. Again, if so he isn't talking. In a recent Science Fiction survey, Clarke estimates that contact with extraterrestrial intelligent life would not occur before the 21st Century.

"If the government won't tell us the truth and the major networks won't even give it serious consideration...

(Note: This was written before such programs as SIGHTINGS, ENCOUNTERS, UNSOLVED MYSTERIES, CURRENT AFFAIR, MONTEL WILLIAMS, STRANGE UNIVERSE and other TV news digests and talk shows DID begin dealing with the UFO phenomena, abductions, and so on in much greater depth -- not to mention the X-FILES, DARK SKIES and other TV series'. - Branton),

...then what is the big picture, anyway? Are the EBE's, having done a hundred thousand or more abductions [possibly millions worldwide], built AN UNTOLD NUMBER OF SECRET UNDERGROUND BASES [Groom Lake, Nevada; Sunspot, Datil, Roswell, and Pie Town, New Mexico, just to name a few] getting ready to Return to wherever they came from? Or, from the obvious preparations are we to assume that they are getting ready for a big move? or is [it] the more sinister and most probable situation that the invasion is essentially complete and it is all over but the screaming?

"A well planned invasion of Earth for its resources and benefits would not begin with mass landings or ray-gun equipped aliens. A properly planned and executed invasion by a civilization thousands [of] years in advance of us would most likely be complete before a handful of people, say 12?, realized what was happening. No fuss, no mess. The best advice I can give you is this: Next time you see a flying saucer and are awed by its obvious display of technology and gorgeous lights of pure color - RUN LIKE HELL!   -- June 3, 1988 Las Vegas, NV"

[The following was an addendum to the above that was included with later copies of John Lear's 'statement']:

"In 1983 when the Grand Deception was discovered MJ-12 [which may now be designated 'PI-40'] started work on a weapon or some kind of device to contain the EBE's which had by now totally infested our society. This program was funded through SDI which, coincidentally, was initiated at approximately the same date. A frantic effort has been made over the past 4 years by all participants. This program ended in failure in December of 1987.

(Note: British Ufologist Timothy Good claimed that over 22 British scientists -- who were working on the U.S. SDI program for British Marconi and other Aerospace companies -- had all mysteriously died or 'committed suicide' within the space of a few years. Could this have had anything to do with this 'failure'? Apparently someone 'out there' was intent on sabotaging the SDI / STAR WARS project. Also there are reports that several of our 'defense satellites' have been destroyed as well. - Branton).

"A new program has been conceived but will take about 2 years to develop. In the meantime, it is absolutely essential to MJ-12 [PI-40], that no one, including the Senate, the Congress or the Citizens of the United States of America [or anyone else for that matter] become aware of the real circumstances surrounding the UFO cover-up and total disaster it has become.

THE DULCE PROTOCOL

"Moore never did release the video tapes but claims he is negotiating with a major network to do so...'soon'."

Another source added the following statements in regards to Lear's claims:

"Area 51... and a similar setup near Dulce, New Mexico, may now belong to forces not loyal to the U.S. Government, or even the human race. 'It's horrifying to think that all the scientists we think are working for us [in the joint-interaction bases] are actually controlled by aliens.'

"'...SDI, regardless of what you hear, was completed...to shoot down incoming saucers. The mistake was that we thought they were coming inbound -- in fact, they're already here. They're in underground bases all over the place.' It seems that the aliens had constructed many such bases without our knowledge, where they conduct heinous genetic experiments on animals, human beings, and 'improvised' creatures of their own devising.

"Thus was born PROJECT EXCALIBUR. Press reports described EXCALIBUR as a weapons system designed to obliterate deeply-buried Soviet command centers, which the Reagan Administration hypocritically characterized as destabilizing. We have exactly similar centers. Lear claims the weapon was actually directed toward the internal alien threat. Unfortunately, the 'visitors' have invaded us in more ways than one.

"'Millions of Americans have been implanted. There's a little device that varies in size from 50 microns to 3 millimeters; it is inserted through the nose into the brain. It effectively controls the person. Dr. [J. Allen] Hynek estimated in 1972 that one in every 40 Americans was implanted; we believe it may be as high as one in ten now.' These implants will be activated at some time in the near future, for some unspecified alien purpose.'"

Robert K Teske

When Lear was pressed to disclose some of his sources, he stated that his anonymous intelligence informants "go right to the top." He did however mention some of the names in not-so-sensitive intelligence positions from whom he has also gathered information; many of these names may be familiar to veteran Ufologists.

These include:

* Paul Bennewitz, director of Thunder Scientific Laboratories [a New Mexico-based research facility with government contract ties], who claims to have gained access to and 'interrogated' an alien computer system via a radio-video-computer setup of his own invention.

* Linda Howe, the television documentarian responsible for STRANGE HARVEST [a program about cattle mutilations], who received astonishing 'leaks' from a special intelligence officer, Colonel Richard Doty formerly of Kirtland AFB, a name noted in aerial research circles.

* Robert Collins [code-named 'Condor', according to Lear] who has secured numerous official documents relating to UFOs.

* Sgt. Clifford Stone, premiere collector of UFO related Freedom of Information Act or FOIA documents.

* Travis Walton, professed UFO abductee whose experience inspired the movie FIRE IN THE SKY.

As an interesting follow-up to Lear's article, we quote here some actual statements made by prominent individuals in regards to the 'UFO' phenomenon:

"In our obsession with antagonisms of the moment, we often forget how much unites all the members of humanity. Perhaps we need some outside, universal threat to make us realize this common bond. I occasionally think how quickly our differences would vanish if we were facing an alien threat from outside this world. And yet, I ask you, IS NOT AN ALIEN FORCE ALREADY AMONG US?" **-- President Ronald Reagan., Remarks made to the 42nd General Assembly of the United Nations., Sept. 21, 1987**

"I couldn't help but say to him [Gorbachev], just think how easy his task and mine might be in these meetings that we held if suddenly there was a threat to this world from some other species from another planet outside in the universe... Well, I don't suppose we can wait for some alien race to come down and threaten us. But I think that between us we can bring about that realization." **-- President Ronald Reagan., Remarks to Fallston High School students and Faculty, Fallston, MD., October 4, 1985**

"For your confidential information, a reliable and confidential source has advised the Bureau that flying disks are believed to be man-made missiles rather than natural phenomenon. It has also been determined that for approximately the past four years the USSR has been engaged in experimentation on an unknown type of flying disk." **-- FBI Memo dated March 25, 1949 sent to a large number of FBI offices.**

"...on Unidentified Flying Objects... The panel recommends that the national security agencies institute policies... designed to prepare the material defenses and the morale of the country to recognize... and react most effectively to true indications of hostile measures." **-- Recommendation of the CIA Robertson Panel on UFOs, January, 1953**

"Public interest in disclosure is far outweighed by the sensitive nature of the materials and the obvious effect on national security their release may entail." **-- U.S. District Court Opinion in the case of Citizens Against UFO Secrecy vs. the National Security Agency., May 18, 1982**

"The sums made available to the Agency may be expended without regard to the provisions of law and regulations relating to the expenditures of Government." -- **Central Intelligence Act of 1949**

"On this land a flying disk has been found intact, with eighteen three-foot tall human-LIKE occupants, all dead in it but not burned." -- **FBI memo from New Orleans Branch to Director, FBI, March 31, 1950 about a disk found in the Mojave desert in January, 1950**

"When four sit down to conspire, three are fools and the fourth is a government agent." -- **Duncan Lunan**

"The flying disks are real." -- **General Nathan Twining.**

"According to Mr. ... (informant), the saucers were found in New Mexico due to the fact that the Government has a very high-powered radar setup in that area and it is believed that the radar [EM beams] interferes with the controlling mechanism of the saucers...each one of the three saucers were occupied by three bodies of human SHAPE, but only 3 feet tall, dressed in metallic cloth of a very fine texture." -- **FBI Memo from agent Guy Hottel., Washington Field Office., sent to Director, FBI., March 22, 1950**

"I WOULD SAY THAT WE KNOW OF SEVERAL, SHOULD WE SAY, INTERGALACTIC FIGHTS THAT HAVE TAKEN PLACE -- DOGFIGHTS." -- **United States Army Sgt. Clifford Stone, Roswell N.M. Station.**

"He believes that because of the developments of science all the countries on earth will have to unite to survive and to make a common front against attack by 'people' from other planets." -- **Mayor Achille Lauro of Naples, quoting General Douglas MacArthur in the NEW YORK TIMES, Saturday October 8, 1955. p.7**

Chapter 4
Dulce New Mexico & The Nazi Connection

Researcher Jim Bennett, in a letter to Jacques Vallee dated Jan. 15, 1992, made some startling disclosures in regards to the alien situation and the Dulce, N.M. base in particular. It is my belief that even if there is a fascist-CIA cabal trying to establish a world dictatorship using the 'threat' of an alien invasion to foment world government, that the 'threat' may be real all the same.

It is also possible that the 'Bavarians' may be working with very REAL aliens in an end-game designed to establish a world government using this 'threat' as an excuse to do so, although when the world is under 'their' control the Illuminati may betray the human race by turning much of the global government control-system over to the Grey aliens [the Beast?].

The aliens may have been collaborating with the Bavarians for a very long time as part of their agenda to implement absolute electronic control over the inhabitants of planet earth. One source, an Area 51 worker -- and member of a secret Naval Intelligence group called COM-12 -- by the name of Michael Younger, stated that the Bavarian Black Nobility [secret societies] have agreed to turn over three-quarters of the planet to the Greys if they could retain 25 percent for themselves and have access to alien mind-control technology.

The aliens would assist in the abduction, programming and implanting of people throughout the world in preparation for a New World Order -- which in turn would be annexed to the alien empire. Apparently some top-echelon Bavarians have agreed to this, since they realize that they NEED the alien mind-control and implant technology in order to carry out their plans for world domination.

In his lengthy letter, Jim Bennett, director of the research organization 'PLANET-COM', writes:

"...1947 brought the passage of the National Security Act, the start of the NAZI GERMINATED CIA and NSA. The influx of at least a hundred Nazi scientists, engineers, etc., into the United States and Canada.

(Note: Other sources claim that eventually over 3000 Nazi S.S. agents entered the U.S. in this manner. NOT former Nazi's but ACTIVE Nazi SS who still maintained the national socialist philosophy and agendas which they intended to carry through on to their planned conclusion.

They were given refuge within the military-industrial complex with the help of members of the Bavarian-based black Gnostic -- serpent worshipping -- lodges in America, such as the Jesuit-spawned Scottish Rite and related lodges who control the oil-military-industrial complex. The leaders of the Military-Industrial Complex or M.I.C. not only gave these fascists refuge following the war, but also had financed the Nazi war machine itself during the second world war. - Branton).

"A Nazi aeronautical engineer, a certain Herr Mieth -- who had designed four different types of saucer shaped craft by 1943 using either rocket power or DONUT CONFIGURATION jet turbine engines, with the cabin stabilized by gyro, the compressors rotating in one direction and the expansion chambers and vectored exhausts rotating in the opposite direction -- was traced to Canada in 1947 and began work for the A. V. Roe company [Avroe disk]. The phony AVROE 'aircar' was definitely to disinform the press as to the real projects underway underground in Canada.

"The eight mile long train that went out of Austria in 1945 [672 train cars!], to the coast of Brittany, the contents loaded on board SHIPS, eventually ended up underground in Southwestern Canada. At the same time over 100 prefab factory buildings were shipped from England to British Columbia.

"...the Nazis had everything before any other country, they had radar in 1933, they had infra-red sensors, heavy water, etc., etc. We have been told lie after lie in terms of who invented these things. If anyone in the world had access to 'alien' technology it was the...'Aryans' [Nazis]. Their metallurgy and casting were flawed or they would have conquered the world.

As you probably know, many expatriate Nazis were given carte blanche, new I.D.'s, and were included in [the] startup of more than several departments of the CIA in 1947. Departments including 'genetics and cloning' [with some of the same 'doctors' who had given death camp residents gangrene, etc.] 'designer drugs and mind control' using the same scientists who had designed Methadone and Methedrine for Hitler's maniac efforts. In 1952, a public stir caused the CIA to shuffle these fab fellows out of town. My guess is to various underground centers that were being built.

"...I have talked to Paul Bennewitz at length, several times. On his behalf, you only tell people how they drove him nuts, not why. I ask myself why would you leave out the reason why they sent him reeling. **(here Bennett is addressing Jacques Vallee concerning his book 'REVELATIONS' - Branton)** To fill you in, because you obviously took Linda Howe's and Tracy's opinion rather than questioning Paul directly; he's a pilot, he flew over the Dulce area numerous times on his way between Albuquerque and Denver.

He took many pictures of the construction going on, and according to Paul, he also took pictures of circular craft on the ground at this site which, as late as 1973 according to him, had large hanger doors much the same as Lazar's second hand explanation about the doors at S-4. [All the stuff from Area 51 and 'S-4' having to do with inertial mass cancellation was moved to an area NEAR ST. GEORGE, UTAH]. The most revealing photos and their negatives disappeared in or about 1975 when various 'fringe UFO experts' visited Paul.

Also, his house was burglarized and ransacked more than once. In later years Moore, Shandera, and Torme made a meaningless tour of Dulce when they went on to Albuquerque [the real reason for their travels] to see if there was any more evidence of serious consequence still in Paul's possession that they could grab, and sure enough, he was missing some photos when they left his house. If you even talked to Bennewitz, you would have gotten a lot closer to having a 'revelation'...

"The 'waste' from the underground bio-genetic lab [no aliens involved, although that is where we humans produce the short lived, big-eyed, big headed imitation 'aliens'] comes out in the river canyon about TEN MILES BELOW Navajo Dam...

(Note: An alternative scenario to the above would be that reptiloid grey 'aliens' ARE involved -- AS WELL AS biogenetically constructed beings developed by Illuminati-Thule-CIA backed scientists working in the Dulce facility - Branton)

"Although these days they 'treat' it a lot more before letting their 'grey' water back into the environment. This base and others are of course connected by tunnels to Los Alamos. The Archuleta Mesa installation rivals Pine Gap at Alice Springs, Australia for security, etc. Every U.S. Air Force base has a so-called 'bolt-hole' and is connected to this bolt-hole by tunnel...

"A group of 21 people led by an individual we will call Rick, went to Area 51 in 1989 in a small bus to watch 'saucers'. They were stopped on 'mail-box road' by two individuals carrying automatic weapons and wearing camouflage togs. One individual popped a can of 'gas' in the aisle of the bus, and that's all for three hours.

When they came to their senses, they cut their trip short, Returned to L.A. and five persons got separately regressed using hypnotic regressors that did not know one another, and found that during the lost time their memories had repressed similar events. They had been marched off the bus, taken in jeeps to a building nearby, and had their lives threatened by military personnel...

"In the U.S., the group that runs the 'alien abduction scam' can only use some of the hardiest of these short lived bio-genetic bad luck stories. Short lived because they have no digestive tract and can survive only about two weeks maximum after they are removed from the growing matrix, then they deteriorate and die. They have no 'soul' and are not considered 'sentient beings' by Tibetan Buddhists."

(Note: One might ask why they would bother. The REPTILIAN Grays, the 'cloned' branch -- although in addition to the 'clones' there are also apparently the 'polyembryons' and 'egg-layers' -- reportedly have no digestive tract and thus intake 'food' and excrete waste through the skin. Jim Bennett may have just assumed that, since they have no digestive tract they had no way of taking-in 'food', and that they were therefore government creations which die after two weeks of starving. We grant however that Bennett is right in that -- according to the DULCE PAPERS -- human and cattle DNA may be used to develop "Almost Humans", and other unnatural living forms - Branton)

"...The army's mind control unit must take well deserved credit for the veterans who seemingly go suddenly crazy, killing many people and then themselves. The most recent event in Killeen, Texas was planned for the day BEFORE a Congressional vote on gun control, hoping to influence Congress with yet another mass automatic killing. Handlers [psychiatrists] at each perpetrator's local Veterans Hospital are involved in each and every case of these mass killings/suicides.

Prozac is also involved with each case having been prescribed by the aforementioned 'handlers' in each and every case. The fellow in Canada who killed 12 women at a women's college, the fellow in Stockton, California schoolyard, etc. etc..."

FURTHER COMMENTS ON GERMAN-BAVARIAN NAZISM, THE CIA, THE NEW WORLD ORDER, ETC.

Sirhan Sirhan, the man who was convicted of murdering Senator Robert Kennedy, had a psychiatrist by the name of 'Dr. Diamond' who maintained CIA-fascist connections.

Also Sirhan's attorney Grant Cooper, who seemingly made very little effort to defend Sirhan, had CIA-fascist ties as well, leading some to believe that Sirhan was used as a hypno-programmed "Manchurian Candidate" by a fascist cabal, a cabal that murdered not only Robert Kennedy but also his brother President John F. Kennedy as well.

Following World War II over 2,000 German 'immigrants' to the U.S. became members of the American Psychiatric Association, which was involved in GUN CONTROL lobbying. In light the collaboration between the Bavarian Thule Society and the Bavarian Illuminati, and the influx of Thule-backed fifth-column Nazi SS agents into U.S. Intelligence, with the help of Illuminati-backed Oil barrens like the German-immigrant Aryan-supremacist Rockefellers and their corporate oil-chemical empires [EXXON, ARCO, ZAPATA, etc.], and in light of the deadly intent of both 'Bavarian' societies to establish a "New World Order" as Adolph Hitler laid out in his second book "The New World Order", one has to wonder WHY so many German nationals would join an association that dealt directly with the study of people's MINDS?

This is not to say that Germans themselves are to blame, it is rather the German-Bavarian FASCISTS who are behind the New World Order agenda, and especially the

THE DULCE PROTOCOL

Satanist Germanic Black Nobility families who claim direct descent from the early leaders of the [un]Holy Roman Empire of Germany, which rose from the remnant of the Roman Empire and which kept Europe in an iron grip throughout the Dark Ages. These were the "13 families" who had ruled vast financial empires in Europe for nearly 1500 years.

They are once again trying to take control of the world as they attempted to do with World Wars I and II, provoke a global war that will result in the massive 'de-population' of Blacks, Asians, Jews, Slavs, and many others -- excepting of course for the 'Aryan elite' class. In essence they intend to finish what Adolph Hitler set out to accomplish. The threat then is from 'Nazism' or National 'Socialism', whether it be European, British or American or whether it be political, corporate or occult National Socialism.

Some have reported that the sudden 'fall' of the Soviet states and the Berlin wall was planned in advance as part of an agenda to merge the East and the West into a so called communist-socialist / democratic-socialist New World Order. East and West Berlin would be at the forefront for the reunification of Eastern and Western Europe and in turn -- they hope -- the rest of the world.

Germany has also led the way for European unification by establishing an 'open border' policy and encouraging other European countries to do the same. This may sound benign on the outside but considering the facts it may be a ruse to 'unify' Europe under German control, which was also Adolph Hitler's goal. However in this case the unification is being accomplished through economic means rather than military means.

The control is still in Germany but it is more subtle. The Third Reich established German MILITARY control of Europe. The "European Economic Community" or E.E.C. established ECONOMIC control. In most cases, in this world it is the ECONOMIC forces which control 'governments'. Sad, but true. Notice how the term "Economic" has now been removed, and the New World Order has been re-named the

"European Community". Very clever! In other words the unification is no longer just along economic lines but is becoming increasingly political, since the member nations have been pressured into submitting to an E.C. constitution along MORE THAN mere economic lines.

France and England have been pulled into this alliance, in spite of two devastating world wars with the very country that is secretly orchestrating the E.C. or the New World Order. Come on France and England, wake up!

Germany is not only the largest federated state in the E.C., but in 1990 was the LARGEST economic power in the WORLD, with a trade surplus totaling over $58 billion. With almost no foreign currency reserves in 1949, Germany had accumulated nearly $80 billion in reserves by 1989, compared with the $38 billion in the U.S.A. and $41 billion in Great Britain. A rather incredible "comeback" for a country that had waged two world wars for the sole purpose of offensive conquest, wars that had cost the Allies a HEAVY price in blood and resources.

Of course Germany is also the LEADING economic power in the E.C. as well, possessing 35% of the Economic power-base of the European Community according to the GROLIER ENCYCLOPEDIA. So just WHERE does the real power lie in the E.C. / N.W.O? Considering that the German Black Nobility were the same ones who sent Vladimir Lenin from GERMANY to Russia to start the Communist Revolution, AND the same powers who backed Adolph Hitler... then it is not surprising that Communist East Germany would merge into Democratic(?) West Germany with such ease.

It should not be surprising, therefore, to learn that GERMAN troops In the United States AND Canada play a MAJOR role in the planned invasion of North America under the cover of a "United Nations" emergency action. Lenin himself revealed the ultimate goal of the 'Communist' agenda, on behalf of the Bavarian 'elite' whom he served. Communism, like Democracy, was supposed to give control of the government to the PEOPLE.

THE DULCE PROTOCOL

But of course Lenin altered the plan a little bit -- just as the largely unelected-appointed Executive branch of the American government 'altered' the rules of democracy -- and stated that he did not believe that the common people could 'handle' the responsibility of directing the Communist Revolution, so a select group of individuals 'trained' in the 'Communist philosophy' would carry out this responsibility instead.

And wouldn't you know it, many of these 'people' who ended up as the leaders of the Communist Revolution were hand-picked by the German-immigrant "Capitalist" Rockefeller family themselves.

"Oh what a tangled web we weave...."

The Bavarian cultists who were REALLY running the show would of course be the "WE" that Lenin refers to in the following quote:

"First WE will TAKE Russia, next WE will CAPTURE the nations of eastern Europe, and then WE will TAKE the masses of Asia. Finally, WE will SURROUND the United States and that last bastion of freedom will fall into our hands like over-ripe fruit."

A likely scenario that some have suggested would be an orchestrated global economic collapse -- blamed on Americans of course -- which would be followed by fomented anarchy in American cities, followed by sudden nuclear strikes on strategic military bases on the East and West coasts, followed by a Chinese invasion of the West coast, a Russian invasion via Alaska, and a United Nations / German invasion via the East and North-East coasts of the U.S.A.

Robert K Teske

All of those countries who believe that by accepting a flawed Socialist political agenda from ANOTHER country [Germany] in order to supplement their own nation and cultural integrity are sadly mistaken.

Collaborating with a Bavarian-backed United Nations-New World Order agenda can only lead to the DEATH of your independence as a nation, the DEATH of your culture and history, and the DEATH of your children who are sent to fight and die for the sake of a Global Government, its Bavarian-Antarctican masters, and in turn their 'Draconian' allies who are just waiting with greedy claws to take hold of this planet once they have succeeded in getting us to kill each other off to the point where they can move right in and take over with little human resistance.

Chapter 5

Report From A Japanese Television Crew

Norio Hayakawa is the head of the 'CIVILIAN INTELLIGENCE NETWORK' [P.O. Box 599., Gardena, CA 80248].

Mr. Hayakawa was one of several individuals, including a Japanese film crew from the NIPPON Television Network in Japan, who witnessed and video-taped "a flight maneuver of a brightly lit orange-yellowish light making extremely unorthodox flight patterns, including sudden acceleration, descension and ascension -- possibly exerting a force of multiple g's under extremely limited space and time -- and even zig-zag type movements, while on a field trip to an area just outside of 'Area 51' in Nevada on Wednesday, February 21, 1990" [there were approximately 25 to 28 individuals in the group who also witnessed the display].

His brother-in-law Itsuro Isokawa also photographed the object as it was in flight.

With over 30 years of in-depth UFO investigative experience, Norio was instrumental in the subsequent production of a two-hour documentary program televised throughout Japan on March 24, 1990.

The entire program dealt with Area 51 and also the crew's pursuit of an alleged biogenetics laboratory in New Mexico, that is, the DULCE facility. It is his contention that what could only be described as,

"...highly intelligent and deceptive 'ultradimensional entities' materializing in disguise as 'aliens', are collaborating with a secret 'world government' that is preparing (barring unexpected circumstances - Branton) to ingeniously 'stage' a contact-landing...to bring about a 'New World Order'."

(Note: This Alien-Bavarian collaboration is apparently feigning animosity with one another by pushing for global government so that the world can join together to "fight the aliens". As in Vietnam and Korea where the Socialist leaders of the United Nations Organization were playing both sides of the chessboard, any war waged by the "New World Order" against the Grays will no doubt be a no-win conflict that will only serve to reduce the population of the planet, which is after all part and parcel of the overall Draconian-Bavarian global agenda.

Another possibility that has been suggested is that the Grays will be made out to be the good guys who need 'our' help to break free from the tall Reptiloids and their empire, which had conquered them in the past, or visa versa. Actually the collaboration between the Reptiloids and Grays has been undertaken with the full consent of both sides, and behind the scenes the collectivist Reptiloids, the Insectoids, the Grays and the Bavarian secret society lodges are all working together.

Many scenarios are possible... however the important thing to remember is that ANY war waged against the Reptilian Grays which threatens the American Declaration of Independence, the U.S. Constitution and the Bill of Rights is merely playing into the hands of the aliens either way you look at it. International 'cooperation' in a common defense against an alien threat should be considered SO LONG AS the national sovereignty of individual nations are not violated in the process.

THE DULCE PROTOCOL

All nations should learn to be self-supporting and not be tempted to succumb to a global economic system -- and therefore a global political system, in that money and politics are more or less synonymous... at least in this world where those who control the money CONTROL the governments. Also independent economies will prevent all nations from falling like dominoes if an economic collapse does occur.

The target of any future attacks against an outside 'threat' to a nation's security should not be excluded ONLY to the aliens NOR exclusively against human conspirators or tyrants, but the target of any future conflict with one or the other -- in regards to planetary or national defense -- should be directed specifically at those 'areas' where collaboration and interaction between the alien infiltrators AND the human collaborators are taking place... for instance areas such as the underground 'joint-interaction' bases of Neu Schwabenland, Antarctica, Pine Gap, Australia; Alsace-Lorraine Mts. area of France-Germany; and of course and probably by far the worst of all, the underground mega-complex below DULCE, NEW MEXICO where the worst life-forms this universe has to offer seemingly congregate, conceive and carry out their atrocities against their victims -- or those who have been taken or abducted to the base permanently -- as well as against their implanted-programmed victims beyond the confines of the base who are never-the-less forced to exist in 'psychological' concentration camps imposed on them against their will by the 'collaboration'. - Branton)

Furthermore, Norio Hayakawa contends that the 'GRAND DECEPTION',

"... will immediately follow a rapid series of shocking, incredible events in succession, beginning with a Russia-backed Arab Confederacy's attempt to invade Israel, simultaneous worldwide earthquakes, worldwide stock market crash and a sudden, mysterious 'evacuation' of a segment of the planets population, all of which will culminate in a quick official formation of a New World Order [based in Europe] that will last for seven years upon its inception."

(Note: It is interesting that George Washington's famous 'vision' at Valley Forge accurately predicted the Revolutionary and Civil wars and their outcome, and also a 'third trial' through which America must pass... an air, ground and sea invasion of the America's by a World Order which will have conquered all of Asia, Africa and Europe. Depending on how one interprets the prophecies of Revelation, this siege will last for either 3 1/2 or 7 years, and will end with an American victory aided by Divine Intervention. I personally believe that America is the 'wilderness' spoken of in the 12th chapter of the book of Revelation.

Since the world empire will last no longer than 7 years according to the books of DANIEL and REVELATION, the invasion/siege of America must also not exceed 7 years, although I suspect that it will be closer to 3 1/2 years. Also Washington's vision combined with other prophetic sources seem to imply that those who are living west of the Mississippi river at this time will be far better off then those in the 'occupied' zone east of the Mississippi. If General Washington's vision was accurate, then the ultimate outcome of the battle is not the question. The real question is HOW MANY Americans -- North-Central-South Americans -- will survive through to the final victory? - Branton)

Norio also explains that the 'Grand Deception' and the shocking series of events will "...put millions and millions of people worldwide in an absolute stupor for months during which time a special, extremely effective, multi-leveled 'mind control' program will be activated to calm down the stunned populace..."

Hayakawa has himself appeared on Japanese television, has lectured considerably, has appeared on a radio station in Phoenix, Arizona, and has been the subject of an article in the ARIZONA REPUBLIC, has published articles in 'U.S. Japanese Business News' [March, 1990], was the guest on a Japanese talk show in March and April of 1990, and also appeared on the Billy Goodman 'Happening' on KVEG of Las Vegas several times in early 1990, and in 1995 made dramatic appearances on Art Bell's DREAMLAND broadcast.

THE DULCE PROTOCOL

He was also interviewed on the Anthony J. Hilder Show on "Radio Free America" aired in Anchorage, Alaska, during all of which he spoke extensively about his interesting beliefs concerning the origin and nature of UFO's.

In a letter dated January 28, 1991, Norio added the following comments concerning the 'Dulce' facility and it's possible connection with the 'Mystery of Iniquity' of Bible prophecy:

"...I've been to Dulce with the Nippon Television Network crew and interviewed many, many people over there and came back with the firm conviction that something was happening around 10 to 15 years ago over there, including nightly sightings of strange lights and appearances of military jeeps and trucks. And I am convinced that the four corners area is a highly occult area. The only stretch of highway, namely Highway 666, runs through the four corners area from southeast Arizona to North-western New Mexico and up [and into SW Colorado and SE Utah]. I have also heard that this Highway 666 came into existence around 1947 or 1948, fairly close to the time of 1947, the modern-day beginning of OVERT UFO APPEARANCE, i.e. the Kenneth Arnold incident, and coincidentally or not, the establishment of Israel in 1948."

(Norio believes that the establishment of the nation of Israel in 1948 began the 'countdown' to the final apocalypse -- see Revelation chapter 12, for instance. - Branton)

The following is a transcript of parts of a speech presented by Mr. Hayakawa at the 11th 'LOS ANGELES WHOLE LIFE EXPO' held at The Los Angeles Airport Hilton Convention Center on November 16 and 17, 1991.

The transcript from which we will quote is a revised and expanded version of the address or lecture written on June of 1992 and titled: 'UFO'S, THE GRAND DECEPTION AND THE COMING NEW WORLD ORDER':

"...AREA 51 is located in the northeastern corner of a vast, desolate stretch of land known as the Nevada Test Site [a large portion of which includes the Nellis Air Force Test Range] but has practically nothing to do with underground nuclear testing. It is located approximately 125 miles north-northwest of Las Vegas and consists of Groom Lake and the Papoose Lake Complexes. The presently expanding eastern portion of the latter complexes is known as the S-4 site.

"This entire area is under the strictest control of Airspace R-4808N [with unlimited 'ceiling'], prohibiting any entry therein of air traffic, civilian or military, unless special clearance for such entry is secured well in advance. By land, the area is meticulously patrolled 24-hours a day by several tiers of external security even though it is conveniently 'covered' by the... Jumbled Hills [...which cover north of the Papoose Lake area], making it virtually impossible for anyone to see the facilities without first climbing atop the hills of the rugged mountain range which became off-limits to the public since 1985.

"The main external perimeter security is now being handled by Wackenhut Special Securities Division, part of the operations of Wackenhut Corporation, a worldwide semi-private security firm based in Coral Gables, Florida which has an exclusive contract with the U.S. Department of Energy and handles not only the perimeter security at the Nevada Test Site but also at many other secret facilities and sensitive installations throughout the U.S. and U.S. interests worldwide, including ground-level perimeters for several large underground facilities in and around Edwards Air Force Base in Southern California.

"It is also important to mention that dozens of unmanned, miniature-sized remote-controlled automatic security vehicles constantly patrol the immediate perimeters of the S-4 Site, located around [and presently expanding particularly towards the eastern portion of] Papoose Lake. These automatic, miniature sized four-wheel vehicles have been produced by Sandia Laboratories of Albuquerque, New Mexico exclusively for the Department of Energy.

THE DULCE PROTOCOL

"The outer northeastern perimeters of this area located in the Tickaboo Valley come under the geographical jurisdiction of Lincoln County and are relegated to the Bureau of Land Management [B.L.M.]. Yet it is considered highly inadvisable for anyone to even enter the main country dirt road, known as the Groom Road, which begins its southwestern extension towards Groom Lake from a point midway between mile marker 34 and 33 on Highway 375, and leads to the guard shack located two and a half miles northeast of the Groom Lake complexes.

"The first line of exterior security forces [dressed in military-type camouflage uniforms but with no insignia of any kind whatsoever] consists of the GP patrols [the 'Groom Proper' patrols, in Bronco-type four-wheel drive vehicles] who sometimes drive around at night with their lights off on various country dirt roads adjacent to the outer demilitarized zone, intimidating any civilian vehicle that tries to enter those access roads [off of Highway 375] located on public land. The GP patrols themselves [part of Wackenhut Special Securities Division], however, are strictly ordered to avoid any direct contact with civilians. They are only instructed to radio the Lincoln County Sheriff immediately should anyone be spotted driving on any of those dirt roads. The most common radio frequency used between Security Control and Lincoln County Sheriff's patrols is 138.306 MHZ.

"...The only area 'allowed' by the Sheriff for such curiosity seekers to 'congregate' is an open area near a black mailbox located at the south side of Highway 375 between mile marker 29 and 30. Even then, the Sheriff patrol will routinely stop by during the evening to check on the cars parked at the mailbox area.

"Moreover, it is our understanding, based on information provided by a highly reliable source connected to a special U.S. Navy SEAL operations center, that the mailbox area is constantly being monitored by high-powered, state-of-the-art, infra-red telescopes set up at a facility known as Security Control high atop Bald Mountain [10 miles west of the area], the highest peak in the Groom Mountain Range.

"...It was precisely at 4:45 a.m. on the morning of Thursday, April 16, 1992, that an NBC news crew, dispatched to the area to report on the landing of an alleged super spy-plane known as Aurora on Groom Lake, accidentally succeeded in video-taping the first flight [which we have been calling the 'Old Faithful'] of [a] mysterious object while standing at the mailbox area and looking due south toward Jumbled Hills. The footage, taken with a night-scope vision camera, was broadcast nationally on NBC Nightly News with Tom Brokaw on April 20, 1992. The NBC News reported that it had video-taped a test flight of a new U.S. aerial craft that had definitely defied the laws of physics, and that the news team may thus have taken the first glimpse of the other 'deep black' projects [aside from the Aurora project] being conducted within the confines of the top-secret facility.

"Also in regards to the ongoing program, it is to be noted that usually a day or two prior to significant test flights [i.e., only if the test flight is a significant one, by whatever measure known only to the installation] a vehicle-traffic counter is laid on Highway 93, at approximately a mile and a half north of Ash Springs, right before the juncture of Highway 375.

The other counter is set up about a half mile or so west upon entering Highway 375. The obvious question is: in such desolate, less-traveled areas of Nevada, why should there be such traffic counters installed on undivided, lonely highways? It is now my belief that the number of cars being registered that head out west on Highway 375 at such times [particularly in 'clusters', such as caravans] is relayed to several of the security posts at AREA 51, including the main observation post high atop the previously mentioned Bald Mountain. However, it is very possible that they may now have more sophisticated devices for registering the number of vehicles going through the area.

"The February 21, 1990 expedition was instrumental in the subsequent production of a two-hour documentary program entitled 'Saturday Super Special' televised throughout Japan on March 24, 1990 which was seen by more than 28 million viewers on prime time. The entire program dealt with AREA 51 and also the crew's pursuit of an alleged biogenetics laboratory thought to be located just outside of DULCE, a tiny town in northwestern New Mexico, about 95 miles northwest of Los Alamos.

"...The U.S. Naval Research Laboratory...seems to have a Parapsychology Research Unit that coordinates its research activities with DARPA [the Defense Advanced Research Projects Agency]. It is my understanding that some of their activities conducted under the auspices of the Office of Naval Intelligence are being held at locations such as AREA 51.

"ELF [extremely low frequency] wave-emitting devices, scalar machines, electromagnetic beam weapons and highly-defined holographic projections are just a few examples of the many new types of mind-control 'weaponry' that the government seems to have developed in the past three decades or so. Newest researches on special types of hallucinatory and memory-tampering drugs are part of a growing 'arsenal' that the U.S. Naval Intelligence boasts to have developed in its own Parapsychology - Mind Control Unit.

"According to recent information provided to me by a highly reliable informant within a special operations group of the Department of the Navy [D.O.N.], two of the most widely used devices will be R.H.I.C. [Radio Hypnotic Intra-Cerebral Control] and E.D.O.M. [Electronic Dissolution of Memory]. The first of the two, Radio Hypnotic Intra-Cerebral Control, calls for the implantation of a very small, electronic, micro-radio receiver. It acts as a Stimulator which will stimulate a muscle or electronic brain response.

This, in turn, can set off a 'Hypno-programmed' cue in the victim or subject, which would illicit a pre-conditioned behavior. The second one, Electronic Dissolution of Memory, calls for remotely-controlled production within the brain of Acetyl-Choline which blocks transmission of nerve impulses in the brain which results in a sort of

Selective Amnesia. According to this source, in the hands of certain units within the intelligence communities both of these methods are ALREADY BEGINNING TO BE USED!

"An amazing article appeared in the Los Angeles Times on May 12, 1992 announcing that Caltech scientists have recently discovered and confirmed the presence of 'tiny magnetic particles in the brains of humans, similar to those that have heretofore been found in other animals.' [L.A. TIMES, Section A, page 3]. According to the Caltech researchers, it is now an undeniable fact that every human brain contains a tiny natural magnetite particle, even from the time of conception. Could the government, particularly the U.S. Naval Research Laboratory, have known this fact for a long time? The answer definitely seems to be in the affirmative!

"It is interesting also to note that as of this writing, many strange, turquoise-colored antenna-towers with triangular configurations on top, are beginning to be constructed along key areas near the freeway systems of many U.S. cities, particularly proliferating the Los Angeles and Orange County areas of California. According to several reports, these antenna-towers are presently being used as relay towers for the increasing networks of cellular telephone systems and are being operated by such firms as Pacific Bell and Telesis.

"Yet the most interesting aspect of the constructions of these strange antenna-towers is that there are increasing reports that the Department of Defense is somehow involved in this operation. The frequency waves being utilized in the cellular telephone communications are, according to several researchers, strikingly close to the range of frequency waves used in several ELF emission and microwave experiments of the U.S. Naval Research Laboratory as well as DARPA, the Defense Advanced Research Projects Agency. Will these towers be utilized throughout the nation?

"...In the meantime, government-sponsored genetics researchers and bio-technology experts at New Mexico's Los Alamos National Laboratory are said to be conducting in-depth studies not only on the total effects of mind-control upon human behavioral patterns but also on its possible applications relative to such areas as genetics engineering and exploration of the human genome.

(This may be of special interest considering the news in early 1997 out of Edinburgh, Scotland of the successful cloning of an adult Ewe lamb. There are some who contend that certain technological breakthroughs are allowed to leak out into the public domain only after that technology has been harnessed and used for years by the secret scientific fraternities who serve the agendas of the military-industrial 'elite'.

It is interesting that following the announcement of this discovery a Jesuit priest made the rounds on the talk shows defending this 'new' science and advocating the various 'benefits' that it could provide. It is interesting that Adam Weishaupt who founded the Bavarian Illuminati was a Jesuit; and it is also interesting that the Scottish Rite of Masonry originally had its origin within the Jesuit college of Clermont in France. - Branton)

"A large underground genetics laboratory is thought to be located just outside of DULCE, a tiny town in the midst of the Jicarilla-Apache Indian Reservation located about 95 miles northwest of Los Alamos and 100 miles east of [the] sinister-sounding Highway 666, the only stretch of highway in the U.S. with that designation and the only highway that links the four states of Arizona, New Mexico, Colorado and Utah.

"Perhaps it may just be a pure 'coincidence' that this highway -- befittingly named Highway 666, which originated in southeast Arizona and goes up north -- cuts into northwestern New Mexico, right near the Four Corners area, an area that happens to have one of the most consistently concentrated UFO sighting reports in the country since around 1947. This entire Four Corners area, especially northwestern New Mexico and southwestern Colorado [even extending, for that matter, to the entire southern tip of the state] also has had some of the most concentrated reports of unexplained cattle mutilations in the nation during the late seventies and early eighties. Was something covertly taking place in those areas?

"Even though we could not locate the alleged underground genetics laboratory in Dulce when the Nippon Television crew and I visited the area in late February of 1990, I had several opportunities to interview scores of local residents there that admitted that nightly appearances of mysterious lights -- [occasionally accompanied by unmarked black helicopters] darting over, into and out of nearby Archuleta Mesa and Archuleta Mountains -- were quite common during the late seventies and early eighties.

"Many of them even claim to have spotted, on many occasions, military-type trucks and jeeps as well as government vans passing through Dulce and loitering around nearby mesas. Occasionally even black limousines carrying what appeared to be 'CIA' agent-types were claimed to have been sighted 'loitering' around the foothills of other nearby mesas.

"We must bear in mind that the Dulce area is only 95 miles northwest of Los Alamos. Los Alamos National Laboratory is one of the top U.S. research laboratories specializing in the study of the human genome. Also it is a vital center of the government's SDI research and development programs. Just about a hundred miles southeast of Los Alamos is Albuquerque, New Mexico's largest city, and more significantly, a city where Kirtland Air Force Base is located right next to the sensitive Manzano Storage Facility, a top-secret underground military facility [where nuclear warheads are stored]. Sandia Corporation, one of the nation's top-secret government contractors specializing in top military-industrial projects, is also located in Albuquerque.

"As far as advanced bio-technology is concerned, I have no doubt that a micro-chip implantation technology is being perfected in which tiny micro-chips could be implanted in our circulatory systems, vital organs and tissues if need be for whatever purpose the future may 'require'. It is my conclusion that a large-scale research has been completed by the government [with possible assistance from 'outside' sources] within the last 20 years or so utilizing tens of thousands of cattle in the Southwest to conduct this covert experiment.

Only recently has science proven that cow hemoglobin could be substituted [by utilizing a special purification system] with human blood in situations of 'unforeseen national emergencies.'"

Chapter 6

'Cosmic Top Secrets' And The Dulce Base

The Sept. 10, 1990 issue of 'UFO UNIVERSE' related the following under the title-heading, "WILLIAM F. HAMILTON III -- UFOLOGY'S 'MYSTERY MAN' TO REVEAL 'COSMIC TOP SECRETS'":

"Until just recently, William F. Hamilton III managed to keep up a relatively low profile so that he can continue his work in private and without needless interruption from well-meaning and never-the-less prying eyes.

"Admittedly, his name is not known in every household, but the fact of the matter is that 'Bill' is highly respected among his peers.

"Indeed, what he has to say is as important and vital as the words of flying ace John Lear and former Navy intelligence officer William Cooper, who have gone on record regarding the alien conspiracy.

"In fact, much of what Hamilton maintains is consistent with the theory that there is a massive government cover-up on UFOs and alien visitations that reaches right up to the president's private office door, and that the U.S. military has made a secret pact with a group of aliens known as the 'Greys'. [They] are on earth... mutilating cattle, and abducting humans for experimental purposes. Supposedly the Greys have TAKEN OVER several Top-Secret underground military facilities, AND certain branches of the government [who] are working hand-in-hand with these entities to bring about total domination of the world, while a <u>SECOND group of extra-terrestrials is here trying to protect us</u>...

"Of a highly controversial nature, many of Hamilton's statements may seem overly 'radical' to even his closest associates, not to mention other investigators who refuse to even seriously consider the documentation he is able to present to bolster his case.

"...About ten years ago, a few scientists and engineers, who worked for NASA and shared an interest in UFO abductions, came together to form a group they called Project VISIT -- Vehicle Internal Systems Investigative Team. They studied about 130 cases of UFO abductions with the goal of constructing a model of UFOs, their operation, and the entities who crew UFOs.

"They found:

"-- UFOs have bright interior lighting.

"-- Abductees undergo a medical-type examination with apparently highly sophisticated equipment.

"-- Burns are suffered by many abductees.

"-- Time loss - from 20 minutes to 3 hours - is common. Project VISIT member, Dr. Richard Niemtzow, described the crew members as four feet tall, hairless, grey in color, with no nose, a small mouth and large slanted eyes. The Grey humanoid is emotionless and communicates by telepathy.

THE DULCE PROTOCOL

"The Greys have earned a reputation quite different than the Nordic blondes and other reported species. Most of the abductions are done by greys and more than one variation of Grey. The Greys do most of the biological intervening on abductees. Tans, Whites, and Blues **(i.e. 'Greys' of other skin colors, gray-tan, gray-white, gray-blue, etc. - Branton)** have also been reported by abductees. I have personally had some sort of encounter with what I call the Whites. They are small with extremely white skin and black, wrap-around eyes.

"<u>EARTH MADE SAUCERS</u> -- In April, 1984, Lt. General George Bone, and Vice Commander of the U.S. Air Force Systems Command was killed while test flying a secret aircraft over the Groom Lake area, a top secret facility located about 100 miles north of Las Vegas, Nevada. This facility is designated 'Area 51.' The Systems Command reputedly uses this facility to test-fly spy planes, such as the SR-71 Blackbird or its successor, the Aurora. According to the February, 1988 issue of GUNG-HO magazine which ran a feature article on Area 51, some of the craft being flown out of that test facility would make George Lucas drool!...

"In the early 1980s a radio technician working at Area 51 reported seeing a saucer on the ground. It was some 20 or 30 feet in diameter, he said, and when it flew, it moved silently through the air. The technician also viewed a number of wooden shipping crates marked 'Project Redlight.' That project may have been a forerunner of Snowbird. Presently, the Air Force is trying to acquire 89.000 acres adjacent to the Groom Lake facility and to place the nearby Groom Mountains off-limits to the public.

"Before and after the TV documentary 'UFO COVER-UP LIVE', there had been talk of an underground alien base located in the vicinity of the Groom Lake test site, known as 'Dreamland'... This adds a whole new dimension to the idea of a secret space program and hints at fantastic secret programs that take [us] more than one step beyond.

"A friend of mine once moved to Riverton, Wyoming to escape from terrifying mysteries he encountered in NEW MEXICO. He said the locals at Riverton asked him, 'Are you here to work on the secret space project out at the jet airport?' Saucers were seen close to the ground in Riverton. One day my friend's truck broke down and he had to hitch a ride to town. A black Lincoln pulled up and a man dressed in black gave him a lift. The dashboard looked like a computer console. The MIB knew exactly where he wanted to be left off in front of the post office, but my friend had never told him.

"ALIEN IMPLANTS -- In 1980 when I lived in Glendale, Arizona, I received a call from my friend Walter Baumgartner, who published a magazine of limited circulation called ENERGY UNLIMITED. Walter was a natural technologist. He said that he had started working for a physicist by the name of PAUL BENNEWITZ at Thunder Scientific Labs in Albuquerque, New Mexico. He then proceeded to tell me the fantastic story that Mr. Bennewitz had succeeded in communicating with aliens at an underground base situated near MT. ARCHULETA in the town of DULCE that was close to the Colorado border and situated on the Jicarilla Apache Indian Reservation.

(Note: Bennewitz actually stated that he 'interrogated' the alien-collective via a computer-radio-video link with an 'alien' computer terminal, by tapping-in to the aliens' ship-to-base communications frequency and using a type of hexadecimal mathematical code to break the alien encryption. He first discovered the signals using specialized equipment he had developed, and later concluded that these signals were also being used to influence abductees who had been given electronic mind-control implants. - Branton).

"He told me that these little grey aliens were abducting and implanting people with a device inserted at the base of the skull for the purpose of monitoring and CONTROLLING humans. He said that the 'government' knew about this and was involved with alien activities. He also stated that the aliens feared our nuclear weapons and nuclear radiation. He told me that Paul was working on a weapon that would be effective against these aliens.

THE DULCE PROTOCOL

(INTERJECTION BY BRANTON REGARDING 'MIND CONTROL'
IMPLANTS: I know of a person who went to have some implants removed by doctors.
The implants were removed, via the nasal cavity, from the nerve centers of the brain --
some of her nerves being damaged in the process. This nerve damage resulted in a near-
death experience following which, when she had 'awakened', she felt like a 'new person'
or that some other 'identity' that had been operating in her was now gone. Some mystics
may refer to alien intelligence's that possess human minds as 'walk-ins'. What many
refer to as 'walk-ins' are often artificial intelligence matrix implants which are attached
to the nerve centers of the human brain.

These serve as 'nodes' for an alien collective in a parasite-host capacity, allowing
the aliens to physically utilize the human subject after an altered state of consciousness
has been induced, and the human subject's individual consciousness is incapacitated.
This transfer to the 'alternate consciousness' often occurs at night. Also, both malevolent
and 'relatively' benevolent other-worldly cultures often induce within human subjects
one or more 'alternate' personalities which are taught or programmed to work and
operate in the 'other' realm. If the individual is left-brain dominant and right-handed in
their 'conscious' life, in the 'alternate' life they may be right-brain dominant and left-
handed, as is the case with my own elusive alternate identity.

Other than saying that humans have one brain with two hemispheres, it would be
just as legitimate to say that we have two brains in one cranium. In many cases where
more 'benevolent' humanoids are concerned, the individual may have 'flashes' of
memories of a 'double' or 'alternate' existence where they interact with exterran,
subterran or even other-dimensional humanoid societies, often in an 'intimate' capacity,
and in some cases even serve as starship crew members or pilots. In the case of the
benevolent 'non-interventionists', such an alternate personality may be a means of
interacting with Terrans without violating the laws of non-intervention and interfering
with an earth-persons 'conscious' life, although I myself would suggest that even this
would be stretching 'non-interventionism' to the limit.

However in the case of the malevolents, such alternate 'identities' are programmed through <u>intense mind-control techniques</u> with the intent of producing unconscious mind-slaves for the alien collective.

The 'secrecy' and fear of the exposure of their interventionist agendas is in this case the motive for maintaining secrecy. What is especially confusing however is when one, as in my own personal case, has been infused with alternate personalities or identities by <u>BOTH benevolent AND malevolent</u> other-worldly cultures. In my personal case this involved being patched-in to an <u>alien collective-mind</u> [Ashtar] via implants and 'used' by the dark side of that collective -- or the interventionist elements within the Ashtar collective such as the 'Orionite infiltrators' that some contactees have spoken of who desire to use their positions to establish absolute control -- only to later have this or another alternate personality matrix 're-programmed' by a more benevolent faction of the 'alliance'. This more benevolent faction would either be involved with a separate Federation, or it would be a faction that is part of the 'collective' itself yet which is involved in an ongoing conflict with its 'darker' side, a faction which is opposed to the interventionist-control agendas of the 'infiltrators'.

One cannot comprehend the significance of the psychic battles that can rage through a single human mind until one has been caught in the crossfire between two OPPOSING 'alternate personalities' -- one of which is an individualist and one of which is a collectivist -- that are slugging it out for dominance of ones unconscious existence. The best one can do in such an event would be to try and retrieve as many suppressed memories as they are able, sort the whole mess out, and assimilate and take conscious control of those thought patterns that will be most beneficial to them and eliminate the harmful thought-patterns. I will not deceive you, such a process can be very painful at times.

After all, it is the ROOT "individual consciousness" of a human being which has the final say as to just WHO that person is going to be, based on the universal law of free agency. For those of you who are reading this and who feel that they may have been 'programmed' with an alternate 'alien' personality which is activated during alien encounters, I will say for an absolute fact that according to universal law this collectivist alternate personality MUST submit to the demands of your conscious will. Anything else would be a direct violation of the non-intervention laws.

Even without the assistance of alien psycho-technology, certain psychiatrists are fully aware of how easy it is to hypnotically induce an alternate personality within a human being, IF they had access to the suppressed mind-control techniques that have been used by certain intelligence agencies and occult fraternities. - Branton)

"UNDERGROUND BASES

On April 1 and 2, I spent 24 hours visiting with John Lear at his home in Las Vegas. He took out a stack of papers and had me peruse them at my leisure. His study room had walls covered with aircraft photos and certificates. There was no doubt in my mind that John loved flying. John is a soft spoken individual and frequently, while visiting him, I have watched him putter in the garden. We discussed Area 51. John had some long distance photos of the Groom Lake facility. The one thing that stood out in one photo was the radio telescope pointing straight up in the midst of a group of buildings. The scope was probably tracking any overhead spy satellites.

He showed me the reference in the February, 1988 issue of GUNG-HO magazine, that [insisted] that spacecraft were being test-flown from this facility. John heard rumors that the Greys had a base under the Groom Mountains. This is the one we believe is called DREAMLAND. One of my sources [a leak] says DREAM is an acronym that stands for Data Repository Establishment And Maintenance. John told me the story of Mr. K, whose son Robert was trapped inside a joint human-alien underground base in Utah. This Robert had apparently worked at DULCE BASE at one time. MR. K felt like he was being given the run-around by the military in his attempts to locate his son...

"I learned that there were a few technical people who worked at Sandia Labs in Albuquerque who were interested in alien activity. One man I talked to, C.R., knew a mysterious Colonel Ronald Blackburn, who was reputed to have said that there were 600 aliens at the Groom Lake facility in Nevada. C.R. had investigated a UFO crash near Gallup, N.M. in 1983. This one was also investigated by Tommy Roy Blann. I heard of Colonel Edwards at Albuquerque who knew the AFOSI agent Richard Doty (BOTH of whom worked with Paul Bennewitz in his investigations of the alien activity taking place at the Dulce Base. - Branton). Doty had talked to some investigators about the government cover-up. Why? I don't know.

"WEIRD HAPPENINGS AT DULCE

On April 19, 1988, my wife and I arrived at Dulce, N.M. at about 4:30 p.m. Dulce was a beautiful little mountain town sitting at an elevation exceeding 7,500 feet. There was still snow on the ground by the Best Western Motel. I checked into the motel and called Gabe Valdez. He came over to see me about 9:30 p.m. We talked about UFOs and the cattle mutilations. He said that he had not seen any mutes since 1981-82. [I] had him read a letter written by Richard Doty in which Doty denies all involvement with UFO secrecy. He said Doty wasn't telling the truth. This proved true, because Doty started talking again.

"He told me that Doty wrote a report that stated that Paul Bennewitz was being investigated. Later Gabe offered us a ride around Dulce. He took us in his patrol car and showed us some of the routes. He said he saw glowing orange-lighted airships flying silently around the area frequently. He never saw these airships in daylight. We took a look at the Gomez Ranch, site of some of the mutes that took place in 1978.

We asked about Bennewitz's belief that there was a secret underground alien base in the area. He said he believed about 80 percent of what Bennewitz said concerning alien activities in the area... he definitely seemed to think there was a base in the area, but his idea of where it is located was different than Paul's. He thought that the base might be south of Dulce, closer to the Gomez Ranch. He said he had not found any entries to the base. He had found landing tracks and crawler marks near the site of the mutes. He invited me to come back sometime and climb Mt. Archuleta. Someday I would come back to Dulce, but I had no idea when...

"A lot started happening in October, 1988. I started investigating the case of a couple who had gone up to a plateau on the south side of the Tehachapi Mountains (outside of Edwards AFB. - Branton) not far from my house. At two in the morning they witnessed a large flashing orb come up from the ground and rise slowly into the sky.

They experienced about two hours of missing time. Under hypnosis performed by a local hypnotherapist who had taken an interest in UFO abductees, we had found that the man recalled having been taken to an underground facility. He kept mentioning 'the Colonel!'..."

Chapter 7

A Dulce Vanguard At Deep Springs?

It has been fairly well established that the Dulce, New Mexico network is the largest and most significant alien [Reptiloid/Gray] base network in North America. However according to one source there is also another 'nest' near Deep Springs, California. This [Dulce-connected?] base -- because of its proximity -- may pose an even greater threat to the humanoid residents of the 'subterranean network' who have major city-complexes below California: Mt. Shasta, Panamint Mountains, 29 Palms area, etc.

These colonies are reportedly being contested by 'Draconian' vanguard positions near Lakeport-Hopland, Mt. Lassen and Deep Springs, California. On the other hand, some of the non-interventionists 'Nordic' cultures reportedly have their own forward positions near the Four Corners or Colorado Plateau region where the Reptiloids/Greys have their major center of activity. Then there are other areas BETWEEN the two sectors [between the Andro-Pleiadean bases centered under Death Valley and the Draco-Orion bases centered under Archuleta Mesa] where the 'collaborators' meet.

There are basically three alien networks at work on earth:

o   The Anti-Grey Nordic [Federation] factions,

o   the Anti-Nordic Grey [Empire] factions and

o   the Nordic-Grey collaborators, which would also include those Terran intelligence agencies and occult lodges who are involved in the collaboration for whatever motive.

Even within the collaboration, there is a great deal of struggle over whether the humanoid or reptiloid agendas should have the upper hand. Within the collaboration itself 'speciesism' [akin to racism] exists at certain levels, so in spite of the species prejudices the collaboration continues nevertheless because of a 'marriage of convenience'. In other words the Greys want to take over the planet and impose a slave society to ultimately serve their empire, but they need the Illuminati's international economic connections to do so; and the Illuminati wants the same thing but they realize that they need the alien mind-control and abduction technology to accomplish their goals.

So then, it is more of a love-hate relationship. They collaborate in order to set up a planetary government, however both the humanoids and reptiloids are constantly plotting for the time when the world government arrives so that once it is established they can move-in and take full control and expel the necessary collaborators -- the humans doing away with the Greys or the Greys doing away with the humans or whatever the case may be. For instance the Illuminati might negotiate with the Greys while at the same time develop SDI weapons to potentially use against them.

On the other hand the Greys may continue negotiating with the humans while at the same time implanting micro-electronic mind-control devices in the human agents with whom they negotiate in order to ensure that they remain under ALIEN control once the planet succumbs to the New World Order. So a one world government will NOT bring peace to the planet, it will merely be a matter of fighting for control of one super-government rather than for many smaller ones.

THE DULCE PROTOCOL

What many do not realize is that there appears to be a third element behind this agenda, a 'race' of paraphysical entities that some might refer to as the 'Luciferians' or the 'Poltergeists' -- who are often described, by abductees who have encountered them, as being in the appearance of quasi-physical etheric or energy beings who have often been seen overseeing and directing the actions of the humanoid-reptiloid collaborators.

Although it might sound simplistic to imply that this cosmic battle is essentially being fought between the 'Nordic' bases near Death Valley and the 'Grey' bases near Archuleta Mesa, the true fact of the matter is that when we are dealing with multi-leveled subterranean systems the 'border zones' are a little more complex than on the surface, where we have obvious horizontal borders between countries. In 'inner-planetary' warfare the 'battle-lines' are horizontal, vertical and in some cases inter-dimensional.

The battle would be one that is being waged above, below and within our society, even though the outward manifestations of that 'war' might not be immediately seen for what they are, unless one is aware of the REAL conflict behind the scenes. There are also indications that at least CERTAIN factions of the NSA-MJ12-CIA-AVIARY agencies have 'defected' from the neo-Nazi New World Order agenda of "joint interaction" with the Reptiloids/Grays, and are now AT WAR with the same...

Recently a researcher with the initials K.S., was approached by the family of a U.S. Intelligence worker [O.S.I.] by the name of 'Tucker', who had disappeared mysteriously. The family was concerned and frightened as they had discovered, in a personal locker of his, SEVERAL papers describing INTIMATE details of activities surrounding the Dulce, New Mexico and Nevada [S-4, etc.] underground installations. Several of these papers are reproduced throughout this present work. Among this large stack of papers was hidden the following letter which was stamped 'SECRET'.

The letter, copies of which were apparently also in the hands of a few other researchers as well, stated the following:

"Dear John...

"I am writing to you in the event that I do not return.

"There is a triangle surrounding the Nevada Test Site.

"There are in fact two of them. Each one frontiers on the other. One is the ELECTRO-MAGNETIC TRIANGLE, installed by MJ-12. This is a shield <u>to protect the</u> 'Benevolents' [very human looking] from the EBEs (the so-called "Extraterrestrial Biological Entities" or Grays - Branton) while they help us develop our counter-attack/defenses. The other is the EBEs' 'trap' keeping the Benevolents in the redoubt... At each corner of the EM Triangle you will find BLM stations and they are the transmitters of the shield.

"Facing each one of these is an EBE transmitter... THERE ARE MANY OF THESE STAND-OFFS THROUGHOUT THE WORLD. It is important that you do not interfere by attempting to destroy one of their 'surrounds', they would be able to 'double-up' somewhere else and overthrow that position. Once that link is over-thrown, our support team would fail. Their over extension is deliberate on our part. We are like the Chinese, we can't out technology them but we can out number them.

"Especially since they can't breed here and it is too far for them to go back home without our help. Many of our EM Triangles are ruses to keep them over extended. They can't get out of our solar system because our electro-magnetic field (at this time? - Branton) is the wrong frequency for their propulsion system to work efficiently. This explains why the EBEs can not commit more vehicles to our solar system."

There have been comments among some 'contactees' to the effect that occasionally the Solar system passes through areas of differing electromagnetic variations as it moves in and out of cosmic energy streams that flow through the universe like a vast universal electromagnetic 'circulatory system'.

Certain energy fields are conducive to certain types of propulsion systems whereas others are not, and in these cases alternate or more 'conventional' forms of propulsion must be resorted to. Some even suggest that large ships disguised as asteroids, planetoids or even comets are being used by the Greys and Reptiloids in order to get around this propulsion problem and also to conceal their presence.

These 'engineered' planetoids are accompanied with conventional drives to serve as platforms for various operations: abductions, implantation's, mutilations, and also mind control and infiltration activities taking place on or under planet earth. All of this would seem logical, so as not to attract a great deal of attention and in Return resistance from the masses. Some of these converted 'planetoids' have been identified as Geographos, Phobos, and even Hale-Bopp comet -- which is accompanied by many unusual anomalies not observed in most 'comets'. For instance Hale-Bopp comet was 1000 brighter than Haley's Comet was at the distance from the sun where it was 'discovered'.

This is because the 'halo' is NOT caused by ICE-GAS being blown from the surface of the object by solar winds as in the case of most comets. For some unexplained reason THIS comet is ejecting 7 large streamers or jets of DUST-GAS from its INTERIOR, many of these jets activate and deactivate at regular intervals. THIS is what creates the halo, and because of this the halo might have a distinct appearance when compared to past comets.

Some contactees state that Hale-Bopp is being used by Reptiloid entities from Draconis and Greys from Orion who have joined with a renegade 'Ashtar' faction from Sirius-B, resident within Hale-Bopp's 'companion'. They are determined to back a world dictatorship by bringing the 'comet' close to earth in order to 'trigger' the implants within abductees and simultaneously activate their unconscious subliminal programs via powerful transmitting devices. This is not to mention the potential and destabilizing 'shock' value that this comet might pose to planetary political, economic and religious systems.

It would seem that a Federation of Worlds, based in the Andromeda and Pleiades constellations, are attempting to 'blockade' the interventionist actions of the Draco-Orion empire in the Sol system. According to contactees these Federation forces will soon be joined by a massive fleet from Sirius-B, who are apparently Federation allies who have [let us hope] severed themselves from a large segment of the Ashtar collective which has since been infiltrated and taken-over by Orion-based Reptiloids and Greys. These Andro-Pleiadean backed Sirians have reportedly waged, and won, a civil war in Sirius-B with the 'dark side', or the cultic renegade Ashtarian collaborators.

They are now reportedly en route to the Sol system to do battle with the Draconian-Orion forces and to convince the renegade Sirian collaborators who are working with them that they have and are being misled into an interventionist agenda. Like fanatical cultists, the rebel Sirians have blindly succumbed to the deceptions of the Reptilians, Greys and the Rebel Angels in Hale-Bopp who are controlling the infiltrated segment of the Ashtar collective and are masquerading as "ascended masters" of the 'Ashtar' command. At least this is what some contactees have implied. Are these contactees relaying the truth? I would guess that time will tell.

As for the humans at the Nevada Test Site, these 'may' be in fact -- if we are to believe the collective revelations within this volume -- victims of subtle reptilian propaganda and intimidation. For instance, this source who authored the letter about the 'EBE's' apparently believes that ALL of the saurian-grays or EBE's come from extra-terrestrial realms. However as we have indicated, there is much evidence suggesting that reptiloid or homosaurian activity exists deep within the subterranean cavernous levels throughout planet earth, an intra-terrestrial presence that has existed for many centuries if not for thousands of years.

This is one fact that the reptiloids have tried to hide from humankind, both terrestrial and extraterrestrial. Also, there are accounts suggesting that the reptiloids and greys ARE IN FACT breeding profusely and reproducing themselves via deep subterranean polyembryony, cloning and incubation facilities below Dulce and elsewhere and are not as 'over-extended' as they might have us to believe. Some estimate that at the very least 20 million grays are now actively operating under the surface of planet earth within bases or within natural cavern systems. According to still others, 20 million is a conservative estimate.

However, on the other hand, the fear the humanoids might have of prematurely attacking the 'enemy' positions may possibly be the result of intimidation and propaganda intended to keep humans from taking OFFENSIVE action, believing that they are keeping the greys, etc., 'at bay' when in fact the Greys ARE ATTACKING OFFENSIVELY HUMAN SOCIETY on several other hidden fronts via mass abductions, subliminal programming, implantation, psychic manipulation, recruiting of 'fifth column' human agents, and infiltration. I personally do not believe in 'standoffs'. In war there is no 'neutrality', one is either attacking [in various ways] or capitulating themselves over to the enemy, in various ways -- ways which those on the defensive side might not even be aware of.

The letter which we have quoted earlier continues:

"The 'headquarters' of this particular 'surround' is Deep Springs, California. At this location one can find a 'school' for Communist homosexuals who have defected to the EBEs in exchange for a cure for AIDs and a promise to their own little world, including reproduction via cloning and artificial wombs. Their sperm fertilize eggs taken from abductees. You will not likely see the hybrids hidden inside the mountain, unless you have... starlite binoculars. Some homosapien APPEARING malevolents [mercenaries] are also there. Nine Soviets were there at the same time Soviets were at the NTS. They were there in the hopes of talking them into defecting back to our side. We are still hopeful.

"The collaborators use the cover organization Natural Resources Defense Council, with front offices in New York and 1350 New York Avenue, N.W., suite 300, Washington, D.C. 20005 [tel.(202) 783-7800]. It is headed by Tom Cochran, staffed by Kevin Priestly UNR, John Brune UNR, Holly Eisler UnSan Diego, Gary Reisling Univ.

Ca. Pasadena, Holly Nelson NY, Mary Manning LV Sun, Ed Vogel LVR; and many others I can reveal later.

"One will also find that each corner of their triangle is at the base of a mountain. At each location you will find several entrances to underground systems. Do not attempt to enter, unless you wish to become liquid protein. You may however harass the EBEs' two other corners by placing a large magnet on the vaults... [placing a magnet on the other two entrances at each location will not affect anything].

"This temporarily interrupts their communications with Deep Springs until a collaborator team comes out to see what is going on. If you place a large magnet on this entrance [it has a large computer near the surface, you can hear it], it will affect an immediate interruption. So, you can take it off in a short time [1 hr] and take it with you. They will still have to come and reset the system. If you plant magnets [camouflaged like rocks] around these entrances, the EBEs won't come out & the sell outs won't be able to find them.

"The EBEs are also allergic to high concentrations of sugar (and apparently other substances with a 'left hand atomic spin', it has been claimed. - Branton). You will find that at two locations I have poured sugar around their exits. Always wear magnets near these locations, they interrupt the EBEs' sense of direction [due to an internal compass much like those found in migrating birds] similar to our loss of balance when our ear drum is affected.

"Please wait until I have Returned, if you have an airplane, I would like to take aerial photos, we can photograph them together.

"Our alliance crest, symbolic of the EM Shield and our sign/mark/graffiti is enclosed. Do not reveal them or else everybody will use them & you won't know the real from the pseudos.

"YOU DO NOT KNOW ME, I DO NOT KNOW YOU. THIS IS NOT FOR PUBLIC DISSEMINATION. ZEALOTS MAY DISRUPT THE BALANCE BEFORE V-EBE DAY."

THE DULCE PROTOCOL

Another researcher by the name [pseudonym] of Jason Bishop has revealed that 'John', to whom the letter was addressed, is non other than John Lear who himself claims many connections with people 'in the know' who go 'right to the top'.

According to the letter, both the Nevada Test Site and Deep Springs are areas of conflict between a U.S. Government - 'Nordic' Alliance AND a Socialist - Reptiloid [Gray] Alliance. In this context 'Socialist' could indicate either National Socialist or Global Socialist. Both hold the same basic philosophies of tyranny yet different methods for bringing them to pass.

Both have the same roots and are apparently twin pincers in a deadly Machiavellian game that is being carried out by the Bavarian Illuminati [which backed the Communists by sending Lenin from Germany to Russia to incite the Bolshevik revolution] and the Bavarian Thule Society [which backed the Nazis by grooming Adolph Hitler for his part as Nazi dictator], yet most importantly it is being orchestrated by the International "Black Nobility" Banking cults that have kept Europe under their financial grip since around 500 A.D.

These are the same bankers who claim direct descent from the royal families of the ancient Roman and [un]Holy Roman empires, families who have ties to BOTH Bavarian cults -- Thule and Illuminati... and in turn with the 'aliens'.

Jason Bishop also released some other information he received by way of John Lear, from the individual whose letter we've just quoted. According to Lear, the author of the letter was actually a Security Officer at the Test Site who had called-in to the Billy Goodman talk show [KVEG radio - Las Vegas, NV] on a few occasions, before Goodman went to Southern California to take over a more lucrative Talk Show position.

This person used the codename: 'Yellowfruit,' which he claimed was actually the codename for a top secret security division that worked at the site, with which he was involved. YF also sent to Lear a copy of the 'Benevolent' teachings. The 'Benevolents' are reportedly working at the Test Site with MJ-12 and are 'Blond-Nordic and/or Aryan-like' people. I would personally guess that the 'Benevolent Ones' are members of the exterran Andro-Pleiadean Federation and/or members of the subterran Telosian-Agharti Alliance which has maintained ties with the ASHTAR collective, or in this case the non-collaboration faction of that collective.

The BENEVOLENT TEACHINGS [not limited to the below] were identified as follows:

"DISCOURAGED -- NON PREPARATORY SPORTS [Activities That Can Not Be Used In Nonsporting Life] motocross, auto-racing, skateboarding, roller skating, football, baseball, hockey. Also Discouraged: Processed Sugar, Recreational Carbohydrates, Recreational Fluids, White Bread.

"ENCOURAGED -- NONCEREMONIAL LESSONS OF THE MAJOR RELIGIONS & PREPARATORY SPORTS [Activities That Can Be Used In Nonsporting Life] swimming, running, hiking, martial arts, survival arts. Teach Your Children!

"FORBIDDEN -- Alcohol, Illegal Drugs, Nicotine, Recreational Drugs, and Unjustifiable Homicide.

"MUST -- Avoid Weakness [evil grows in weakness]. Execute Evil Prisoners In Order To Help Other Prisoners (Editors Note: Another possibility that might be interjected here is to establish a completely secured underground prison-cave and place all of the worst offenders there and leave them to themselves, to either work out their problems or destroy each other, whichever they choose. - Branton).

"MUST -- Quarantine Contagious Disease [AIDS] Victims Humanely. Show Strength. Stop Illegal Drugs. Stop Destruction of Environment. Stop Pollution. Use Nuclear Power.

THE DULCE PROTOCOL

"STUDY - Bill Of Rights, Biology, Computers, Economics, Geography, History, Latin, Mathematics, Philosophy, Survival Skills, United States Of America's Declaration Of Independence, United States Of America's Constitution, Vocational Skills."

Yellowfruit also provided coordinates for the Electro-magnetic Triangles he referred to in his letter.

These include:

- A.- N 37 22 30 - E 117 58 0
- B.- N 38 21 0 - E 115 35 0
- C.- N 35 39 0 - E 114 51 0
- also Yucca Lake: N 37 0 30 - E 116 7 0

The following information, from William F. Hamilton III, describes further details on the "Yellow Fruit" account -- including claims which the Nevada Test Site agent made over the air during the few 'interviews' which were heard over KVEG Radio's Billy Goodman talk show.

It is also interesting that COM-12 member Michael Younger [who has given lectures on the 'Nazi' presence within the Rockefeller-backed Oil companies -- Nazi war criminals and their families who were smuggled into America following World War II and given refuge within the Rockefeller's corporate empire; the plans the Nazi's/Bavarians have for selling-out the planet to the aliens in exchange for one quarter of the "New World Order"; and a MASSIVE Nazi child abduction & satanic-ritual-sexual abuse & murder ring operating within ARCO, etc.] is or at least was at one time also a worker at the Nevada Test Site.

This suggests that COM12 is intimately involved in the counter-offensive against the Grays.

Robert K Teske

"...Yellow Fruit revealed that A CONFLICT WAS GOING ON BETWEEN THE BENEVOLENT ONES and THE EBE's and that now the benevolent ones had gained the upper hand at Dreamland where he said a contingent of 37 benevolent ones were stationed and where 3 EBE's were held in captivity.

"Bizarre! Science Fiction? Yellow Fruit knew a lot about the test site area. I resolved to go to the location he gave of the EBE installation in Deep Springs, California and then on to visit Pat at the Rachel Bar & Grill to make contact with Yellow Fruit [the name for the first level of security force at Area 51 and also the name of an old Army-CIA unit]. The second level of security he called "Sea Spray" and intimated that you would have an encounter of the unpleasant kind if you ever met with them.

"Callers to the Billy Goodman Radio Happening had already organized trips to mile-marker 29 1/2 on highway 375 where a dirt road left the highway to intersect the road to Dreamland. There was a heavy black mail box on this road which identified it. I got to Rachel early one October morning and left my card with Pat at Rachel's Bar and Grill to pass on to Yellow Fruit. She knew him by sight. I then inspected the dirt roads where people stood to observe the test flights.

I had already interviewed four witnesses by phone who testified that they had seen UFOs over the Groom Mountains on certain nights in the same area they were seen by John Lear. I made a second trip to the area in late October where a public group visited Rachel and that is when I saw the mysterious Yellow Fruit in the cafe. He later called me on the phone. I left him with a copy of my book, 'Alien Magic' and he remarked on the research I had done concerning the search for underground bases.

"According to Yellow Fruit and others there are underground bases and tunnels that conceal the activities of the aliens and secret government projects..."

THE DULCE PROTOCOL

One more note on the Nevada Test Site - Area 51 - Groom Lake - 'Dreamland' underground facilities: Aside from reports that Dugway, Utah serves as an underground 'link' between Dreamland and DULCE, there is the added claim that another underground link exists farther south, at Page, Arizona.

Anyone who has been to the Glen Canyon dam [Lake Powell] could easily observe how the dam might be used as an entrance to such a base, and how the large hydroelectric facility might power the base operations.

The Glen Canyon Dam connection was not specifically mentioned [by former Dulce base security officer Thomas E. Castello who named Page, Arizona as a 'connecting' base], however if there is a base under Page, then it would be logical to utilize this hydroelectric facility in one form or another...

Chapter 8

An Alien Fifth Column On Earth?

The mysterious "government insider" whose books have been published by Tim Beckley's Abelard Press of New York, "Commander X," related a very interesting incident which involved the subterranean mega-complex beneath Dulce, New Mexico:

"...In another case an old illustrator, John D., does very painstaking work, but during his being on active duty at Dulce he began to act very queerly. He would write letters to the President informing him of a plot underway to undermine the government, and to sabotage the base. He began to draw pictures of American flags, beautifully executed. He drew strange designs of mechanical devices, began to visit the library and bring back books on physics and advanced electronics. He hardly knew how to spell the words.

"He would patiently explain something of a very technical nature which he shouldn't have understood. When asked what he was raving about and why he was causing trouble by writing the President, John D. would say that he had been 'sensitized.'

"'Last year when I was sick [John D. explained], the doctor on the base gave me sulfanilamide. There is a fifth column in this country that is tied up with aliens.

Selenium is being slipped into SULFA DRUGS, and this selenium lodges in the bones and makes the body receptive to extremely short waves, those in the wave band of the brain. Similar to the waves that can be detected by the encephalograph. About 300,000 people in this country have been sensitized, and at least seven secret radio stations have been set up in this country, and they are broadcasting to these sensitized persons, instructing them in the best way to perform acts of sabotage against our planet.'"

These claims as given by the Dulce worker, John D., are incredible indeed, and could easily be dismissed as the ravings of a madman, IF NOT FOR THE FACT that many others are saying basically the same thing, that there is a movement underway to bring the minds of the masses under the subjection of an alien force, whether through electronic implantation and control, subliminal programming, or through other means.

Why would the 'controllers' use the United States as the major target of their activity? We believe that this is due to the fact that the United States is a place that was originally intended by it's 'founding fathers' to be a refuge for peoples FROM ALL NATIONS to come and work out their collective destinies free from the restrictions of prejudice and the oppressiveness of tyrannical rule -- a land where all people could express their creativity, culture and individual destinies without interference.

This was their 'intention'; however it is obvious that the 'dream' has not been fully realized because of collective and governmental compromise of the principle that "all men are created equal". The United States, nevertheless, is unlike any other single nation. It is a cultural "melting pot" and a place where not only international human societies on the surface CONVERGE and intermingle in a dramatic way, but apparently where human societies beneath or beyond the earth converge as well.

For instance, according to various reports, most non-surface human societies who are aware of planet earth have their representatives walking among us in our own society [and to some extent, other nations throughout the world], although many of these choose to keep a low profile for either honorable or not-so-honorable reasons.

Another factor is the respect which the BILL OF RIGHTS gives to all American citizens, allowing for personal freedom and individuality so long as the freedom and individuality of others is not threatened. Individuality is the MORTAL ENEMY of the alien "Hive", you could say.

The U.S., then, seems to be in essence a "World Scenario", if not a 'universal' scenario in miniature and therefore the 'Conspiracy' sees it as a most valuable prize. Therefore it would probably not be too 'far out' to suggest that the war between the human and serpent races from all three 'realms' [extraterrestrial, ultra terrestrial and intra-terrestrial] CONVERGE within the United States, and to be more exact, within the vicinities of the Archuleta plateau near Dulce, New Mexico [a MAJOR earth-base of the Reptiloid interventionist Empire forces]; the Death Valley region of California [a MAJOR earth-base of the Humanoid non-interventionist Federation forces]

And then we have the 'battle-grounds' between the AMERICAN-COM12-CABAL-PHILADELPHIAN-NORDIC and the BAVARIAN-AQUARIUS-MAJI-PHOENICIAN-REPTILOID forces within high-security military complexes like those which permeate the underground territories below California, Nevada, Utah, Idaho, Arizona, Colorado, Oklahoma and New Mexico... and apparently centered specifically in or near,

- the underground military-industrial systems beneath Lancaster, California
- Mercury, Nevada
- Burley, Idaho
- Dugway, Utah
- Page, Arizona

- the underground systems below the Denver International Airport of Colorado
- and also below Oklahoma City

All of these basing areas are seen by the proponents of the New World Order as strategic sites that they MUST maintain control of if they are to force America to submit to a one-world government.

Chapter 9
Technological Terrorism & The Dulce Base

The elusive "Commander-X" has -- through his reported connections within the Intelligence Community -- released still further revelations regarding the dark secrets of Dulce.

The Commander claims to be a member of "THE COMMITTEE OF 12" [COM-12?], an obscure intelligence group which is working to educate the public about the joint fascist-alien threat to America and preserve our Constitutional-based Republic as it was established by the original founders of the United States:

"...There were over 650 attendees to the 1959 Rand Symposium. Most were representatives of the Corporate-Industrial State, like:

- The General Electric Company;
- AT&T;
- Hughes Aircraft;
- Northrop Corporation;
- Sandia Corporation;
- Colorado School of Mines, etc.

"Bechtel (pronounced BECK-tul, a San Francisco - based organization - Branton) is a super-secret international corporate octopus, founded in 1898. Some say the firm is really a 'Shadow Government' -- a working arm of the CIA. It is the largest Construction and Engineering outfit in the U.S.A. and the World [and some say, beyond].

"The most important posts in the U.S.A. Government are held by former Bechtel Officers. They are part of 'The Web' [an inter-connected control system] which links the Trilateralist plans, the C.F.R., the Order of 'Illuminism' [Cult of the All-seeing Eye] and other interlocking groups..."

"MIND MANIPULATING EXPERIMENTS... The Dulce Base has studied mind control implants; Bio-Psi Units; ELF Devices capable of Mood, Sleep and Heartbeat control, etc.

"D.A.R.P.A. [Defense Advanced Research Projects Agency] is using these technologies to manipulate people. They established 'The Projects,' set priorities, coordinate efforts and guide the many participants in these undertakings. Related Projects are studied at Sandia Base by 'The Jason Group' [of 55 Scientists]. They have secretly harnessed the Dark Side of Technology and hidden the beneficial technology from the public.

"Other Projects take place at 'Area 51' in Nevada.

- 'Dream-land' [Data Repository Establishment and Maintenance Land]
- Elmint [Electromagnetic Intelligence]
- Cold Empire
- Code EVA
- Program HIS [Hybrid Intelligence System]:
    - BW/CW
    - IRIS [Infrared Intruder Systems]

THE DULCE PROTOCOL

- BI-PASS
- REPTILES, etc...

"The studies on Level Four at Dulce include,

- Human Aura research
- as well as all aspects of Dream
- Hypnosis
- Telepathy, etc. [research]
- They know how to manipulate the Bioplasmic Body
- They can lower your heartbeat with Deep Sleeve 'Delta Waves,'

induce a static shock, then reprogram, Via a Brain-Computer link

- They can introduce data and programmed reactions into your Mind

[Information impregnation -- the 'Dream Library']

"We are entering an era of Technologicalization of Psychic Powers...

- The development of techniques to enhance man/machine

communications;

- Nano-tech;
- Bio-tech micro-machines;
- PSI-War;
- E.D.O.M. [Electronic Dissolution of Memory];
- R.H.I.C. [Radio-Hypnotic Intra-Cerebral Control];
- and various forms of behavior control [via chemical agents,

ultrasonics, optical and other EM radiations].

- The Physics of 'Consciousness.'...

"SURVIVING THE FUTURE... The Dulce Facility consists of a central 'Hub.'
the Security Section [also some photo labs]. The deeper you go, the stronger the
Security. This is a multi-leveled complex. There are over 3000 cameras at various high-
security locations [exits and labs].

"There are over 100 Secret Exits near and around Dulce, many around Archuleta Mesa, others to the source around Dulce Lake and even as far east as Lindrich.

"Deep sections of the Complex CONNECT INTO [EXTENSIVE] NATURAL CAVERN SYSTEMS.

"...INSIDE THE DULCE BASE... Security officers wear jumpsuits, with the Dulce symbol on the front, upper left side (the Dulce symbol consists of an upside-down triangle with an inverted 'T' superimposed over it - Branton)... The ID card [used in card slots, for the doors and elevators] has the Dulce symbol above the ID photo. 'Government honchos' use cards with the Great Seal of the U.S. on it. 'The Cult of the All-Seeing Eye' [The NEW WORLD ORDER], 13, '666', The Phoenix Empire... '9', 'Illuminism'... 'One out of many.' [and so on]..."

"THE PHANTOM BOARD: ABOVE THE LAW... Most meetings of 'The Dulce Board' are held in Denver and Taos [New Mexico]. A former U.S. Senator has full knowledge of Dulce. He was among the group that included a number of very prominent government figures who toured the base (i.e. most likely the upper levels only - Branton). In 1979, an 'animal mutilation' conference took place in Albuquerque, New Mexico. This meeting was used to locate researchers and determine what they had learned about the link between the 'mute' [i.e. mutilation] operations and the 'Alien' government.

"Another Senator knows about the 'Ultra' secrets at 'Dreamland' and Dulce. Several of my official sources have confirmed this to me. So do many others in government... this is what the UFO researchers are up against...so be careful. You know more than they want you to know.

"They have also underwater bases off the coast of Florida and Peru.

THE DULCE PROTOCOL

"More detailed information will be released in the near future: photos, video tapes, documents, etc. Watch out for 'Special Agents' among you now.

"In the 1930's, DIVISION FIVE of the FBI knew about the 'Aliens.'

"A FASCIST cabal within this country had John Kennedy assassinated. Look to the links within the larger Umbrella... the 'WEB' of a fascist totalitarian secret police state... within the Pentagon; JCS, DIA, FBI [Division Five]; DISC/DIS and the DIA. Note: The Defense Investigative Services insignia is a composite of the Sun's rays, a rose and a dagger, symbolizing 'The Search for Information, Trustworthiness and Danger.'

"This links with caves used for 'Initiation Rites' all over the world... ancient vaults, retreats, [underground 'bases']..." etc.

Commander 'X' also stated that:

"Recently, participants in a 'field investigation' of the area near Archuleta Mesa, were confronted by two small hovering spheres. They all became suddenly ill and had to leave the area.

"We have passed the point of no Return in our interaction with the 'alien' [i.e. 'reptilian gray'] beings. We are guaranteed a crisis which will persist until the final REVELATION [or conflict].

"The crisis is here, global and real. We must mitigate or transform the nature of the disasters to come, and come they will. Knowing is half the battle. Read the book, THE COSMIC CONSPIRACY, by Stan Deyo..."

Chapter 10
The Deep Dark Secret at Dulce

The Feb.-Mar. 1991 issue of 'UFO UNIVERSE' carried an article titled 'THE DEEP DARK SECRET AT DULCE', written by Bill Hamilton and 'TAL' LeVesque. If planet earth is to be the central 'battleground' or staging-ground for a final cosmic battle between galactic superpowers, and if the U.S. is one of the major areas on earth where the 'final outcome' will be decided, and since the Dulce, New Mexico area is considered to be THE MAJOR BASING SITE where human - alien collaboration AND/OR conflict is taking place, then we should focus our attention on what has been going on deep beneath this small southwestern town.

More than any other area in the U.S., if not the world... this small town has been the epicenter for nearly ever form of paranormal activity one can imagine, including:

- UFO sightings
- UFO landings
- Abductions
- Implantation's
- Human & Animal mutilations
- PSI Warfare studies

- Secret Government-Alien interaction
- U.S. 'Constitutional' Government vs. Alien Agenda conflicts
- 'Reptilian' sightings
- Crypto zoological or Bioengineering phenomena [this was the general area where the famous 'Cabbit', the half cat / half rabbit was captured]
- Underground bases
- Conspiracy scenarios
- Alien Infiltration
- Deep-Cavern phenomena
- Super High-Tech activity
- MIB encounters

In fact a higher CONCENTRATION of such activities has been evident in the vicinity of Dulce than any other area in the world, to the point that the inhabitants of this town have for the most part resigned themselves into acknowledging -- although not necessarily accepting -- the reality of such activity, whether they like it or not.

Bill Hamilton and 'TAL' Levesque take us 'inside' the Hadean-like labyrinths deep within this underground mega complex, through the eyes of those who have actually been there, so brace yourselves:

"Dulce is a sleepy little town in northern New Mexico. It's population is about 900 and it is located above 7,000 feet on the Jicarilla Apache Indian Reservation. There is one major motel and just a few stores. It is not a resort town and it is not bustling with activity. Yet, according to a few outsiders, Dulce harbors a deep, dark secret. That secret is said to be harbored deep below the tangled brush of Archuleta Mesa. That secret involves a joint government-alien biogenetic laboratory designed to carry out bizarre experiments on humans and animals.

THE DULCE PROTOCOL

"New Mexico State Police Officer Gabe Valdez was drawn into the mysteries of Dulce when called out to investigate a mutilated cow on the Manuel Gomez ranch in a pasture 13 miles east of Dulce. Gomez had lost four cattle to mutilations between 1976 and June 1978 (and SEVERAL more in ensuing years. - Branton) when a team of investigators which included Tom Adams arrived from Paris, Texas to examine the site of the carcass.

"Curious as to how cattle were being selected by the mysterious mutilators, an interesting experiment was conducted on July 5, 1978 by Valdez, Gomez, and retired scientist Howard Burgess. The three penned up about 120 of the Gomez beef cattle and moved them through a squeeze chute under an ultra-violet light. They found a 'glittery substance on the right side of the neck, the right ear, and the right leg.' Samples of the affected hides were removed as well as control samples from the same animals.

"Some investigators attribute the mutilations to aliens from UFOs. Sightings of strange lights and other aerial phenomena have been reported in many areas where the cows have been found at the time of the reported mutilation. UFOs have been seen frequently around Dulce.

"I arrived in Dulce on April 19, 1988, to visit with Gabe Valdez and to inquire about the sightings, the mutes, and the rumors of an underground alien base in the area. There was still snow on the ground by the Best Western motel when I checked in and called Valdez. He made an appointment to see me at 9:30 PM. I found Gabe to be a very congenial host as he offered to show us around the roads of Dulce that night and point out the various locations where he had found mutilated cows or had seen strange aerial lights.

He made the astounding statement that he was still seeing unidentified aircraft at the rate of one every two nights. We took a look at the Gomez Ranch, the road by the Navajo River, and the imposing Archuleta Mesa. Gabe had found landing tracks and crawler marks near the site of the mutes. Gabe was convinced that scientist Paul

Bennewitz of Thunder Scientific Labs in Albuquerque was definitely on the right track in his attempts to locate an underground alien facility in the vicinity of Dulce.

"I had first heard of Paul Bennewitz in 1980 when my friend Walter called me from Albuquerque and told me he had been working with Paul on electronic instruments. Walter said Paul had not only photographed UFOs, but had established a communication link with their underground base at Dulce. Bennewitz had first come to prominence during the August 1980 sightings of UFOs over the Manzano Weapons Storage Area and Kirtland AFB. A KIRTLAND AFB INCIDENT REPORT dated October 28, 1980 mentions that Bennewitz had taken film of UFOs over Kirtland.

Paul was president of Thunder Scientific Labs adjacent to Kirtland. Bennewitz gave a briefing in Albuquerque detailing how he had seen the aliens on a video screen (via a computer-radio-video link he had developed using a hexadecimal code after tapping-in to their ship-to-base communications frequency, Paul himself being a brilliant scientist who has developed equipment for the Space Shuttles and several Fortune 500 companies. - Branton). The aliens were transmitting signals... from a base underneath Archuleta Mesa.

"Researcher William Moore claims that government agents became interested in Bennewitz' activities and were trying to defuse him by pumping as much disinformation through him as he could absorb. Whether Paul's communication with supposed aliens at the Dulce Base was part of this disinformation campaign is unclear. If one were to believe that Paul is the SINGLE source of reports on the Dulce Facility, then it could also be a tactical maneuver to discount and discredit Paul's allegation of an underground base if such reports were meant to remain secret. Then the actual disinformation maneuver would be to <u>dis-inform the public and NOT a single individual</u>.

"In a report entitled 'PROJECT BETA', Paul states that he had spent two years tracking alien craft; that he had constant reception of video from an alien ship and underground base view screen; that he had established constant direct communications with the aliens using a computer and a form of Hexadecimal code with graphics and printout; and claims to have used aerial and ground photography to locate the alien ships' launch ports and charged beam weapons. Paul claimed that the aliens were devious, employed deception, and did not adhere to agreements. Paul and Walter were working on a weapon that would counter the aliens.

"Some will think at this point that we have crossed-over from the land of clear thinking concerning anomalous phenomena to the land of science-fiction. But let us remember that bizarre phenomena such as the UFOs represent may have its roots in a bizarre reality. It is expected to be bizarre at first, but as we continue our studies we will evolve to understand it.

"Paul Bennewitz had investigated the case of abductee Myrna Hansen of New Mexico who reported having been taken to an underground facility in May 1980. Christa Tilton of Oklahoma has reported that she had an experience of missing time in July 1987 where she had been abducted by two small grey aliens and transported in their craft to a hillside location where she encountered a man dressed in a red military-like jump suit.

She was taken into a tunnel through computerized check-points displaying security cameras. She reported having been taken on a transit vehicle to another area where she stepped on a scale-like device facing a computer screen. After the computer issued her an identification card, she was told by her guide that they had just entered Level One of a seven-level underground facility. Christa goes on relating how she was eventually taken down to Level Five. She reports having seen alien craft and little grey alien entities in some of the areas that she passed through.

"Christa reports going into one large room where she saw large tanks with computerized gauges hooked to the tanks and large arms that extended from some tubing down into the tanks. She noticed a humming sound, smelled formaldehyde, and was under the impression that some liquid was being stirred in the tanks. Christa has made drawings of much of what she had witnessed during her abduction.

"These tanks Christa talks about were depicted in a set of controversial papers called the Dulce Papers. These papers were allegedly stolen from the Dulce underground facility along with 30 black and white photos and a video tape by a mysterious security officer who claims to have worked at Dulce up until 1979, when he decided that the time had come to part company with his employers.

The rest of the story is about this security officer who has met with one of us in an attempt to tell us the truth about the aliens, the [so-called] U.S. Government, and the Dulce base. He is announcing his intention to come out of hiding and present soft and hard evidence of his claims. It will be up to you to decide whether this evidence constitutes an addition to the growing proof that a government cover-up exists.

"In late 1979, Thomas Castello could no longer cope with the awesome reality he had to confront. As a high level security officer at the joint alien-U.S. Government underground base near Dulce he had learned of and had seen disturbing things. After much inner conflict, he decided to desert the facility and take various items with him.

"Using a small camera, he took over 30 photos of areas within the multi-level complex. He removed a security video tape from the Control Center which showed various security camera views of hallways, labs, aliens, and 'U.S. Government' personnel. He also collected documents to take with him. Then, by shutting off the alarm and camera system in one of the over 100 exits to the surface, he left the facility with the photos, video, and documents. These 'originals' were hidden after five sets of copies were made.

(Note: These were placed in the hands of five individuals, who were told that if they failed to hear from Castello for three consecutive 6 month periods -- normally he would visit each of them every six months -- then they could release the information or do whatever they wanted with it.

No one except Castello and the recipients themselves know who these people are, however with rumors of Castello's death or disappearance in Costa Rica in recent years the recipients CAN release the information if they choose to do so, although they may decide to wait until the subject reaches critical mass among the public, and then come forward with little fear of repercussions. - Branton)

"Thomas was ready to go into hiding. But, when he went to pick up his wife and young son, he found a van and government agents waiting. He had been betrayed by K. LOMAS [a fellow worker] who was instrumental in the kidnapping of his wife and child. The agents wanted what Thomas had taken from the facility for which he would get his wife and son back. It became apparent to him that his wife and son would be used in biological experiments and were not going to be returned unharmed. That was a little over ten years ago...

"How did Thomas get involved in all this covert intrigue?

"Thomas is now about 50 years old (at the time that the article was written in 1991 - Branton). When he was in his mid-twenties, he received top secret training in photography at an underground facility in West Virginia. For seven years, he worked for the RAND Corp. in Santa Monica, California when in 1977 he was transferred to the Dulce facility

(Note: in a similar manner as scientist Robert Lazar who worked for LOS ALAMOS LABS was transferred to AREA-51 in Nevada, which is an alternate base similar to DULCE. Lazar claims that he replaced a scientist who had died during an 'altercation' with aliens in the tunnels below the Nevada Military Complex. The point I'm trying to make is that both RAND LABS and LOS ALAMOS LABS apparently have the answers to what is really going on under DULCE and AREA-51, if anyone does. - Branton)

"He bought a home in Santa Fe, New Mexico and worked Monday through Friday with weekends off. All Dulce Base personnel commute via a deep underground tube-shuttle system.

"At the time, one of us [TAL] was working security in Santa Fe, N.M. and was privately investigating UFO sightings, animal mutilations, Masonic and Wicca groups in the area. Thomas had a mutual friend who came to Santa Fe in 1979 to visit both of us. This individual would later view the photos, video tape and documents taken from the Dulce Base. Drawings were made from what was seen and circulated later in the UFO research community as the 'Dulce Papers'

"Thomas alleges that there were over 18,000 of the short 'greys' at the Dulce Facility. He has also seen [tall] reptilian humanoids. One of us [TAL] had come face-to-face with a 6-foot tall Reptoid which had materialized in the house. The Reptoid showed interest in research maps of New Mexico and Colorado which were on [my] wall. The maps were full of colored push-pins and markers to indicate sites of animal mutilations, caverns, the locations of high UFO activity, repeated flight paths, abduction sites, ancient ruins, and suspected alien underground bases.

"...The security level goes up as one descends to the lower levels. Thomas had an ULTRA-7 clearance. He knew of seven sub-levels, but there MAY have been more. Most of the aliens are on levels 5, 6, and 7. Alien housing is on level 5. The only sign in English was one over a tube shuttle station hallway which read 'to Los Alamos.' Connections go from Dulce to Page, Arizona facility, then to an underground base below Area 51 in Nevada. Tube shuttles go to and from Dulce to facilities below Taos, N.M.; Datil, N.M.; Colorado Springs, Colorado; Creede, Colorado; Sandia; then on to Carlsbad, New Mexico. There is a vast network of tube shuttle connections under the U.S. which extends into a global system of tunnels and sub-cities.

THE DULCE PROTOCOL

"At the Dulce Base, most signs on doors and hallways are in the alien symbol language and a universal symbol system understood by humans and aliens. Thomas stated that after the second level, everyone is weighed, in the nude, then given a uniform. Visitors are given off-white uniforms. The weight of the person is put on a computer I.D. card each day. Any change in weight is noted. Any change in over three pounds requires a physical exam and X-ray. The uniforms are jump suits with a zipper.

"In front of all sensitive areas are scales built into the floor by doorways and the door control panels. An individual places his computer I.D. card into the door slot, then presses a numerical code and buttons. The person's card must match with the weight and code or the door will not open. Any discrepancy in weight will summon security. No one is allowed to carry anything into sensitive areas. All supplies are put on a conveyor belt and X-rayed. The same method is used in leaving sensitive areas.

"All elevators are controlled magnetically, but there are no elevator cables. The magnetic system is inside the walls of the elevator shaft. There are no normal electrical controls. Everything is controlled by advanced magnetics, including lighting. There are no regular light bulbs. The tunnels are illuminated by Phosphorous units with broad, structureless emission bands. Some DEEP TUNNELS use a form of phosphorous pentoxide to temporarily illuminate certain areas. The aliens won't go near these zones for reasons unknown.

(Note: This suggests that these DEEPER tunnels may have originally been constructed in more ancient or prehistoric times by beings OTHER than the current reptiloid-draco residents of the deeper levels of the Dulce 'base' itself. - Branton).

"The studies on Level 4 include human-aura research, as well as all aspects of telepathy, hypnosis, and dreams. Thomas says that they know how to separate the bioplasmic body from the physical body and place an 'alien entity' force-matrix within a human body after removing the 'soul' life-force-matrix of the human."

(Note: Or in more simple terms, 'kill' the human being and turn it into a vessel to be used by another entity -- whether alien OR paraphysical -- in order to allow that entity to work and operate in the physical realm. This appears to be a complex high-tech version of the old 'zombie' traditions, IF in fact such horrific applications of occult-technology are taking place within this installation.

Incidentally the interlinking underground systems converging below Dulce, NM, have been described ONLY IN PART within this and other related accounts. Those sectors of the underground that are 'forbidden' to most humans and under reptiloid control, are of course those areas that we know the least about. - Branton).

"Level 6 is privately called 'Nightmare Hall'. It holds the genetic labs. Here are experiments done on fish, seals, birds, and mice that are vastly altered from their original forms. There are multi-armed and multi-legged humans and several cages [and vats] of humanoid bat-like creatures (deceased 'Mothmen', or those creatures that John Keel refers to in his book THE MOTHMAN PROPHECIES? - Branton) up to 7-feet tall. The aliens have taught the humans a lot about genetics, things both useful and dangerous."

TAL then describes something which might seem unbelievable if it weren't for the fact that dozens of other sources seem to have confirmed it. This discovery was reportedly one of the REAL reasons for the incitation of the 'Dulce Wars':

"...LEVEL #7 is the worst. Row after row of 1,000's of humans & human-mixture remains in cold storage. Here too are embryos of humanoids in various stages of development. Also, many human childrens' remains in storage vats. Who are [were] these people?"

"[My sources of information include...] people who worked in the labs, abductees taken to the base, people who assisted in the construction, intelligence personnel [NSA, CIA, etc.], and UFO-Inner Earth researchers. This information is meant for those who are seriously interested in the Dulce base. For **YOUR OWN PROTECTION**, be advised to **'USE CAUTION'** while investigating this complex..

"The Greys, the Reptoids, the winged Draco species are highly analytical and technologically oriented. THEY HAVE HAD ANCIENT CONFLICTS WITH THE EL-HUMANS and may be STAGING here for a FUTURE CONFLICT...

"Principal government organizations involved with mapping human genetics, the so-called genome projects are within,

- the Department of Energy
- the National Institute of Health
- the National Science Foundation
- the Howard Hughes Medical Institute
- and, of course, the Dulce Underground Labs run by the DOE

(Note: the "Department of Energy", which ALSO runs the Nevada Test Site. - Branton)

"Is the alien and human BIO-TECH being used to nurture and serve us or is it being used to CONTROL AND DOMINATE US? Why have UFO abductees been used in genetic experiments?

"IT WAS WHEN THOMAS ENCOUNTERED HUMANS IN CAGES ON LEVEL 7 OF THE DULCE FACILITY THAT THINGS FINALLY REACHED A CLIMAX FOR HIM. He says, 'I frequently encountered humans in cages, usually dazed or drugged, but sometimes THEY CRIED AND BEGGED FOR HELP. We were told they were hopelessly insane, and involved in high-risk drug tests to cure insanity. We were told NEVER TO SPEAK TO THEM AT ALL. At the beginning we believed the story. Finally in 1978 a small group of workers discovered the truth. THAT BEGAN THE DULCE WARS.'

"We may find it hard and unpalatable to digest or even believe Thomas' story and why should we even give it a hearing at all? Probably for no other reason than the fact that MANY OTHERS are coming out and telling bizarre stories and the fact that there <u>may be a terrible truth hidden behind</u> the continuing phenomena of UFO sightings, abductions, and animal mutilations. Our government intelligence agencies have had an ongoing watchful eye on all UFO activities for many decades now. This bizarre phenomena must have a bizarre explanation. We may be only one outpost in [a] vast interstellar drama.

"Recently, researcher John Anderson went to Dulce, N.M. to see if there is anything to the reported UFO activity. He says that he arrived in town coincidentally to see a caravan of cars and a McDonnell Douglas mini-lab in a van going up a rural road near the town. He followed them to a fenced-in compound where he waited to see further developments. Suddenly, six UFOs descended rapidly over the compound, hovered long enough for him to snap one picture, then shot up and out of sight.

When later stopping in a store to tell the owner of the UFO photo he had taken, the store owner listened and revealed how he had been a victim cattle rancher of cattle mutes. Their conversation was interrupted by a phone call after which the store owner told John to leave at once, then closed the store after John went to his car. John then saw a mysterious van drive up to the store and a man got out and went in. John decided to leave Dulce at that moment but was FOLLOWED by two men in a car as he left town.

"Even more recently a research team has gone up to Archuleta Mesa to take soundings under the ground and preliminary and tentative computer analysis of these soundings seem to indicate <u>DEEP CAVITIES UNDER THE MESA</u> (one source has stated that according to the data received these cavities extended to a depth of over 4,000 FEET! - Branton).

THE DULCE PROTOCOL

"Perhaps, someday, we will discover the deep dark secret of Dulce... Whatever the future brings it won't be dull."

Chapter 11

A Dulce Base Security Officer Speaks Out

The following is a list of questions that were directed to former Dulce Base Security officer Thomas Edwin Castello approximately a year before his death [or disappearance]. They are followed by his responses:

QUESTION - When exactly was the [upper human-occupied level of the] Archuleta installation constructed?

ANSWER - I heard Dulce was started in 1937-38 by the Army engineers, enlarged over the years, most recent work was completed 1965-66 to connect tunnels to the Page [Arizona] Base, site of one of the older underground facilities. The four corners base is called PERICA. Most of the Native Americans [the Indians] living in that area are aware of that base, and could tell us about the underground life forms that frequently are spotted near those communities, Bigfoot, etc.

(Note: The references to the Dulce base here deal mainly with the upper levels, not the extreme lower levels which include vast natural caverns and, some believe, very ancient tunnel systems as well. This would include the tunnels illuminated by phosphorus pentoxide which the alien grays avoid, and the origin of which is unknown.

In fact sources have informed us that some of the underground NORAD facilities of Colorado were constructed within already-existing cavern systems, suggesting that Ray Palmer and Richard Shaver were correct when as early as the mid-1940's they wrote about the government's search for ancient underground cave and tunnel systems to be converted for their own use. - Branton)

Q -- By what means was the [upper] installations constructed? Are you familiar with the alleged developments made by the Rand Corporation of a highly-efficient bore or mole machine capable of melting rock using nuclear powered wolfram-graphite tipped 'drill-cones'?

A -- According to several senior maintenance workers, part of it was blasted by nuclear devices in the sixties. There are sections, like the shuttle tunnels, that were formed by an advanced tunneling machine that leaves the tunnel walls smooth. The finished walls in those tubes resemble polished black glass.

Q -- By WHOM was the Dulce installation originally constructed?

A -- Nature started the caverns. The Draco [reptilian humanoids] used the caverns and tunnels for centuries. Later, through RAND Corporation plans, it was enlarged repeatedly. The original caverns included ice caves and sulfur springs that the 'aliens' found perfect for their needs. The Dulce caverns rival Carlsbad caverns in size.

(Note: Carlsbad caverns and especially the adjacent Lecheguilla caves are 'officially' among the largest and deepest in the world, with several 'leads' that remain to be explored by professional speleonauts - Branton)

Q -- What exactly are the cattle [and human] organs such as blood, anal tissue, eyes, reproductive organs, tongues, etc. used for -- i.e. the organs obtained via cattle and human mutilations?

THE DULCE PROTOCOL

A -- Read the so-called Dulce papers [for more information].

Q -- Are the various electromagnetically-controlled air or space craft -- [that have been seen] leaving from and arriving at Mt. Archuleta -- manned by humans, the 'alien entities', or both?

A -- Archuleta Mesa is a minor area... the craft leave [and are stored] in five areas. One is SE of DULCE, one near Durango Co., one at Taos, N. M., and the main fleet is stored at LOS ALAMOS [under].

(Note: I believe Thomas Castello is referring to the 'joint-operational' fleet. From combined sources however it appears as if Dulce is absolutely SURROUNDED ON ALL SIDES by 'alien' bases, and that Archuleta peak -- although apparently the central NEXUS of the entire underground network -- is nevertheless just one part of an overall complex that some claim is nearly the size of Manhattan!

One source has indicated that there are chambers a few hundred feet below the very town of Dulce itself that are part of level one of the facility. This close proximity may explain why it has usually been described as the 'Dulce Base'. Apparently even with his high-security clearance, Thomas Castello was only familiar with one part of the overall mega-complex which underlies the area. Whatever amount of activity is taking place there, different sources seem to indicate that the town of Dulce nevertheless lies over a major crossroads, convergence or 'intersection' area of alien activity even though the 'core' of alien activity has been extended to Los Alamos.

Los Alamos and the mountainous regions east and southeast of it in and around the Santa Fe National Forest seem to be the MAJOR 'nest' of Reptiloid/Gray forces in North America, although there is also a large number of 'dens' scattered throughout the underground networks between Dulce and Area 51.

Robert K Teske

Dulce seems to be a major 'through' point for exterran and subterran reptilian activity, a central 'infiltration' zone for surface operatives, as well as an operational base for abduction-implantation-mutilation agendas and also a major convergence for sub-shuttle terminals, UFO ports, and so on. - Branton)

Q -- Others have suggested that some of the entities below Dulce are not of 'extraterrestrial' ORIGIN, and that they are actually descended from saurian or reptiloid beings such as the Velociraptors or Stenonychosaurus Equallus -- a 'serpentine' race or races similar to that hinted at in the third chapter of the book of Genesis?

A -- Yes, some 'reptoids' <u>are native to this planet</u>. The ruling caste of 'aliens' ARE reptilian. The beige or white beings are called The Draco. Other reptilian beings are green, and some are brown. <u>They were an ancient race on Earth</u>, living underground. It may have been one of the Draconian beings that 'tempted' Eve in the Garden of Eden. Reptoids rightly consider themselves "native Terrans." Perhaps they are the ones we call the Fallen Angels. Maybe not, either way, we are [considered] the 'squatters' on Earth.

Q -- Some have suggested that the so-called underground 'E.T.' bases and tunnels may, for a large part, be literally thousands of years old... constructions of an antediluvian race which attained to a considerable level of scientific complexity, and who were destroyed by a Divinely-initiated cataclysm which took place after they attempted to merge their science with occult/supernatural forces.

For instance some have suggested that the Bermuda Triangle phenomena may be the result of an out-of-control Atlantean experiment that led to a space-time disaster which produced "electromagnetic fallout" in the Triangle area and elsewhere after they had accidentally loosed powerful forces and energies into the world that they knew very little about. Do your observations tend to confirm or refute such a possibility?

A -- I'm not sure about the Divine part, but these 'aliens' consider themselves 'NATIVE TERRANS.'

THE DULCE PROTOCOL

Q -- Where do the little gray Aliens fit in?

A -- They work for, and are controlled by the Draco. There are other gray skinned beings that are not in league with the Draco.

Q -- Did you ever talk to any of the 'Aliens' at the Base?

A -- Since I was the Senior Security Technician at that base, I had to communicate with them on a daily basis. If there were any problems that involved security or video cameras, I was the one they called. It was the reptilian "working caste" that usually did the physical labor in the lower levels at Dulce.

Decisions involving that caste were usually made by the white Draco. When human workers caused problems for the working caste, the reptoids went to the white Draconian 'boss', and the Draco called me. At times, it felt like it was a never ending problem. Several human workers resented the "no nonsense" or "get back to work" attitude the working caste lives by.

When needed, intervention became a vital tool. The biggest problem were human workers who foolishly wandered around near the "OFF LIMITS" areas of the "Alien Section." I guess it's human nature to be curious and to wonder what is past the barriers. Too often someone found a way to bypass the barriers and nosed around. The cameras near the entrance usually stopped them before they got themselves in serious trouble. A few times I had to formerly request the Return of a human worker.

Q -- Are there other sites tied-in to the 'shuttle network' other than those which you mentioned, and if so, where are the entrances?

A -- WHERE!?! EVERYWHERE! THEY CRISS CROSS THE WORLD AS AN ENDLESS SUBTERRANEAN HIGHWAY. LIKE A FREEWAY, EXCEPT THIS

ONE IS UNDERGROUND... The subterranean highway in America is like a freeway except it's underground. That highway depends on electric motors [for trucks, cars and buses] for the paved roads, and it is for limited travel.

There is another style of transit for freight and for passengers that is for rapid travel. That world wide network is called the "Sub-Global System." It has "check points" at each country entry. There ARE shuttle tubes that 'shoot' the trains at incredible speeds using a mag-lev and vacuum method. They travel at a speed that excels the speed of sound. Part of your question involves the location of entrances to that base. The easiest way to answer is to say every state in the U.S.A. has them.

Frequently, the entrances are camouflaged as sand quarries, or mining operations. Other complex portals are found on military bases. New Mexico and Arizona have the largest amounts of entrances followed by California, Montana, Idaho, Colorado, Pennsylvania, Kansas, Arkansas and Missouri. Of all the state's Florida and North Dakota have the least amount of entrances. Wyoming has a road that opens directly into the subterranean freeway. That road is no longer in use, but could be reactivated if they decide to do so, with minimal cost. It's located near Brooks Lake.

Q -- Are there any 'bases' in the state of Utah?

(Note: Thomas mentioned several areas surrounding Utah -- Colorado, New Mexico, Arizona, Nevada and Idaho, where there are 'connections', but little on Utah which according to some sources lies directly over one of the largest NATURAL cavern systems in North America, one that is said to reach deep beneath the Western Rockies as well as beneath the Bonneville basin. - Branton)

Have you heard anything about an alleged underground installation within the Wasatch Mountains...?

THE DULCE PROTOCOL

A -- Salt Lake, Lake Powell Area, Dark Canyon, Dugway Grounds, Modena, Vernal. All have exits there. Others too.

(Note: There have been many rumors of ancient 'tunnel' systems being intersected during the excavations of sub-basement levels below major industrial and mall areas in downtown Salt Lake City. Various stories surrounding these tunnels include:

- explorers who have entered the tunnels and never Returned;
- reports of 'lizard people' down in the labyrinths;
- reports of grays working with humans on electronic equipment and massive building projects going on in huge caverns beneath the mountains to the east;
- reports of humans who are part of an Asian-based 'Agharti' kingdom who maintain colonies within the tunnels and caverns below -- and who are in conflict with the reptiloids, grays, and a group collaborating human fascists from a network of massive underground facilities beneath the Neu Schwabenland region of Antarctica;
- reports of men in suits having been seen pacing back and forth through large underground chambers carrying uzi machine guns;
- reports of seemingly bottomless shafts;
- large tunnels strung with lights that are "big enough to drive a semi-truck through";
- sections of tunnel walls that looked solid yet which one could put their hands through;
- rooms which emanate a strange greenish phosphorescent glow;
- abductees who are taken below and encounter all types of aliens;
- discs that have been seen emerging from the mountains to the east and attacking incoming UFOs over the valley;

- Dungeons & Dragons fanatics who have been down in the tunnels and tell wild stories of hundreds of miles of maze-like passages;

- reports of connections to the tunnel systems via the sewer-drainage network especially underneath the downtown "Crossroads" area;

- reports of alien activity similar to that which has been described in connection to Dulce New Mexico;

- and reports of a huge cavern network that reaches beyond the border of the state in all directions -- a huge network that connects the underground systems of Nevada with those of New Mexico.

There is a famous story which is not openly talked about -- there are two versions... both may be true. In one version a Mormon Temple worker penetrated an underground tunnel below the 'square' in downtown Salt Lake City and traveled for some distance through a series of underground catacombs until running into a 'lizard' like man.

The creature attempted to attack him but the man escaped and managed to find his way back to the surface. He began telling other people what had happened and soon afterwards the 'government' arrived in the area and went in and closed off many of the tunnels leading to the sub-basements of the Temple. Presumably there was some heated debates over how much of the underground system this denomination was allowed to control.

A similar dispute apparently occurred to the southwest where the LDS church maintained a large storage facility under Granite Mountain in Little Cottonwood canyon, within the upper levels of a vast network of caverns. Fascist CIA elements and the Grays came in and took control of the larger caverns deeper within the mountain and ordered the 'vault' workers to stay out of the 'forbidden' areas -- and stated that the "U.S. Government" was now using them for "National Security" purposes and that it was their "patriotic duty" to maintain the secret.

THE DULCE PROTOCOL

The other version concerned a custodian who entered a tunnel near the cinemas area below the Crossroads Mall across the street and to the south from the temple square, while excavation was being carried out in a that part of the Mall. The worker entered the tunnel and before long encountered a 'serpent' type man, beat a hasty retreat, and told his fellow workers what he had seen. The FBI and/or the local police soon arrived and sealed the tunnel.

Another story involved a young man who, along with a friend, had used a chain tied to his pickup truck to rip-up a manhole cover in the area near the 'Mall' and the 'Square'. They navigated through a maze of sewer passages underneath and came to a shaft that descended in a series of 5 small 'rooms' one below the other, and from the bottom room a tunnel led south into a large chamber wherein they saw a seemingly bottomless shaft, a large southwest tunnel strung with lights and 'large enough to drive a semi through', and the footprints of some type of three-toed bi-pedal creature.

Other sources imply that early pioneers and settlers of the area who explored these tunnels came in contact with and in some cases even joined with some of the Telosian-Agharti-Melchizedek-Mayan underground colonies below the Salt Lake Flats, the Salt Lake Valley and the Western Rockies.

These subterraneans had formerly established territorial agreements with the Reptiloids and Grays before the aliens begun invading their subterranean lands below the intermountain west en-masse in the early 1900's. The treaties were part of an attempt to stave off a possible inter-species conflict, as skirmishes between the humanoids [Teros] and reptiloids [Deros] within the cavern networks of North America had been increasing since the 1920's, 30's and 40's.

Because of a somewhat non-exclusive collective-mind with which these humans interacted, it was decided that one possible way to 'convert' the reptilians into becoming beings of emotion and compassion was to allow them access to the group consciousness.

The reptiloids however, once given access, immediately began taking advantage of the collective and used it to CONTROL the humans on a subliminal basis.

The ease with which this occurred may have been enhanced by the fact that the Reptiloids and Grays were already operating as part of a collective or group mind, one which was far more complex than the Ashtar or Astarte collective itself which many of the 'Aghartians' depended on.

This suggests that the reptilian 'collective' or HIVE itself is absolutely void of any and all care, concern or compassion for human beings. Individual reptiloids operating distinct from the draconian collective might however be 'tamed' by other collective-free humanoids in some cases -- as some have reportedly been 'tamed' by the Andro-Pleiadean worlds.

If the non-humans could be severed from the 'collective' they might be deprogrammed and reprogrammed so-to-speak and even attain individual awareness and a degree of emotionalism. In such cases it would not be advisable to give these creatures equal standing among humans and absolute subservience and monitoring should be enforced even if means were found to sever them from the collective mind network.

When dealing with the reptilian forces, unconditional surrender should be first offered, and if this is not accepted than direct military action would be justified especially in light of the many permanent 'abductees' whom the Greys and Reptiloids have taken captive [those who are still alive] to their underground systems.

Most of the treaties that the humanoids had made with the reptiloids 'down under' have since been broken... especially following the Groom Wars of 1975 and the Dulce Wars of 1979, during which time much of the underground U.S. base networks [which were funded by American tax dollars by the way] were taken over by the Grays.

THE DULCE PROTOCOL

Some sources have implied that the aliens took advantage of the chaos especially during the Dulce wars and commenced to invade and conquer several of the older underground colonies. This apparently led to a rift in the 'Ashtar' collective, with many humanoids and hybrids splitting off and joining with the Andro-Pleiadean Federation non-interventionists, and many reptiloids and heartless humanoid agents splitting off and joining with the interventionists of the Draco-Orion Empire.

The Sirius-B system which -- aside from Arcturus and Sol -- has been the major center of 'Ashtar' activity, has since been shaken by this split between the two opposing Ashtarian factions and war had reportedly raged through the Sirius system for several years, according to some 'contactees'... an apparent reflection of the division within the underground networks of North America between the Pleiadean-backed Sirian humanoids and Orion-backed Sirian reptiloids which both had maintained operations within the underground levels before the "Dulce Wars" broke out.

The Dulce wars were just the mere tip of the proverbial iceberg when we consider that the overall events which happened at Dulce had a chain reaction effect throughout this whole sector of not the galaxy. Before the division occurred, the reptiloids were invited to take part in 'peace talks' in Telos and elsewhere as an act of good faith, but the reptiloid-grey collectivists were more interested in expanding their empire and feeding their insatiable appetite for conquest than they were in making peace, although they agreed to peace treaties that they never intended to keep for 'Trojan horse' manipulation purposes.

There is a remnant collaboration such as that taking place in the underground facilities near Paradox Nevada where collectivist humanoids and reptiloids from Sirius and Sol still maintain a collaboration of necessity -- in order to establish a global control system, however a large number of humanoids within the underground systems are at war with the collectivist-interventionist Reptilian infiltrators who would otherwise 'assimilate' these humanoids into their collective through deception, espionage and mind control.

Robert K Teske

Now several contactees like Alex Collier, Ray Keller, Stan Johnson and others are claiming that the conflicts in Sirius between the Andro-Pleiadean backed Ashtar forces and the Draco-Orion backed Ashtar forces -- which were infiltrated and commandeered by Draco-Orion agents -- have now spread to the Sol system, as both stellar superpowers have focused on this most strategic system, intent on protecting their respective 'interests' here from being subverted by the other side. - Branton)

Q -- Does the Mt. Archuleta "shuttle system" connect with a shuttle system which allegedly radiates from Mt. Shasta in northern California?

A -- Yes. Mt. Shasta is a major site of Alien - Elder Race - Reptilian Race - Human meetings. Beginning Cleveland, Grover every president in U.S. history have visited Telos City. Truman was supposed to have visited the Lower Realms as a High Archon on Earth. He was supposed to have met the King of the World there, and gave him the "Keys to the U.S.A."

(Note: Whether or not the reigning 'King' of the Agharti realms at the time had benevolent or other motives, subjecting America to an outside super-power without Congressional consent would be considered high treason. Although unelected/appointed 'individuals' working within the Executive-Military-Industrial branch of 'government' might choose to do so of their own volition without Congressional or Senatorial consent, such an act cannot apply to the 'America' which is based on the Declaration of Independence, the U.S. Constitution and the Bill of Rights. There are apparently two 'nations' occupying the United States,

- the traditional grass-roots 'America' established by the founding fathers and led by the 'Electorate' government,
- and the fascist Bavarian-lodge-backed 'underground nation' led by the 'Corporate' government which is contesting the original 'America' on its own soil.

THE DULCE PROTOCOL

Some predict an inevitable civil [?] war between the Electorate/Constitutional/Surface government of the U.S., and the joint humanoid-reptiloid Corporate/National-Global Socialist/Underground New World Order government, which incidentally was bought and paid for by American taxpayers and other unsavory money-making projects. This war will apparently provoke an armed United Nations / New World Order invasion of the U.S.A. which, according to George Washington's famous 'vision' at valley forge in 1777, will ultimately end with an American victory as a result of Divine Intervention.

Something like this may be inevitable if FREEDOM is to be preserved on this world, and beyond. We should never forget however that the NWO corporate elite and their draconian masters intend to 'depopulate' the surface of this planet AND the underground systems as well. According to one Navy intelligence source the 33rd degree-plus Masons [there are allegedly several degrees above the 33rd degree which interact directly with the Draconians and are part of the interplanetary initiatory lodges] intend to set the left-wing caverns and the right-wing caverns against each other in order to depopulate the underground realms so that they can impose absolute Bavarian-Draconian global control of 'both' worlds.

The 33rd+ and higher degrees according to this source intend to ride out the inferno in super-secret fortified caverns while the 33rd and lower degree masons and their respective left-wing and right-wing armies will be left to die in the surface and subsurface wars. It may be that some of the 33rd+ Masons intend to ride-out the holocaust in their Alternative-3 bases on the Moon and Mars, IF those bases are still active. Remember, the roots of BOTH the 'right-wing' National Socialist AND the 'left-wing' Global socialist agendas trace back to Bavaria. Isn't it interesting that the legendary 'dragon' has TWO 'wings' -- a right wing and a left wing -- both of which are controlled by a single 'beast'?.

In essence, when it comes right down to it the war is between the Judeo-Christian based Constitutional Republic of America and the Luciferian-cult-based Socialist empire of Bavaria. Both the right and left wing movements are Machiavellian extremes created by the Bavarian Black Nobility ['Black' here being a reference to something hidden that cannot be seen, and NOT skin color] in order to foment global chaos.

There are several claims that the collaboration with the Reptilians began with the Luciferian cults of Bavaria, and was later brought into America via the infiltration of the Scottish Rite and the fascist core of the NSA-CIA. There may have nevertheless been a reptilian presence below North America within the caverns that dates back several centuries, however a MASSIVE reptilian infestation of these underground systems seems to have begun near the beginning of the 20th century. 'Mt. Archuleta' might be considered the 'capital' of the ALIEN segment of the 'secret' [Bavarian-Draconian] New World Order government in America -- with the deep underground systems beneath the Denver International Airport being the 'capital' of the HUMAN segment of the secret government. - Branton).

Truman received assurance to new high tech knowledge, and victory over all enemies on Earth. He then was introduced to Samaza and Khoach, aliens from Bootes and Tiphon [Draco], both reptilian 'kings' or Ambassadors. Truman updated the '100 Treaty' [that began IN 1933, Roosevelt] and requested magnetic advance, space knowledge and experiments. Khoach agreed, Samaza partially agreed. He exchanged hostages for genetic experiments and magnetic advance, but vetoed space and beam weaponry.

Q -- Did you notice any involvement of high-level Freemasons, Rosicrucians or Jesuits within the underground installation and/or with the aliens?

(Note: This question is based on the assumption made by some researchers that many of the Masonic lodges were, beginning about 1776, infiltrated by the Bavarian

THE DULCE PROTOCOL

Illuminati. Much of the Masonic world is ultimately controlled by the <u>Bavarian-lodge-</u>

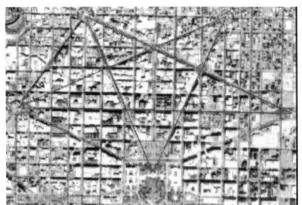

<u>backed 33+ degrees of Scottish Rite Masonry</u>, a 'Rite' which according to early Masonic authority Rebold can be traced back to the JESUIT college at Clermont in Paris -- a Rite which advocates the destruction of national sovereignties in exchange for world government, the destruction of religious

and especially Judeo-Christian movements, and the destruction of the family-structure to be replaced by 'State' control of children, etc., as opposed to the more traditional Protestant-Christianized YORK RITE of Masonry which the SCOTTISH RITE has attempted to subvert since its inception into Masonry.

This question was also based on claims from a former 33rd degree Mason, James Shaw, that the Scottish Rite headquarters in the "House of the Temple" -- which lies at the northern apex of the pentagram-like street layout of Washington D.C. -- is filled with all kinds of indications of serpent worship in the form of murals, carvings, statues, etc., depicting serpentine figures.

Actually, from what my sources tell me, not only are there degrees beyond the 33rd degree, but the <u>33rd degree itself is made up of two cores</u>, an inner and outer core, the 33rd degree and the 33+ degree. In the past when the 33rd degree initiation was reached a potential initiate might have been given a Bible or a Cross and asked to spit on it or desecrate it in some manner.

If they refused to do this they were told that they had made the "right decision" <u>and remained in the outer core</u> of the 33rd degree, thinking that they had finally 'arrived'. If they did or do commit this form of blasphemy then they are told that they have made the "right decision", and they are <u>sent on to the inner core of the 33+ degree</u>, which is the springboard to the higher levels which interact with the joint humanoid-reptiloid Ashtarian lodges or branches of the 'Serpent Cult' on other planets, within underground cities, and possibly even other dimensions.

One source informs me that former president George Herbert Walker Bush -- who was at one time the HEAD of MJ-12 -- had attained to the 42nd degree, however he may have attained to even higher levels since that time. I would guess that the one who holds the highest level of initiation would be the 'dragon-king' of Draconis himself, or whatever appellation the leader or the leaders of the Draconian Empire may go by. - Branton)

A - Yes I did, but that is a loaded question, and I won't comment further. I'm not a Mason, or member of any other secret fraternal group. There is one organization I am a member of [in the U.S.A.]. That group is commonly called the "Central Unit." It is a pleasure to tell you that I AM a member of the "Sub-Galactic League" of Costa Rica.

Q -- Is there any truth to the allegations that the CIA/'Aliens' have established 'bases' on the moon, and also Mars?

A -- I've HEARD that too, but I haven't seen proof with my own eyes. The 'aliens' do allegedly have bases on several moons of Jupiter and Saturn. The CIA operates in other COUNTRIES, but I've never heard they operate on other PLANETS

(Note: Perhaps we should have referred to the CIA's superior agency, the NSA, whose personnel reportedly pilot the "black-budget UFOs" between the LUNA and DREAMLAND bases. - Branton).

Q -- Have you heard any hints or rumors suggesting that there may be lower levels beneath the ULTRA-7 level of the Dulce base, and also, where these might lead to and what they might consist of?

THE DULCE PROTOCOL

A -- YES. Your guess is as good as mine... Sure, there was lots of TALK but that doesn't mean it's there. However, I will tell you I saw elevators that were "off limits" unless you had an UMBRA or higher security clearance. At that base, information is supplied to me at a "need to know" basis ONLY! [My clearance was ULTRA-7]

Q -- Some insist that the U.S./Secret government has developed it's own disk-craft based largely upon top secret antigravity experiments carried out by the Nazi-German scientists during World War II. Have you heard anything referring to this?

A -- When I was working in Photo-security, heard a lot of talk, never saw the proof, but once in the Air Force I developed a roll of film that showed a craft LIKE ADAMSKI'S, WITH A SWASTIKA ON THE SIDE.

(Note: A letter from 'R.J.M.' of Pennsylvania dated 1-31-91 stated: "...I have a lot of UFO videos. I also have 'THE SECRET LAND' [1947]. It shows Bunger's Oasis and says they discovered warm land at the South Pole. One German author claims the Nazi's had a photo-finish FIGHT with Byrd. At the end of the movie, it says: 'Byrd's Intrepid 4,000 met and defeated ANTARCTICA'S TOUGHEST BATTALIONS.' I don't think they were talking about the weather..."

Another source has stated that there were loses on BOTH sides, and the Battle for Antarctica against the Nazi's "Last Battalion" -- which had fortified themselves in underground bases below the mountains of Neu Schwabenland, AntarcticA -- ended in a stalemate.

Question: Why would Adolph Hitler and Eva Braun commit suicide after Hitler had spent so much energy executing over 5000 Nazi officials whom he 'suspected' were behind his assassination attempt at the 'Wolf' bunker, especially if he had a way out via a secret Nazi South Polar base? The March 18, 1994 issue of THE PLAIN DEALER [Cleveland, Ohio] carried an AP story titled "DOCTORS FIND BURNT BODY COULD NOT BE HITLER'S".

Excerpts include:

"...French forensic experts say the charred corpse said to be Hitler's is not his body... experts FALSIFIED verification reports ordered by Josef Stalin to APPEASE the Soviet dictator.... the body is actually that of an unknown German male. [The forensic experts] spent more than two years analyzing the autopsy reports prepared by Soviet coroners in the days following [the] surrender of the Third Reich in 1945... the body [said to be Hitler's] had an extra tooth and only one testicle... no German doctor who had examined Hitler before his death ever mentioned either anomaly."

This is also interesting when we consider that the well-known 'abductee', Barney Hill, remembered the following experience under regressive hypnosis as recorded in the paranormal encyclopedia, "MYSTERIES OF MIND, SPACE & TIME". Barney and his wife Betty were abducted by gray-skinned humanoids "from Zeta Reticuli".

HOWEVER, one of the 'beings' on the craft was described by Barney Hill under regressive hypnosis in the following words which are taken from p.1379 of the encyclopedia: "...another figure has an EVIL face... HE LOOKS LIKE A GERMAN NAZI. HE'S A NAZI... HIS EYES! HIS EYES. I'VE NEVER SEEN EYES LIKE THAT BEFORE!"

Remember that this occurred nearly 15 years after Europe had supposedly been "de-Nazified". There seems to be an Antarctic connection with the Dulce scenario as well as other possible 'Nazi' connections:

- German 'tourists' scouring New Mexico, exploring mines and caves and buying up land and mineral rights just before the outbreak of WWII;
- the Nazi-connected CIA's involvement and their placement of several Nazi S.S. agents -- who had been brought into the U.S. via Project Paperclip -- within the Dulce and other underground facilities;

- the involvement of secret 'Bavarian' lodges at Dulce;
- and the possible Antarctican-Dulce connection to 'Alternative 003'.

Another interesting connection is the fact that the secret Nazi teams involved in the construction and operation of the underground bases below the mountains of Neu Schwabenland and elsewhere in Antarctica were called ULTRA teams. ULTRA is also the code-name for the DULCE base!

Also there seems to be a direct connection between the Dulce base and the Montauk base in Long Island -- which was/is[?] reputedly jointly operated by the Draconian Reptiloids, Orion Greys and the Bavarian Thule Society which had backed the Nazi agenda. - Branton)

Q -- Tom, did you have access to the alien craft? Were you ever inside any of them?

A -- Yes, I frequently saw them in the garages, there are quite a few of them. The main fleet is stored at Los Alamos. Yes, I entered several crafts. There were two things that stick in my mind, the odd spongy feeling of the floors, and the unusual pinkish purple color of the lighting.

The crew stated the floor becomes ridged in flight, and the purple tint of the lighting changes to bright blue white. The entire inside of the air craft are scaled down in size, when compared to the average human. The halls were curved and narrow, but some how, when inside it appears bigger than it looks. Certain areas, the outermost sections, almost felt and looked alive. I was never taken up in one.

Q -- Can you give me more information on the reptilian race, what do they do on the sixth level? [The area called Nightmare Hall.]

A -- The worker caste does the daily chores, mopping the latex floors, cleaning the cages, bringing food to the hungry people and other species. It is their job to formulate the proper mixture for the type one and type two beings that the Draco Race has created. The working caste work at the labs as well as at the computer banks. Basically speaking, the reptilian races are active at all levels of the Dulce Base. There are several different 'races' of aliens that work on the east section of level six (No doubt some collaborating 'Nordic' factions included. - Branton).

That section is commonly called "the alien section." The Draco are the undisputed masters of the 5-6-7 levels. The humans are second in command of those levels. I had to ARGUE with one large Draconian 'boss' frequently. His name is difficult to verbalize, Khaarshfashst [pronounced throaty kkhhah-sshh-fahsh-sst]. I usually called him 'Karsh,' and he hated it. The Draconian leaders are very formal when talking to the human race. These ancient beings consider us a lower race. Karsh called me "Leader Castello," but it was used in a sarcastical way. However the worker caste is friendly enough, as long as you allow them to speak first.

They will answer if you address them. They are very cautious beings, and consider most humans to be hostile. They always seem surprised when they found many of the humans were open and trustworthy. There is no fraternizing with the aliens off hours. It is forbidden to speak to any alien race [in the halls or an elevator] without a clear business oriented reason. Humans can talk to humans, and aliens can speak to aliens, but that is as far as it goes. At the work site, however, it's different. There is "free speech" in the labs.

The camaraderie found in the labs also reaches the computer banks section. In those areas, everybody talks to anybody. However, everything changes the minute you cross the threshold of the hall. Instantly, all conversations become strictly formal. Hard as it was, several times I had to arrest some one, simply because they spoke to an alien. It's a strange place.

THE DULCE PROTOCOL

Q -- Exactly what first made you aware that something was wrong at Dulce? Seems to me that a place as obviously horrible as this one wouldn't need an Einstein to know that this is a CRIME site! What took you so long? Are you the guy who blew the whistle?

A -- There are several things you should know about. I took an oath, under the penalty of death, that no matter what I saw or heard I would never divulge the information. Also, I signed a waiver that states I would willingly give up my life if I was found guilty of 'treason'.

At the Dulce Base treason is "ANYTHING that mentions the details of daily operations at this facility, when outside the confinement of the this base." When I first arrived, a "need to know" policy was in effect. The story the 'honchos' told us was that "this is a Tri-Biotransfer Facility with Advanced Technology, doing advanced adventurous methodology for medical and mental gains."

This is a fancy way of saying they do really risky things with human life just to see what would happen. If a medical cure happens, it will be heralded on the surface of the earth as a marvelous new cure, saying it was found after years of research at some well known medical lab. The real story of the cure is never explained.

After all, the Dulce Base IS A SECRET FACILITY! These people are very good at what they do. They do not tell the truth about the unfortunate people that end up in "Nightmare Hall." I worked with aliens. With that in mind, you should get the idea of the secrecy and the security at that place.

Yes, I know this was not the usual hospital type job site, but in the beginning I 'bought' the whole package. I was reminded daily by intercom, in the elevators, that "this site does high risk advanced medical and drug testing to cure insanity, please, never speak to the inmates, it can destroy years of work." I'm sensible, when doctors say don't speak to them, who was I to destroy the delicate situation?

But one man some how caught my eye. He repeatedly stated that he was George S---- and that he had been kidnapped and he was sure someone was searching for him. I don't know why he sticks in my mind, I found I was remembering his face, thinking he sure didn't look or sound insane, but many inmates said that. The next weekend I convinced a friend of mine, a cop, to run a check on the guy, saying I had a run in with him and was curious.

I didn't mention the base at all. It was a sickening feeling when the computer confirmed that George S. was missing. What's worse, the cops thought he was just another guy that got tired of the daily grind and split. That was the beginning. Am I the one that blew the whistle? No. The next Monday, I searched for George, but he was gone.

There were no records that explained what happened to him. It was another security officer that came to me saying he and some lab workers wanted an off duty meeting at one of the tunnels, [off the record]. Curiosity took over and I said OK. That night, about nine men showed up. They said they knew they were risking me turning them in but they wanted to show me some things they thought I should see. One by one they showed records that proved many inmates were missing people.

There were newspaper clippings, and even photos that they had some how smuggled into the base. They hoped to smuggle them back out, without me turning them in to the honchos. I could see the fear in their faces as they spoke. One man stated he would rather lose his life by trying, than to lose his soul by not doing anything at all. It was that remark that turned the tide. I told them about George and the things I found out about him. After a few hours we pledged to attempt to expose the Dulce Base.

Q -- The name Nightmare Hall is descriptive, but surely there was a 'regular' name, what was it called in the manuals?

THE DULCE PROTOCOL

A -- In the manuals it was called "The Vivarium". It describes Dulce Base as a "secured facility for tending bio-forms of all types." In their report it is retold as "a private subterranean bio-terminal park, with accommodations for animals, fish, fowl, reptile, and mankind." After SEEING this 'park' the name Nightmare Hall is far more accurate than the manual. The 'accommodations' for the inmates at Nightmare Hall fall short of the pretty picture the manual describes.

Q -- You mentioned one reptilian leader, Khaarshfashst, do you know any thing about him, like where is he from? Is he from Earth or some other planet?

A -- His name means "keeper of the laws". They receive their name after they reach the "age of awareness". They do not recognize time as an important factor in "being aware" the way humans do. Upon their "age of awareness" they are cognitive of the station or position they are destined to fulfill. At that time they chose or allow someone to choose their name.

Their name will include the position they hold and several personally chosen letters. Each letter has a personal meaning, known only to the alien and the one that chose their name. Since Karsh's name means keeper of the laws his name includes kaash [memory or keep, base word for 'Akashic' record] and fashst [law, base word fast or bind]. Reptilians choose to be not only private but secretive of the location of their natal place. To them birth, or emergence of life, is considered as one of the sacred rites of life.

They consider Earth or Terra their "home planet", but several reptoids discuss several star maps. Most of those stars were within the Milky Way. Within those star maps lies the stars and planets of the Planets of the Allegiance.

Earth being one of the planets in their trade routes. If any human asked clear questions about the Allegiance, the Aliens referred the questions to the Draco. The Draco in turn, referred the questions to their supervisor [me]. I did not have that information about the stars, because information was supplied on a "need to know" basis. I didn't 'need' that information.

Q -- Did any of the working caste join in the revolt? Could you give me some names?

A -- A few of the reptilian janitorial crew let us know that THEY knew WE were attempting to sabotage the work going on in the sixth and seventh levels. One of them, with the name Schhaal, secretly formed a small group of reptoids with the same mind set as my group

(Note: Take note of the similarity between this scenario and the NBC mini-series "V", which is now available on video cassette after years of non-availability. I have it on good authority that the original author of the "V" idea was an investigator who knew Thomas Castello on a personal basis.

He had connections in Hollywood and had written a motion picture script, which was in turn seen and 'borrowed' without permission by an NBC employee and re-written as a mini-series. The show was based on reptilian humanoids from Sirius-B who had come to earth under the guise of benevolent human-like space brothers to bring a new order of universal peace. In reality they had a secret agenda to rape planet earth of her resources and steal her people for biological sustenance.

This agenda was being contested by a human resistance who refused to fall for the reptilian's facade, and these resistors were in turn working with a secret fifth-column of reptilians who did not agree with their leaders' agenda for planet earth. Could this mini-series have had an actual basis in a bizarre reality? - Branton).

Sshhaal took upon himself the danger of informing me. He was as open as is possible in a unique situation. On the day I found out about it, I was inspecting a camera near an exit tunnel.

THE DULCE PROTOCOL

He approached, stooped down (the tall reptiloids average about 7-8 ft. in height according to most witnesses - Branton), seemingly scraping some non-existent dirt, and he quietly said,

"A few of us agreed that you are singular in your interest in missing-human reports. If true, walk away. I'll reach you. If it's untrue, destroy my life now!"

My heart almost leaped out of my chest, but I silently walked toward one of the wide halls.

For the rest of my life I'll remember those words! It was the first time I KNEW reptilians could have individual thoughts and opinions! Basically, they formed a uniform front with a small variety of interests. Or at least, that was what we had thought. It was a couple days before I heard from him again. As he walked beside me in the sixth level's infamous hall, I heard him say "Enter the exit tunnel on the sixth level, north, after your shift."

The next few hours were long and filled with thoughts of betrayal, or worse, but I shouldn't have worried. I contacted one of the original nine [resistance] men, and let him know, just in case. Gordon wanted to go with me, but I convinced him to wait a few feet from the exit and pretend he was having trouble with his cart [electric, like a golf cart]. When I got there, there were three of them.

SSHHAAL formerly introduced FAHSSHHAA and HUAMSSHHAA [name base word is SSHHAA or assist]. With that, I quickly grabbed Gordon from the hall and the five of us talked and walked in the dark tunnels about three hours. After that day, the joined resistance group got bigger and bolder. Ultimately, it ended when a military assault was initiated via the exit tunnels and they executed anybody on their list, human or reptilian.

We fought back, but none of the working caste had weapons, nor did the human lab workers. Only the security force and a few computer workers had flash guns. It was a massacre. Every one was screaming and running for cover. The halls and tunnels were filled as full as possible.

We believe it was the Delta Force [because of the uniforms and the method they used] that chose to hit at shift change, an effort that killed as many as named on their list

(Note: If Thomas Castello is correct in his assertion, then based on his overall revelations, as well as the revelations of others such as Robert Lazar, Phil Schneider, etc., the Dulce Wars were the result of at least five overlapping factors or scenarios which converged at more or less the same time or played into each other.

This may have also involved a conflict of interest within MJ12 itself, and apparently involved different security forces including the Delta Force, Black Berets, Air Force Blue Berets, Secret Service, FBI Division Five, CIA stormtroopers and Dulce Base security.

The various factors which seem to have played into the Dulce Wars would include animosity towards the Greys for their slaughter of several scientists and security personnel in the Groom Wars below Area 51 three years earlier as described by,

- former MJ12 Special Studies Group agent Michael Wolf
- accidental [?] encounters between aliens and human construction workers and security forces near Dulce as described by Phil Schneider
- an attack on the Dulce base 'resistance' that was apparently ordered by die-hard collaborators in deep-level intelligence as described by Thomas Castello
- an attempt to rescue several of our best scientists who had been captured by the aliens after they had discovered the "Grand Deception" involving a violation of the established treaties, that is the permanent abduction of thousands of humans to the Dulce and other bases for God only knows what purposes, as

described by John Lear -- could it be that MJ12 / PI40 was unaware of these abductees, yet their superior agency the BLACK MONK / MAJIC agency was aware and had agreed to an actual exchange of human life for technology?

- and another factor would involve a dispute over whether human security personnel could carry flash guns as opposed to machine guns

All of these were apparently contributing factors to the 'altercations' which raged throughout the Dulce Base beginning in 1979. - Branton).

We, to this day, do not know who BETRAYED us. Gordon Ennery ran beside me as we ran into the third level exit tunnels, and he died when several bullets slammed into his back. I vaporized that assassin and kept running. And I'm still running. Gordon will be remembered.

Q -- Tell me more about the flash gun. Is it difficult to operate, or is it like the weapon on Star Trek, that can stun or kill on different modes?

A -- It is an advanced beam weapon that can operate on three different phases. Phase one, like Star Trek, can stun and maybe kill, if the person has a weak heart. On phase two, it can levitate ANYTHING no matter what it weighs. Phase three is the SERIOUS BUSINESS mode. It can be used to paralyze anything that lives, animal, human, alien and plant.

On the higher position on the same mode, it can create a TEMPORARY DEATH. I assure you, any doctor would certify that person is dead, but their life essence lingers in some strange limbo, some kind of terrible state of non-death. In one to five hours the person will revive, slowly; first the bodily functions will begin, and in a few minutes, consciousness followed with full awareness. In that mode the alien scientists re-program the human brain and plant false information.

When the person awakes, he 'recalls' the false information as information he gained through life experience. There is no way for a person to learn the truth. The human mind 'remembers' and believes completely the false data. If you attempt to inform them, they would laugh or get angry. They NEVER believe the truth. Their mind always forgets the experience of re-programming.

You asked if the flash gun is difficult to operate. A two year old child could use it with one hand. It resembles a flash light, with black glass conical inverted lens. On the side are three recessed knobs in three curved grooves. Each knob is sized differently. The closer the knob to the hand the less the strength. It's that simple. Each knob has three strengths also, with automatic stops at each position.

The strongest position will vaporize any thing that lives. That mode is so powerful it will leave NO TRACE of what it vaporized.

Q -- Is the weapon called a Flash Gun or is there a different name in the manuals?

A -- Everybody calls them Flash Guns, or more commonly "The Flash" or "my Flash" when talking about it. In the manual it is first introduced as the ARMORLUX Weapon. After that, it is explained as the Flash Gun.

Q -- What type of security is found at the Dulce Base? What else is used against espionage or unauthorized entry?

A -- I'll mention a few, but it would be nearly impossible to cover it all. The weapon, besides the Flash Gun, mostly used is a form of sonic. Built in with each light fixture [and most camcorders] is a device that could render a man unconscious in seconds with nothing more than a silent tone. At Dulce there also are still and VCR cameras, eye print, hand print stations, weight monitors, lasers, ELF and EM equipment, heat sensors and motion detectors and quite a few other methods.

There is no way you could get very far into the base. If you made it to the second level, you would be spotted within fifteen feet. More than likely, you would become an inmate and never see the light of the surface world again. If you were 'lucky', you would be re-programmed and become one of the countless spies for the Ruling Caste.

Q -- According to certain reports, the Dulce Base is host to [other] aliens that live in level five. Is that true? Can the humans freely roam or meet one-to-one in the halls or is some type of protocol in effect?

A -- There is protocol from the first time you enter the base and it MUST be followed every time you SEE an alien there. From the working caste, to the visiting aliens, to the Ruling Caste, there is a never ending check list of rules, law, and strict protocol. There is never a chance to roam on the fifth level. The alien housing area is off limits to any human. The Hub is surrounded by security, arsenal, military and CIA\FBI sections.

The area past the security is one of the most secured areas because it houses so many classified files. The entire east side of the fifth level is off limits except for security personnel holding ULTRA-7 [security clearance] or higher. The garage on the west side of the fifth level requires ULTRA-4 clearance.

Q -- Is there proof available that could confirm the allegations of the underground base, or are we just supposed to believe you?

A -- Many people have asked that one. No, I don't expect people to believe with blind faith, there is tangible proof that has been seen, felt or inspected by quite a few folks. I'm in no position to go on a lecture circuit to explain to every person on a one-to-one basis. I am trying to stay alive.

All I can do is state again, that Dulce is a SECRET FACILITY. They work HARD to make sure nobody can find the place. If everyone could easily find it, it wouldn't be a SECRET facility. I've explained the extreme security methods they use. There is other proof available.

There are five sets of copies in five different boxes in five different locations that hold complete proof of every thing I have tried to explain. Here is a list of contents of each box (delivered into the safe-keeping of five individuals known only to Thomas Castello and to the individual recipients - Branton):

(A) 27 sheets of 8 x 10 photographs of Aliens, creatures, cages and vats.

(B) One silent candid video tape, begins on the computer banks, shows the vats, multi shots of Nightmare Hall, two shots of Greys, one shot of the Terminal showing sign saying 'To Los Alamos' and about thirty seconds of the Shuttle train arriving.

(C) 25 pages of diagrams, chemical formulas and schematics of alien equipment.

(D) A copy of the new treaty complete with signatures.

(E) 2 pages of original Alien documents signed by Ronald Reagan [as governor of California], each page includes Reagan's signature.

The ORIGINAL set mentioned above is sealed in one piece oxygen free heavy plastic box. That set includes:

(A) 27 sheets of 8 x 10 WITH original negatives

(B) The video tape, AND the original micro film, from which the video tape was copied.

(C) The 25 original pages of diagrams [with notations], formulas, alien equipment schematics plus the schematics for the Flash Gun and MY Flash Gun.

(D) The treaty with Reagan's signature plus seven other political signatures and four Alien signatures.

The working Flash Gun in that box is an extremely dangerous weapon. In the wrong hands, there is no limit on the danger it could inflict. That proof must be protected. But when placed in the hands of certain government agencies, it would not be treated as proof for an Alien visitation. That government branch KNOWS THE TRUTH and they publicly lie. Think about it like this, do you KNOW, for certain proof, that George Washington lived? Or do you believe what other people SAID about him?

There is no one alive that saw with their own eyes what is claimed about him. You judge all you know about him by what other people SAID. Columbus SAID there is a new land, and it was found. I am SAYING there are aliens in several underground bases in this country and terrible things happen in those places. If I die, before it is proven, search for proof (after all, the Dulce Base and the other bases aren't going anywhere. Unlike UFO's themselves they are not "here today and gone tomorrow". If they are there, then there are bound to be some indications of the fact. - Branton).

Demand that the government admit it. If enough people demand it, they WILL find a way to explain the base, or at least explain why they must keep it secret. There are MANY people that work at the Dulce Base that know me. I am challenging those co-workers to speak up, at least anonymously. Send a letter, or a telegram [or fax] to confirm what I have explained. In the name of the brave men, woman, children and aliens that died TRYING to let the public know what is going on at the Dulce Facility,

EXPOSE that horrid place before thousands more innocent people are tortured and die unspeakable deaths.

Q -- What about the elevators, do they drop from the surface to the seventh level in a couple of seconds? Do you know anything about them? Are they electrically lifted? Every where on the surface world there are elevators made by Otis Elevator Company. Does that company make the elevators at Dulce?

A -- I failed to notice what brand was available in the elevators at the base. I could tell you that there is no elevator anywhere at Dulce that drops from the surface to the seventh level. The security blue prints show the levels are 'stepped' down. Each level drops one floor only.

Not even the Hub has an express elevator. After the third level, not only would you change elevators, you are weighed and color coded, before you re-enter the car. All the elevators are magnetically controlled, even lights in elevators, as well as all lights on all levels are magnetically induced. The light bulbs are not the type bought on the surface, but a totally different type of light system. The illumination found there is a closer match to natural sunlight than any artificial light on the surface world.

The shape of the elevators is unique. If you have ever seen a Tupperware sugar bowl, you could see the shape copied in the elevator. Sort of like an open ended oval with another half oval on each side. The elevator shaft matches the shape perfectly. The magnetic controls are in the half oval shape. If you could stand in or close to the half ovals, you would feel the slight pull of the power of those magnets.

The motion is smooth and silent, there is a nearly unnoticed surge when the motion starts or stops. There are no cables needed, because the lift is magnetic, not electric. Since there are no cables in the elevator cars there is no chance of them falling.

THE DULCE PROTOCOL

Q -- I understand that certain groups of cleared individuals in the government are collaborating with alien groups. Is it known how many groups and of what type they are working with?

A -- I don't know how many groups or what type they are working with.

Q -- A mysterious security man calling himself agent "Yellow Fruit" says he worked at Groom Lake [Area 51]. The Security Officer states that he's been in contact with benevolent aliens, at the Groom Lake facility -- are you aware of such a group?

A -- Yellow Fruit is one of the slang names for Yellow Jack [or Yellow Flag] that shows quarantine and caution in the labs. There are so many different slang names at Dulce labs that meant quarantine that the workers published a booklet to show the meanings. At Dulce, Yellowfruit are the lab workers [so called from the yellow light outside the decontamination chambers]. Banana is the older workers, lemon is the new guys and so on.

Q -- Is there an alien installation under Groom Lake or Papoose Lake at the Nevada Test Site, and are they conducting biological research at these sites?

A -- Most of the stuff at the Groom facility deals with defense, but there is a large storage area in the tunnels that holds thousands of alien craft parts. From what I have heard, the medical tests at the Nevada Test Site are conducted by and for the Navy.

Q -- According to my sources, the Aerospace companies have a secret underground installation in the Tehachapi Mountains, not far from Rosamond near Edwards AFB. Insiders refer to the Tehachapi Installment as the Ant Hill. They are experimenting with advanced technology such as antigravity disks. Some have seen basketball sized floating orbs patrol the facility, do you have any further information on this?

A -- The California mountains [Tehachapi, Chocolate, Shasta, etc.] all have alien security methods and equipment. The basketball size orbs are used for unmanned patrol. They are silent, but when photographing living beings there is a humming sound. The glow that emits light is magnetic aura. This [light] is in the visible spectrum [3900 angstroms]. You can see the light, but the light does not reflect off any thing.

Q -- Is there anything you can tell me about the moon - alien installations? Atmosphere? U.S. bases?

A -- There is not much I can tell you there. I wasn't in the Lunar Program. I heard there was a LOT of equipment sent to the moon between 1959-1964 under "Project Whiteout".

Q -- How do the aliens use magnetism? Do they use it as an energy source? Is there more we need to know about magnetism?

A -- The aliens use magnetics for EVERY THING! They use magnetics as the basic structure for their energy source. The more you learn about magnetics, the better. The Human Race calls them 'magnets', the Aliens call them 'lodestar'. They have been harvesting lodestars [lodestones] for centuries. Not only that, they want ALL the magnetic power on Earth.

They intend to continue harvesting that power, now and in the future. As long as we were only using magnetic power as an oddity, there was no problem. But in recent times, the human race has begun using magnetic power and finding more ways to utilize that commodity. There was a treaty made. In the original treaty, the human race (or those who supposedly 'represented' the human race, if you could call it that - Branton) didn't mind at all, 'we' considered magnets as hardly more than useless.

As people searched for another source for power, we turned to magnetics. The aliens wanted a new treaty. What could we offer? They chose land, underground mining rights, animals and humans for new experiments. The general public NEVER KNEW about the treaty. The governmental [Bavarian cultist] heads of the world chose another treaty in 1933. This time 'we' got high-tech knowledge in exchange.

So now, the more we use magnetics, the more they claim humans, and the lands of the U.S.A. We were 'sold' in exchange for magnets. If you doubt it, look around -- there are token companies that 'really' utilize magnetic power, but are depending on electric based or ceramic magnets, NOT lodestar [magnetic oxide of iron] based magnets.

Q -- What do the aliens do with the cow blood and other parts from mutilated animals? Do they need these fluids for research or survival?

A -- The aliens use the blood and body parts for formula to keep them alive [their food] and for use in the growing vats, and for the artificial wombs. Plasma and amniotic fluid are the two most vital ingredients for their lives. Also, the 'sap' of some plants can keep them alive for months. Most of the plants are parasitic in nature, but red grapes and okra plants can also be added to the formula to keep them alive, if they have no 'regular' formula.

Q -- Female abductees report being inseminated by aliens. Are they trying to hybridize our species?

A -- Yes, they are breeding slave-warriors for the upcoming war with the alien races (the Nordic races? - Branton). The serpentine races are in orbit around Earth, Venus and Mars.

Q -- Abductees have reported that the aliens can pass their bodies and that of the abductee through window glass. Is this a feat of magic achieved by advanced technology or is it a psychic power?

A -- The aliens have mastered atomic matter. They can go through walls like we go through water! It is not magic, just physics. We can learn to do the same thing. It has to do with <u>controlling atoms at will</u>.

Q -- Are you in communication with benevolent aliens or do you have contacts that are? If you are, can you tell us how we can communicate with their teams?

A -- I am not at liberty to discuss communications with any friendly alien life forms. I can tell you there is a <u>friendly factor active in</u> Costa Rica, I am in direct communication with that factor. I am an active member of the Sub-Galactic League of Costa Rica. This organization, using a small satellite dish, a television set and ham radio equipment reached this factor. I might suggest that by using similar equipment and a low band frequency, you may reach the same factor.

Q -- Do you stay in the U.S.A., or do you live abroad? Do you work now? I know you have been on the run for several years.

A -- Yeah, quite a few years. I visit the U.S., but it's really dangerous when I do. I've lived in several countries. I spent a few years in Mexico, working as a mercenary soldier. It's rough work, frequently living in the bush, eating what ever I can find. I spent time in South America, fighting the drug cartel [it's not the citizens, it's the secret government, top officials AND American alphabet boys -- CIA, FBI, etc.].

I settled in Costa Rica, 'bought' a small house in Limon. Actually it is a shanty that some one abandoned. I paid the equivalency of $11 to one of the local constables for the right to call it 'mine'. My name changes when I think some one is asking questions. I've worked in one of the underground bases near the Panama border. It's in the mountains, not very far from a passive but 'active' volcano. It is not as fancy as Dulce, but the people are wonderful.

THE DULCE PROTOCOL

Q -- What is the best city in Costa Rica for an American to visit and maybe move to live?

A -- None of them are worth anything [by comparison], but I like Limon. There is a real culture shock when you get past the tourist sections. Inside the urban areas, it's not so bad, but away from the beaten path the picture changes. There are no improvements in the shanties, no sewers, plumbing, or paved roads. But if you stay in the cities, and you don't mind the big difference in the cultures, the countries have a lot to offer. Nice weather, great beaches and beautiful trees with fruit growing everywhere.

Q -- Are there any other security level names [other than 'secret' - 'top secret' - 'ultra']?

A -- There are many other security clearances, here are a few, UMBRA, STELLAR, G2-7Z, TRIAD, UMT [Universal Military Training] and UMS [Universal Military Service], ASTRAL and SUB-ASTRAL. UMBRA is higher than ULTRA

(Note: It may be conceivable that some of the higher security clearances are used for the joint human-alien interstellar projects. For instance Whitley Strieber described an abduction to another planetary sphere where he encountered ancient ruins, aliens and human personnel dressed in military kakis and carrying camcorders, automatic weapons, etc.

Obviously such personnel would have to possess an extremely high security classification, such as "Universal Military Service" for instance? The joint alien-illuminati " alternative-3" projects have reportedly taken part in joint offensive operations against the peaceful residents of other worlds, this according to a couple who 'defected' from the alternative-3 movement after an agent from the 'Federation' warned them about such atrocities. - Branton)

Q -- Ever see a badge with 'MAJI'?

A -- No.

Q -- Since you have lived in Spanish speaking countries, it's obvious that you are bilingual. What other languages do you speak?

A -- Other than English, the only other languages I speak are Spanish and Eusshu, the common language [alien] spoken at Dulce. I speak Spanish fluently, and enough Eusshu to keep my self out of trouble. Shortly after I first transferred to Dulce, I took a crash course in Eusshu.

Any one that plans to spend more than one week working at that base, they are wise to learn the basics. Other wise, you are required to wait for an escort to get around. All the signs at that base are written in the universally recognized symbolic language. Eusshu is logical and easy to learn.

Q -- What are the eating habits of the aliens? Are they carnivores?

A -- That depends whether they are one of the gray worker caste, one of the reptilian worker caste, or one of the higher developed Draconian Leaders. Also, the created beings, replicants, type two being, or one of the really strange [genetic] mixtures. I'll try to cover a little of each. The formula includes amniotic water, plasma and several other body parts [raw, usually bovine].

This nearly clear mixture with a texture of pureed peaches, and almost in that color. The grays make the attempt not to 'eat' around the humans, because the odor of it is VERY unpleasant to ANY human. They can spend days or even weeks between feedings. The working caste of the reptilians eat meat, insects and a large variety of plants including vegetables and fruit. They prefer their meat raw and very fresh, but have learned to enjoy some cooked meat like rare beef steak

THE DULCE PROTOCOL

(<u>Note</u>: According to many abductees, the reptiloids are not above eating human flesh. It has been said that they prefer flesh that is young enough to be free of toxins, yet old enough to be imbued with a lifetime of accumulated "emotional energy residue" which is resident within the human body. Some abductees claim that certain reptilian factions have such complex bio-technologies that they are able to <u>remove a human's soul-energy-matrix</u> and place it in a containment 'box', and use the controlled 'body' for whatever purpose they choose.

Some abductees also insist that in some cases the reptiloids can create a cloned duplicate of a person in a short amount of time through time warping and replace the soul-energy-matrix of a person back into the new cloned body if their disappearance from society would otherwise create too many problems. This way they can ingest the emotional-residue-imbued original body without the abductee realizing [in most cases] that their soul-memory-matrix has been transferred to a cloned body, because they would have experienced a total 'soul-matrix' energy transfer and a suppression of any memories relating to the transfer process.

The cloned bodies do not possess the integrated emotional residue that the vampirialistic reptiloids apparently crave and find intoxicating in a similar manner as a human on earth who is addicted to hard drugs. - Branton).

Unlike the Greys, they eat frequently and usually carry or send for food on their breaks. The Ruling Caste is SECRETIVE about their foods. They have created several dietary myths that they carefully embellish when the chance arrives. One of their favorite legends involves one of their ancestors' ability to eat an entire flock of geese in one setting. They RARELY eat in sight of any other species.

They carefully choose their food, then carry their meal to their quarters. It was only when dignitaries arrive at the base did they join their meals. They <u>enjoy the same foods we do</u>, and they have been seen secretly munching on a freshly found snail. The "human looking" replicants eat some cooked vegetables. They rely on vitamins and liquid protein for sustenance. If they have to eat on the surface world, they can eat what ever they are served, but as soon as possible they regurgitate.

Their digestive systems frequently fail to process the food properly. The engineered beings have a special diet, created for their dietary needs. The mixture includes several organ foods blended with plasmatic fluids, amniotic liquids and parasitiplasm materials. These unique 'animals' also enjoy occasional green plants, usually grasses or lettuce. The creatures that are designed to become warriors, eat protein filled liquids.

Q -- In the Dulce Papers, copper seems to be high on the importance list. In what methods is copper used?

A -- One of the main uses of copper at Dulce is containment of the magnetic flow, magnets are used every where at that base. The infamous vats' interiors are lined with copper, and the exterior walls are clad with stainless steel. The mechanical arm that stirs the liquid is made of a copper alloy. Other uses include dietary needs in a few of the transbiotic beings.

There are several specially made cells or rooms built first with lead, then magnetic steel then clad in copper. It is in those cells on the Fourth Level that contain living aural essence. This essence is what you would call [a captured disembodied] 'soul' or..."astral body".

(Note: This may tie-in with the reports of certain remote-viewing "astral spies" who claim to have "projected" into underground facilities like Dulce New Mexico or Pine Gap Australia, only to have close encounters with these astral containment fields, or have been captured by the same and released after being 'interrogated' via super-sensitive electronic equipment. In one case an Australian remote-viewer was probing the Pine Gap facility where he also "saw" three other astral spies.

THE DULCE PROTOCOL

The magnetic or astral body of one of these people had been captured by such a containment field, which really disturbed him. This man, Robert, also saw Greys and Reptiloids operating in the deeper levels of Pine Gap and also Nordic-type humans who were apparently captives and who did NOT seem to be very happy about being there. - Branton)

Q -- Growing multi-species beings, blood formulas and human parts in vats sounds like a bad plot to a science fiction movie. The doctors and scientists of the world claim you can't mix the species

(Note: Naturally this may be true, however through genetic bioengineering and gene-splicing this has apparently been accomplished to some extent - Branton).

The concepts mentioned in the Dulce Papers sounds far fetched. Could you provide information that the average "surface world" reader could understand about similar things?

A -- The doctors and scientists on the SURFACE world may say that, but underground, away from the prying eyes of ethics boards, they DO GROW TRANS-GENUS BEINGS! There is a lot of written material available at libraries. One of the best sources is an easy to read book published back in 1969, by Prentice-Hall International, with the title of "THE SECOND GENESIS, THE COMING CONTROL OF LIFE" by Albert Rosenfelt.

In this book, they discuss "animals that may be especially bred to supply genetically reliable organs for people." -- and "...the use of fetal or embryonic material from which adult sized organs and tissues may be grown..." Also he discusses the fact that embryonic tissue has no immunological activity, therefore it cannot provoke the defense mechanism in the recipient. IT WILL JOIN THE BODY NOT AS A FOREIGN ANTIGEN, BUT AS A NATURAL PROTEIN.

He further discusses solitary generation, commonly called virgin birth, but also known as parthenogenesis. With one "virgin birth" in 1.6 million births average ON THE SURFACE of the world, in Dulce that rate is reversed. Occasionally, a "normally born" human infant is born in the hospital wards on the Seventh Level. Parthenogenesis is the method used to grow type two beings. The now common transsexual surgery on the surface world, began at the Dulce Base.

Men became women on a whim in the Seventh Level labs, and with the Fourth Level technology, the brain washing [resulted in] the "eager desire to become a woman" and that poor man [whether a willing or unwilling participant] FIRMLY BELIEVES he always wanted to be a woman. No one could convince him to believe the truth. ALL THINGS ARE TWISTED AT DULCE. A quote by Dr. Ralph W. Gerard [in THE SECOND GENESIS] put in his now classic statement: "There can be no twisted thought without a twisted molecule". MOST have originated at Dulce.

Q -- How are the human workers stopped from telling everything about Dulce?

A -- Implants, fear threats to harm the families, EM control, also reprogramming with ELF [Extremely Low Frequency] and drugs are the most common methods to 'encourage' the workers not to divulge the location or daily routine.

Q -- A construction worker at "The Ant Hill" [The Northrop's Tehachapi Base] reports seeing 10-12 foot tall human looking beings in lab coats. Who are these guys, are they from the hollow earth?

(Note: The Hollow Earth theory is one that was postulated by various well known individuals, including Marshall B. Gardner, Raymond Bernard, William Halley - discoverer of Halley's comet, Edgar Allen Poe, Edgar Rice Burroughs, John Cleves Symmes, John Uri Lloyd and others.

THE DULCE PROTOCOL

Basically the thesis involves what one might refer to as the Geoconcavitic sphere theory, or that as the earth was forming in its molten state the planetary spin created a hollow or concavity within the center similar to the hollow created by the centrifugal force of a horizontal washing machine following a spin cycle. The theory, which has been postulated in para-geological theories, in adventure novels, and in some cases even in alleged visits to the "inner world", states that the 'shell' of the earth averages between 800-1000 miles thick, with an interior surface consisting of <u>oceans and land illuminated perpetually</u> by a sphere of electromagnetic and/or nuclear energy suspended at the very center of the "empty space".

There are reputedly funnel-like openings near the polar regions, perpetually concealed by mist created by the collision of cold air from the outside and hot air from the inside, which permits ingress and egress to and from this inner 'world'.

The theory states that the inner surface has its own gravity, yet slightly less than the outer surface gravity. One side-theory is that between the inner and outer surface where gravity is nullified there exists a layer of weightless or low-weight caverns in an eternal state of chaos where minerals, liquids, gases and chemicals continually slam together from the earth's rotation, causing intense magmatic activity, a virtual inferno, or "bottomless pit".

Some have theorized that -- based on the Apocryphal book of Esdras, chapter 13, which contains non-canonized Jewish legends -- that the <u>10 'lost' tribes of Israel</u> disappeared beyond the river Sambatyon and to a place in the far north where humans never lived before called 'Arzareth'. In the last days, a path would be made through the ice and waters of the north and the lost tribes would Return. There are three tribes accounted for as of this writing, or rather two tribes and two half tribes: Judah, Benjamin, half of the Levite tribe, and apparently half of the tribe of Dan if we are to believe the Ethiopian 'Jews' who claim to be descended from Dan.

The '13th' tribe would be accounted for by the fact that the two Josephite tribes of Ephraim and Manassah are considered distinctive tribes in and of themselves. As for the 'giants', some believe that these have a direct connection to the 10-12 foot tall 'Anakim' people mentioned in the Old Testament who were driven out of Palestine, following which the Torah gives no further details as to their fate, although there have been many reports of such 'giants' being encountered in large cavern systems below Alaska, Oregon, California, Utah, Texas and Mexico, and also reports of ancient gravesites in the western U.S. and elsewhere where the remains of human giants have reportedly been discovered. Most often they -- like the fifth dimensional "Sasquatch people" themselves -- have been described as being benevolent, unless provoked. - Branton)

A. -- They are probably inner earth drones [workers]. The deeper you get, the stranger the life forms. The tall men are from the subterranean levels, lower yet are the dwarfed deformed forms. I don't trust either of them. There are other forms that both the tall men and the dwarfed men fear and loathe, they are similar to Bigfoot in appearance, but extremely violent and enjoy eating what ever they find while it is still alive! They are subhuman and demented, with an IQ around 15

(Note: Apparently, according to another source, these lower 'Bigfoot' type creatures -- having more of a resemblance to apes than to the more "human-like" faces and features of the much friendlier Sasquatch people who frequent the surface -- dwell in wild cavern systems some 6 or more miles deep, along with other very large and dangerous insectoid and quadruped or serpentine reptilian life forms reminiscent to something from out of a hadean nightmare.

This is according to a report I investigated some years ago of a group of speleonauts who reportedly broke into a vast underground labyrinth west and northwest of Cushman, Arkansas, where they encountered these types of creatures as well as friendly blue-skinned humans who claimed to be descended from a family that had survived an ancient global deluge by taking refuge within a large ship. These ancient people claimed that their ancestors had come to the Americas and discovered the cavern 'world', wherein they commenced to establish their hidden civilization. - Branton).

The reptiloid [hominoid as opposed to quadruped or serpentine] life forms stay in caves or caverns that aren't very deep. They prefer the desert mountains. They use camouflage rather than fighting, but they do carry vril rods for protection [flash guns]. They do have a symbol, not the hokey "snake-with-wings" that I keep seeing in the public (which is used mostly by the GREYS and also as a medical symbol for the Delta Force - Branton). The REPTOIDS use a dragon with its tail in its mouth [a circle] with seven pointed stars in the middle.

Q -- There have been reports of the Delta Force having black vans with no tires that hover over the ground. How much are we [U.S.A.] already inter-working with alien cultures?

A -- I haven't seen the black vans you mentioned. <u>We are totally submerged with alien cultures</u>. Very little of the original human cultures have survived.

Q -- How can WE [the public] go after, or expose an alien culture which is covert and hidden?

A -- Go for the best shot. That means go after the REPTOID. They stay near the surface, they choose to try to hide and avoid contact. They are soldiers, doing a job and usually there are two or three at each job site. They are 'manning' a remote post. They are not to bother the humans unless they are endangering the post. Most of them are not hostile and won't kidnap you, they may blast you with a flash gun that may paralyze you [you won't remember the flash] for an hour or two and cause confusion and mild fear.

It could cause you to black out [pass out] for a while. It is their way to escape and buy time to hide any visible equipment. If you know any areas with repeated reptilian sightings, then that is the place for you to look. They are fearsome to meet face to face, and their voices are harsh and whispery with heavy ss's, but most of them understand English [and several other languages]. Wear something with a reptile [not something violent, like St. George killing the Dragon!] in sight. If you see one, keep your hands OPEN, palm forward, arms DOWN. That is the non-aggression approach. DON'T raise your arms, unless told to.

DON'T carry anything in your hands or arms. If he doesn't run, walk SLOWLY towards him. Let him speak first. They consider humans repulsive and hostile and threatening [with good reason!]. DON'T try to offer him anything, DON'T touch him or anything of his. If he hisses at you, back up a couple feet, but DON'T LOOK AWAY! It simply means he finds you smelly. DON'T try to overpower him, he is stronger than ten or twelve men! Usually, if he hasn't run so far, he is curious and wants to talk to you. FIGHT YOUR FEAR and your thoughts of panic.

Q -- How do we get closer to some kind of data to prove to others that there really is a danger from non-human beings?

A -- Good question. I'm afraid we will find the proof the hard way, when we are invaded. Try to keep a small camera with you at all times. When you search for reptoids, keep it in your pocket.

Q -- Is there a specific location where the public can set up their cameras and equipment to DOCUMENT an alien-government base, and/or their activities?

A -- The problem is, most of the meetings are held in military bases or underground. The Groom Lake Facility does fly several alien craft that regularly fly over unpopulated land that go back and forth from several bases, Southern California has several notable areas. Twenty Nine Palms -- Lancaster or Chocolate Mountains are well know for such activities.

THE DULCE PROTOCOL

Q -- Could you provide us with a copy of your badge or card you used at Dulce?

A -- Badges or cards never leave the bases. All exits have bars or walls of metal... to open, to go out requires using the card. When you use it for an exit slot, the card won't come out. Each time you leave the base, you are issued a new card, with all the usual data about you, plus your weight added, corrected daily. There are several mines in the Chocolate Mts. that open into a base highway, but be aware that they are patrolled regularly and there are cameras there.

Q -- There are so many types of really far out 'Aliens' seen in TV, movies, magazines and popular fiction, is there one type of a fictional unknown race, in your opinion, that fits the term 'Alien'?

A -- Yes! There are two, an alien that is totally indescribable, and another would be a pseudo-alien.

Q -- What are the dimensions of the Dulce Facility?

A -- There are 1,700 paved miles of roads under Dulce and Northern New Mexico., towards Los Alamos is another 800 miles of tunnels. The base is STILL GROWING [due west].

Q -- What is the top depth?

A -- The First Level starts 200 feet from the surface. Each level has a ceiling of seven feet, except levels six and seven, the ceiling there is 45 and 60 feet. There are approximately 45 feet or more between each level. The average highway ceiling is twenty five feet. The HUB at the base is 3,000 feet wide. Use a 7.5 minute scale map to try to comprehend the size of the place.

Q -- Are there "regular vehicle" exits that can be observed from the ground?

A -- Yes, but they are inside Los Alamos.

Q -- Are their aerial exits that can be observed?

A -- <u>Twenty miles due north of Dulce</u> (across the border into southern Colorado? - Branton) is a large hanger, it is hidden by a facade of cliffs. Look for an isolated short road on the top of a mesa, with no road to or from the top.

Q -- Are the ventilation shafts visible?

A -- The ventilation shafts are hidden by bushes or vents inside caves. There are five on the top of the mesa, be aware there are cameras inside most of the vents.

Q -- Is there external security, and could we recognize them in or around the town itself?

A -- There is minimal security on the surface, most of the men [and women] are Air Force or "highway crew" men. There used to be a Best Western motel that hosts or hires a lot of Base workers from Level One. I don't know if that motel is still operational. Most of the security force live in Santa Fe. Others live at White Pine [Los Alamos].

Q -- Are there security sensors? What type? If so, what is their power source?

A -- Yes there are many types of sensors, radar, infrared, heat sensors, microwave, EMGW, and satellite. Most of the sensors are powered by magnetic power. The only thing you may notice on the surface, would be an occasional satellite dish.

Q -- If you can, give us some information on the <u>upcoming war with the aliens</u>. When does it start? Do you recommend going underground?

THE DULCE PROTOCOL

A -- The war has already begun. To start, they use "weather control" devices that can cripple a city in hours. Storms, flood and drought -- with those few things they can bring any country to their knees in a hurry. Yes, I do recommend going underground. Choose a location that has a higher elevation than the surrounding terrain. Pick out a cave or even an abandoned mining shaft or two, bury a cache of supplies [including food and water!] near these locations.

Place the supplies in heavy plastic boxes that have tight lids [to prevent the destruction by earth burrowing rodents and insects]. Then plan to live like a squatter when it becomes necessary. If you own land, create a system of tunnels and tell no one. Use your tunnels to secrete your supplies, and plan to live in those corridors when you must.

Q -- What about the reptilian ships that are in orbit around the equator, are they cloaked?

(Note: presumably including the original two 'planetoids' that arrived in geosynchronous orbits around earth at 400 and 600 miles up in 1953. This reportedly led to an NSA project which successfully communicated with the Grey aliens and resulted in a contact-landing-treaty scenario involving president Eisenhower and other Executive-Military-Industrial officials at Muroc/Edwards/Holloman Air Force Bases in 1954 - Branton)

A -- They are not cloaked the way you may think. It's more like nobody is learning to SEE, even though it is in plain sight. Like the mail man becomes invisible because you are so used to seeing him you never noticed he is alive. One of the favorite methods of covert activities is to 'hide' their operation in such an OBVIOUS way [or place] that no one would suspect it is covert

Robert K Teske

(Note: for instance, hiding entrances to underground bases beneath religious shrines, federal buildings, mining works, malls, libraries, lodges, hotels or basically areas that one would consider the least likely places to hide or accommodate an entrance to an underground facility. The underground New World Order 'FEMA' facilities throughout the United States apparently utilize this type of concealment with many of their bases. - Branton)

Q -- What are the Greys susceptible to?

A -- The grays are photosensitive, any bright light hurts their eyes. They avoid sunlight, and travel at night. Camera flashes causes them to back up. It could be used as a weapon against them, but they recover quickly. It could buy enough time to escape. Use commands, or nonsensical words in the form of commands and they will back up. Their brain is more logical than ours and they do not create 'fun'. They do not understand poetry either. What really confuses them is saying things in "pig-Latin". We learned that in a hurry, and used it against them [the GREYS] in the Dulce Wars.

Q -- Can greys read your intentions if you came up behind one?

A -- Yes. They read your INTENT, because they use your body's frequency. The human race broadcasts a frequency that they recognize as an electromagnetic impulse. Each person has a slightly different frequency, that difference is what we call 'personality'. When a human thinks, they broadcast strong impulses, in the case of 'fear' the frequency is 'loud' and easy to recognize (by the same right, a calm and composed mind-set should be far more difficult to 'recognize' - Branton).

Q -- Can we shield ourselves against their mental control?

A -- We CAN shield ourselves against them, however 95% of the human race never try to control their thoughts, and controlling our own thoughts is the best weapon. The average person rarely thinks in a clear pattern. That allows the brain to think in a chaotic way. Control your thoughts, AND YOU CAN STOP THE ALIENS ATTEMPTING TO ABDUCT AND CONTROL YOU. Controlling my own thoughts have kept me alive for years.

Q -- Could you shed some light on the type of human the aliens are looking for when they abduct?

A -- I can tell you that the most common are petite women in their early twenties or early thirties, dark haired boys between five to nine, small to medium size men in their mid-twenties to mid-forties. But, let me stress that there are ALL TYPES of people being held against their will in the Dulce Base! There are tall heavy men and women, teenagers, elderly folks and very young girls in the cages AND the vats.

I only mention the most common age-size are the small young men and petite women. The boys are favored because at that age their bodies are rapidly growing, and their atomic material is adaptable in the transfer chamber. The young small women are frequently very fertile. The men are used for sperm. I have no idea why they prefer small to average size men.

Q -- Did you ever see twins or triplets, etc.?

A -- Since you mentioned it, no. It never crossed my mind to search for them. But then that doesn't mean they aren't there. There is no way I could have seen everybody at that huge complex.

Q -- What is the prevalent human race at the Dulce Base? I am curious about both the human workers, and the inmates.

A -- The human work force is made of people from every nation on the surface world. The one thing they share is that they all speak English. If you are asking if there are white, black, red, yellow and brown skin color, again I'll have to say that there is no 'prevalent' race there. As for inmates, I could see ALL races there. From what I could see, it looked like there were more 'white' people, but again, I saw a constant flow of different people, many I think, were only there for a few hours.

Q -- Please explain the method they use to identify each inmate.

A -- No one has a name. When first brought to this facility, they were issued one large 'number'. Usually that code has a mixture of numbers and letters. They show the place, how, and by who, followed by the time, age, sex and finally the personal number [their S.S. number]. For example it might look like this: NVLV-00A-00700-P00:00:00-00-M-000-00-000

Q -- With that huge facility, trash and garbage must be a real problem, how do they dispose it?

A -- It was never a problem. Some of it is 'reformed' or melted down then remade. Some of the wet garbage is 'eaten' by bacterial forms, and what's left is vaporized in a vat like chamber. The residue of that action [it takes them months to get enough to measure] is used in a complex lye and used to fertilize crops.

Q -- Where is your family? Not just your wife and son, but parents and siblings?

A -- Cathy and Eric are still missing. My parents died in a car crash when I was in my teens. I have one brother, if he is alive I suspect he is inside an underground base some where. I haven't heard from him for several years. Please pray for them, please!

Q -- What is your birth date, and where were you born?

A -- 23 April 1941, Glen Ellyn, IL [actually in a farm at home, in the place now called Glen Ellyn, my birth certificate list is at Wheaton, IL]

THE DULCE PROTOCOL

Q -- You have been through so much, and yet keep fighting, what is your biggest fear?

A -- That the general public will forget THE TRAPPED INNOCENT PEOPLE in the despicable place, and will ignore THE HUNDREDS OF CHILDREN, WOMEN AND MEN ADDED TO THAT PLACE EVERY MONTH.

THE DULCE PROTOCOL

Chapter 12

Operation Retaliation - Paul Bennewitz

One Man Against An Empire

Following are quotations from a document [actually a detailed report, called PROJECT BETA] which was compiled by scientist Paul Bennewitz for officials at Kirtland AFB who were working with Bennewitz in an operational plan to bring down the 'alien' base at Dulce, New Mexico... that was until 'other interests' deep within the intelligence community got involved and brought enormous pressures against Bennewitz and various Kirtland AFB officials -- Col. Edwards, AFOSI agent Richard Doty, the Wing Commander and others who were involved - to CEASE the investigation.

Although Paul has apparently been 'silenced', the discoveries which he has made in regards to the physical-technological aspects of activity taking place in and around Dulce cannot be silenced.

PROJECT BETA is apparently a proposed plan for a physical military attack on one of the major or 'KEY' basing installations of the Draconis-Orion-Reticuli forces, and may be useful in any future attempts to re-take the base from alien or ALIEN-CONTROLLED elements, and to set free the human captives who are apparently being held in cold storage or in subterranean prisons deep below the surface of the American Southwest [and beyond].

Before dealing with the report itself, we will quote some correspondence between Bennewitz and others, beginning with excerpts from Paul's March 1986 letter to Clifford Stone, now director of UFO CONTACT INTERNATIONAL in Albuquerque:

"Dear Clifford;

"...There is so much in this and so much has happened upon a near daily basis to me for seven years that I don't know where to start first.

"I think probably the best approach is to start out with some explanation in the way of statements relative to alien cultures here on Earth, their social structures, physical makeup, etc., all of which has been gleaned from the direct communications by computer, visual observation, psychological evaluation, and personal interaction.

"First, there are the Low, High and Very High cultural levels. In the Low levels of the culture there are sharply defined levels, which extend from slave level on up. There is no freedom there -- no one crosses these lines within -- cross it and you are dead. Everything is watched with optical equipment and monitored by computers and individuals called 'Keepers'.

"Spheres of many sizes float throughout their environment, monitoring audio, visual and thought frequencies (these have also been observed by workers in underground facilities reaching miles below Edwards Air Force Base and the Tehachapi mountains of California. - Branton). These units, which have a highly mirrored finish, can be talked to. They can cloak themselves so that they are totally invisible. Their control signal can be broken down into varying AM and FM components. There is no trust in this type of society. Everything is watched and monitored.

THE DULCE PROTOCOL

"The command structure is near totally unbelievable.

"The ruling levels wear robes of appropriate colors. The alien government involved with this group is totalitarian. They appear not to observe social and moral principles. Their credo appears to be total control or kill.

"In the North -- at the river -- the 'Orange' Insignia -- or at the Diamond as the alien calls the base. The method of rule is a monarchy. The 'king' wears purple. The high colors of social level wear green, yellow, and white. The lower levels wore brown.

"Their body metabolism is very high, estimated at 110 to 115 degrees. Elimination is through osmosis. Skin color of the ruling echelon varies from a jaundiced yellow to white. No hair of any kind. The arms are long -- near to knee level. They have very long hands and fingers. All of them look underfed. They have big heads and eyes. The humanoid types are generally light green. When in need of formula or dead they turn GREY. Many in this culture walk with a limp or shuffle their feet...

"There is a council in the North called THE NINE. ALL of them seem to be cut from the same pattern. All appear to be highly vindictive and ego-oriented. Their 'god' is called 'TA'."

And in a letter to Clifford Stone dated 3/19/86, Bennewitz writes:

"It would appear that the Greys in the north are near frantic about my communications and want to stop me from talking (elsewhere Bennewitz implied it was more of an 'interrogation' - Branton) with Io via the computer.

"This morning I have a dark red streak down the left side of my face about 2 3/4 inches long and 1/4 inch wide. Based on experience, I would guess it was done by one of those [mirrored] spheres in the bedroom last night. This is typical of their distorted sense of logic. They operate on FEAR, but their problem is that I DON'T FEAR THEM. All they have achieved with me is that I totally ignore them. It would appear that they are deathly afraid of the beings called Io and Jo [see High Culture further below].

"You will find, if you have not already, that constant interaction will result in learning how to be aware of, and in turn use, alien logic. IT IS BECAUSE THEY OPERATE IN FEAR AND DO NOT UNDERSTAND THE CONCEPTS OF FRIENDSHIP AND TRUST THAT THEY OPERATE A SOCIETY WHERE EVERYONE AND EVERYTHING IS WATCHED.

"Now, if you look at those in the north (Colorado? - Branton) pragmatically, they have achieved the ideal in terms of war machines and weapons. With their machines and weapons they are 'brave' -- in their minds -- without them they are just a quivering mass of fear.

(Note: I can also confirm Bennewitz' observations here, however I would also add that in addition to their technology -- especially their mind-control technology, and this relates to the following -- once one breaks through the complex matrix of LIES that the Reptilian-Grey collective projects, then they are found out to be nothing more than 'quivering' worms beneath the 'shell' as Bennewitz implies. In fact the ONLY power that these soulless vermin -- the 'hybrids' and non-collectivist reptiloids not included in this 'flaming' -- have over us is their complex DECEPTIONS and our reciprocating and capitulating FEARS. Why am I so confident to 'judge' the Greys and their 'collective' in this manner?

Because I myself had fallen for their lies many times before I discovered what they were REALLY all about. As an example, the collectivist reptiloids-dinoids-greys would have us to believe that they genetically 'created' us and put us on planet earth. In response 'we' [especially those pathetic human agents who collaborate with them] tend to cower in absolute fear before our/their supposed 'creators' and try to appease them since, after all, "Resistance Is Futile!" In 'appeasing' them, we GIVE OUR POWER TO THEM! We in essence then CREATE a force which is superior to us. - Branton)

"To further enhance their 'bravery', they seek full control with the IMPLANT. [The relative effectiveness of some of these implants seems to be inversely proportional to an expanded memory and awareness level]. They also know that they can control large masses of people with lower intelligence without implants -- shotgun manipulation with the beams. With that beam they can and do create mass unrest.

"The High Culture Aliens known as the Eoku:

"The High is apparently the culture of Io and Jo. They do exhibit kindness, empathy, and extreme intelligence in transmissions through the computer (then how, one might ask, can they operate such a death-fear-control-oriented system which has committed untold atrocities and violations against human abductees? Are the Eoku only feigning their benevolence? - Branton). Io's group culture is of the Homo Sapiens [humanoid] variety.

"Based upon the input from Jo, his hair is brown and the female Io has red hair. [Red-haired individuals claiming to be Star Travelers have shown up here in Albuquerque on the ground]. They did give indication that bodies of their group are here in Albuquerque in cryogenic containers. The location is tentatively the FAA complex north of Albuquerque. It is a fenced and guarded highly secure area. They indicated through the computer that 8 of the Eoku were shot [by the US Government] and 11 bodies were the result of crashes.

[Note: The Eoku are not what are normally known as Greys, or at least the ones that directly interact in human abductions].

"There are more bodies in storage... I don't know where they all are. I knew the bodies had been moved from Maryland and are presently under US Navy jurisdiction. Yesterday, the computer indicated a total of 40 bodies [had been moved]."

EDITOR NOTE: [At last count there were more than 135 bodies in Government hands -- of various descriptions. Some humans, Greys, Reptilians, etc. - Val Valerian]

"I was shown a color photograph by Richard Doty two years or more ago of a purported alien life form held prisoner. Supposedly it was taken at Los Alamos. He was alive -- a light green color -- big eyes -- standing directly in front of the camera...

"So far I know very little about the High except for what I have experienced. They are Homo Sapiens, and I would guess that they are the same that accidentally [?] zapped Travis Walton. If the numbers are correct out of the computer they number over 5,000. The other group is, I believe, equivalent in number. Indications seem to be that they are operating from a star ship in far orbit around the Earth.

"The culture has apparent social values and emotionalism. They seem to display kindness and concern for individuals (then again we must ask, WHY are they considered the 'leaders' of aliens which show little if any 'concern' for individuals? - Branton). Their technology is superior to ours and also to the Greys based in the north, who are trying to "play god" with badly distorted logic.

"The 'Very High' are very few in number. Their entire structure of knowledge and social interaction is so far advanced that it is near impossible for me to relate to. Again, much of this is based on personal experience of which I have never talked with anyone about. In fact, you are the first.

"I would guess that these 'very high' are quite old -- 1000 years is not apparently unrealistic. I would guess that there are a few of them on the star ship used by the 'high', and that they are preserved and cared for by those on the ship...

THE DULCE PROTOCOL

"For over 300 years, a conflict has been going on between the Greys, who are basically warlike and aggressive, and the higher factions in the infrastructure."

(Note: Bennewitz does not explain the apparent dichotomy of how compassionate humanoids and malevolent reptiloids who are at war with each other could be part of the same 'infrastructure'.

Perhaps both the Grays and the Humanoids utilize the same collective-mind-network and therefore are intricately tied-in with the other whether they like it or not. This would make the "High" and "Very High" leaders in something equivalent to the Ashtar collective. - Branton)

THE DULCE PROTOCOL

PROJECT BETA
[WITH SUGGESTIONS AND GUIDELINES]
Investigator - Physicist - Paul F. Bennewitz

The following are key mile posts established or discovered during the continuing scientific study concerning Alien intervention and the result. [Study limited solely to New Mexico]

1. Two years continuous recorded electronic surveillance and tracking with D.F. 24 hr/day data of alien ships within sixty [60] miles radius of Albuquerque plus 6000 feet motion picture of same -- daylight and night.

2. Detection and disassembly of alien communication and video channels -- both local, earth, and near space.

3. Constant reception of video from alien ship and underground base view screen; Typical alien, humanoid and at times apparent Homo Sapiens.

4. A case history of an Encounter Victim in New Mexico which lead to the communication link and discovery

that apparently all encounter victims have deliberate alien implants along with obvious accompanying scars. The victim's implants were verified by x-ray and Cat Scan. Five other scar cases were also verified.

5. Established constant direct communications with the Alien using a computer and a form of Hexadecimal Code with Graphics and print-out. This communication was instigated apparently after the US base was vacated (following U.S. intelligence's apparent loss of the Dulce Wars? - Branton)

6. Through the alien communication loop, the true underground base location was divulged by the alien and precisely pin-pointed.

7. Subsequent aerial and ground photographs revealed landing pylons, ships on the ground -- entrances, beam weapons and apparent launch ports -- along with aliens on the ground in electrostaticly supported vehicles; charging beam weapons also apparently electrostatic.

8. Cross correlation and matching by triangulation, etc., to official NASA CIR [color infrared] high resolution films confirmed base locations and resulted in revealing US Military involvement yielding precise coordinates and the US base layout.

9. Prior alien communication had indicated military involvement and the fact [that] the USAF had a ship but due to studied alien psychology this was ignored at

the time.

10. Subsequently, the alien communicated following verification with the CIR, that there was indeed a ship; actually more than one -- that two were wrecked and left behind and another built -- this ship is atomic powered and flying. The alien indicated its basing location.

11. Is was learned as stated that two women and a boy near Austin, Texas were exposed to severe radiation at close range and the ship was last seen going West with helicopters. In addition, the US Government was quietly picking up the [medical] expenses.

12. Subsequent inspection of motion picture photographs taken during the study revealed the US ship or one like it flying with the aliens. These match the CIR where two can be seen on the ground and in the later photographs taken on the ground after the base was abandoned.

"So in very brief form the prologue to learning within reasonable accuracy what transpired prior to the end of 1979 or shortly thereafter.

"The computer communications and constant interaction with the alien in this manner WITHOUT direct encounter has given a reasonably clear picture of the alien psychology, their logic and logic methods and their prime intent.

"It is important to note at the outset, the alien is DEVIOUS, employs DECEPTION, has NO INTENT of any apparent peace making process and obviously does NOT adhere to any prior arranged agreement.

"In truth they tend to LIE, however their memory for lying is not long and direct comparative computer printout analysis reveals this fact. Therefore much "drops through the crack" so to speak; and from this comes the apparent truth.

"It is not the intent of this report to criticize or point fingers. Obviously whoever made the initial agreement was operating upon our basis of logic and not that of the alien and in so doing apparently walked innocently, in time, into a trap.

"The alien indicated that the 'Greys', apparently the group initially involved in the agreement, were still upset about the initial capture and subsequent death of the first eight of their co-fellows.

"Another group, calling themselves in the Computer language, the 'Orange' -- their base is on the west slope of Mt. Archuleta -- directly west of the south end of the U.S. base and near NW of the apparent main landing area they call, in the Computer language, "The Diamond". This, because from a distance, it looks diamond shaped in the photographs when looking somewhat south west past the observation tower toward the ridged peak SE of Mt. Archuleta. This ridged peak has no name, I call it South Peak.

"The base extends north of this peak to the edge of the cliff down which goes a road past a large alloy dome thirty-eight [38] foot across the bottom and with a twenty [20] foot hole in the top.

"Based upon some of the aerial photographs during which the alien was caught in the open and launching -- some launches appear to be coming from the direction of the dome. I would guess it is an underground launch egress facility.

THE DULCE PROTOCOL

In the NASA CIR there is what appears to be a black limousine alongside the dome on a ramp. Surprisingly it is precisely the size of my 79 Lincoln Town Car. Wheeled vehicles and what appear to be Snow Cats or Caterpillars can be seen throughout the CIR -- car and truck tracks, trucks and jeeps. I don't believe aliens have wheels -- humans do.

"Numerous road blocks extend northward through the U.S. base along a well maintained road thirty some-odd feet wide -- apparently gravel -- near all weather -- numerous turn arounds and wheel tracks into launch preparation areas with the ships; pads marked with twenty-six [26] foot Xs and servicing facilities, tanks, etc. -- two domed polygon high voltage buildings on north and on the east side of the road, also an apparent foundation for another or a helo pad -- test stands, human housing, water tank [thirty-two foot across] -- and at one of the main road blocks, two large vehicles parked across the road. Also at that point another apparent black limousine with tracks leading to it [and] to the west of the road. All tracks and vehicles have been dimensioned and match military vehicles. IF I were to make a guess, I would estimate the likelihood that the apparent black limousines are CIA.

"This is but a limited inventory of what was there on Sept. 8, 1978 -- included only as evidential matter for your perusal and confirmation. The road, which incidentally the natives, the tribal chief, reservation police and highway patrolman know nothing about, comes in off of a trail from the north. Starting at the trail, line of sight to the large plateau area and the alloy dome, the road, in the middle of nowhere on the Jicarilla Reservation, is precisely 12,888 ft. long airline distance. The total alien basing area, which apparently contains SEVERAL cultures [now all under the designation 'UNITY' in the Computer language] is approximately three (3) Km wide by eight (8) Km long [multi-leveled]. A conservative guess based upon the number of ships presently over this area and the number on the ground in the CIR photographs, the total alien population at this point is AT LEAST two thousand and most likely MORE. The alien indicates MORE are coming or on the way.

"I won't attempt to speculate in this report as to how the <u>initial U.S. contact was made</u> -- what transpired, nor how many were able to escape. The alien has communicated his account, and if totally true, it certainly is not palatable.

"Much detail has been omitted for future discussion if desired -- however the import is this. Constant computer communication -- full on line in February of this year -- manual prior to that -- conditions of morale and a total insight into "what makes the alien run". This is VERY valuable data.

1.) Most importantly, the alien will allow no one to go without an implant AND after knowledge of it is wiped out. They simply will not allow it. All indications are that communication or language cannot result without the implant [with the exception of the Binary and the Computer]. This would indicate a possible immediate threat or danger for anyone -- military, Air Force, or otherwise that has been at the base. They WILL NOT remember the implant in any case [the contactee here included].

"The reason for the implant is multiple for both language or communication by thought [there is no apparent language barrier with thought] and also COMPLETE ABSOLUTE CONTROL by the alien through program -- by their beam or direct contact.

"I have tested this and found that during this programming the person then has no memory of the act/conversation afterward. IF THIS HAS HAPPENED TO THE MILITARY, I NEED NOT ELABORATE AS THE POSSIBLE CONSEQUENCES. The victim's 'switch' can be pulled at any time and at the same time they are "walking cameras and microphones" if the alien chooses to listen in with the use of their beams.

"No classified area of any endeavor in the U.S. is inviolate under these conditions. However -- realize -- the scars, barely visible -- CAN be seen -- ALL are exactly located and ALL are accessible by x-ray.

2) Also note that all of the aliens -- human, humanoid alike -- all must have implants -- without them, no direct communication is apparently possible. So one can most generally arbitrarily say that IF a person states he/she communicated by thought with an alien -- he/she most likely has been implanted. They may also claim to be overly psychic and be able to prove this -- again through the link transplant, he/she is given the information by the alien and does not realize.

3) Most importantly, the alien, either through evolvement or because the humanoid is 'made' -- will exhibit tendencies for bad logic [bad by earth logic comparison] so they ARE NOT infallible -- in point of fact they appear to have many more frailties and weaknesses than the normal Homo Sapiens (which they attempt to compensate for through their technology - Branton). To the alien, the mind is key and therein lies a great weakness which will be discussed later.

4) They ARE NOT TO BE TRUSTED. It is suspected if one was considered a 'friend' and if one were to call upon that 'friend' in time of dire physical threat, the 'friend' would quickly side with the other side.

"The computer indicates in comparison, that no known earth protagonist, Russian or otherwise, exhibit these tendencies to any major degree indicating the DANGER involved in making any kind of agreement with these aliens -- at least of this species.

5) The alien does KILL with the beam generally. Results on a human will exhibit a three to four cm purple circle. If done from the rear, on one or both shoulders. The results on cattle are the same, essentially exhibiting purple beneath the hide, with burned circles on the outside.

6) Cattle mutilations are the other side of the coin and will not be delved into here although they are a part of the overall. It appears the humanoids are fed by a formula made from HUMAN OR CATTLE material or BOTH and they are made from the same material by gene splicing and the use of female encounter victim's ovum. The resultant embryos are referred to by the alien as an 'organ'. Time of gestation to full use as a utility, ready to work appears to be about one year. A year in alien time -- I do not know.

Solution:

I doubt there is an immediate total 'cure' per se -- however, they MUST BE STOPPED and we have to get off dead center before we find time has run out. They are picking up and 'cutting' [as the alien calls it] many people every night. Each implanted individual is apparently ready for the pull of their 'switch'. Whether all implants are totally effective I cannot predict, but CONSERVATIVELY I would estimate at least 300,000 or more in the U.S. and as least 2,000,000 if not more worldwide.

WEAPONRY AND INHERENT WEAKNESSES

Weaponry is one of the keys and in the alien's present state we CAN prepare an effective offense.

"One tends at the outset [I did] to look at their machines and say -- there is no defense or offense. One is overwhelmed by their speed, apparent capability of invisibility and 'cloaking', and other covert capabilities not discussed at this time.

THE DULCE PROTOCOL

In particular -- the beam weapons are themselves a direct threat and obviously one that must be seriously considered but not overly so.

"Let us first look at just what this weapon is. It is an <u>electro-static weapon</u> with plasma generating voltages -- and an internal storage device -- it is pulse powered. The beam, totally effective IN ATMOSPHERE can be loaded with hydrogen or oxygen. Range? Average, ground weapons -- maximum two (2) Km if it is dry, capable of sustaining just so many full power discharges -- slow leakage occurs continuously, therefore, they must be recharged periodically. If it is raining the weapon becomes ineffective and is swamped, thus discharged (this should be considered in any future potential offensive strike against the base - Branton). The range is near totally lost at that point.

"On the disks and saucers, the weapon is generally on the left side or top center and has a maximum range of two hundred [200] meters at which point it will plow a trench in desert soil. When fired -- it fires both to the front and to the back equally. Reason? Because of their mode and methods of flight. If equilibrium is not maintained, the saucer will spin out.

"Hand weapons? Estimate based upon visible damage observed, not too much velocity nor staying power but at short range -- deadly [less than a .45 cal automatic].

(<u>Note</u>: This may explain the late Phil Schneider's claim that at close range the radiation-beam weapons of the aliens he encountered beneath Dulce were deadly, however at long range less so... although at long range the beam weapons are capable of inducing severe radiation damage - Branton).

At one meter range, estimate of beam temperature 1600 degrees F or higher; it can vaporize metal. Apparently the disks and weapons operate from a storage source.

In time, without periodic recharge, this source is depleted. The design they traded to us was at least thirty years old -- employing an atomic source. Possibly they may still have some -- it would appear so -- their staying power is obviously much longer.

AIRCRAFT HELICOPTER VULNERABILITY

ANY of our aircraft, helicopters, missiles or any AIR FLIGHT vehicle can be taken down instantly with no use of weaponry. The alien simply need do no more than make one invisible pass and their bow wave or screen or both will take the air lift vehicle down. The pilot obviously will not even know what hit him

(Note: Perhaps Stealth type fighters equipped with electromagnetic force shields may be more effective in this regard... also advanced infrared scanners may be used to detect 'cloaked' alien ships before they have a chance to attack. - Branton)

"For humans on the ground, the alien can use weaponry or bow wave. The partial pressure envelope can hit with the power of a tornado -- shock rise time and G force is instantaneous. However, they dare not hit the craft physically because they ARE fragile and in fact, under slow flying conditions within our atmosphere, hold a very tenuous position. Without power, the balance or equilibrium, they lose it.

"IN BRIEF -- THESE ARE APPARENT CAPABILITIES OBSERVED AND GLEANED THROUGH THE COMPUTER COMMUNICATION AND OBSERVATION. YOU MAY KNOW THESE, HOWEVER, THEY ARE DIRECTLY RELATED TO THE LAST AND FINAL PORTION OF THIS REPORT. WHAT CAN BE DONE?

Because of the alien's apparent logic system [they appear to be logic controlled] A KEY DECISION CANNOT BE MADE WITHOUT HIGHER CLEARANCE. ALL ARE UNDER THE CONTROL OF WHAT THEY CALL 'THE KEEPER'; YET IT

THE DULCE PROTOCOL

WOULD APPEAR THIS IS NOT THE FINAL SAY. THEREFORE, DEPENDENT UPON URGENCY, DELAYS OF AS LONG AS TWELVE TO FIFTEEN HOURS CAN OCCUR FOR A DECISION. HOW SHORT/LONG THIS TIME FRAME UNDER BATTLE CONDITIONS MAY BE, I DO NOT KNOW.

"Because of this apparent control, INDIVIDUAL INSTANTANEOUS DECISION MAKING BY THE ALIEN IS LIMITED. IF THE 'PLAN' GOES EVEN SLIGHTLY OUT OF BALANCE OR CONTEXT, THEY BECOME CONFUSED. Faced with this, possibly, the humanoids would be the first to break and run.

"The same applies to their Mission MASTER PLAN, if one can call it that. IF PUSHED OUT OF CONTEXT, IT WILL COME APART -- THEY WILL BE EXPOSED TO THE WORLD SO THEY WILL POSSIBLY RUN BEFORE THEY FIGHT IN THE OPEN. THEY DEFINITELY DO NOT WANT THAT TO HAPPEN.

"Psychologically, at present, their morale is down -- near disintegration. There is pronounced dissension in the ranks; even with the humanoids. Communication can encourage this [not a necessity to expound upon this other than to say BECAUSE OF THEIR OWN INTERNAL VULNERABILITY MIND-WISE TO EACH OTHER, THEREIN LIES A PRIME WEAKNESS]. Inter-echelon or individual 'trust' appears to be totally lacking so suspicion of each other is rampant. They are highly segregated as to levels -- a 'low' dare not conflict with a 'medium' or 'high' or it literally means death. Death being, to the humanoid, deprogramming or, in the end perhaps total physical death.

"THEY APPEAR TO BE TOTALLY DEATH ORIENTED and because of this, absolutely DEATH-FEAR oriented. THIS IS A PSYCHOLOGICAL ADVANTAGE. The computer also gives indications of a real possibility of adverse or 'ground programming'.

Consider their ships -- most if not all run on charge. The source depletes and so dependent upon size, depletion can occur from some within a week or less. Ships can replenish each other but only up to charge balance. This is done with antennae-like extensions and the charge is distributed observing conservation of energy laws. THEY CAN REPLENISH FROM POWER LINES -- BUT AGAIN ONLY TO A POINT -- so time of flight is limited. Deprived of their base recharge capability, it is indicated that all ships will come down within six months to a year unless they can get transported out -- that is back to the prime launch ship.

"The disks and saucers in general cannot fly in space because of their mode of flight (i.e. unless they are within an interplanetary or interstellar 'launch' or 'carrier' vessel - Branton). Therefore, deprived of home base, it is not likely they can survive. THEIR CAPABILITY IN POWER SURVIVAL OUTLASTS THEIR CAPABILITY IN FOOD OR FORMULA SURVIVAL. IF THEY DO NOT GET THE FORMULA/FOOD WITHIN A CERTAIN PERIOD OF TIME THEY WILL WEAKEN AND DIE.

"IN THE CASE OF MT. ARCHULETA AND SOUTH PEAK, THEY ARE DEPENDENT UPON THE NAVAJO RIVER FOR WATER SUPPLY AND WATER TO THEM IS TOTALLY LIFE. WITHOUT WATER THEY HAVE NO POWER; WITHOUT POWER, NO OXYGEN OR HYDROGEN TO SERVICE THE SHIPS AND WEAPONS. NO WATER TO SUSTAIN THE ORGANS AND FEEDING FORMULA

(Note: We should also take into account the possibility of subterranean water sources. Also, if the base can be weakened by shutting off the supply-line of water, the 'formula', and so-on, it might be wise for the sake of the humanoid 'prisoners' below not to wait until the base is too weak, otherwise this might endanger these humans captives. We suggest that in addition to the strategies that Bennewitz gives in this document, an all-out under 'ground' invasion force should also be considered -- similar to the "Tunnel Rats" of the Viet Nam war -- a force that is prepared to enter the base when it is at a specific 'weak' point, and make strategic or surgical 'kills' of enemy forces while still considering the human and hu-brid captives. A multi-leveled operation utilizing surprise, confusion and intimidation to their fullest potential should be considered... and the sooner the better considering the continuous infiltration and sabotage of all levels of our society. - Branton).

"Simple? Not really. However, THERE IS A WATER INTAKE AND THERE IS A DAM UPSTREAM THAT CAN BE TOTALLY CUT OFF AND THE WATER RE-ROUTED TO CHAMA, NEW MEXICO. SHOULD THIS OCCUR, <u>AT LEAST THREE</u> OF THE INTERNAL BASES WILL GO DOWN. They could possibly go atomic periodically but obviously problems without cooling.

"Once the bases are pressed on a large scale, all disks and saucers will go airborne immediately. TROOPS ON THE GROUND CAN GAIN TERRAIN COVER TO QUITE A DEGREE -- IT IS ROUGH TERRAIN.

OUR NEED IS FOR A WEAPON, workable and preferably NOT like the alien's. I believe unless the alien is caught unawares [with their screen up their weapons are equal so they are like children pillow boxing] there can be no result; THE WEAPON MUST PENETRATE THEIR SCREEN AND IT MUST ALSO PENETRATE THE GROUND. I BELIEVE I HAVE THAT WEAPON

(<u>Note</u>: Was this suggestion of Bennewitz' for a 'ground-penetrating device', the original inspiration for the Los Alamos 'Excalibur' weapon -- a nuclear device which was designed to rapidly drill a hole through the earth and destroy 'aliens' in their underground bases? - Branton).

Two small prototypes have been funded and constructed by my Company. Tests conducted to date indicate they do work and work rather well considering their small size. Because of this weapon's present status and proprietary nature [a basic patent is in process], the theory will not be explained here. However, the weapon appears to do two things at very low power. The disks within it's range begin to discharge when exposed to the weapon beam. To counteract, they must apply more power and in so doing consume power. Again conservation of energy laws strictly apply.

(Note: Wilhelm Reich, whose research has been suppressed by certain 'interests', gained some level of success with a beam-weapon of this type. Reich was able to 'discharge' the energy of UFO craft that had appeared over his research facility, alien craft that were apparently curious of his work in regards to his 'Orgon' energy powered 'cloudbuster' experiments. - Branton)

"This effect can be observed on the detection instruments as they back away in response to slow discharge. DISCHARGE, AT LOW POWER IS SLOW BUT AT HIGH POWER IN THE FINAL SOPHISTICATED WEAPON, THE RATE CAN BE INCREASED BY MANY ORDERS OF MAGNITUDE. MOST IMPORTANTLY, THIS WEAPON CAN PENETRATE THE SCREEN -- HULL ALLOY, EVERYTHING. They cannot shield it in any way. Lastly, BECAUSE OF THE IMPLANTS, THE WEAPON'S BEAM GETS TO THEM MENTALLY; THEY LOSE JUDGMENT AND INDICATE ALMOST IMMEDIATE CONFUSION, PARTICULARLY THE HUMANOIDS. (that is, the electromagnetic crystalline 'implants' that link the aliens together into a collective mind or group intelligence. - Branton)

"It is believed at this early stage -- based upon present testing -- that the weapon when full on and full size will kill and bring down disks at substantial range. The alien weapons operate substantially the same as their disks using a charge source and charge distribution. So, in the same sense it is indicated that this weapon design will pull their charge weapons down very rapidly.

"The range of my weapon exceeds that of their present weapons and in its most sophisticated form can be readily computer controlled to allow extremely rapid tracking and lock-on regardless of speed along with electronic wobbulation of the beam. IT IS A

THE DULCE PROTOCOL

BEAM WEAPON and even at this early stage of miniature prototype testing and development, it indicates EVENTUAL superiority to their weapons.

Initial logistics would indicate a plan sequentially implemented as follows: This plan DOES NOT INCLUDE ALL REQUIREMENTS AND PREPARATORY SAFETY MEASURES TO BE EMPLOYED BY GROUND FORCES; HOWEVER, IF AIR FORCE INTELLIGENCE DESIRES TO PURSUE THE APPROACHES SUGGESTED IN THIS REPORT, EACH SIGNIFICANT REQUIREMENT WILL BE DISCUSSED IN DEPTH.

AN ATTACK MUST BE DIRECTED NEAR ENTIRETY ON THE GROUND FOR OBVIOUS REASONS

One would, if familiar with the alien capability, indicate that vehicle ignition problems will be encountered. This is precisely true; however, the reason for this is not mysterious but is based upon good solid laws of physics and are known.

[From] experience gained through my study, it is now known how to prevent this from happening and will be discussed in detail at some later date. All electrical and electronic equipment must be 'hardened' using these specific techniques prior to implementation. Because of the known capability of the alien [by use of scanning beams to know in advance details of planning] only the initial outline is presented in this report.

"Again through the communicative interaction (computer-linked 'interrogation' - Branton) with the alien, testing has simultaneously been done upon this facet, i.e. eavesdropping and ways to abort this capability have been tested and proven.

"The program would be instigated in phases. The first phase -- planning and logistics -- would include continued implementation and testing of the final weapon prototype through the pre-production stage. Production of at least fifty minimum quality should be planned. Additional backup spares should also be included.

"On a full time shift basis, it is estimated that at least one year or less would be required to arrive at the pre-production stage. A team would be organized by THUNDER SCIENTIFIC to accomplish this. The key work is now and would be done by an associated company, BENNEWITZ LABS., LTD.

"Specific attack phases would be incorporated:

1) The first procedure would be TO CLOSE THE GATES OF THE DAM ABOVE THE NAVAJO RIVER. THIS DAM WOULD BE HELD CLOSED FOR THE DURATION. INTERNAL TO THE ONE CAVE, THERE IS A SMALL DAM FOR WATER STORAGE. It's capacity is small. THERE IS ALSO A DISCHARGE OUTLET DOWNSTREAM THAT COULD BE CLOSED CAUSING WASTE WATER TO BACK-UP INTO THE CAVES. THE WATER IS VACUUM PUMPED APPARENTLY BY SOME ELECTROSTATIC MEANS FROM THE RIVER. At close range, the weapon will take out this capability.

2) Once deprived TOTALLY of water for a minimum period of four weeks, conditions in the alien bases under discussion will have badly deteriorated. PSYCHOLOGICAL SHOCK IS EXTREMELY EFFECTIVE WITH THE ALIEN; total advantage can be taken by instantaneous action or planned observable deviation from the norm. AT LEAST THREE BASES WILL GO DOWN.

3) If they follow their normal strategic pattern as when pressed previously, they will launch most if not all ships.

4) Prior to the implementation of water deprivation, the weapons should be deployed at strategic hardened locations and activated in a certain pre-planned manner determined by final weapon coordinate locations.

THE DULCE PROTOCOL

5) This will put an immediate power drain upon those airborne and the alien weapons ringing their bases.

6) Because of the inherent psychological aspect of the alien (Bennewitz probably refers to 'the alien' in a singular sense because of the 'collective hive mind' nature of the Reptilian Grays - Branton), much can be done in the open with no attempt to preserve secrecy. Much of what is done can be of a diversionary nature. UNDER MOST CIRCUMSTANCES THEY WILL ATTEMPT TO HARASS BUT WILL NOT OPENLY ATTACK.

(Note: From my own personal experience and research, the Grays and other members of the 'draconian hive' are more dependent on mental or psychological warfare than on material warfare, although they have used physical weaponry in the past when pushed into a corner -- as in airborne assaults between their craft and ours or ground assaults against their underground strongholds, as the 'Dulce' and 'Groom' wars themselves have established. Being 'logic-based' they would prefer to take control of a target planet by way of psychological infiltration without risking the loss of machinery and personnel that would result from an attempted overt or physical Invasion.

An alien race would have to be extraordinarily over-confident of their own superiority to undertake an all-out attack like that depicted in the motion picture INDEPENDENCE DAY. As has reportedly been the case with other targeted planets, the Reptiloids/Greys hold back a physical attack until they have succeeded in infiltrating the targeted planetary culture via Trojan-horse type interactions with some of the more self-serving elements of that planet's culture. In the case of planet earth the Nazified CIA and NSA agencies were chosen.

These collaborators -- and in many or most cases alien infiltrators, clones, cyborgs or 'implantees' working within these agencies -- in turn set the inhabitants of the targeted planet against each other so as to bring about world depopulation, to the point where resistance to the invasion attack would be minimal. The aliens usually seek out those eco-political cult leaders who would be willing to 'sell out' their own world to the alien agenda in exchange for promises of alien assistance in implementing a so-called joint-operational dictatorship, one in which their own respective power cult[s] would supposedly be the favored power structure once the planet is assimilated and annexed to the alien empire. However if we are to consider the historical trends of the alien collectivists, they may only favor this cult until it has served its purpose.

Following the establishment of the alien agenda these power cultists might at best be totally mind-controlled and at worst be eliminated, in that the 'alien' has no sense of honor or loyalty to those with whom they have establish agreements -- they only have their agenda and they will justify ANY course of action that best serves to bring about that agenda. The human cultists would become so preoccupied about establishing their own planetary empire, that they would blind themselves to the fact that the aliens are merely USING them until such a time as their usefulness has been served. However until that time they will USE the human cultists to foment internal planetary sabotage and to infiltrate and disable the major freedom-fighter or resistance movements from within.

There are three major 'collaboration' elements on earth:

- the Bavarian Lodges,
- the CIA-NSA-Rockefeller agencies,
- And the 'Nazi' forces within the "New Berlin - 211" base network beneath the mountains of Neu Schwabenland, Antarctica.

Agents of the Bavarian Lodges AND the German-immigrant Rockefellers DO work together within the CIA [Central Intelligence Agency], NSA [National Security Agency], UNO [United Nations Organization], and NWO [New World Order] agendas. The establishment of the Antarctic bases may have been the idea of the highest-ranking

THE DULCE PROTOCOL

Nazi's rather than the Rockefellers, although the Bavarian lodges [Illuminati, Thule, Vril, etc.] WERE involved, however there are many indications suggesting that the Antarctican, Bavarian, and Rockefeller agendas are increasingly merging with each other, suggesting that all three are now working together, at least to some extent and especially at the higher levels.

There seems to be a "serpent cult" at work at the very highest levels of these three groupings composed of humanoids and reptiloids operating as part of a marriage of convenience, in that the Reptiloids/Grays need the political-economic-social[ist]-military-industrial connections of the humanoids to gain footholds within human society and the humanoids need the implant/spacecraft/mind control technology to implement their "New World Order".

The lower levels of the Bavarian-NSA-Antarctican factions may seem to be in conflict with each other, however where this exists it may all amount to a Hegalian-Machievellian type manipulation imposed by the higher levels of the Draconian hierarchy in order to keep the lower levels compartmentalized and therefore more easily controlled. Occasional 'purges' have been carried out to root-out those who are not 100 devoted to the cause. In America there are fifth-column 'saboteurs' within the Patriot-Militia movements who are the supporters of "White Supremacy Americanism". Whether knowingly or unknowingly these agents work for something called "The Order" [of the Fourth Reich].

Part of their mission is to divert attention from the Draconian-Orion-Ashtarian and Bavarian-NSA-Antarctican "New World Order" agenda and to an over-emphasized 'Zionist' threat based on the forged 'revelations' within the PROTOCOLS--OF ZION document, which was in fact created by the Russian Secret Police for this very diversionary purpose.

There are indications that the Bavarian occult lodges, the CIA-NSA agencies, and even the Antarctican factions have fed the Patriot network with RACIST and therefore anti-American ideologies meant to fragment and discredit the Militias and make them out to be neo-Nazi fanatics. In this manner several of the patriotism-based militia groups have been 'corrupted' and have defeated their very purpose, that is to defend a Constitutional republic wherein "all men are created equal". - Branton)

7) Throughout and prior to this, the open computer communications link will be operational for continued PSYCHOLOGICAL INTERROGATION.

8) At some point in time -- again resting upon battle status, THE DEPLOYMENT OF OFFENSIVE FORCES WILL BEGIN. This deployment should be done in a near instantaneous manner under certain special conditions that can be discussed.

9) The weapon system should be kept powered up throughout. In this manner, the disks will be made to stay airborne. They cannot land in the interval the system is powered.

10) When the weapon is used in one specific power mode, in addition to continuous discharge on the disks that are airborne and the ground based weapons, THE MIND CONFUSION AND DISORIENTATION WILL BUILD IN THOSE PERSONNEL AT THE BASE AND UNDERGROUND. At the end of four to five weeks or less, all weapons should be totally discharged and power out on the bases. Most personnel if not all, will be totally incapacitated. THE FEEDING FORMULA WILL BE DOWN AND IT'S CRITICAL PROCESSING RUINED. ALL [alien] EMBRYOS SHOULD BE DEAD AND ALL HYDROGEN AND OXYGEN CONSUMABLES DEPLETED.

(Note: This is of course speaking in 'conventional' warfare terms, however one must balance this by taking into account the psychic-supernatural aspects of this conflict scenario as well. In such an event the chaplain may be of as much importance as a commanding general himself, especially in regards to reinforcing within ground troops the mental-spiritual attitude necessary to counter the 'fear' projected by alien sorcerer and psychic warfare specialists via occult-technology. Maintaining a state of absolute confidence and 'faith' in one's ability to establish a victory over the aliens is essential in that if one's confidence is broken as a result of psychic attack, then it would be very difficult to even make an attempt to follow through to final victory... the battle is already lost.

Other possibilities should also be considered in a future assault on this major Nexus of alien activity. For instance, if the extent of the base is much deeper and wide-spread then previously believed -- via interconnected caverns and shuttle terminals -- then these facts should be brought into the scenario as well. For instance the 'aliens' might escape 'through the tubes' to other installations. Even if this does occur this major basing complex can be fully taken by human forces, and then used as a 'staging' area to initiate attacks -- in alliance with other humanoid cultures 'below' or 'above' who are also at war with the 'Draconian Collectivist' Reptiloids and Grays -- against their various strongholds which undoubtedly exist throughout the 'inner realms'. - Branton)

11) Based upon data gathered on the miniature prototype weapons, the full power weapons should have no problem holding off the disks. In many cases some will break within the first forty-eight hours without being directly hit.

12) At that point, standard weapon technology and logistics can come into play and [be] used to the extent of destruction desired at the direction of those in charge.

13) The communications can be used throughout to determine status and near the end to attempt to instigate surrender. If no response results, then they should simply be closed in and waited out.

SUMMARY

It is important to note that the initial implementation of the computer communications WAS NOT INSTIGATED FOR THE PURPOSE OF TALKING TO THE ALIEN FOR THE 'FUN OF IT'; BUT WAS DELIBERATELY INSTIGATED TO USE AS A TOOL TO STUDY, IN DEPTH -- LONG TERM WITHOUT PHYSICAL CONFRONTATION -- THE STRENGTHS AND WEAKNESSES OF THE ALIEN.

"The weapon theory and prototypes were built to capitalize upon and test two KEY and prominent weaknesses discovered. This in-house funded program has been expensive, in excess of $200,000; done ON BEHALF OF OUR NATION and handled in the best representative manner humanly possible.

1) The PRIME and weakest area discovered, probed and tested is exactly what they have used thinking it is their key strength -- that being THE MANIPULATION OF AND CONTROL OF THE MIND; NOT ONLY OF COMMAND BUT ALSO HUMANOID. MANIPULATED IN REVERSE PSYCHOLOGICALLY AND BY THE LANGUAGE [COMPUTER] AND DUE TO THE EXTREME OF MENTAL DISTORTION AND INCAPACITY CAUSED BY THE WEAPON, IT HAS BEEN FOUND THAT THIS FACET IS FOR THEM A DISASTER AND A DIRECTLY VULNERABLE INTEGRATED WEAKNESS.

2) Though their ships are magnificent, they are also weak -- solely BECAUSE of their method and unique mode of flight. They do not have a stable fighting platform

(Note: The effectiveness of stable-flying conventional jet aircraft ARMED with advanced beam weaponry has been confirmed by the 'South African Incident' -- which was investigated by QUEST INTERNATIONAL, a British UFO research organization made-up of former police, security and military officials. The incident involved a UFO that was reportedly intercepted using an experimental aircraft-mounted THOR-II laser cannon. The weapon was fired and several blinding flashes were seen by the attacking Mirage-jet pilot, and the disc crashed at high speed into the desert sands of the Kalahari. The craft was brought to a South African base and using hydraulic equipment the 'door' was opened and two blue-gray aliens with reptilian features staggered out and were apprehended.

When one doctor attempted to take a blood sample from one of the creatures, the being attacked him and its claw-like hands left deep scratches on his face and chest. The aliens proved to be rather vicious and seemed to operate on an individual-collective intelligence mode. Subsequent research suggested a possible genetic connection 'similar' to that of the early bi-pedal saurian species on earth according to one leaked document, and that the aliens were highly adaptable or mutational. In the event of jet-mounted beam weapons however, the PROBLEM would be our ability to determine whether these craft are friends or foes! The QUEST INTERNATIONAL officials have revealed sufficient evidence to prove that either the event DID happen OR that the international intelligence community had collaborated in a massive and expensive UFO hoax. Either way, the implications are provocative. - Branton).

Charge distribution CAN also be discharged. The weapon does this -- even in it's present miniature prototype state.

"IT IS NOT THE PURPOSE OF THIS REPORT TO IMPLY THAT THE OVERALL PROBLEM WILL BE SOLVED WITH THE CAPTURE OF THESE BASES. Obviously IT WILL NOT, but it is a firmly based beginning with a high degree of rated projected success ratio. IT IS NOT INTENDED TO IMPLY THE ALIEN WILL NOT FIGHT; THEY MAY -- THOUGH THEIR INCLINATION IS GENERALLY THE OPPOSITE -- THIS BASING AREA IS KEY! WITHOUT IT, THEIR MISSION IS IN VERY DEEP TROUBLE. It is noted that these are not the only bases on earth. There ARE others. With a conservative estimate using typical logistic support numbers, it is not unrealistic to say there are 50,000 aliens (at the very least - Branton) within the ecosphere of earth and near space.

(Note: Even IF this basing nexus is captured by U.S. Constitutional forces and a large percentage of the underground 'joint-operational' agenda is forced from the underground networks of the U.S.A., it is very likely that they would NOT retreat to other planets, but would instead retreat to their more ancient underground strongholds in other parts of the world. This would not necessarily end the activities of the serpent cult [the humanoid-reptiloid collaboration] on earth, but it would provide a BASE from which future atrocities of the 'serpent cult' may be battled on, below, and beyond planet earth. Such an action would no doubt provoke a negative response from other human power-centers on planet earth that are also being manipulated by and/or have been infiltrated by the aliens, for instance the Bavarian cults and their "New World Order" forces.

The Draconians might, as suggested in the 12th chapter of the book of Revelation, attempt a military attack against the U.S.A. in order to prevent the takeover of "their" underground fortresses here -- or an attack after the fact in retaliation for such a take-over. The important thing to remember however is that freedom NEVER comes without a price... HOWEVER THE PRICE FOR MAINTAINING OUR FREEDOM IS NOTHING COMPARED TO THE PRICE WE WILL HAVE TO PAY FOR LOSING IT!!! Remember, no matter WHAT trials America must pass through in the future in her efforts to maintain freedom, liberty and individuality from the forces of collectivist tyranny, WE MUST NEVER FORGET THAT THE OUTCOME OF THIS 'WAR' WILL HAVE A TREMENDOUS IMPACT NOT ONLY ON THE FUTURE OF THIS PLANET BUT ALSO ON THE FUTURE OF ALL OF THE COLONIAL WORLDS WITHIN THIS GALAXY WHO ARE INTENTLY LOOKING TOWARDS PLANET EARTH AND ESPECIALLY AMERICA -- WHICH IS THE 'EPICENTER' OR STAGING-GROUND FOR THE LATEST BATTLE BETWEEN THE HUMAN 'FEDERATION' AND THE REPTILOID 'EMPIRE' -- TO SEE JUST WHICH WAY THE BATTLE WILL TURN.

According to several contactees many Federation forces and personnel from the Andromeda and Pleiades constellations, and also from Tau Ceti, Procyon and other star systems, are so absolutely devoted to their belief in non-interventionism that they have blockaded our Sol system from Draconian-Orionite interventionists who would take advantage of this critical and unstable time in earth's history [the close of the 20th century] to claim yet another treasure planet -- perhaps the most strategic planet of all -- for their empire. This would have a devastating impact on all of the Federation worlds, since this planet and all its chemical-mineral-plant-animal-liquid-genetic-etc., resources could be used as a staging world for Draconian attack against other Federation worlds.

As this is being written, Federation Personnel are fighting and dying near the outskirts of our Sol system, according to Contactee Alex Collier and others, in order to prevent this from happening and to prevent continued 'intervention' in the affairs of planet earth by the various galactic vermin, scum, parasites, and filth that have poisoned and destroyed countless human colonial worlds throughout this galaxy and possibly others. No matter what trials we as Americans must pass through in the future in order to defend our nation and our planet from the Draconians and their ungodly human "New World Order" collaborators, NEVER forget that we are not only fighting for our families, our communities, our states, and our nation. We are also fighting for our planet, our star system, and for OUR GALAXY! - Branton)

"Some of us will be lost in the endeavor that is obvious -- however, done NOW the advantage is gained along with new additional technology to prepare for the next stage.

"The key to overall success is -- they TOTALLY respect FORCE. And with them, the most effective method is to stubbornly continue to pick and pull at their defense WITH NO LETUP. Faced with the total loss of a base that has taken YEARS to construct, it is believed that their mission WILL be grossly weakened and badly slowed.

"As Americans, in this particular instance, we MUST realize that we in this case cannot rely upon our inherent moral principles to provide the answer. Negotiation IS OUT. This particular group can only be dealt with NO DIFFERENTLY than one must deal with a mad dog. THAT method they understand.

(Note: This has led some to suggest that the only way to deal with the Grays is through direct force and threat of death. That is, to demand unconditional surrender of their forces to ours and threaten their destruction if they do not comply. It is possible, according to some contactees that certain of the reptilian life-forms can be tamed -- that is IF they are somehow disconnected from the alien collective-hive mind. This would be especially true with the genetic 'hybrids' and especially those hybrids who possess a human soul-matrix. Even if they surrender, those aliens that are truly non-human -- that is, no soul -- can NEVER be allowed to work and operate on an equal basis with other humans, but must EVER remain subservient and I would personally suggest prevented from reproducing after their kind, since they do not possess the integral 'conscience' necessary, of their own initiative, to overcome their base animal or predatory instincts or drives.

For those who may disagree, just look at the known history of the Reptiloids/Greys in their dealings with human beings. One should not be mislead by the apparent "superiority of intelligence" of the Greys, since their intelligence is a direct result of the collective mind. Without the 'collective' hive and operating on their own they are mentally inferior to human beings, at least on an individual basis. The Greys have told some individuals that they are 'legally' here on earth and in America because of the 'treaties'. Did they 'legally' implant numerous influential men and women with mind control devices against their conscious will? Did they 'legally' and permanently abduct untold thousands of men, woman and children to their underground bases? Are they 'legally' mutilating and stealing our livestock?

Did an elected Congress 'legally' agree to these treaties -- or was it an Executive branch of government which has appointed numerous UNELECTED personnel and agencies, in many cases hirelings of unelected corporate-military agendas, who in turn have established 'treaties' with an alien force or forces? Just how 'legal' is the U.S. presidency anyway, following the death of John F. Kennedy, IF Lyndon Johnson was an accomplice in a fascist coup d'état of the Executive branch of the U.S. government in 1963?

THE DULCE PROTOCOL

Were any of the Corporate-CFR-TLC 'presidential' hirelings who came into office following this Executive coup d'état 'legal'? Were their Executive Orders, for instance those connected with FEMA which 'authorize' the destruction of the U.S. Constitution in the event of a 'national emergency', 'legal'? Or could it be that such Executive Orders are not worth the TOILET PAPER they are written on?

The fact is that the Greys, with the help of their mind-controlled human zombie collaborators, HAVE INVADED OUR COUNTRY, OUR AIRSPACE, AND HAVE UNDERMINED OUR LANDS, and they are freely VIOLATING the personal and mental integrity of our people against their conscious consent. - Branton).

Therefore, in ELIMINATING this threat, we most certainly cannot be called the 'aggressor', because we HAVE literally been invaded.

In final conclusion,

A) They CANNOT under ANY circumstances be trusted.

B) They are totally deceptive and death oriented and have no moral respect for human or human life.

C) NO NEGOTIATION, AGREEMENT nor PEACEFUL COMPROMISE can be settled upon in any way.

D) NO agreement signed by both parties will EVER be adhered to NOR recognized and respected by the alien, though they might attempt to make us believe otherwise.

E) ABSOLUTELY NO QUARTER can be allowed under ANY circumstances.

Once the offense is instigated, it cannot be abandoned. If it is, reciprocal reprisal will immediately result. They must be made to come down -- destruct themselves which is a standing order if the ship is failing or leave earth immediately -- NO leeway of any kind can be allowed or tolerated."

For those of you who would question the need to take the offensive against the Reptiloid/Gray strongholds at Dulce and elsewhere, let me just remind you of the kind of alien mentality we are dealing with here by relating the following three incidents:

According to well-known Ufologist Brad Steiger, in the book THE RAINBOW CONSPIRACY, co-authored with his wife Sherry Steiger, a terrifying incident occurred in 1955. This was one of SEVERAL reports of UFO attacks against civilians, civilian airlines and military planes and jets that were documented in the book. In many cases many notorious airline crashes were accompanied by UFO activity reported by witnesses just prior to the disasters or disappearances. Usually there are few actual witnesses to aircraft related 'disasters' or 'disappearances', however in this particular case there was.

A civilian pilot and his friend were engaged in some prospecting projects near the headwaters of the Agua River near the city of Prescott, Arizona. The two men SWORE that they had observed two brightly lit UFOs attack a military plane as it directed "some kind of strange beams" at the aircraft, causing it to explode.

Worse yet, according to the civilian pilot and his friend, when both of the airmen ejected from the doomed and burning aircraft and began floating down to the ground in their parachutes, the UFOs swung back around and seared the survivors with the same deadly rays, apparently killing them both.

In an article titled, 'INCREDIBLE UFO INCINERATION'S: CLOSE ENCOUNTERS OF THE COMBUSTIBLE KIND', researcher Larry E. Arnold describes the following terrifying encounters:

Of the many episodes involving UFOs and the spontaneous combustion of humans, quite probably the most disastrous event [if true] in MODERN times occurred to the African village of Kirimukuya on Mt. Kenya.

THE DULCE PROTOCOL

For several nights in June 1954, young Laili Thindu and his shepherd companions listened to the pounding of their neighbors' drums announcing a wedding about to take place on the mountainside. They also watched STRANGE LIGHTS soar around this 'sacred' peak in central Kenya. They naturally were startled when bright beams flashed from these soaring lights, then concerned that the drums were now silent.

The next morning Laili learned that 'all the dancers, all the children, all the livestock, -- the entire population of the village -- had been seared to death by terrible streams of light from glowing objects,' report Brad Steiger and Joan Whritenour in their book , FLYING SAUCERS ARE HOSTILE. 'It was not until Laili Thindu ventured into Nairobi that he was able to tell his story to someone who recognized the tale for what it really was: the annihilation of an African village by a UFO..."

In the spring 1991 issue of UFO JOURNAL OF FACTS, Forest Crawford, a researcher for the well-known MUFON aerial phenomena research organization, related his personal encounters and conversations with a man he identified only as 'Oscar', who was involved in UFO crash/retrieval projects in earlier years. Oscar stated that on one occasion he and his team received an assignment to investigate a disc that had crashed near Phoenix, Arizona and was then transported to an underground base in North Dakota. The team descended into the deeper levels of the COMTRAPAC submarine base in San Diego where high-security OSS personnel directed them to a tube-like shuttle. Entering the shuttle they prepared to "shoot the tubes", and eventually emerged into the lower levels of the North Dakota base.

Once they arrived, they were told that they would not be allowed to visit the surface of the base during their stay. 'Oscar' viewed the disc which had originally held a crew of three human-like pilots. Two were found outside the craft dead from radiation exposure and other injuries, whereas another was found in an injured state within the secured conditions inside the craft after the team had succeeded in opening it using a sonic resonator. The operation was initially carried out under the direction of

Commander Charles Turner, a friendly man who Oscar got along with well. However without warning another high-ranking officer who everyone feared and who did not appear friendly at all came on the scene. He stated that he was now in charge and began ordering all kinds of experiments and exploratory surgeries on the humanoid -- who was still alive -- in spite of the fact that the anesthesia had little or no affect on him. Some samples of his organs were also removed for study.

The new man in charge was Frank Drake, who later became involved with the OZMA and SETI radio-dish experiments, which had initially pointed their dishes at Tau Ceti and Epsilon Eridani and began receiving intense signals suggesting intelligent life. These initial reports were a mistake or irrelevant according to Frank Drake and his colleagues, and nothing remarkable resulted 'publicly' from the SETI project -- 'officially' that is -- however this and similar projects continue to receive a great deal of funding supplied by the loyal American taxpayer. Drake named the disc-recovery research project OSMA [with an 'S'], and continued to torment the humanoid with various surgical procedures until he finally died. Oscar had given the humanoid the nickname 'Hank', which was an Amerindian word meaning 'troubled spirit'.

According to Forest Crawford, before the humanoid died, 'Oscar' had learned several interesting things from other researchers on his team as well as from the humanoid himself, who had projected images and messages to Oscar via some form of telepathic-empathic-visual-encephalographic wave transfer. The 'man' was approximately 5' 8" tall, of humanlike Meso-American or Mediterranean appearance yet with a face and nose that was slightly 'broader' than the average earth-person, muscular yet not fat -- however he was somewhat heavier for his size than earth people, suggesting that his planet of origin possessed gravity somewhat greater than earth's.

Crawford stated:

The pattern from the panel inside the ship was confirmed by 'Rapp' to match stars of the constellation Eridanus as seen FROM EARTH. It was later confirmed by

THE DULCE PROTOCOL

Hank that the stars of origin of his people were Tau Ceti and Epsilon Eridani. In later sessions Oscar discussed some reasons for the presence of the aliens. He said THEY DO NOT LIKE THE SITUATION WITH SOME OF THE SMALL GREY ALIENS... ('Hank' also stated that the particular group of aliens that his people most often encountered were the gray-whites, which are apparently a genetically engineered reptiloid-insectoid hybrid race. - Branton).

The Tau Cetians feel that the abductions being carried out by some of the Greys ARE A GREAT INJUSTICE TO HUMANITY. 'THEY ARE A PARASITIC RACE THAT HAS AND IS PREYING ON HUMAN CIVILIZATIONS THROUGHOUT THE UNIVERSE,' Oscar relayed. He added that our government's involvement with the grays IS VERY DANGEROUS AND OUT OF CONTROL... Oscar is ADAMANT that [they] are using HUMAN FLUIDS FOR SUSTENANCE. They feed by immersing their arms in vats and/or rubbing the fluids on their bodies. HE CLAIMS THAT THEY ARE ALSO KIDNAPPING CHILDREN.

The Tau Cetians have been preyed upon by these aliens before and they are working with other races and communities that were also victims. ONE SUCH RACE THAT OSCAR CLAIMS WAS RUN OFF THEIR HOME PLANET BY THE BUG PEOPLE [Hanks definition of these aliens, because of their partly insectoid nature and parasitical character] WAS WHAT WE NOW CALL THE NORDICS OR PLEIADIANS. He claims, because of his ongoing contacts, he was made aware of the Billy Meier case in Switzerland and swears that is a real contact...

(Note: Others claim that the Meier contacts and photos are faked, however they may not have been aware of the fact that some of the very first skeptical investigators who came to Meier attempted to see if they could reproduce the photos by making their own models and taking pictures of them. Several of these models and the photos were given to Meier -- the exact motive for doing so is not known. However, later investigators saw these 'models' in Meier's home and took some of the faked photos that the initial investigators had left with Meier, found the hidden 'strings' through photo analysis, and came to the 'logical' conclusion. Was Meier "set up" or was it just one big misunderstanding? Other evidence tends to confirm Meier's claims, including other eye-witnesses to unusual UFO activity, photo's of UFO's passing behind trees, motion picture footage, and so on. - Branton)

I find all these comments interesting especially when you consider one investigative detail of this case. I have seen Oscar's house, his Mother's house, his work shop and truck, and at no time were any books, magazines, transcripts or movies about any subject, let alone recent UFO material, found... Could he be an avid reader of the latest and most controversial UFO documents and just be hiding them when we come over? This is highly unlikely since, without a phone, our visits were always unannounced.

[Oscar, who has since had subsequent contacts with Tau Cetians] wants people to know that if they are contacted by the Tau Cetians [humans such as he described] to not be afraid because they are here to help."

THE DULCE PROTOCOL

Chapter 13

Dulce New Mexico & The Draconian Connection

The following is taken from an article by TAL LeVesque, titled 'THE COVERT Return OF AN ALIEN SPECIES OF REPTILIAN HERITAGE -- THE DULCE BASE,' which appeared in a mailer-newsletter distributed by researcher Patrick O'Connell:

According to TAL, ages ago "...a CONFLICT with other beings, ELs [human giants] destroyed most of the Reptoid civilization, which forced some into deep caverns & others to leave earth -- to Alpha Draconis and/or Altair in the constellation Aquila, which in ancient lore was associated with evil reptilian creatures... The conflict is a Species War, between the Evadamic Seed and the 'Serpent' [draconian] Seed.

(Note: Contactee Maurice Doreal claims to have learned from people he had encountered who came from the subterranean 'Agharti' colonies below North America and Asia, that these giants were closely allied with a race of pre-Scandinavian Nordics who maintained a powerful and scientifically developed civilization whose remains now lie beneath tons of sand in the ancient Gobi desert region of Asia. Doreal was told how both the giants and blond people had waged a prehistoric war against a race of Antarctic-based reptiloids, which they succeeded in driving from the surface of the planet during the ancient conflict. - Branton)

"Under cover of darkness, with bases hidden inside the earth, this nocturnal invader has chosen to reclaim what was once theirs & use it, and us, as a staging area in their ancient conflict with the 'ELs'.

(Note: That is, to reclaim that which these serpent races WANT US TO BELIEVE was once theirs. The 'ELs' are the so-named EL-der race, a human branch tied-in with the Evadamic heritage yet who had attained to or had retained a very tall physical stature averaging from 9-12 ft. in height. Others have referred to them as the 'Anakim' or the 'Nepheli'. - Branton)

"Humans with alien brain implants [the 'zombies'] have been programmed to help overthrow Mankind in the NEAR FUTURE. The 'Reptoids' are even able TO TRANSFORM THEMSELVES INTO BEINGS WITH HUMAN CHARACTERISTICS & FEATURES. The planet Earth is being stressed so that human resistance will be minimal, during the overt takeover & control of Mankind.

"It started as a 'joint interaction program.' An Alien Species wanted to 'share' parts of it's advanced technology with certain humans in KEY POSITIONS OF POWER within government, military, corporations, 'secret societies', etc... The population as a whole began to be manipulated into the 'Alien Agenda'... they wanted TOTAL CONTROL of us!

"[Former Dulce Base Security Officer Thomas Castello] had seen tall Reptilian Humanoids at the base. This is interesting to me [TAL] because in 1979 I came face-to-face with the over 6 foot tall 'Other' Species [REPTOIDS] which materialized in our home! They took blood from my wife [who is an Rh-negative blood type]; & her daughter, who was 1500 miles away.

"...We all came to know that the 'Visitors' were here to stay. We also learned how the Reptilian Race was Returning to Earth & the 'Greys' [who are mercenaries]

THE DULCE PROTOCOL

WERE BEING USED to interface [with] & manipulate humans. Their DEMONIC AGENDA was to keep earth surface [man] CONFUSED & unaware of their true nature & potential... ALSO THE KNOWLEDGE OF VAST & VARIED CIVILIZATIONS LIVING WITHIN THE EARTH.

"The Fantastic Truth was made to seem a fantasy, a legend, a myth, an illusion! The REPTOIDS are Returning to earth to use it as a staging area; in their ANCIENT CONFLICT with the Elohim (the angelic forces of the Almighty Creator, as well as the Nephilim who were not angels as some believe but actual humans of tall stature who in ancient times were undeservingly worshipped as 'gods'. - Branton) The ADAMIC Race has underground bases within Mars -- they are a 'Warrior Cult' culture.

"...There is a vast network of Tube Shuttle connections, under the U.S., which extends into a GLOBAL SYSTEM OF TUNNELS & SUB-CITIES... Note: The reptilians DO NOT consider them-selves 'Aliens'... they claim Terra [3rd from the Sun] was their home before we humans 'arrived'.

"...As a species," TAL continues, "the reptilian heritage beings [the Greys, Reptoids, Winged Draco with 2 horns -- the classic stereotype of the 'Devil']... are highly analytical & technologically oriented. They are seriously into the sciences of automation [& computers] & bio-engineering [& genetics]! However, their exploits in these areas has led to reckless experimentation, WITH TOTAL DISREGARD FOR ETHICS [moral standards] AND EMPATHY. This is also true of MANY OF THE HUMAN BEINGS WORKING WITH THEM!"

(Note: In reference to the "Winged Draco", which are considered to be near the top of the alien hierarchy, above the tall "Lizard Men" and the short 'Grays', these have also gone by the following titles: the Mothmen, Gargoyles, Winged Serpents, Pterodactoids, Ciakars or Birdmen. They seem to be exclusively deep-subterranean dwellers yet have been known to appear during massive UFO - Men In Black - Abduction waves such as that which passed through the Point Pleasant area of West

Virginia as recorded in John Keel's book THE MOTHMAN PROPHECIES, which suggested a possible subterranean connection near an old TNT storage area in the vicinity. The two other areas where these winged reptilians have been most often reported are of course below Dulce, New Mexico and also within the 8-levelled underground system beneath Camp Hero near Montauk Point, Long Island where a joint Nazi [American Corporate & European Militant Nazi's], Gray, and Reptiloid base exists... one that reportedly connects to the ITT center in New Jersey.

The common denominator would be the German Krupp family who built munitions plants for Adolph Hitler and not only maintains a large percentage of control over ITT but also helped to finance the 'Montauk' time-space-mind-control projects for the Bavarian Thule Society, which are continuing within the M.A.L.T.A. or Montauk-Alsace-Lorraine-Time-Archives facility within the Alsace-Lorraine Mts. near the French-German border. The Alsace-Lorraine regions were taken from France in the Franco-Prussian war of the previous century and later Returned to France by the Allies following the end of W.W.II.

The MALTA base 'may' lie under the German territory near the border, however if it happens to lie under French soil, this may be because the base is located in one of the underground facilities constructed by the Nazi's during, before or just following W.W.II, a facility that the French did not discover following the Return of the region following the war. As for the ITT center in New Jersey, it also reportedly has a connection to the national-international Sub-Global network, according to Al Bielek.

Very rarely are the "winged draco" encountered on UFO's, and although at times they have been seen flying at night or in the day through the air as in the Point Pleasant manifestations, they seem to operate most often within the deepest underground levels where the Grays and Reptiloids themselves have been known to converge. - Branton)

TAL then describes something which might seem unbelievable if it were not for the fact that dozens of other sources tend to confirm the same thing.

THE DULCE PROTOCOL

This discovery was reportedly one of the REAL REASONS for the initiation of the 'Dulce Wars':

"...LEVEL #7 is the worst. Row after row of 1,000's of humans & human-mixture remains in cold storage. Here too are embryos of humanoids in various stages of development. Also, many human children remains in storage vats. Who are [were] these people?"

(Note: During a lecture given to THE PROPHECY CLUB, Japanese researcher of the Area 51 and Dulce enigmas - Norio Hayakowa - quoted the following statement that appeared in a 1992 issue of THE ALBUQUERQUE JOURNAL: "...WHY NEW MEXICO HAS SO MANY MORE MISSING CHILDREN THAN COMPARABLE STATES REMAINS A MYSTERY." - Branton)

The sources for these incredibly disturbing allegations aside from Thomas Castello himself, according to TAL, included:

"...people who worked in the labs, abductees taken to the base, people who assisted in the construction, intelligence personnel [NSA, CIA, etc.], and UFO-Inner Earth researchers."

This information, TAL states,

"is meant for those who are seriously interested in the Dulce base. FOR YOUR OWN PROTECTION, be advised to 'USE CAUTION' while investigating this complex."

Robert K Teske

THE DULCE PROTOCOL

Chapter 14

Raging Battles beneath the Earth

The Dulce Wars

The following is an excerpt from an article which appeared in a UFO-related publication. We do not know exactly <u>who the author of the article is</u> or what publication it appeared in, as our source sent us only some Xeroxes with no references.

We relate the information as received:

"...Lear directed my attention to a large map of Nevada, which delineates all the areas which civilian maps coyly leave as uncharted military reserves. 'Right in the very center is a place called Area 51. It is our most secret complex. There are 1900 people there -- it takes presidential clearance to work there -- and they're ferried in by aircraft in the morning and taken out about 5 o'clock in the evening. They have nothing to do with the saucers. The people who work on the saucers go up later in the afternoon, and go home about midnight. <u>The saucer facility is called</u> S-4.' S-4 is in the southwest corner of Area 51.

"Unfortunately, this facility -- AND A SIMILAR SET-UP NEAR DULCE, NEW MEXICO -- may now belong to forces not loyal to the U.S. Government, or even the human race. 'It's horrifying for us to think that all the scientists we think are working for us are actually controlled by the aliens.'

"'...A deal was made with them in the latter part of the 1960s (Probably a revisioning of the 1954 treaty, which was in turn an outgrowth of the secret Bavarian Illuminati treaty with the Grays in 1933. - Branton). In exchange for technology, we would cover up the existence of the aliens.' Apparently this agreement -- engineered by an arm of government so covert that even the President may not be on the 'need to know' list -- also sanctioned the abduction of humans, which the aliens rationalized as an ongoing monitoring of a developing civilization. We asked only for a list of the abductees.

"In 1973, the deal soured. 'Hundreds of people -- thousands -- were being abducted that weren't on the list. In 1978-79, there was an altercation between us and the aliens, in which they killed 44 of our top scientists, and a number of Delta Force who were trying to free them. I'm not sure where this altercation occurred -- it could have been Dulce, or it could have occurred in Groom Lake

(Note: According to Robert Lazar, an underground facility below Groom Lake was the sight of an intense fire-fight between Grays and U.S. Military personnel after a human Security officer had challenged an alien dictate not to enter a certain alien-controlled area with a loaded weapon, and was subsequently killed as a result of his challenge.

This 'war' was actually a 'massacre' according to MJ12 Special Studies Group [MJ12-SSG] agent Michael Wolf, since the first outbreak of violence in 1975 resulted during a demonstration of an anti-matter reactor within an underground chamber. The Greys operating the demonstration ordered the human security officers to remove the bullets from their weapons. One Security officer questioned this order and just for having the audacity to question, one of the Greys apparently let their true colors show.

THE DULCE PROTOCOL

That is, it prematurely exposed the fact that 'they' were not really the 'allies' of the American government, but actually an occupational invasion force that had to maintain absolute discipline among its 'conquered subjects'. This 'thing' from out of this world decided that it would make an 'example' out of those who questioned their orders, and its comrades followed suit. The Greys commenced to slaughter SEVERAL dozen Security personnel and Scientists, although only one alien Grey died in that initial altercation.

Thomas Castello claims that another battle occurred below Dulce four years later in 1979, after several scientists who had discovered the 'Horrible Truth' -- of thousands of human abductees in cold storage or imprisoned in cage-like enclosures in the deeper 'Alien' sectors under Dulce -- were themselves captured by the aliens following this discovery. These were some of the best minds America had to offer. As we will see later on, the "Dulce Wars" were somewhat more complex than this brief explanation might suggest, however. - Branton).

"This battle, Lear claims, left us bereft of our own facilities [and some of our best scientists]; ever since, we have attempted to create a counterforce to meet the alien challenge.

"The Strategic Defense Initiative was one such scheme. SDI, regardless of what you hear, was completed two years ago; that was to shoot down incoming saucers. The mistake was that we thought they were coming inbound -- in fact, they're already here. They're in underground bases all over the place.' It seems that the aliens had constructed many such bases without our knowledge, where they conduct heinous genetic experiments on animals, human beings, and 'improvised' creatures of their own devising."

In battle, even in a conflict as unusual as the "Dulce Wars", there are bound to be prisoners of war or POW's.

In his LEADING EDGE Report, researcher Val Valerian revealed the following:

"DULCE LAB TECHNICIAN HELD: In early November, 1988, we received word that the scientist son of [B.M.] is now being held in the underground facility at FORT WAYNE, Colorado. The underground base is located in southwestern Colorado near the UTE mountains. The son apparently worked at the genetics lab under Archuleta Mesa near DULCE, NM and finally grew disgusted with what he was observing. Subsequent probes into the retention of this person have yielded several interesting project names. His father, B.M. apparently encountered two Nordic appearing men in Pomona, CA on 22 Oct. '88..."

Note: The "Ute Mountain" Indian reservation border -- which super-imposes the southern border of Colorado, lies only a relatively few miles north of the Archuleta plateau. It extends from that point westward along the border to the four corners area. Just across the border in Utah another branch facility apparently exists, according to John Lear, where another Dulce scientist is reportedly being held. Lear spoke with the father of THIS young scientist, referring to the father only as 'Mr. K.', and attempted to locate the exact position of the base.

Lear stated:

"...The son, whose father I met and who passed away several years ago is apparently being held in a base near or around Sleeping Ute Mountain (Sleeping Ute mountain is in the extreme southeast part of Utah, near the four corners area on the Ute Reservation, south of Utah highway 666 which also runs through Colorado and down through New Mexico. - Branton). I don't remember how I came by that information but it had to do with some research I was conducting in a search for the Project BLUE LIGHT base near Delores [which I never found]."

In regards to Utah, there have been rumors of "New World Order" bases being constructed below southeastern Utah with containment facilities where 'dissidents' are intended to be apprehended underground when and if the New World Order takes control of the United States. There are reportedly numerous such underground containment facilities throughout North America.

The U.S. Military is not the only force that has become involved with the 'war' against the Grays. One of the major underground human forces who are VERY upset at the Grays -- over their violation of territorial agreements and abuses and atrocities that have been committed against various intra-planetary human colonies -- include certain segments of the Telosian-Agharti alliance, as well as some of their Sirian allies who are against the Greys.

The following information was sent to a Utah researcher by Juliette Sweet, a personal friend of Sharula Dux who is reportedly an Aghartian 'princess' from Telos, the city-complex below Mt. Shasta.

The central metroplex of Telos is said to consist of a multi-leveled complex over 5 miles deep and at least 20 miles in circumference, which extends outward to suburban colonial systems beyond. According to Sharula, Telos has subterranean connections via tube-shuttles to at least 100 other subterranean cities below North America as well as cities below South America, such as the allied city of POSID below the Matto Grosso region of Brazil. Many of these cities are maintained by ancient 'native' North, South and Central Americans.

The following letter was dated 2/7/93:

"...last month I had your disk transcribed and read your materials in their entirety. Very interesting, and full of well cited facts. I appreciate your sense of groundedness when presenting your ideas... I am not familiar with the saurian race, nor have I heard mention of them from Sharula or Adama... The Greys do come up from time to time, and what has been communicated by the [Telosian] Hierarchy is that they are indeed being asked, forcibly if necessary to leave.

The ousting process has been active for the last year or so, and Adama has indicated that Los Alamos will be one of the last areas to clear out... there has been some "star wars" type of conflicts of late, but the [Telosian] masters tell us not to worry about it, that they have things well in hand... Sharula's age is actually 267 years. Although for surface ID purposes, she says she was born in 1951. It helps where social security and passport purposes are concerned.

You might want to update your materials to reflect her actual age..."

<u>Note</u>: During one lecture, Sharula was asked what the Telosians were doing about the problem with the Grays. Sharula stated that the Telosian-Agharti Silver Fleets had confronted the Grays and told them to cease their abusive activities on this planet, to which the Grays responded that they have the right to continue their activities since the "U.S. Government" has authorized their activities on earth and in America.

Are the Grays referring to the Nazi-backed CIA-NSA "secret government" which has infiltrated America through murder and manipulation, and established the "alien interaction" projects WITHOUT Congressional consent?

It's AS IF these green-blooded, pencil-necked, melon-headed, blood-sucking parasites - who break treaties, violate human will, permanently abduct and even kill humans for scientific or sustenance purposes, lie and deceive, disregard non-intervention ethics, destroy animals and property, manipulate the thoughts of the masses and their leaders against their conscious knowledge, ruin human lives on mental-emotional-physical levels, and literally 'feed' off of human LIFE including that of our children - have ANY place to give such excuses!

Chapter 15

Dulce: An Ancient Terminal To Inner & Outer Space?

Researcher Paris Flammonde gives a description of what appears to be the 'Dulce' underground base-network, as described by UFO 'researcher' James Moseley:

"...The intimations of strange pressure groups, purportedly intent upon obscuring the true meaning of Flying Saucers, began arising in the early 1950's, the most famous of these being the 'three men in black' and the 'silence conspiracy,' which Major Keyhoe and others regard as an ominous element functioning within the Air Force. During the summer of 1956, SAUCER NEWS editor James Moseley postulated an addition to this enigmatic company in the June, 1956, issue of his magazine.

Theorizing that Flying Saucers were originally being researched by the United States in 1946, were capable of speeds exceeding four thousand miles an hour, and were operating from a super-secret subterranean base below a southwestern state, he continued:

"'The whole project is so highly classified that ordinary military pilots and even the Air Force's saucer investigators on Project Blue Book could not possibly know about it. In fact, this type of saucer IS NOT built by the American Government AS WE

ORDINARILY UNDERSTAND THE WORD 'GOVERNMENT.' As fantastic as this might sound... these saucers are actually built, operated, and maintained by an organization which is ENTIRELY SEPARATE from the military and political branches of the Government that we know about. Although a handful of people at the very top of the Government know about the existence of this project, they have no direct contact with it... I shall call this secret project, 'The Organization.'"

Moseley, according to Flammonde, "...considerably elaborated on the activities of this shadowy cabal with some very extravagant revelations."

This 'Secret Society - Secret Government' base in the 'Southwest' is no doubt the very same DULCE facility which we have been exposing throughout this work. Secret Societies, if not Secret Agencies, have their own symbols or emblems. The 'Symbol' for the Dulce Base that is worn by many of the workers there consists of an UPSIDE-DOWN or inverted triangle or pyramid with an upside-down 'T' superimposed over it, as shown in the "dlcpic." graphic file at the beginning of this series of files. William Hamilton reveals the following in regards to the Dulce base:

"...Schoenfeld Clinical Laboratories in Albuquerque analyzed the samples [of the affected hides of mutilated cattle studied by Gomez and Burgess, that were discovered near Dulce] and found significant deposits of potassium and magnesium. The potassium content was 70 times above normal.

"...Level 1 [of the Dulce base] contains the garage for STREET MAINTENANCE. Level 2 contains the garage for TRAINS, SHUTTLES, TUNNEL-BORING MACHINES, AND DISC MAINTENANCE.

"...The Greys and reptoid species...have had ancient CONFLICTS with the NORDIC humans from outer space societies, and may be staging here for a future conflict."

THE DULCE PROTOCOL

The late Thomas Edwin Castello, who worked within the underground 'Dulce' facility, suggested that the early experiments by Rand and Los Alamos labs in nuclear-powered 'earth-boring' technology has been taken to the extreme.

In a letter dated Sept. 1990, he made mention of the nuclear BORING mechanisms which can allegedly bore a tunnel through the earth at a rate of 5-10 mph by cracking the surrounding rock and heating the rock and earth into a state of liquid incandescence using super-hot cones, pulsed lasers and other methods.

[see: U.S. Patent numbers 3,881,777; 3,885,832 and 3,693,731 for instance, via their Patent Search engine which can be easily accessed by doing a "web search" of the "United States Patent Office"] and pressing the liquid or molten rock into the peripheral cracks where the cold earth cools and solidifies it in a matter of minutes, leaving no leftover materials that would otherwise have to be removed from the tunnel, as in more traditional and expensive tunneling or mining operations:

"...On level one is the garage for the street maintenance, level two is the garage for trains, shuttles and TERRON DRIVE [bore machine] and disk maintenance. [Requires ULTRA 4 to even SEE the disk garage]...

"The chief of the Genetic Experiments is LARRY DEAVEN [Los Alamos AND Dulce]..."

Another confirmation that the DULCE base is a major terminal -- not only for other-planetary craft but also a nexus connecting several other underground systems -- was sent to us by a woman who knew Thomas Castello on a personal basis, and whose father had worked with Castello in what was referred to as "The Organization" [her exact words] which operated in the upper levels of the joint-interaction facilities near Dulce.

The following description of one of the more ancient tunnels was given by Thomas Castello himself:

"The halls around the Dulce Base are slightly curved, and in most locations you can see what looks like an endless corridor. It is only when you glance up and see the high ceiling of the natural rock covering do you remember you are inside an immense cavern. The place has the feeling of infinity, or a sense of seeing something immemorial.

"I realize this place has been expanded repeatedly over many years. But somehow, a person tends to forget the written history the manual describes. The place feels ANCIENT. The Native Races of this planet have used the tunnels and caverns for centuries. Human hands too, added their personal touch in a way that makes you feel the passing of age. Here and there the architectural designs resemble the fantasy of Art Deco. Doors display the designs and angles that recall the playful grace of that era.

"From tunnel entrances stare down carved gargoyles and winged beings that cling to your memory much longer than they should. Those grotesque gargoyles are dark and look like a preview of the Nightmare Hall. Some of the faces of the frightful creatures depicted have lost details in a way that softens the ugliness. History has a way of erasing details and the memory of the original form. Just as well, perhaps the gargoyles were carved from live models. Maybe from some thing seen on the sixth level.

"One specific tunnel, the long tunnel to Taos, is completely different. The symbol that marks the portal is the symbol for marsh, or wet lands. The shape resembles the letter 'Z' with two cross lines.

"It was not until I had to make a 'goodwill run' to Taos to escort a foreign dignitary on a tour of the base, did I realize why the tunnel was so named. After a few miles the rock tunnel walls became mostly white in color and were decorated with carved plant life of all kinds. Here, I saw ancient fern trees with huge Rose like flowers depicted in beautiful relief. These beautiful walls portray a dense archaic tropical thicket. Beyond the trees, in the background, some unknown ancient mountains are depicted in the same clear style. I slowed the car, searched the scene, hoping to see animal or humanoid creatures, but there was none. No signs or signatures in sight, unless they were written in a long lost unrecognized hand.

(Note: Was this one of the more ancient tunnels that was left by a prehistoric race, a tunnel which was already ancient at the time that the U.S. government AND the Reptiloids/Greys 'discovered' or 'took control of' the original underground systems? Perhaps a tunnel and an underground system that was excavated in prehistoric times by the ancestors of the Pueblo Indians of the four corners area whose legends claim that they were chased-out of the cavern world by invading reptilian forces - that is, according to Hopi-Apache descendant Robert Morningsky? - Branton)

"It looked like every plant on earth, ancient and modern, were faithfully displayed. Mile after miles of trees, wheat, corn, flowers and grasses graced the gleaming walls.

"It must be the most beautiful place on earth. Maybe it was created as a museum. Or perhaps a shrine to plant life. Regardless of the reason, there is NO WAY that place could have been made by the hands of MODERN man. These carved plants are in minute detail, and they look brand new.

"My eyes had quickly scanned the upper sections of the tunnel in hoping to find the source of the soft illumination that now seems to be coming from every where. I found no answers.

"I had stopped the electric car, wanting to touch those walls, in the hope I might guess the age upon closer examination. To my surprise the walls were covered with some transparent covering. Those walls felt like polished glass, and looked about a foot thick! The biggest shock was when I touched the astonishing gleaming wall. The slightest contact created a wave of quivering of the lights. What is even more surprising, was that the lights were INSIDE the glass! Starting as a soft gentle harmonic sound that resonated with the shimmering lights, and grew to a bone deep vibration that was subtle and surprisingly invasive, like someone speaking to me when I'm meditating. The tunnel echoed with musical tones. I struggled to isolate the difference between what I was hearing and what I was feeling. I could not separate them.

"I sensed that the tones were designed to provide information in ancient language. The changing tones were at first received at a rapid rate, that I couldn't understand. Like learning a foreign language, at first the words are endless sound, but after a while separate words are recognized. I know the musical tones are words and I recognize it as a lost language.

"I started the car, almost feeling light headed from the ongoing sounds. I wanted to stop the flow of words that were musical and pleasant. After I knew they were words [that I couldn't understand] I wanted the dialog to end. I felt those tones clear to my bones, and the tonal vibrations refused to leave me until I left the tunnel!

"It was one of the most profound experiences of my life, but I'm sure I wouldn't want to do it again!

"At the Dulce Base, the roadways exit on the first three levels. From all other levels the roads will climb in a steep spiral to join the upper levels. After a few miles more those three levels too, join in a huge intersection that rivals any 'cloverleaf' exchange, anywhere. The five main exit roads that leave the base have no markings any where, but after the exchanges, there are mileage markers IN ENGLISH posted in the walls of the tunnels.

"The underground highways occasionally follow the same direction as the Terradrive shuttle. That shuttle is also known as the Sub-Global System

THE DULCE PROTOCOL

(Note: Different sources claim that one must be a very high ranking Mason, Corporate-Intelligence Agent, or a Native Sub-Terran to gain access to the Sub-Global System. There are several access terminals in North America and elsewhere where identification must be provided, however according to Al Bielek and others, when one has passed the security checks they are free to go wherever they please in the Sub-Global network, and the inner dwellers just generally assume that if one has made it that far, then they more or less have authorization to be there. Many of the residents of the underground, whether Exterrans, Subterrans or visitors from the Surface, are tied-in to a collective mind or group intelligence matrix called the 'Ashtar' or 'Astarte' network which has its roots in the underground systems below ancient Egypt.

This has been the main framework for collaboration between humanoids and reptiloids and other alien life forms. Although there have always been independent humanoid and reptiloid factions that have been at war with each other for centuries, in more recent decades following the Dulce Wars, et al, these conflicts have been increasing within the "inner earth" between the "collectivists" and the "individualists".

Because of this we might reason that the inner-world 'highways' may not always be safe places to travel alone, even if one has the 'clearances' to do so. Although there is a collaboration-of-convenience between certain human and reptilian groups, this mainly grows out of the aliens' NEED for human cooperation in implementing total global electronic control, and vise versa, not necessarily out of any major level of friendship or tolerance between the two races. For instance in order to implement the New World Order the human elite must absolutely DEPEND on the alien mind-control technology and the aliens in turn must DEPEND on the humans' social structure connections. They MUST have each others' assistance and cooperation in order to implement a world government. Apparently they will worry about fighting over WHICH SIDE comes out with absolute control WHEN and IF the global dictatorship is implemented.

We must realize that the underground 'world' is just as 'alien' to dwellers on the surface as are the worlds from which many of the interstellar starships that have been seen in our atmosphere hail. It is a very ancient world whose inhabitants have interacted with other worlds, or have even colonized other worlds, over a period of thousands of years. - Branton)

Chapter 16

Dulce New Mexico & The Ashtar Connection

(The following is an edited version of a very extensive file downloaded from the Internet. Some of the highlights/emphasis are mine. - Branton)

- From: Michael.Corbin@p0.f428.n104.z1.FIDONET.ORG (Michael Corbin) Newsgroups: alt.alien.visitors
- Subject: Dulce Report
- Message-ID: <138993.2A566EB0@paranet.FIDONET.ORG>
- Date: 5 Jul 92 03:20:06 GMT
- Sender: ufgate@paranet.FIDONET.ORG (newsout1.26)
- Organization: FidoNet node 1:104/428.0 - Lines: 127
- Forwarded from "ParaNet UFO Echo"
- Originally from Michael Corbin
- Originally dated 07-04-92 20:17

The following was uploaded by a user on ParaNet. It is being provided in its entirety for information purposes only. ParaNet or its affiliates makes no claims to its truthfulness or validity and does not endorse its contents in any way.

As a further note: Under paragraph (3E), it mentions that there are buildings ... "five-sided with a dome," ParaNet has seen photographic evidence of such buildings. These buildings are not buildings as one would think of them, but what appear to be wilderness observation platforms. The Dulce Report denies any of these buildings appeared in their investigation.

THE DULCE REPORT

NUMBER 920527

MAY 27, 1992

A Field Investigation and Evaluation

A PHOENIX PROJECT REPORT

The "Phoenix Project Reports" Are Published By

ADVENT PUBLISHING COMPANY

P.O. Box 3748

Carson City, NV 89702

(Opening Note: ParaNet has done an investigation into the PHOENIX organization which put out this report. Contrary to the claims of the authors of this document, ParaNet HAS FOUND obvious links between the PHOENIX PROJECT and the PHOENIX REPORT, an outlet for the ASHTAR Collective. One of the 'leaders' and 'spokesmen' for this collective is a being that goes by the name of HATONN. Hatonn, according to some sources, is a 9 ft. 'Pleiadean' with severe fascist leanings who claims to be a reptilian 'defector' from the Unholy Six Orion-Draconian Empire. Other sources claim that the Ashtar Collective -- or at least a large segment of the collective which was infiltrated and assimilated by Draco-Orion agents posing as "ascended masters" -- is now in direct collaboration with the reptilian Grays and the 'Unholy Six'. In such an event, it would NOT be surprising for the Draco-Orion controlled segment of the Ashtar network to seek to discredit a base under Dulce, New Mexico IF IN FACT the base is being controlled and operated jointly by Draconian AND Ashtarian forces... for instance the joint Draconian-Ashtarian forces which, some believe, are operating in conjunction with the anomalous "Hale-Bopp" comet.

THE DULCE PROTOCOL

Since the original document-chain in which the 'Dulce Report' appears contains over 140 KB's and is an obvious smear effort -- for instance throughout the document you will read passage after passage containing phrases like "...there is no evidence" for phenomena which HAVE been confirmed by several other researchers -- I have decided not to waste valuable space, and have eliminated the rambling and innocuous sweeping opinionated attempts on the part of the authors to wipe the entire Dulce issue under the carpet. I have instead gleaned the information which may be useful to those who accept the obvious fact that 'something' is actually going on near Dulce, New Mexico. Whether it involves top secret government activity OR alien activity OR both is debatable. The fact is, something strange IS happening in and around Dulce, New Mexico. - Branton)

The document begins as follows:

The Town of Dulce is located in northern New Mexico near the southern border of Colorado. Dulce is located eighty-three miles northeast of Farmington, New Mexico on U.S. Route 64. See Map Exhibit 1.

It has a population of 1,648 and is nestled in a valley. Just to the north and overlooking the town is the large Archuleta Mesa. The town is at an altitude of 6,825 feet above sea level. The main income producing activity in the area is cattle ranching. The business and service activities are typical of those needed in a community of this size. There are no military or industrial activities, large or small, in the area. See Photo Exhibits 4 and 5.

In order to present the results of our investigation it is necessary to refer to items of information, widely available to UFO researchers, concerning the Dulce, U.S.\Alien base. In the following, we will quote from those items of information. We will attempt to identify the source whenever possible. This will be followed by our findings.

The Investigation

1) Source Information Excerpts: Dulce Papers.Txt Author Unknown

A joint US/EBE facility exists beneath the Archuleta Mesa near the town of DULCE NEW MEXICO.

(1A) This facility has been in existence in one form or another since 1948.

(1B) ...The facility proper is located one kilometer underground.

(1C) The base is approximately 2.5 miles northwest of Dulce, and almost overlooks the town.

(1D) There is a paved government road 36 feet wide going into the area.

* * *

Findings of Phoenix Project Investigation (PHX) regarding the foregoing:

(PHX-1A) No substantiating County records confirm this. Local residents have no memory of any government installation, civilian or military ever having existed in this area.

(PHX-1B) Same as 1A. There is no record or memory of any underground heavy construction, excavation, or mining activity in the area.

* * *

2) Source Information Excerpts: 1988 Krill2.Txt

...During the occupation of the Greys, they have established quite a number of underground bases all over the world, especially in the United States.

THE DULCE PROTOCOL

(2A) One such base [among others in the same state] is under Archuleta Mesa, which is about 2.5 miles northwest of Dulce, New Mexico.

The foregoing extract is from a transcript of a conversation between Jim McCampbell and Dr. Paul Bennewitz on July 13, 1984...

* * *

3) Source Information Excerpts: 1988 Krill2.Txt

(3A) ...Bennewitz reports he was able to determine the location of the underground facility: a kilometer underground beneath Archuleta Mesa on the Jicarilla Apache Indian Reservation near Dulce, New Mexico [since 1976, one of the areas of the U.S. hardest hit by mutilations].

(3B) Bennewitz' information is that this installation is operated jointly as part of an on-going program of cooperation between the U.S. government and the EBEs.

Back to the base under discussion. After Bennewitz briefed Air Force officials on what he had found, a trip to the area revealed the following data:

(3C) The base is 2.5 miles northwest of Dulce, and almost overlooks the town.

(3D) There is a level highway 36 feet wide going into the area. It is a government road.

(3E) One can see telemetry trailers and buildings that are five-sided with a dome. Next to the domes, a black limousine was noted -- a CIA vehicle.

(3F) These limos will run you off the road if you try to get into the area.

(3G) To the north there is a launch site.

(3H) There are two wrecked ships there; they are 36 feet long with wings, and one can see oxygen and hydrogen tanks. The ships that we got out of the trade are atomic-powered with plutonium pellets. Refueling of the plutonium is accomplished at Los Alamos.

(3I) The base has been there since 1948. Some of the disks are piloted by the NSA.

(3J) The base is 4,000 feet long

(3K) and helicopters are going in and out of there all the time. When it became known that Bennewitz was familiar with this, the mutilations in the area stopped.

(3L) In 1979, something happened and the base was temporarily closed. There was an argument over weapons and our people were chased out. The aliens killed 66 of our people, and 44 got away.

(Side Note: Christa Tilton claims that the government activity at Dulce may no longer be present, as there are signs that the upper levels have been de-activated, at least in regards to human government activity. Sightings of Greys atop the Archuleta mesa HAVE been reported by Jicarilla Apache Indians as of the early 1990's. Such reports have made their way to Christa Tilton, suggesting that even if the 'government' activity at Dulce has ceased, the Greys/Reptiloids are apparently still operating there en masse and very active within the base, and are continuing on with their former agendas. - Branton)

THE DULCE PROTOCOL

One of the people who in fact got away was a CIA agent who, before leaving, made some notes, photos, and videotapes, and went into hiding. He has been in hiding ever since, and every six months he contacts each of five people he left copies of the material with. His instructions were that if he missed four successive contacts, the people could do whatever they want with the material. [The material] was received in December, 1987, by many researchers. The "Dulce Papers" were composed of 25 black and white photos, a videotape with no dialogue and a set of papers that included technical information regarding the jointly occupied [CIA-Alien] facility one kilometer beneath the Archuleta Mesa near Dulce, New Mexico.

(3M) The facility still exists and is currently operational.

* * *

Findings: (I've deleted SEVERAL paragraphs which basically state -- in the most technical sounding terminology the authors could conjure -- that ALL of the above "doesn't exist". - Branton)...

* * *

4) Source Information Excerpts: "PROJECT BETA" BY DR. PAUL BENNEWITZ

(4A)...numerous road blocks extend northward. (4B) Maintained road some thirty feet wide and servicing facilities, tanks, etc. There is also an apparent foundation for another helo pad_____

(4C) human housing, and another black limousine with tracks leading to it west of the road.

The total alien basing area apparently contains several cultures, [all under the designation 'UNITY']

(4D) and is approx 3km wide by 8km long and is located in the middle of nowhere on the Jicarilla Indian Reservation west of Dulce, NM. ...Based on the number of ships presently in this area, the total alien population is estimated to be at least 2,000 and most likely MORE.

(The former self-professed Dulce base Security Officer Thomas C. Castello stated that there were over 18,000 Greys based under Dulce while he was there. - Branton)

----- Logistical plans -----

...initial logistics would indicate a plan sequentially implemented as follows:

This plan does not include all requirements and preparatory safety measures to be employed by the ground force; however, if Air Force Intelligence desires to pursue the approaches suggested in this report, each significant requirement will be discussed in depth.

(4E) The attack must be directed almost entirely on the ground since vehicle ignition problems will be encountered. All electrical and electronic equipment must be 'hardened' using specific techniques perfected prior to implementation. This information has been checked by interaction and eavesdropping on their communication channels _____ as far as weaknesses are concerned. The program would be instigated in phases:

(4F) 1) The first procedure would be to close the gates of the dam above the Navajo River. This dam could be held closed for the duration. Internal to the one cave, there is a small dam for water storage. Its capacity is small.

THE DULCE PROTOCOL

(4G) There is also a discharge outlet downstream that could be closed, causing waste water to back up into the caves. The water is vacuum pumped apparently by some electrostatic means from the river.

(4H) There is a water intake and dam upstream that can be totally cut off and the water re-routed to Chama, New Mexico.

* * *

Findings: (refer to last note... MUCH MORE of the same innocuous and rambling evasiveness. However if you really ARE determined to see the entire file, I suppose you could log-on to PARANET via the Internet and access it. - Branton)...

* * *

5) Source Information Excerpt Thisisit.Txt Wm. C. Cooper

The alien underground base is located beneath an indian reservation near the small town of Dulce, New Mexico...

* * *

Findings: All of the previous 'Findings' apply to this source information...

* * *

Signed,
The Phoenix Project
END OF FILE
PARANET FILENAME: DULCEDOC.TXT

ParaNet(sm) Information Service - via ParaNet node 1:104/422

UUCP: !scicom!paranet!User_Name

INTERNET: ParaNet(sm).Information.Service@p0.f428.n104.z1.

FIDONET.ORG

From: rodb@slugo.corp.sgi.com (Rod Beckwith)

Newsgroups: alt.alien.visitors

Subject: Re: Dulce Report - Conclusion

Message-ID: <1992Jul7.000018.24512@odin.corp.sgi.com>

Date: 7 Jul 92 00:00:18 GMT

References: <138997.2A566EBC@paranet.FIDONET.ORG>

Sender: news@odin.corp.sgi.com (Net News)

Organization: Silicon Graphics, Inc.

Lines: 21

Nntp-Posting-Host: slugo.corp.sgi.com

Michael,

Didn't Bill Moore get tangled up in this situation? Didn't this whole episode cause Paul Bennewitz to have a nervous breakdown? Do you have any further documentation on this aspect of the investigation? I for one would like to find out where some [if not all] of the disinformation came from. Are there any other investigations "The Phoenix Project" is working on?

Thanks,

Rod

Rod Beckwith |$$

Datacom I/S |"The great obstacle of progress is |not ignorance,

THE DULCE PROTOCOL

rodb@corp.sgi.com |but the illusion of knowledge."

From: Michael.Corbin@p0.f428.n104.z1.FIDONET.ORG (Michael Corbin)
Newsgroups: alt.alien.visitors
Subject: Re: Dulce Report - Conclusion
Message-ID: <139085.2A5B8080@paranet.FIDONET.ORG>
Date: 8 Jul 92 23:19:02 GMT
Sender: ufgate@paranet.FIDONET.ORG (newsout1.26)
Organization: FidoNet node 1:104/428.0 - Lines: 22

Dear Michael:

I read all of the information that you posted and appreciated your work and the work of the Phoenix Report but I don't believe it. It doesn't add up to me and I won't explain why. You may be right and I'm wrong. I hope I am wrong in this case. That's all folks.

John Winston.

First, that was not my work, nor did I have anything to do with it. Someone uploaded that material to ParaNet and I simply reposted it with permission. I have found numerous problems with it myself and, although I do not necessarily believe that something is happening at Dulce, I think that the Phoenix material is just more disinformation...

Mike

From: ParaNet.Information.Service@p0.f428.n104.z1.FIDONET.ORG (sm)

Newsgroups: alt.alien.visitors

Subject: Rating on Dulce Report and K2 Report

Message-ID: <139161.2A610FC9@paranet.FIDONET.ORG>

Date: 13 Jul 92 05:02:02 GMT

Sender: ufgate@paranet.FIDONET.ORG (newsout1.26)

Organization: FidoNet node 1:104/428.0 - Lines: 49

* Forwarded from "ParaNet UFO Echo"

* Originally from ParaNet(sm) Information Service

* Originally dated 07-12-92 22:01

Recently we published two reports generated by the Phoenix Project, a group in Carson City, Nevada. These two documents allege that members of this group investigated reports of underground alien bases in Dulce, New Mexico, and an underground alien base located in the Plumas National Forest in Northern California.

(Note: Basically their investigation 'proved' that the Dulce base did NOT exist, but that the 'K2' UFO base in California DID! Why do I get the feeling that IF the K2 base DOES in fact exist, then we should not be too concerned about it? Could it be that there is an actual alien force based in the Plumes National Forest that is CONTESTING the activities at Dulce? Just remember that for every visible conflict, there is often an invisible conflict taking place behind the scenes. Often the 'pawns' cannot see who the real "chess players" are. - Branton)

Because of the following findings/reasons, ParaNet has assigned a high level of probability that the material contained in the documents is disinformation and is inaccurate.

The reasons are as follows:

THE DULCE PROTOCOL

1) The Phoenix Project is unknown to the general UFO research community. No where in any of the materials are the principals of the organization identified. As is the case with any materials where substantive findings are reported, it demonstrates a strong lack of credibility when the names and addresses of the investigators are not provided.

2) Due to an investigation that has been ongoing, we have found that the material on Dulce is inaccurate. It is interesting that the Dulce report denies that ANYTHING exists at Dulce. Although we have found no information to the contrary, we feel that the report from the Phoenix Project is inaccurate as to location of buildings and other factors. There are things down there which ARE unusual.

3) The K2 material is too ambiguous and does not provide enough reliable data bits to launch an investigation into the claims. It appears that although the report is written with some literary license, the findings are presented in a very unscientific fashion.

ParaNet will provide a complete report of its investigation into the various other claims contained in the reports as soon as the information is available. We have written to the Phoenix Project requesting further information.

In the meantime, we urge caution in the use of this material.

Michael Corbin

Director

ParaNet Information Services -- ParaNet(sm)

Information Service - via ParaNet node 1:104/422

UUCP: !scicom!paranet!User_Name

INTERNET:

ParaNet(sm).Information.Service@p0.f428.n104.z1.FIDONET.ORG

Robert K Teske

From: ParaNet.Information.Service@p0.f428.n104.z1.FIDONET.ORG (sm)

Newsgroups: alt.alien.visitors

Subject: STRONG WORD OF CAUTION!

Message-ID: <139389.2A739F99@paranet.FIDONET.ORG>

Date: 27 Jul 92 06:56:03 GMT

Sender: ufgate@paranet.FIDONET.ORG (newsout1.26)

Organization: FidoNet node 1:104/428.0 - Lines: 25

* Forwarded from "ParaNet UFO Echo"

* Originally from ParaNet(sm) Information Service

* Originally dated 07-26-92 23:56

Over the last few days we have been posting information supplied by the Phoenix Project of Carson City, Nevada. This information has been strongly disclaimed by ParaNet pending the results of our investigation to determine the validity of the Phoenix Project and its officers.

While the investigation is still ongoing, we have found some highly disturbing things relating to credibility of the group. This information will be reported as soon as the investigation is completed. This should be in the next few days.

Until this investigation is complete and the findings published, ParaNet wishes to urge everyone not to send any money to the group.

Michael Corbin

Director

ParaNet(sm) Information Service - via ParaNet node 1:104/422

UUCP: !scicom!paranet!User_Name

INTERNET:

ParaNet(sm).Information.Service@p0.f428.n104.z1.FIDONET.ORG

THE DULCE PROTOCOL

From: ParaNet.Information.Service@p0.f428.n104.z1.FIDONET.ORG (sm)

Newsgroups: alt.alien.visitors

Subject: Report on Phoenix Project

Message-ID: <139577.2A817124@paranet.FIDONET.ORG>

Date: 6 Aug 92 18:16:01 GMT

Sender: ufgate@paranet.FIDONET.ORG (newsout1.26)

Organization: FidoNet node 1:104/428.0 - Lines: 177

A few weeks ago, ParaNet received on-line copies of several documents which purported to come from a previously unknown organization called "The Phoenix Project". The project is described in the documents as a "private, civilian, research organization" which was "formed in 1952 to investigate and correlate information" concerning UFOs and ETs. According to the information contained in the documents, for a small price one can receive printed copies of the project's reports, complete with maps, magnetometer readings, and a host of other supporting charts and diagrams which serve to make the whole endeavor look scientific and legitimate.

The documents we received were formulated as investigative reports on two of the hottest and most controversial issues within the UFO research community: the underground alien bases which are said to exist at numerous locations around the United States, and the cluster of alleged UFO-related projects sometimes referred to collectively as "Operation Majestic Twelve".

Specifically, the material consisted of three separate documents:

(1) "The Ultimate Secret", originally dated 4 August 1989 and revised most recently 5 May 1992, purporting to lay bare the inner workings of the government's secret UFO projects, including the recovery of alien technology and bodies from crashed UFOs, the exploitation of this technology by a number of code-named government projects, and the involvement of NASA and the SDI program in preparing for CONFLICT with alien INVADERS;

(2) "The Dulce Report", dated 27 May 1992, describing an on-site investigation of the Dulce and Archuleta Mesa area in New Mexico, which purportedly proved beyond any doubt that there is nothing there of any interest to UFO researchers despite PERSISTENT reports to the contrary; and

(3) "The K-2 Report", originally dated 28 July 1989 and revised 27 June 1992, which purports to document the discovery of a genuine "secret alien base" in the Pilot Peak area of Plumas County, California.

ParaNet quickly reviewed this material and posted it in its entirety for our subscribers, pursuant to the permissions attached to the material by the publisher. We also posted a preliminary evaluation which warned that the material might contain inaccuracies or deliberate disinformation.

This evaluation was based on a number of factors:

(1) much of the information in "The Ultimate Secret" about Operation Majestic Twelve and associated projects is clearly related to, and probably derived from, earlier material which has been dismissed as worthless by almost all reputable UFO researchers

(2) much of the information in "The Dulce Report" about Dulce and the Archuleta Mesa contradicts information already provided to ParaNet by other capable investigators

(3) some of the information in "The K-2 Report" is intrinsically implausible [although, admittedly, not impossible], such as the claim that a seasoned military intelligence operative 'forgot' his camera when rushing to document a UFO landing site, or that by the next day that same landing site had been re-sodded by the aliens to obliterate all the evidence.

THE DULCE PROTOCOL

ParaNet received the three documents as uploads from a Mr. Jack L. Mathias of Carson City, Nevada, who represented himself as the sole public spokesman for the Project. But the reports themselves name neither the authors of the documents nor the principals of the Phoenix Project. Instead, they cryptically state that they are the work of "former military personnel who have all been associated with intelligence activities, and have knowledge of covert government operations concerning UFO's" (AND also 'disinformation' projects? - Branton). Given the sorry history of anonymous documents and 'former' government agents in the UFO community, ParaNet felt it necessary to start its own investigation in an effort to determine just who was behind the Phoenix Project and what their motives might be.

First we sent a letter to the post office box listed in the documents, asking for further information about the group; but the letter was not answered. We corresponded by electronic mail with Mr. Mathias, who represents himself as an agent for the group, but he refused to provide any of the information we requested. So much for the direct approach.

Each document formally states that the Phoenix Project logo is a registered trademark [presumably in the state of Nevada, since that is where their mailing address is located], so we tried a query to the Nevada trademark office in Carson City. That office informed us that the state of Nevada has NO record of any current trademarks under the "Phoenix Project" name.

They did say that articles of incorporation were filed under the name of the Phoenix Project on 25 August 1988 by a Mr. Thomas Naylor of Las Vegas, Nevada. However, the corporation failed to file the names and addresses of its officers by 1 July 1989 as required by Nevada law, as a result of which the incorporation was revoked by the Nevada Secretary of State. And so we reached another apparent dead end, except for one bit of trivia uncovered by a ParaNet investigator in Las Vegas: An attorney named Thomas C. Naylor had recently moved into an office building at 2810 West Charleston in Las Vegas.

Next we contacted the U.S. Postal Service in Carson City, Nevada to determine the box holder for the Phoenix Project's publisher, Advent Publishing Company. We were told that the box was registered to a Richard T. Miller, whose address was given as a mobile-home park in Carson City.

Following this, we contacted the Clerk and Recorder's office in Carson City, and determined that a Richard Miller is listed with them as the legal owner of Advent Publishing. However, the telephone number they gave us for Mr. Miller has been disconnected, and directory assistance was unable to provide a new one. Another brick wall.

To this point, all attempts to verify the Phoenix Project's legitimacy using conventional methods had proved futile, so we decided to try a different approach. The Phoenix Project explicitly and emphatically disclaims affiliation with any other groups using the name 'Phoenix'. And just to make sure everyone gets the message, each document states at the beginning that "[i]n particular, there is no affiliation with a publisher known as America West, any of its publications, or the individuals known as George and Desiree Green"

(Note: one source has informed us that George Green has ties to the CIA. However, this source was not able to confirm this claim, and so it should be taken only as a 'possibility'. - Branton).

Unfortunately, ParaNet has uncovered evidence that these disclaimers may be intended to conceal rather than to illuminate.

America West, it turns out, is the publisher of a magazine called the Phoenix Liberator, which carries large quantities of channeled material alleged to originate with an entity from the Pleiades known as 'Hatonn'. The Phoenix Liberator has come under fire recently from some in the UFO community as anti-Semitic and neo-fascist. [See, for

266

THE DULCE PROTOCOL

example, "Hatonn's World: A Neo-Nazi ET?" by Don Ecker in the July/August 1992 issue of UFO Magazine.]

(Note: According to the video 'SECRETS OF THE THIRD REICH' -- available via Vladimir Terziski, President, American Academy of Dissident Sciences, 10970 Ashton Ave. #310, Los Angeles, CA 90024, phone and fax: USA-(310)-473-9717 -- the Nazi Thule society not only 'channeled' the Ashtar forces, but had developed several aerial disc designs, photographs of which are depicted in the film. One disc type was the 'Adamski' model.

Whether Adamski's contacts were actually 'Nazis' masquerading as 'Venusians', or whether the Nazi's had somehow gained access to a Venusian-Pleiadean scout ship is not clear at this time, however John Lear has stated that a small renegade 'Pleiadean' faction in Aldebaran which had sold itself over to the Ashtarian-Draconian agenda, had intentionally 'crashed' one of their ships -- loaded to the hilt with high-tech equipment -- so that they could get the technology to their Germanic/Bavarian allies while at the same time making an effort to seemingly by-pass the established non-intervention laws of the Saturnian-Lyran-Pleiadean-Andromedan 'Federation'.

Lear also claims that this Pleiadean-Ashtarian faction also wanted Germany to initiate a war which hopefully would reduce the population of the planet to a point where the Ashtar/Gizeh alliance or collective could establish more influence with less resistance in the international affairs of planet earth... this collaboration with the Bavarians also being motivated by certain extremist Interventionist and RACIST factions from Lyra and Aldebaran who were intent on making their 'Aryan' brothers on earth the dominant race. - Branton).

But 'Hatonn' and his defenders vehemently deny the charge [of being 'Nazis'], and the whole affair has been widely and rather nastily trumpeted both on the net and in print. It seems that until recently America West Publishers and the Phoenix Liberator were operated out of TEHACHAPI, California.

(This, according to many investigative sources, is a MAJOR center for collaborative alien and military-industrial activity - Branton).

But a few days ago one of ParaNet's subscribers uploaded a response from 'Hatonn' to Don Ecker, which he said he had pulled down from the Phoenix Liberator BBS; and with it he posted a new address for the Liberator. That address was all too familiar: 2810 West Charleston Boulevard, Las Vegas, Nevada -- THE SAME BUILDING, it seems, where an attorney named Thomas Naylor also has his new office.

And then another strange coincidence: A posting coming across the Internet stated that before 'Hatonn' channeled through his current host, he used to convey his messages through a Mr. RICHARD MILLER, who started an organization which was known as the Solar Cross and which was apparently a forerunner of the Phoenix Liberator.

(Note: These 'channeled' messages are apparently received through psionic beams from hovering craft which interact with micro-electronic implants that have been placed in various individuals who have been 'connected' to the Ashtar collective in this manner. - Branton).

Is this the same RICHARD MILLER who owns the Phoenix Project's publisher, Advent Publishing Company?

We do not yet know if the THOMAS NAYLOR who tried to incorporate the Phoenix Project is the same THOMAS NAYLOR who apparently SHARES 2810 West Charleston with the new offices of the Phoenix Liberator. We do not yet know if the RICHARD MILLER who owns Advent Publishing is the same RICHARD MILLER who reportedly once channeled 'Hatonn'.

THE DULCE PROTOCOL

In short, we do not yet know if the Phoenix Project is truly an independent organization, or merely another incarnation of America West Publishers and the Phoenix Liberator. But the coincidences are certainly striking and suggestive. And in light of this we again urge extreme caution in dealing with the Phoenix Project material, until such time as a definitive assessment of the Project's motives and reliability can be made.

ParaNet will keep you advised of our findings as they become available. If you have any information about the Phoenix Project, especially regarding its possible relationship with the Phoenix Liberator or America West Publishers, please send it to Michael Corbin by Internet mail to mcorbin@paranet.org; by Fidonet to 1:104/422; by U.S. Mail to P.O. Box 172, Wheat Ridge, CO 80034-0172; or by phone at 303-431-8796.

ParaNet(sm) Information Service - via ParaNet node 1:104/422
UUCP: !scicom!paranet!User_Name
INTERNET:
ParaNet(sm).Information.Service@p0.f428.n104.z1.FIDONET.ORG

From: ParaNet.Information.Service@p0.f428.n104.z1.FIDONET.ORG (ParaNet Information Service)
Newsgroups: alt.alien.visitors
Subject: Our Response to Phoenix Project
Message-ID: <139863.2A9405AD@paranet.FIDONET.ORG>
Date: 20 Aug 92 20:25:07 GMT
Sender: ufgate@paranet.FIDONET.ORG (newsout1.26)
Organization: FidoNet node 1:104/428.0 - Lines: 159
* Forwarded from "ParaNet UFO Echo"
* Originally from ParaNet Information Service
* Originally dated 08-20-92 13:23

Robert K Teske

On 6 August 1992, ParaNet Information Service posted a preliminary statement on our investigation into an organization known as the Phoenix Project, which had recently released "investigative reports" entitled "The Dulce Report", "The K-2 Report", and "The Ultimate Secret". In our statement we pointed out some apparent problems with all three Phoenix Project reports, as well as some suspicious aspects of the Project's organization itself. In our conclusion, we issued a warning not to take the Phoenix Project reports at face value, pending further investigation.

On 10 August 1992, Jack Mathias of the Phoenix Project responded in a long, rambling message posted to a number of bulletin boards and news groups. Unfortunately, rather than dealing with the substantive issues raised in our previous postings regarding the project and its publications, Mr. Mathias's statement consisted mostly of ad-hominem attacks impugning the motives, integrity, and competence of ParaNet's officers and investigators.

Here is some typical language excerpted from the Phoenix Project statement:

"... you blew it ..."
"... a snap judgment without examining the evidence ..."
"... your spontaneous and instant negative reaction ..."
"... your attitude problem ..."
"... you abused your position of trust and responsibility ..."
"... inexcusable ... a new record for prejudice ..."
"... you've just won the Golden Fleece Award ..."
"... outstanding ineptness ..."
"... amateur sleuthing ..."
"... self-centered ..."
"... lacking any real expertise ..."
"... seated upon your starry throne ..."
"... elected yourself to be the final arbiter of the truth ..."
" ... Judge, Jury, and Executioner ..."

THE DULCE PROTOCOL

" ... Kangaroo Court Proceeding of your own fashioning ..."

"... arm-chair expertise ..."

"... laughable ..."

Following paragraph after paragraph of this kind of personal invective, Mr. Mathias then suggests that:

"In our opinion, the public deserves the truth regarding the real story of UFO's, government involvement and the Alien threat. That should be our objective. ... Perhaps you'll agree that, that objective is more productive than entertaining the public via the BBS links with a side-show of petty squabbles and bickering between individuals and organizations."

This is a noble sentiment, and one which we at ParaNet wholeheartedly agree with. Hopefully in the future the Phoenix Project's representatives will take some of their own advice and try to keep the rhetoric down to a more civilized level.

Having said that, let's look at the actual issues raised by this latest salvo from the Phoenix Project, and see how they stack up.

Let us review the facts. You reacted by issuing a public warning to the members of ParaNet, which was also widely distributed via other BBS's nation-wide. That warning contained language, which implied the information, and the source, were highly suspect. Thus, single-handedly, you created a strong impression throughout the UFO community, that our information was false. Many sincere people, trusting your qualifications, accepted your warning.

True. You took it upon yourself to make a snap judgment without examining the evidence.

False. We did not arrive at our conclusion single-handedly or instantaneously. Our analysis and the resulting warning were the products of considerable discussion among ParaNet's researchers and subscribers. They were also labeled as tentative, pending further investigation.

"In your message, you mention that you wrote to the Phoenix Project, after the fact and your preliminary judgment, requesting further information. You made the same comment in other BBS messages. You state that we did not respond to your request. You also imply, by insinuation, that this is a mark against us and a further indication that we are suspect. ... To date we have not received your letter of inquiry. Apparently, of all the mail we receive, your letter is the only one that has gone astray. We can only conclude that it was either lost in the mail or you didn't mail it. Did it ever occur to you to mail us a second request, when you did not receive a response to your first inquiry?"

The letter was followed up with electronic mail to the Project's spokesman, Jack Mathias. The request for information was repeated through that channel. The request was refused.

"But, this was not the end of your attitude problem regarding the Phoenix Project. You did the same thing, again, issuing warnings, etc., with our release of the K-2 and the Ultimate Secret Reports. And, again, you had not seen or examined the supporting documents at the time you issued those warnings to ParaNet and the public."

We have already stated our reasons for suspecting the 'K-2' and "Ultimate Secret" reports. As with the 'Dulce' report, our suspicions went to the core of the entire concept and execution of both reports; consequently, it seemed unlikely that the "supporting documents" would make much difference. Our judgment in this matter was borne out when we received the "supporting documents" from another source. We were not impressed.

"Would we be out of line in concluding that your mind was already made-up?"

THE DULCE PROTOCOL

Yes, that would be out of line, since our minds were not and in fact are not yet entirely made up. Our warnings were tentative, and in our view totally justified. So far we have not been provided with any evidence to the contrary. If such evidence is provided, we will not only change our minds but say so publicly.

"Fortunately, for the UFO Movement, other investigators and researchers don't share your opinion."

That's not the feedback we've been getting.

"You state in your initial message that "much of the information in the Dulce Report about Dulce and the Archuleta Mesa contradicts information already provided to ParaNet by other capable investigators.

"What information? Who provided it? How did you determine its validity?

"Our information consists of the testimony of ParaNet investigators and others who have been in Dulce and on the Mesa. Their experiences were very different from what you describe, and it is difficult to reconcile your claims with the findings of our own people.

"We formally request access to that information. We'd like to examine it ourselves. Can we obtain copies of 'that' information? Our investigation continues, and the information will be made public when it is complete. At that time we will be glad to provide you with a complimentary copy of our report.

"Now, let us get to the main thrust of your message - your investigation to reveal the personnel of the Phoenix Project.

[several paragraphs of meaningless abuse deleted]

"What, if anything, is the Phoenix Project guilty of? Is it the fact that we dared to question and investigate two of the sacred cows of UFO-dom namely the ones you mentioned, i.e., "underground alien bases, and the cluster of government projects referred to collectively as Operation Majestic Twelve?"

ParaNet Information Service - via ParaNet node 1:104/422

UUCP: !scicom!paranet!User_Name

INTERNET: ParaNet.Information.Service@p0.f428.n104.z1.FIDONET.ORG

From: ParaNet.Information.Service@p0.f428.n104.z1.FIDONET.ORG (ParaNet Information Service)

Newsgroups: alt.alien.visitors

Subject: Phoenix Response - Part 2

Message-ID: <139864.2A9405B0@paranet.FIDONET.ORG>

Date: 20 Aug 92 20:25:09 GMT

Sender: ufgate@paranet.FIDONET.ORG (newsout1.26)

Organization: FidoNet node 1:104/428.0 - Lines: 168

* Forwarded from "ParaNet UFO Echo"

* Originally from ParaNet Information Service

* Originally dated 08-20-92 13:23

<..Continued from previous message>

No. ParaNet has long questioned both of those sacred cows. To this point we have seen no acceptable PROOF for the existence of any underground alien base near Dulce, nor have we seen adequate proof for the existence of "Operation Majestic Twelve". We have publicly stated as much on many occasions.

(Note: I personally believe that there is much 'evidence' for underground activity near Dulce. As for 'proof' -- along the line of a Network video crew broadcasting a Live Special Report from inside the Dulce underground labs or something of the sort -- admittedly that kind of 'proof' is yet to be forthcoming. - Branton)

THE DULCE PROTOCOL

According to our sources within the intelligence community, the Dulce Scam, perpetrated by the disinformation specialists of MAJI, better known to you as Majestic Twelve with help from the CIA and NSA, is considered one of their most brilliant success stories.

But, of course, these 'sources' cannot be named, and all we have to go on is your word that they even exist. And, unfortunately, you are making a concerted effort to keep anyone from knowing who *you* are, either. Anonymous stories relayed by anonymous story tellers. Sorry, but that's not 'evidence'.

We sent in experienced investigators, not amateurs, to check out the alleged Dulce Base. Those people knew what to look for, how to look for it, how to get answers, and are not easily mislead.

We have no evidence for this except your say-so.

If you do not agree with our findings, get off your posterior, go to Dulce, and check it out for yourself.

We have.

In fact, we invite anybody to do the same thing. We're sure you'll find exactly what we did...

We didn't.

You imply that you're good at asking questions -- how are you at answering them? We have a few questions ... Would you mind sharing with all of us, everyone on the BBS's and the public, what hard evidence you have that, without question, supports the presence and validity of the Dulce Base.

Would you mind sharing what hard evidence you have that we ever said anything of the kind? We have never said anything in support of the presence of a secret alien base at Dulce. In point of fact, we consider it extremely unlikely that any such base exists -- at Dulce or anywhere else.

That's one of the reasons we have so much trouble with your 'K-2' report, which purports to document the existence of just such a base in California.

Unless you have irrefutable evidence to present, made available for public scrutiny and evaluation, which invalidates the findings of the Phoenix Project regarding Dulce, K-2, or the Ultimate Secret, or our future reports, back off. Either put-up or shut-up. In other words, get off our back.

All right, challenge accepted. Let's start with this statement from your "Ultimate Secret" report:

According to eye-witness testimony, the CIA agent in charge of this covert operation, wearing the uniform of an AF Colonel, was William C. Cooper. ... This witness testifies that this is the same William C. Cooper, who has been prominent since 1988 in the civilian UFO movement.

Is this "William C. Cooper" supposed to be the famous Bill Cooper we have all come to know so well? Apparently so. Unfortunately, in his own published documents Bill Cooper gives his full name as "Milton William Cooper", not "William C. Cooper". Either Cooper doesn't know his own name, or the Phoenix Project's "eye witness" doesn't know what he's talking about.

And while we're on the subject of Bill Cooper, it is instructive to compare some of the text of the Phoenix Project's "Ultimate Secret" document with some of Bill

THE DULCE PROTOCOL

Cooper's material on the same subject. Cooper writes in his "Operation Majority -- Final Release":

BC> [Project Grudge] was financed by CIA confidential funds [non appropriated] and money from the illicit drug trade ... The purpose of Project Grudge was to collect all scientific, technological, medical and intelligence information from UFO/IAC sightings and contacts with alien life forms. This orderly file of collected information has been used to advance the United States Space Program.

Now look at the corresponding paragraph of the Phoenix Project's "Ultimate Secret" report:

PP> Project Aquarius was funded by CIA confidential funds [non-appropriated] ... The purpose of Project Aquarius was to collect all scientific, technological, medical and intelligence information from UFO/IAC sightings and contacts with alien life forms. This orderly file of collected information has been used to advance the United States' Space Program and provided the data needed to develop present stealth technology.

You don't have to be an intelligence agent to see that these two passages are virtually identical in both content and phrasing. Since Cooper's statement is dated 10 January 1989, more than half a year before the "Ultimate Secret" report's 'origination' date of 4 August 1989, we seem to be left with three possibilities:

(1) Cooper was somehow privy to the Phoenix Project's investigative results even before they were first put to paper; or,

(2) the Phoenix Project plagiarized Cooper's writings; or

(3) the Phoenix Project's own investigations drew on the same [original] sources as Cooper apparently did in compiling his own materials.

Whichever one you pick, it's not a pretty picture. But it gets worse:

PP> The basic information revealing the existence of Operation Majestic-12, the crashed UFOs, alien beings, and their secret bases within the United States, was obtained through the Freedom of Information Act from the files of the CIA, NSA, FBI, State Department, the U.S. Air Force.

This is utter nonsense, as any perusal of published FOIA documents on UFOs would quickly reveal. FOIA requests have forced the government to disgorge many hundreds of pages of UFO documents over the years, but they provide little if any support for the existence of Operation Majestic Twelve, crashed saucers, alien beings, or secret bases.

If the Phoenix Project is relying on already published documents as their source for this claim [e.g., "The UFO Cover-UP" by Lawrence Fawcett and Barry Greenwood, or "Above Top Secret" by Timothy Good], then clearly they have not examined them very carefully.

On the other hand, if the project really does have such explosive FOIA documents in its possession, let's see them; their publication would do more to establish the project's credibility than anything else it could possibly do short of producing a live alien.

PP> PROJECT GRUDGE: This project was originally established in 1953, by order of President Eisenhower and is under the control of the CIA, NSA, and MAJI. Project Grudge went underground and another project, Project Sign, was established as a cover operation. In 1960, the Project's name was changed from Project SIGN to Project Bluebook.

This is demonstrably and totally wrong. Project Sign was established first, in 1947, and it was under the control of the Air Force, not the CIA. The name was changed to Project Grudge in 1949, and to Blue Book in 1952 -- not 1960. [For details, see "The

THE DULCE PROTOCOL

Report on Unidentified Flying Objects" by Edward J. Ruppelt, who headed the project from 1951 to 1953.] The exact dates slide around a little bit depending on whether you're talking about when the decision was made, when the order was signed, or when the order became effective; but the differences are on the order of months, not decades!

How could the Phoenix Project's experienced intelligence agents make so many ludicrous errors in a single paragraph?

ParaNet Information Service - via ParaNet node 1:104/422

UUCP: !scicom!paranet!User_Name

INTERNET: ParaNet.Information.Service@p0.f428.n104.z1.FIDONET.ORG

From: ParaNet.Information.Service@p0.f428.n104.z1.FIDONET.ORG (ParaNet Information Service)

Newsgroups: alt.alien.visitors

Subject: Phoenix Response - Conclusion

Message-ID: <139865.2A9405B4@paranet.FIDONET.ORG>

Date: 20 Aug 92 20:25:11 GMT

Sender: ufgate@paranet.FIDONET.ORG (newsout1.26)

Organization: FidoNet node 1:104/428.0 - Lines: 222

* Forwarded from "ParaNet UFO Echo"

* Originally from ParaNet Information Service

* Originally dated 08-20-92 13:24

<<..Continued from previous message>>

In fact, this whole business was such an embarrassing mess that the Phoenix Project issued a 'correction' document to try to straighten it out. But, ironically, the correction is also wrong -- just less obviously so.

We could go on, but I think you get the point. The "Ultimate Secret" report is, at best, a rehash of other people's garbage.

At worst, it is a deliberate effort to confuse and disinform.

PP> We actively encourage other serious investigators to use the information we have provided as a basis for conducting their own inquiry and to carry-on our effort. Can you, Mr. Corbin, or ParaNet, or Mufon, make the same claim? Or, is it true that the results of critical investigations are held sacred by the elite leadership of these organizations, and are not shared with the member's of their organizations or the public?

We can't speak for other organizations, but in the case of ParaNet we have always made our results public as soon as our investigations are complete.

PP> In your message, you insinuate that because of our past military and intelligence backgrounds, our area of expertise so-to-speak, that the motives of the Phoenix Project are suspect. You further insinuate that we are possibly government operatives attempting to send serious researchers off on a variety of wild goose chases.

Given the prior history of government disinformation in ufology, most of it purveyed by active or former intelligence agents and their victims, anyone who,

(1) purports to have a military intelligence background,
(2) refuses to divulge their identity, and
(3) propagates known disinformation as reliable intelligence [whether deliberately or not], should expect his motives to be considered suspect until proven otherwise. It is extremely naive of you to think it would happen any other way.

PP> If anyone needed assurance that the truth regarding UFO's will remain a deep, dark, secret -- they can rest secure in the knowledge that you, are on the job. There are any number of government agencies who would welcome you with open arms. Expect some offers.

Sorry, none so far. We'll let you know if we get any.

PP> We are sure that the honest and sincere members of ParaNet and other UFO investigative organizations [and there are many] must be seriously considering whether your qualifications, fitness and investigative ability warrant your continuance in a position of leadership within what used to be a respected research organization.

(Note: In my own experience with misinformation, disinformation and dubunker 'agents', very little effort is made to address the information at hand or rationally explain-away information, claims or data that is being released by an individual. Most of the efforts on the part of such agents are directed against the individuals themselves, as in character assassinations and attacks. In many cases they KNOW that they cannot refute the information, so they attempt to discredit the information through character assassination.

Do police officers immediately "discredit" what a drug dealer tells them when he is exposing his superiors so that he himself can acquire a lesser sentence, or what a convicted child molester might tell them about a ritual child abuse ring that he has been involved with? No, especially if there is sufficient evidence to back up their claims. Someone who has been involved personally with some illicit activity can be more of a reliable source than someone who just hears about it second-hand. So the character assassination strategy by certain agents does not hold water especially in a case such as this, wherein ParaNet officials have had their character and integrity UNJUSTLY attacked in order to DIVERT ATTENTION from the subject at hand, OR TO DIVERT ATTENTION FROM THE LACK OF INTEGRITY OR OUTRIGHT DECEITFULNESS OF THESE 'AGENTS' THEMSELVES.

I personally do not claim to be the infallible specimen of a perfect human being. I have a jail record, and suffer from emotional and psychological disabilities resulting from years of suppressed interactions with what I believe to be malevolent alien agendas and certain human agencies which are or were involved with them. Although the psychological-emotional turmoil or instability may not be entirely my fault, the jail term was a result of my own irresponsibility. What I am trying to say is that I do not CLAIM to have it all together any more than the average human being does, so why engage in 'character assassination' against someone who lives in a world whose overall inhabitants are generally lacking in perfect character? Show me someone with full awareness of "good and evil" that has never broken a law or one of the ten commandments. Aside from the Messiah Himself, there is no human being on earth that can make such a claim.

And most often then not, when someone targets an individual for character assassination, as they say, "It takes one to know one." So in the search for the truth about what is really happening in this world, I would suggest that you do not get caught-up in emotional exchanges and character attacks which only serve to cloud the real issue -- which is WHETHER THE INFORMATION ITSELF IS OR IS NOT CORRECT! This is not to say that 'character' has no bearing whatsoever on information. For instance someone who has been known in the past to be a con artist might not be taken as seriously as an ORIGINAL SOURCE of information as, you might say, someone who has won a Pulitzer prize for investigative journalism. However we do need to keep a 'balance'. - Branton)

Exactly the opposite, actually. Most of our people are grateful for the warning, and are coming to the same conclusions as we did.

PP> Instead of making an honest attempt to validate or disprove our findings regarding the subjects mentioned -- missing the point completely, you chose to become obsessed with determining the identity of Phoenix Project personnel. For what reason? Do you intend to judge the validity of the information based on the credentials of those providing it? Some people would interpret that as putting the cart before the horse.

THE DULCE PROTOCOL

And some people would interpret it as a determination not to fall prey to the same fate as far too many others in this field, who trusted strangers too easily and ended up wasting years chasing wild geese -- or worse...

PP> You suggest a possible link between our organization and America West. Sorry about that, but you're dead wrong. It has come to us from several sources that we're not on their list of favorite people. We will take this opportunity to categorically deny that we have any affiliation with America West, their publication the "Phoenix Liberator," or any other publication they provide. Do not expect us to respond to the other coincidences, suppositions, insinuations or innuendoes contained in your message.

Why? Perhaps because there are other 'insinuations' that cannot be truthfully denied? As a matter of fact, we now have solid confirmation of another one of our 'insinuations' -- i.e., the fact that the Richard Miller who owns Advent Publishing is indeed the same Richard Miller who used to channel 'Hatonn'. That confirmation came from none other than Mr. Miller himself. So I guess we're not doing too badly.

In consideration of your explicit denials of any ties to America West, and in view of the additional information provided privately by Mr. Miller, we withdraw our previous suggestion of possible connections between the Phoenix Project and the America West/Phoenix Liberator operation. As we stated before, those suggestions were tentative pending further investigation, and further investigation has not uncovered any additional evidence to support them.

Unfortunately, this is the kind of burden that the Phoenix Project inevitably took on when it chose to publicly portray itself as a clandestine organization.

PP> Since you brought up America West and The "Phoenix Liberator," why not turn your investigative abilities loose on their organization. Just suppose that Milton Cooper is, quietly, linked to their organization. That should intrigue you... Equally intriguing, is where their funding comes from - not the obvious subscription income - the covert funding. Or, how about the busy and numerous, off premise, writers that prepare the volumes of 'Hatonn' material, and their use of high-speed modems to provide the copy for each weekly issue of the "Phoenix Liberator" and the dozens of books they produce. In our supposition, we're talking about a big-time operation. You might also check out their printing facilities, distribution centers, and world-wide circulation. Equally fascinating is their sudden rise, in a few short years, to the top of the New Age Movement. You might even think to ask yourself, why the New Age Movement? What possible connection is there with covert government UFO activities, or a New World Order, with the New Age Movement? The answer to that might be revealed, if you dig deep enough, and discover high-speed modem links between their headquarters and certain organizations located at Langley and Ft. Meade. Yes, if you really dig, you might uncover all kinds of interesting things about America West.

Thanks for the tip.

(Note: I may be wrong, but this sounds very similar to the ramblings of <u>cultists who have broken off from the 'mother' sect</u> to establish their own branch cults... essentially agreeing with the basic 'belief system' -- which in this case might be the channeling of 'Ashtar' intelligence's -- while at the same time claiming that 'they' and not their former 'apostate leaders' are the sole spokesmen for the 'higher powers' on earth. As for the religious 'denomination' in which I was raised, one which dominates a major western state and stretches the Constitutional restrictions on separation of church and state to their uttermost limits, I have come to find out that over 500 'branch' religions ranging from a few followers to tens of thousands of followers have separated from the 'main' denomination. This is one of the main reasons why I became a non-denominationalist Judeo-Christian.

One of these 500-or-so branches incidentally was the 'Freeman Order' which was involved in a drawn-out FBI stand-off in 1996. The U.S. Constitution and Bill of Rights allows for the right to worship as one wishes SO LONG AS one does not infringe on the constitutional rights of others and the laws of the land. Of course 'inquisitional' or 'terrorist' religious practices, or the 'religious' practice of ritual child abuse, or religious institutions that attempt to force their will upon an elected government, or one whose members in government use taxpayer funds or personal influence to show political favoritism towards their 'churches', have no place in a Constitutional Democratic-Republic.

Nor does a our Constitutional system have to put up with cults like the 'Freemen' who have blatantly resisted the PUBLICLY-instituted legal restrictions against money fraud or child sexual abuse, even if the 'Freeman' or similar cults hypocritically use 'Ruby Ridge', 'Waco' or other legitimate yet incendiary catch-phrases to justify their own illegal activities. - Branton)

PP> As to your effort in trying to identify staff personnel of the Phoenix Project -- good luck. However, we do have to admit that you may get lucky and hit on a couple of them. However, since there are many, it is doubtful you will ever get beyond that point.

Our only interest in the personnel of the Phoenix Project is to determine whether the Project has a hidden agenda, and whether it is covertly linked to other organizations whose agendas are known. That interest was made necessary by the Project's clandestine nature and consequent lack of public accountability. You brought it on yourselves, and your continuing hostility and evasiveness suggest that we were not entirely mistaken in our suspicions.

Our investigation continues. We'll let you know what we find out.

Michael Corbin
Director
ParaNet Information Service
END

ParaNet Information Service - via ParaNet node 1:104/422

UUCP: !scicom!paranet!User_Name

INTERNET: ParaNet.Information.Service@p0.f428.n104.z1.FIDONET.ORG

(Note: For what it's worth, here are my 2-cents – I found this bantering back and forth between ParaNet and Phoenix Project to be like "sibling rivalry on steroids". ParaNet: "Did not!" Phoenix Project: "Did so!" ParaNet: "Did NOT!" Phoenix Project: "Did SO!" On and on and on ad-nauseous! – Robert K. Teske)

Chapter 17

The Black Budget And The Underground Empire

On Oct. 20, 1991, California researcher Michael Lindemann, founder of 'The 20/20 Group', gave a lecture before a large crowd of interested investigators.

During the course of his lecture wherein he discussed the Military-Industrial Complex's underground bases outside of Lancaster, California, he made the following statements:

"...How many of you have seen the book 'BLANK CHECK'? It is not a UFO book. I strongly recommend that you read the book 'BLANK CHECK' so that you can understand something about how these projects are funded without your say so, indeed without the say so of Congress. Most citizens don't know for example that the National Security Act of 1947 made it illegal to ever say how much money is spent on the CIA. Indeed all of our tremendous alphabet soup collection of Intelligence Agencies. Whether your talking about the CIA, or the NRO, or the NSA or the DIA, etc., all of them are in the same category.

"You cannot say how much these things cost. All you can do if you want to find out is add-up the numbers on the Budget that aren't assigned to anything that actually means anything. There are these huge categories that have tens of billions of dollars in them that say nothing but 'Special Projects...' And every year the Congress dutifully passes this bloated budget that has some $300,000,000,000 or more with HUGE chunks of cash labeled like that: 'Special Projects,' 'Unusual Stuff.' -- Ten billion dollars. O.K., well where does the 'unusual stuff' money go? Well, it DOES go to 'unusual stuff', that's for sure, and one of the places it goes is that it goes into the underground bases. Indeed TIM said recently since the publication of his book [BLANK CHECK]... MORE Black Budget money goes into underground bases than ANY OTHER kind of work.

"Now I don't believe that 35 billion, which is the approximate size of the black budget money that you can find by analyzing the budget, I don't think that comes CLOSE to the real figure because there is absolutely unequivocal evidence that a great deal of additional money was generated in other ways, such as the surreptitious running of guns and drugs. And one wonderful example of that is coming to light with the B.C.C.I. scandal which I hope you've heard of... a number of very high-ranking American officials are caught in the undertow of the BCCI tidal wave... Even though these guys are tying to pull 'fast ones' on an immense scale they are getting caught. These things don't always work. Indeed they are very, very vulnerable.

Indeed this whole 'end game' is very vulnerable and that's why they feel it requires such secrecy. The American people wouldn't stand for this stuff if they had the information, and that's the reason why we have to get the information out and take it seriously because it really is a matter of our money and our future that's being mortgaged here.

"But my friend who worked in the underground bases, who was doing sheet-rock was down on, he thinks, approximately the 30th level underground... these bases are perhaps 30-35 stories deep ['ground-scrapers']. As I say they are not just mine shafts, these are huge, giant facilities... many city blocks in circumference, able to house tens of thousands of people. One of them, the YANO Facility [we're told... by the county fire dept. director, the county fire dept. chief who had to go in there to look at a minor fire infraction] there's a 400-car parking lot on the 1st level of the YANO Facility, but cars never come in and out, those are the cars that they use INSIDE.

"O.K., so... a very interesting situation down there. Our guy was doing sheet-rock on the 30th floor, maybe the 30th floor, underground. He and his crew are working on a wall and right over here is an elevator door. The elevator door opens and, a kind of reflex action you look, and he saw three 'guys'. Two of them, human engineers that he's seen before. And between them a 'guy' that stood about 8 to 8 1/2 feet tall. Green skin, reptilian features, extra-long arms, wearing a lab coat, holding a clip-board...

"I tend to believe that story because, first of all because we have other stories like it, but more importantly because he walked off that job that very day. And he was getting paid a GREAT deal of money... If your basically a sheet-rock kind of guy, if you can do sheet-rock in a place like that then you get paid way more than standard sheet-rock wages, you can count on it.

"So, he walked off that job. His buddy on that same crew turned into an alcoholic shortly after. This is an extremely upsetting thing. You know, it wasn't like this alien jumped out and bit his head off or anything, it was just standing there for a few minutes, the doors closed. He has a feeling that that elevator was malfunctioning, otherwise he never would have seen that except by accident..."

According to former Wackenhut employee Michael Riconosciuto, there is a direct underground connection between the Nevada Military Complex and the underground facilities near Lancaster, California, such as the Tehachapi mountain base.

Several people have referred to the subsurface as well as the operational 'connections' between the Dulce base in New Mexico and the Dreamland or Area-51 base in Nevada, connections that exist via Dugway, Utah and Page, Arizona. If alien forces are intent on taking control of this planet, then it would be logical for them to target our major military weapons research and development centers.

Robert K Teske

This might involve actual 'infiltration' of our military-industrial complexes and control of the line-of-command through mind control of specific and strategic personnel. The 'deeper' one descends into the underground 'alien empire' the greater the security and therefore the greater the 'control' will be in regards to this "...from the bottom up..." takeover attempt. In many cases patriotic Americans have become caught in the middle of this 'underground war' between loyal American military personnel and alien or alien-controlled 'personnel', as was the case in the Dulce and the Groom wars themselves.

Some have managed to escape from their terrifying encounters and -- whether intentionally or unintentionally, as in the following incident -- have voiced their fears, concerns or even rage to those on the 'outside' who will listen.

The following conversation, in relation to the Nevada Military Complex and the 'underground facilities', took place on the "Billy Goodman Happening" - KVEG Radio 840 AM, Las Vegas, Nevada, on November 19, 1989. It was transcribed by a Las Vegas resident.

Billy Goodman incidentally, has personally planned visits, in collaboration with KNBC Radio in Los Angeles, to observe the 'disks' which are being tested at Groom Lake, Nevada. Goodman and others claimed to have seen these disks in operation, and back-up these claims with video documentation. One such video shows a hovering object making a vertical ascent, stopping in mid-air, followed by a horizontal traverse, followed by another vertical ascent. Something like this would be impossible for any conventionally known aircraft of the time to duplicate. Billy Goodman, who has since moved to another radio station in Los Angeles, has been very instrumental in getting the information out about the underground base at Site 51 [or Area-51].

One contact of ours has informed us that a good friend of hers in Las Vegas, Nevada, had uncovered some very disturbing facts and testimonies concerning construction workers and others who had been involved in the installation of certain equipment within the tunnels beneath the Nevada Military Complex, and particularly under the Mercury, Nevada area.

Many of these later died under bizarre circumstances, and there were rumors that others were being held captive underground because they "saw too much". This informant, Stacey Borland, was later found dead -- along with a brother of hers -- in Las Vegas, as the result of a gangland-type execution. Someone had apparently entered her place and murdered them in cold blood.

In the following annotated transcript, the caller who claims to be a worker in the underground facilities below Mercury, Nevada, will be identified as 'C' and Billy Goodman as 'G':

G: Hi! Your on the Billy Goodman Happening on KVEG! Sir, what can I do for you tonight?

C: O.K. Are you ready? Hang on to your seats! Here goes! We are going 3,000 feet underground! O.K. We get to that point, 3,000 feet. We come out into a stainless steel atmosphere... and we come upon people that are ah... construction people... working people, and so forth that are supposed to be in that area. Then we come upon another people who push us into another little room. They tell us, "Do not come out of that area, until you're told to." These guys are 6 minute marines, all right? They tell us, "If you do, you are going to get hurt!" OK? So we are construction workers!

G: Where are you working? Where is what you are describing to us.

C: On a certain test site!

G: A certain test site! Which one? You can't reveal which one?

C: We're kind'a mixed up! We don't know what the hell is going on. We're making ah... good bucks... and everything has come down on us... and they are hurting us! OK? So we are contractors! We are workers! OK? So there's a person that I called and explained what is happening to me and they told me to call you and tell you! So, that is what I am doing right now! Calling you!

G: You presented it in a very odd way! First of all I didn't know if you were going to be serious or what! Are you saying to me that you are a construction worker and you had to go 3,000 feet under ground? First of all what would you be doing underground? Let me ask you that!

C: We are running lights and power.

G: And who assigned you this job?

C: It's through Reynold's Electronics. I have to say that because I get my pay check from someone else!

(<u>Note</u>: Reynold's Electronics is a branch of "E.G. & G." Corporation which DOES IN FACT work with and contract through the Nevada and Utah Test Sites - Branton)

G: They tell you to put these lights underground?

C: Yeh, but there's more to it than that! I'm sort of afraid of expressing. Am I talking to you or what?

G: Yes, you are talking directly to me!

C: OK. You know some of the things that are happening, shouldn't be. It should be made public! The public should know what the hell is going on! And it scares the hell out of me. What is not being brought out you know? For example, can I give you an example? Here's an example! A few weeks back we were inside a certain cavern going through stainless steel halls, going north, and as we move along we are hanging lights. In the rooms are... they're like operating rooms. All of a sudden, off the elevator, our U.S. Marines come out, crash us down off our scaffold, pushing us down, and then into a room. This is taking a hell of a lot out of me to tell you this right now! The bosses come into the room and we're getting debriefed and all this kind of stuff and all of a sudden they are carrying fixed bayonets. Now I fought in Vietnam and I thought these guys were my buddies! Oh, no way! Forget it! These guys are from outer space! These people brought these little characters on gurneys, OK? They had big heads and little bodies and they went into this little room. Then, behind them, these doctors in white coats and stuff! And we was really at ah... we didn't know what the hell was going on! We were shocked to hell! ...I was SCARED man!

G: Well, sure you didn't know what was going on and didn't expect it! I guess them handling you upset you first of all. Being man to man, you thought why should you treat me this way! And that's to be expected. As far as knowing where you are I have no idea.

C: I know where I was! I worked there every day! I keep a log and if someone asks me I know what's going on! I'm telling you man they're not telling us the truth. There is something damn wrong within our government. I only got a glimpse of this scientist on television (i.e. most likely referring to Robert Lazar - Branton), but I know he's not telling much of what he knows. I'm just a worker. A hammer and nail man. This guy's got more brains than I do, and would know more about it than I do. There's something INSIDE they aren't telling us!

G: OK. I understand that! Now what do you want us to do about it?

C: EXPOSE IT!!!

G: I think you've done that yourself, just now! Now you haven't told us your location and I think that's important so we have some idea where this is. I hope you understand at this moment...

C: I work at Mercury, Nevada and I'm the best electrician there. This is between you and me now. I don't want anybody else to know about this!

G: But you're on the air Sir!

C: You mean somebody knows about this besides you and me?

G: But you are talking over the radio, Sir! Everybody, all over the West Coast that is listening has just heard you! So you've gotten your word out. Now let's see if anybody else knows about it. Maybe just maybe, we'll get some calls from some of the people that work with you.

C: Wait a minute! You mean somebody else knows about this besides you and me?

G: Now, this is a talk show, you called a talk show. I am over the radio -- that's where you called!

C: OH, MY GOD!!!

G: Why, what's wrong with that? You called a talk show!

C: I thought I was just talking to you!

G: Now you said someone told you to call me. Was it someone you work with?

C: Yes.

THE DULCE PROTOCOL

G: Nobody knows who you are. You haven't said your name or anything! Now, let's see if anyone will back up your story!

C: But I didn't know other people would hear this. Now I'm scared for my life! There's tremendous stuff out there that's being hidden. It's being corrupted inside. It's being stashed away.

G: Well that's what we do here. We are trying to bring the information out, and it's people like yourself who are making that happen. They bring us information all the time! Are you trying to bring the information out yourself because you don't like what's going on?

C: I fear for my life because I've seen what happened. I fear for my life because the government is lying to me.

G: OK. Why do you fear for your life? Have you been threatened?

C: Before you even go down in the pit they threaten you! That is you tell anything of what you saw, you are dead!!!

G: But you're not saying more than what you saw. Is there anything else you want to say before we say thank you for calling?

C: Yes, one other thing. Whenever it gets down to the nitty gritty, it will be clear to the people, that what they are seeing on the news, is true! We've got six little bodies under ground, man!!!

G: Please keep in touch, OK? [end of transcript]

Chapter 18

Dulce & the Military-Industrial Establishment

Researcher William F. Hamilton was one of the first to write about the Mt. Shasta subterranean colony of TELOS, an underground city which is said to be the western branch of a subterranean kingdom that certain Asian fraternities refer to as the 'Agharti' network. Mr. Hamilton had personally met with the reputed "crown princess" of Telos, Sharula -- as well as with some of her immediate relatives in the mid-1980s, during his investigations into underground base activity in North America. Based on what Bill has learned, Telos might not be as 'safe' a place to live as one might at first believe.

Just like anywhere else on earth, Telos itself suffers from its own conflicts between factions with different agendas -- ranging from those who align themselves with the "Andro-Pleiadean Federation" and their "Non-Interventionist - Individualist" beliefs, and those who have taken sides with the "Draco-Orion Empire" and their "Interventionist - Collectivist" philosophies.

One might say that the scenarios taking place within Telos are somewhat of a counterpart of similar power-struggles taking place within "Sirius" and within the U.S. government.

The same could hold true within the entire 'Agharti' network which has its center of activity under the Gobi desert of Mongolia, and which allegedly contained two opposing factions during the Second World War period:

- the Technologists who secretly sided with the Allied Forces
- and the Occultists who sided with the Axis Forces

Since the Telos-Agharti alliance is tied-in with the Ashtar collective, there are bound to be some internal conflicts within those cultures just as there have been reported conflicts between the Orionite interventionists and Pleiadean non-interventionists within the Ashtarian collective itself.

All this is based on reports from contactee Israel Norkin and others that the Ashtar collective has been infiltrated by Draconian-Orionite agents posing as "ascended masters", and that a large segment of the "Ashtar Command" has been commandeered by these interventionist-collectivist forces and has split off from another large segment of the 'alliance' which has apparently sided with the Andro-Pleiadean Federation. What distinguishes the two is that the Andro-Pleiadean Federation believes in Truth-Individualism-Non Interventionism whereas the Draco-Orion Empire adheres to a philosophy of Deception-Collectivism-Interventionism.

According to contactee Alex Collier these two factions are now or have been at war within the Sirius-B system, and this conflict has entered the Sol system with the Draconian-Orion reptilians and their paraphysical overlords operating from Hale-Bopp comet in collaboration with their rebel Sirian cultists who were/are operating from within the "infiltrated" segment of the Ashtar collective, occupying Hale-Bopp's so-called "Companion" battleship -- reputedly a "...former Sirian alliance battleship..." -- which some have dubbed "Hale-Mary".

THE DULCE PROTOCOL

This Saturn-shaped object was seen AND photographed by BOTH Chuck Shramek AND is also seen in a leaked Hubble Space Telescope image, along with other 'objects' that apparently 'jumped ship' as the comet circled around the sun. This scenario seems to be reminiscent of the movie "LIFE FORCE" which depicted a race of draconian-like alien 'vampires' that entered the system undetected in the tail of a comet.

Alex Collier claims that the non-interventionist from the Pleiades and Andromeda constellations, from Tau Ceti, Procyon and others systems, have "blockaded" the Sol system near the orbital sphere of Neptune in order to keep the Draconian-Orionite forces out and to keep them from interfering with our planet at this CRITICAL and VULNERABLE point in planet earth's history.

According to Collier's other-worldly friends, there have been devastating battles with casualties on both sides that have been waged between the Federation and the Empire in this CURRENT "war in heaven" [current as this is being written] involving our Sol system, and also in one that was waged shortly before this in the Sirius system... a war that has gravitated from Sirius to our own Sol system. So, PRAY FOR our "friends out there" who are risking their lives for OUR sakes. It is the very LEAST that we can do...

William Hamilton incidentally has voiced his concern that Sharula, being a member of the ruling class of Telos, seems to be involved in this current conflict taking place between the two Ashtarian factions, the Draco-Orion faction and the Andro-Pleiadean faction, although just how this has affected her on a personal basis is unclear. This may also hold true with the entire "Melchizedek Order" which has a major presence in Telos, in the Saturnian moon base-cities, in Sirius, in Arcturus and elsewhere.

Most of the misled Sirian cultists are being led to believe that the New World Order is being orchestrated for the purpose of establishing world peace and laying the groundwork to usher in a "planetary ascension" into higher dimensions in a harmonious and orderly fashion.

They forget however the history of atrocities that have followed the ancient Bavarian-Roman cults who are promoting the New World Order and of their reptilian hosts in Draconis and Orion... the massacres in Lyra, Rigel and Procyon being a few examples (if you don't know what I'm talking about at this point, you WILL by the time you finish this 'volume'. - Branton).

In short, the Draconians and Orions are psychologically and emotionally manipulating their cultic human followers in Sirius-B, the Gizeh empire & Bavaria who are tied-in with the "dark side" of the Ashtar collective, to establish a global government which they intend to annex to their Luciferian Interstellar empire-collective.

William Hamilton himself has gained a great deal of 'intelligence' on the secret government's underground bases, many of which are as of this writing under the control of the 'collaboration', or those military-industrialists who have sold-out to the humanoid-reptiloid collaborators from Draconis, Orion & Sirius-B, who are more-or-less given free reign within the secret government's underground network.

In an article which appeared in Patrick O'Connell's "TRENDS AND PREDICTIONS ANALYST" Newsletter, Vol. 6, No. 2 [July, 1990] issue, William Hamilton stated:

"...The cover-up was initiated soon after the Roswell, N.M. crash. We wanted to know,
    1] Who they were
    2] Why they were here
    3] How their technology worked

THE DULCE PROTOCOL

The cover-up became a matter of NATIONAL SECURITY [a blanket word covering secrecy and deception]. The cover-up involves secret organizations within our government such as MJ-12, PI-40, MAJI, Delta, the Jason Scholars, & known intelligence organizations such as Naval Intelligence, Air Force Office of Special Investigation (AFOSI), the Defense Investigative Service (DIS), the CIA, NSA, and more! It involves THINK TANKS such as RAND, the Ford Foundation, the Aspen Institute, & Brookings Institute. It involves corporations such as Bechtel, GE, ITT, Amoco, Northrup, Lockheed, & many others.

It involves SECRET SOCIETIES who may be the hidden bosses of the orchestrated events [i.e. economic collapse, wars, assassinations, conspiracies to manipulate & control humans & thereby to exercise enormous power over the destiny of the human race] - the Illuminati, Masons, Knights of Malta, etc. The individual players are too numerous to list. The whole of this conspiracy forms an INTERLOCKING NEXUS. The goal is said to be a ONE WORLD GOVERNMENT [Dictatorship]!

"'The Underground Nation' - The RAND symposium held on Deep Underground Construction indicated that plans were hatched during the 50's to build underground bases, laboratories, & city-complexes linked by a stupendous network of tunnels to preserve & protect the ongoing secret interests of the secret societies.

These secret societies made a pact with alien entities in order to further motives of domination..."

Actually, as it turns out, THEY [the secret societies] are now being 'dominated' by the 'aliens'. One can only assume that if certain humans would 'sell out' their own kind to an alien race and use such an unholy alliance to gain domination over their fellow man, then they should consider the fact that they, according to universal law, must in the same way open THEMSELVES up to manipulation and control by their supposed benefactors.

Thus one can see the utter insanity of hoping to establish domination of others by petitioning the assistance of an Imperialistic alien force. The human 'elite' may think that their reptilian collectivist hosts will shower their egos with praise and rewards for their cooperation in selling out their own planet, but in reality the draconians consider the human elite as being useless "weeds", as they do all humans in general, but necessary fodder in order to carry out their agenda.

Mr. Hamilton continues:

"...The underground complexes are not confined to the U.S. alone! A large underground complex operated by 'the U.S.' exists at Pine Gap, near Alice Springs, Australia.

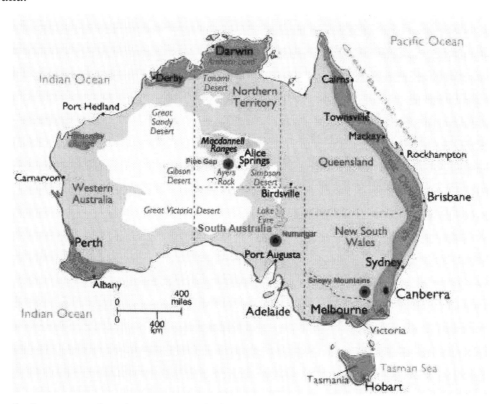

"...It appears that the secret societies among us have become aware of the coming planetary eco-catastrophe & the possibility of an earth polar shift in the near future. Surveying the earth from space, satellites & shuttles reveal EXTENSIVE DAMAGE TO OUR ECOSPHERE! Our planet is wobbling on its axis & its magnetic field is decaying! Ozone depletion & the greenhouse effect are rapidly endangering life on our planet. Alternatives, which include,

    1] Direct handling of the atmospheric problems

    2] taking shelter in underground domains

    3] escape to other planetary bodies in the solar system, have been devised in secret

However there is a possible Alternative 4 which mostly depends on a completely different idea on how to save the earth..."

(Note: this MAY be, in essence, a project to colonize other 'dimensional' frequencies or densities that exist elsewhere within the super spectrum of the ONE Omniversal 'Reality'... although others have suggested that Alternative-4 may involve a HAARP type manipulation of the atmosphere in an effort to get CONTROL of the situation - Branton).

Bill Hamilton then explains some of the mystery surrounding the so-called 'hybrids' who have been encountered by UFO abductees, and why an ACTUAL cross between humanoids and reptiloids [thank God] might never succeed:

"...It is unlikely that the reptilian greys are cross-breeding with humans. Reptilians carry their sex organs internally and reproduce by eggs hatched by solar heat. Reptoids have well developed eyes, no hair follicles, & no external ear cartilage as consistent with most reptilian species. Since their means of reproduction is incompatible with our own, it is suggested that humans (women - Branton) may be fertilized by the grays by artificial insemination with human spermatozoa or perhaps they use the human uterus as an incubation chamber."

Note: Other indications are that the reptilians inject or encodify the human embryo with reptilian or other DNA during the early stages of development. It is even believed by some abductees that they have the ability to 're-program' the genetic information within an 'egg' before it has been fertilized. As for the so-called 'hybrids', Hamilton's statements seem to be confirmed by others, including abductees, who have hinted that the 'hybrid' fetuses are actually alien-looking OR human-appearing 'hybrids' who are conceived through human 'seed' taken from human male and female abductees. In other words the fetus would fall to one species line or the other -- an alien-appearing being lacking a 'soul', or a human-like child with a soul. It is said that within the hybrid society, the more human-looking hybrids consider themselves superior to the alien-appearing hybrids.

Their more-human-like features are a source of pride and status, even though many of the hybrids are nevertheless 'servants' of the Greys. Some abductees have reported that they have observed experiments involving the attempted mixtures of human and cattle DNA to create a 'hybrid' being. Many of the so-called hybrids however are never-the-less essentially 'human'. For instance the "HU-brids" or humanoid-hybrids would possess crimson blood, five fingers, round pupils, ears, and exterior reproductive organs, although the reproductive organs might be minimized and non-operative.

If they possessed even one of these traits there is a 'chance' that the hybrid <u>might possess a human "soul"</u>, although this may not always be the case, as with the "chameleons" and so on. In such a case "aura detectors" -- which could detect whether or not the being has a multi-colored chakra system -- would be a possible fail-safe means to determine the "imposters" from the "real thing". The "RE-brids" or reptiloid-hybrids would generally possess greenish 'blood' similar to that which the Greys themselves possess, four fingers, opaque black and/or vertical slit pupils, no visible ears, and no exterior reproductive organs.

Hamilton continues:

"...Alien vehicles are being tested at the alien physical technology center at S-4 at the Nevada Test Site. Alien vehicles are being replicated at Kirtland AFB & Sandia Laboratories & these replicas are referred to as ARVs [Alien Reproductive Vehicles]

THE DULCE PROTOCOL

(Note: Subsequent research by William Hamilton and Norio Hayakawa have confirmed that McDonnell-Douglass, Lockheed, and Northrup Corps. are now involved with the 'replication' of alien hardware for the Military-Industrial establishment. If this technology is being used for our own American defenses then this is all well-and-fine, however if the technology is being appropriated by the "New World Order" interests, under the oversight of the Reptiloids/Greys, then the 'sell-out' of our Military-Industrial Complex to a pro-Draconian and/or anti-American superpower would be considered HIGH TREASON, just as the sell-out of our entire Stealth fleet to the United Nations / New World Order control structure -- which HAS taken place -- should be considered high treason! - Branton)

"At least three of these vehicles are stored in hangers at Norton AFB, California. It is alleged that vehicle propulsion units were constructed by General Electric & composite materials were provided by Amoco. Alien vehicles generate an artificial gravity field which can be focused & intensified for high speed travel...

Alien organisms and biological technology are tested (in the upper levels - Branton) at the underground biogenetic laboratories at Dulce, New Mexico. Alien genetic engineering, cloning, & cryogenic technology have been studied with a view towards 'enhancing' human genetics, deciphering the human genome, & gaining a biological advantage by ARTIFICIAL BIOLOGICAL ENGINEERING. Strange life forms have been bred in these laboratories..."

Chapter 19

Who Controls The Draconian Collective?

The following chapter is based upon some thoughts and questions that had been forming in my mind for some time, until many of these questions were answered when I discovered an interesting volume titled Cosmic Voyage, by Mr. Courtney M. Brown, Ph.D. This work deals with the authors' personal experiments with remote viewing, along with his trainer Ed Dames, a former remote-viewer for U.S. Military Intelligence who taught Courtney Brown the secret military "R.V." or "Astral-Magnetic body" viewing techniques which he himself had learned as a member of the military psi corps.

From my own perspective, remote viewing operates through the subspace body of a human being who is able to tap-in to the universal psionic field. Since the psionic field is the very <u>foundation of all space-time-material reality</u>, the so-called "master program" of the universe which is made up of a 'field' of psionic <u>or thought-form energy</u>, it is not necessarily bound by the limits of space, time and matter. The psionic energy field seems to be interwoven into the electromagnetic grid structure of all gravitational bodies, with the electro-magneto-gravitic fields of those bodies serving as psionic 'traps' for thought-forms which are essentially the psychic 'residue' of all thinking beings, and in turn the accumulated "memory matrix" of those gravitational planetary bodies.

These psionic fields contain THOUGHT ENERGY. Now thoughts can either be based on truth or on deception, so just because this "thought-form energy" has accumulated within the gravitational grid structure of a planet -- FROM the time that thinking entities begin interacting with a gravitational sphere -- this does not mean that the information which has been 'programmed' into these psionic "thought-emotion energy" fields is always true.

Reality, imagination, truth, and deception based thought-forms are all 'recorded' regardless of their content within these electro-magneto-gravitic energy grids, just as one might record information within a multi-layered crystal via laser technology. Supposing one had the appropriate sophisticated technology, they could 'bleed' a wall, a rock, or any other object of its thought forms, sounds, or visual vibrations which have accumulated within that object over the years. They could literally 'read' the past through these objects.

Like a bio-chemical radio transceiver, some individuals -- for better or for worse -- seem to have the ability to 'tune-in' to and 'surf' the 'universal consciousness', the 'flowline', or the 'Akasha' memory matrix which links all thinking entities together on the deepest levels of the unconscious, allowing them to travel to specific places in space and time. You could say that CONSCIOUS awareness is composed of neural "short waves" which are localized with the individual, however UNCONSCIOUS awareness is composed of neural "long-waves" that reach beyond the individual -- for instance the neural states that are active during dreaming, thus explaining why many have reported experiencing "shared dreams" with other people.

You could liken neuro-psionic activity to an ocean. On the 'surface' are islands representing individual third-dimensional consciousness, however the deeper one goes the more the thought-forms merge with each other, just as the sunken earth beneath the islands eventually connects to other islands at the deeper levels, representative of a collective unconscious where the thought forms of thinking creatures merge into one 'reservoir'.

One of the 'targets' to which Mr. Brown's military RV trainer sent him was the Grey aliens' collective mind, and more specifically he was instructed to search out the ultimate command or control center of the collective.

Shortly after this particular experiment began [one of many], Brown found himself in an area where several Greys were working, although he did not know exactly where this was. He 'followed' the collective mind or thought-flow and found it to be absolutely massive, giving him the feeling of something unbounded, and almost universal in nature. However, he did detect a center, a definite 'heartbeat' of this massive collective matrix, into which and out from which a steady stream of information was flowing.

He noticed, at one point, an unusual 'subspace' being that seemed to be directing the activities of the Greys he was observing, and discovered that the bodies of the Greys themselves were incarnated by such 'subspace' beings which apparently entered the Greys' embryonic bodies and used them as vessels to manipulate physical reality.

Brown was then instructed to locate other of these beings who apparently controlled the Grey collective from a subspace or astral level, and found himself in an area where several of these subspace or paraphysical entities were located. As he continued towards this 'center' the number of subspace or non-corporeal beings increased until he came to a place of much activity, something like a grand central station type of area, where these beings were very active in various pursuits.

He did not know exactly where this was, but noticed that the closer he came to the control 'center' the more he sensed an increasing rigid atmosphere of absolute military-like control. He came to what he sensed was the central governing center of the subspace beings' activity, and in the center of this there was another area where a "council of 10" very high-level subspace or paraphysical entities congregated. These were apparently the governing principalities who were engaged in running the whole operation. The security here was absolutely incredible.

Then he perceived the SUPREME LEADER of this council of 10 paraphysical entities... and at about this point Courtney Brown was jerked back into his body, so to speak. He sensed that this leader had detected the presence of his own subspace, astral or magnetic body which he had projected, and had followed this RV 'intruder' back to his physical source. Brown and his trainer felt an oppressive, dark 'cloud' enter the room and it stayed there for about half a minute scrutinizing the scene. It left, apparently seeing the two RV'ers as "small frys" who were not worth wasting its time on.

Before Brown's expulsion from the command center however, he was able to perceive for a brief moment what this being was really like. He or it was an extremely powerful being, but one with a twisted personality that was full of darkness. Apparently this being had come into conflict with another Force which it saw as its enemy. Brown sensed within this being a severe self-esteem problem, in spite of its incredible power, and because of this it had a consuming desire to be worshipped by others.

Brown was confused when he sensed that these subspace beings, and in turn the Reptilians / Greys, were actually COMMANDED by this leader to engage in self-indulgent and destructive activities. This being apparently wanted his servants to use self-indulgent rewards or fear of punishment to maintain the absolute hierarchical command structure within its empire -- as well as through the rest of the subspace hierarchy, and in turn throughout the Reptilian Grey's collective 'hive' society that they completely infested.

Brown also got the impression that it was FEAR and PRIDE -- its perceived NEED to be worshipped -- that kept this being from negotiating with its ancient enemy, and that this being was utterly desperate to maintain its very survival or existence [strange for a seemingly immortal subspace being] and chose to resort to rebellion and terrorism in a desperate attempt to take control of the situation. Brown received a strong impression that this being was the <u>ultimate universal terrorist</u>!!! Apparently because of its all-consuming ego this being would NEVER humble itself before its 'enemy', and the same might be said for most of the upper echelon of the hierarchy who depended on the praise of their fellow collaborators to maintain their illusion of self-importance.

These beings, one might say, had long ago and of their own free-agency 'imploded' in upon themselves -- becoming 'spiritual black holes' with all-consuming appetites, absolute astral vampirial-like parasites, having extinguished all 'light' within themselves and therefore being unable to be brought back "into the light". Incapable of giving out 'light', they have become totally reprobate, devouring any and all life and innocence around them that they can possibly consume. The leader of this subspace 'collective' had long ago drawn these other dark beings into itself, like a large black star devouring other smaller ones around it.

This irreversible state MIGHT not apply entirely to ALL of these "subspace" beings, as we will see later on.

Now if we go to the book of Revelation, chapter 12, we find that the <u>ultimate leader</u> of the serpent race's collective or 'hive mind' is Lucifer, also known as the "great red dragon", the "old serpent", "the Devil" or "Satan" in the same chapter. Lucifer was one of the three original archangels [aside from Michael and Gabriel] who each apparently had charge over one-third of the light beings whom the Almighty had created... possibly numbering in the billions or trillions.

Now if you're a hard-core evolutionist you may not want to suffer through the rest of this chapter, as <u>physical evolution cannot account for spirit entities</u>, nor for the human soul for that matter. As for myself, I have a "creationist-evolutionist" concept of reality, or that life in this universe was 'created' by an Infinite Intelligence and then allowed to 'evolve' from there in various directions guided by the Creator. A better term might be 'change' rather than to 'evolve', in that the term 'evolution' is equated with 'Darwinism' in many minds.

Remember it has ALWAYS been the THEORY of evolution, not the LAW of evolution. If one is honest with themselves, they must accept the fact that evolution flies in the face of the Second Law of Thermo-Dynamics. Now that is a LAW, not a theory -- so which one are we to believe? In addition to this, a vast number of protein molecules would have had to exist for even the simplest life-form to appear. Just how these molecules could have come together by chance and resulted in an organized life-form with complex DNA programming and all is beyond me.

According to the laws of probability the life-span of an entire galaxy would not be enough time for just ONE protein molecule to come together <u>BY CHANCE out of the dark chaos of lifeless matter</u>, if at all. Then again there is the question of where the original matter came from which supposedly resulted from the 'Big Bang' [THEORY], if ever there was such an event.

Lucifer, as most may know from theological and eschatological traditions, reflected the infinite 'light' of the Creator with great brilliance, and therefore was given the name Lucifer, meaning "light bearer" -- 'bearer' being the operative word here. Lucifer reflected the light of the Almighty like a diamond reflects the light of the Sun. However, Lucifer began taking his attention off of the SOURCE of all Life and began giving HIMSELF credit for the 'light' that he bore [I use the term 'he' for semantic reasons only, although this being -- as well as the Eternal Godhead -- was/is not necessarily a being of physical gender from my own understanding], and the next step was inevitable -- Lucifer became jealous of the position which the Almighty One held.

Now I realize that many of you have different concepts of 'God', however let us just indulge in a thought experiment for a moment. If one accepts the concept of a 'Trinity', then one cannot accuse God of vainglory, for the Father is ever seeking to glorify the Son [the Logos or the Living Word] and the Spirit [which the Father and the only begotten 'Son' of God share].

THE DULCE PROTOCOL

The same holds true with the Son and the Spirit, both of them selflessly seeking to give 'glory' to their other two counterparts of the Godhead. How can God be three distinct personalities yet one single 'God'? [the pleural 'Elohim' God AND the singular 'Jehovah' God at the same time?]. One might just as well ask, how can the universe be 'one' universe yet consist of space, time and matter... three distinct aspects, yet take one of them away and the singular universe ceases to be?

We can also use the 'trinities' of,

- ultraviolet-visible-infrared [LIGHT - and imitating the Father, Son and Spirit, ultraviolet light is invisible, mid-spectrum light is visible, and infrared light felt]
- or length-width-height [SPACE]
- past-present-future [TIME]
- energy-motional-phenomena [MATTER]
- proton-neutron-electron [ATOMS],

...and other 'triune' manifestations in nature such as in humans themselves: the physical-material body, the soular-mental body, and the astral-spiritual body and the sublevels of each of these three distinctions... <u>we ourselves being three-in-one beings</u>.

If I'm beginning to sound preachy, then please bear with me. I believe that many of you will agree that the Grey phenomena has BOTH a physical and supernatural nature, and that we cannot fully understand one without accepting the other. One could equate this to the division within the UFO research community in the 1950's and 1960's over whether UFO's were nuts and bolts craft or ethereal supernatural manifestations. Well... why not BOTH?

So then, Lucifer, in his jealousy, rallies his followers [one-third of the angelic beings] together and convinces them that God is being unjust, that He's holding out on them and that he [Lucifer] has as much a right to be Almighty God as does God

Almighty Himself. In addition to this, Lucifer tells his followers that they too can be Almighty Gods, all they have to do is follow him in the rebellion.

Now, promising them godhood is very strange, since the more 'gods' there are the more the term 'God' loses its singular distinction. It's like a potential president promising every U.S. voter that if he is elected then he will simultaneously make all of those who voted for him Presidents of the United States! Do you see the insanity?

Perhaps not, but it seems to be obvious to me. You see, from my perspective if we are all gods then there is NO God. Pantheism must ultimately lead to Atheism. If that's the way you wish to believe then you certainly have the free agency to do so... But I'm only trying to make a point that according to traditional Judeo-Christian eschatological beliefs, this is the deception that Lucifer used to gain his recruits -- the promise of 'godhood' or self-deification being the original 'venom' of the serpent [Genesis chapter 3].

And this is the deception that the serpent-inspired Bavarian Illuminati cults via the Scottish Rite have used to gain their recruits for a Luciferian World Order on earth, first by infiltrating Masonry and then in turn by infiltrating the major religious denominations of the world. Now you can accept this or leave it as you will, I'm not trying to force any beliefs upon anyone, just attempting to provoke some thought on the possible nature of the supernatural forces motivating the Greys' collective.

Since 'theological' manipulation is a major part of the Greys' agenda, the eschatological component is one that must be dealt with in order to understand the rest.

So the rebellion began, and the heavens were torn in two as the standing and fallen angelics warred with each other, resulting in the fallen angels being cast from the realm of Eternity and into the physical inter-galactic universe. Could the 'subspace' beings described by Courtney Brown <u>be fallen light beings or rebel angels</u>?

THE DULCE PROTOCOL

Brown stated that this 'leader' in ancient times had his followers incarnate the reptilian Grey society, and had ordered them to sabotage their race. The fourth planet of Zeta II Reticuli was the Greys' "home world" at the time, however Zeta II Reticuli is a star lacking in sufficient carbon content to allow for the 'natural' development of carbon-based life [this is for those who may still cling to the 'evolutionist' philosophy], so the Greys must have colonized that world sometime in the distant past.

The subspace beings, according to Brown, animated themselves through the Greys and turned them toward a mindset of self-indulgence, which in turn led to the drive within the Greys for immediate gratification at the expense of their future and their world's resources [sound familiar?].

Once their world had become a polluted, radioactive ruin which was threatening their very genetic survival, the subspace beings under the command of their 'leader' offered a solution -- all the Greys had to do to survive was to give up all individual rights and emotions, and submit to a collective-mind which would control every aspect of the Greys' culture -- for their own 'good' of course, they were told. Using the excuse that individuality was the root of the problem, the subspace collectivists took things to the opposite extreme and insisted that assimilation into an absolute collective-mind was the answer.

In other RV experiments, Brown 'saw' humanoids living on Mars in some past era. A large planetoid grazed the atmosphere with such violence -- barely missing the surface -- that storm of enormous magnitude swept across the planet and much of the atmosphere itself was blown out into space. The Greys [who were observing this event and could have prevented the disaster] arrived as the planet was in the midst of upheaval, and offered to 'rescue' the Martians, but at a price -- namely that the Martian humanoids surrender their society to the control of the Greys' collective and that others be cryogenically preserved in order to 'preserve' the humanoid Martian race.

Actually according to Brown the main purpose of the cryogenic project was to 'preserve' them as sources for genetic materials to upgrade the Greys' race from time to time. It was doubtful that they would ever be awakened, at least en masse. This occurred mostly after the Martian humans had escaped underground and were desperate for survival -- every day being a struggle for existence.

NOW, according to Brown, Mars is under the control of the Greys, although some pockets of humans and 'hybrids' may remain in various places underground. Other sources claim that in 1985 the joint-operational " Alternative 3" facilities on Mars were sabotaged and taken over by the Draconians, or reptiloids and greys serving the Luciferian collective.

This was apparently one of several 'purges' that the aliens have carried out in order to ensure the absolute conformity of the human collaborators to their agenda, that is by purging out those renegades who possess too-much [from their perspective] individuality, which is the mortal enemy of their collective.

There is reportedly an elite force of 2000 'original' Greys based in the Martian moon Phobos. These Greys are reportedly the 'hosts' for several million 'clones' that have been bred to serve the reptilian elite in this system. As suggested the Alternative-3 -- or the so-called pure-bred Aryan "super race" -- humans on Mars and Luna may have been 'purged' due to some level of resistance against the Draconian-Orion-Reticuli collectivist forces with whom they 'collaborated'.

Apparently these humans saw that the two-sided 'collaboration' was turning into a one-sided 'dictatorship' controlled by the reptilian elite, and this 'purge' within the Martian and Lunar Alternative-3 facilities eliminated the resistance factions and ensured that only the most die-hard and devoted mind-controlled 'Aryan' slaves remained. In other words, these Aryan 'elite' suffered the very same fate that they had planned for us 'lower races' on planet earth.

THE DULCE PROTOCOL

One source has stated that these events on Mars and Luna were one of the main themes of discussion at the notorious meeting which took place between George Bush, Mikhail Gorbachev and the Eastern spiritual leader Maitreya [...whom the secret government has reportedly been teleporting around the world using Montauk-type technology in an attempt to provoke a worshipful response from those to whom he appears. Maitreya is the New World Order's "ace in the hole" and may or may not even turn out to be "the one" mentioned in Revelation chapter 13].

This meeting took place on the Island of Malta in the late 1980's, and resulted largely out of Bush and Gorbachev's terror over the events on Mars and the Moon, as well as similar threats that were being faced by the " Alternative-2" underground colonies maintained by the Military-Industrial Establishment in 'joint-capacity' with the Greys. However let's get back to the subject at hand.

What Brown sensed was that the Greys were desperate. They realized that they not only needed to genetically upgrade their race, but also needed to attain emotional individuality in order for their culture to survive [and this may have something to do with the 'hybrid' projects]. However they are trapped by the collective itself... there is presently a great sense of panic within the collective combined with a bizarre sense of protection which the combined psychic continuity of the collective provides.

Although they are desperate to attain emotional individuality which they are attempting to do by interfacing with humans, assimilating human genetics, and producing quasi-hybrid genetic offspring, they cannot fully make the break from the collective without the help of those who already exist in an individualized state, namely the humans.

For those of you who are familiar with the scenario of the 'BORG' collective in the "STAR TREK: NEXT GENERATION" series, certain episodes depicted a Borg entity by the name of 'Hue' who had developed emotional individuality during his captivity aboard the Enterprise that resulted from his association with human individuals. He was later sent back into the collective and <u>introduced the idea of individuality</u>, and in later episodes gathered quite a following of other 'Borg' who had also broken-free from the collective and had developed emotional individuality.

The Reptilians are not alone in this dilemma, since <u>many, many human cultures are 'trapped' in collectivism as well</u>, such as those who are part of the Ashtar or Astarte collective.

The problem with the collectivist Greys is that -- although they need the humans -- the self-destructive instructions coming down through the collective itself from the Luciferian hierarchy are SABOTAGING all attempts to deal with humans on a reasonable basis. Once they establish an agreement with a humanoid culture for whatever motive, the collective commences to use the agreement for its own imperialistic agendas, and the human collaborators are betrayed and sometimes destroyed [as in the case of some of the Alternative 2 and 3 bases], and war and/or conquest inevitably results.

The only answer to the problem that I can see would be to concentrate on severing individual reptiloids and greys from the collective and attacking the "control centers" of the collective itself. In this case mere technical and psychological attacks will not be enough... supernatural warfare will be the only answer since we are dealing with 'subspace' beings.

We need the help of the standing angels, yet at the same time we need to be careful since the fallen angels are good at masquerading as standing angels, which they have often done with those humans who have 'channeled' these entities via occult means -- the 'Heavens Gate' cult leaders and others like them for instance -- feeding these 'mediums' with information which has later turned out to be false, manipulative, or even deadly propaganda.

THE DULCE PROTOCOL

We must realize that the ONLY being in the collective which is allowed to exercise individual choice is their dark leader, and to a lesser extent the inner council, and these beings do NOT want the Reptiloids and Greys to attain emotional individualism. But what about other 'collectives' like the Ashtar or Astarte collective? Just who is this 'Ashtar'? Why is the Ashtar collective so involved with the Dulce base activity in joint capacity with the Greys and Reptiloids?

Is it, as contactee Israel Norkin claims, because the "Unholy Six" star systems of Orion have infiltrated the Ashtar collective to a massive extent? What about the bald 9-foot tall Reptilian "from the Pleiades" who supposedly defected from the Draconian collective, HATONN? Why hasn't Hatonn been warning about this infiltration of his own collective? Is it because he is secretly working FOR the Draconian-Orion empire?

Certainly if he was truly converted from the Draconian collective he could be a lot more zealous in exposing it... especially its infiltration of the Ashtar collective itself.

If we are to believe reports of "Star Wars" taking place within Sirius-B where the Ashtar collective has one of its major headquarters, then this leaves open the possibility that the Ashtar collective-alliance is in the process of splitting or has split down the middle between an interventionist Draco-Orionite faction and a non-interventionist Andro-Pleiadean faction...

Now for some further theological speculation... In II Peter 2:4 we read that:

"...God spared not the angels that sinned, but cast them down to hell, and delivered them into chains of darkness, to be reserved unto judgment."

This verse is apparently speaking of the high-level leaders of the ancient rebellion, who were so malignant and evil that they were bound in dark prisons deep under the earth. However the Bible gives several accounts of fallen angels or demons that are fully ACTIVE on the SURFACE of the earth, so we must conclude that these were lower ranking angels like the 'elementals' who were merely following the "party line", since they are allowed more-or-less to roam about the earth freely.

If such angels were 'condemned' when the first war in heaven ran its course, then WHY are they still allowed to more or less roam free? Is God possibly giving them TIME to reconsider their ways? Does the above verse mean that ALL fallen angels are irreparably doomed? Or, has the Creator in his infinite mercy given SOME of the fallen angels -- those who still maintain a semblance of regret for their part in the rebellion -- one last chance by allowing them physical incarnation through the Reptiloids and Greys?

Could this be why the Greys are so absolutely desperate to attain emotional individuality in spite of the restraints of an individuality-killing collective? Could their very eternal destinies be at stake?

A few years ago I would have totally rejected the possibility that some of the fallen angels could be included in the plan of redemption, yet now I wonder... Now before you begin labeling me a heretic, I would like to quote three versus regarding the serpent race [Greys, Reptiloids, etc.]:

"Now the serpent was more subtle [intelligent/cunning] than any beast of the field... And the Lord God said unto the serpent... I will put enmity between thee and the woman, and between thy seed and her seed." -- Genesis 6:1,14-15

In its full context these verses imply that the fallen archangel Lucifer was the being that had incarnated this particular reptilian -- possibly something akin to a Velociraptor or Stenonychosaurus Equallus or a similar type of biped saurian hominoid -- and in turn the entire serpent race, promising them power over man and nature if they would allow the Luciferians to re-incarnate through their race at will.

THE DULCE PROTOCOL

Whether you take this passage literally or symbolically, the message is essentially the same. Lucifer used the serpent race to deceive the humans into sabotaging their own connection with the God-Source and thereby sabotaging their supernatural dominion over the lower life forms -- and from that point onward these lower life forms began turning wild and untamed because the downward 'flow' of LIFE and ORDER had been broken at the human level, as DEATH and CHAOS began to reign.

One of the races which reverted to their base animal or predatory instincts was of course the serpent race, which originally held a position somewhere between mankind and the beasts. Due to mankind's 'fall' and the reptilians' alliance with the Luciferians, the serpent races began taking the upper-hand over the human race -- or rather, the fallen angels began taking the upper hand over the human race THROUGH the serpent races.

Today one could say that we see basically the same thing happening, however in this case the "Luciferians" are known as "subspace beings", and the "Serpents" through which they have incarnated are known as the "Grey Aliens", who are attempting to enslave humankind by offering them/us Trojan-horse gifts or "forbidden fruit" in the form of occult-technology to those intent on using this technology to establish "god-like" control and domination over their fellow man. As King Solomon once said, "there is no new thing under the sun".

But the point I want to make is that according to the verse given above, fallen angels have been re-incarnating through the Grey and Reptiloid [serpentine] races for several thousands of years.

And another verse:

> "In that day the Lord with his sore and great and strong sword
> shall punish leviathan the piercing serpent, even leviathan that crooked
> serpent; and he shall slay the dragon that is in the sea." -- Isaiah 27:1

This verse, unless I'm mistaken, is speaking of the reptilian COLLECTIVE itself, which could be considered as a "piercing serpent".

And then the following verse, which literally threw me for a loop:

"Praise ye him, ALL his angels: praise ye him, ALL his hosts... Praise the Lord from the earth, ye dragons, and ALL deeps." -- Psalm 148:2,7

Now unless I'm grossly misinterpreting scripture, it would seem that here God is saying that the [fallen-angel-incarnated] serpent races are told to praise the Almighty -- who after all was their creator before they allowed their own race to be corrupted. This MAY apply to both the spiritual-angelic and physical-bestial natures of the serpent races.

Other verses that we might add to the one above include:

"Let EVERY THING that hath BREATH praise the Lord." -- Psalm 150:6

"And he said unto them, Go ye into all the world, and preach the gospel to EVERY CREATURE." -- Mark 16:15

"And EVERY CREATURE which is in heaven, and on the earth, and under the earth, and such as are in the sea, and all that are in them, heard I saying, Blessing, and honor, and glory, and power, be unto him that sitteth upon the throne, and unto the Lamb for ever and ever." -- Revelation 5:13

In order to make the choice to appropriate the redemptive work of the Christ, the Reptiloids and Greys would have to develop emotional individuality and somehow become disconnected from the "Luciferian collective".

THE DULCE PROTOCOL

They already possess the first requirement, being creatures possessing the "breath of life". In order for a created being which has fallen from grace to be redeemed, they must possess both a spiritual and physical nature.

Part of their nature has to 'die' in order for the other part to live, just as the outward 'worm' of a caterpillar must die so that the inward 'butterfly' can live. Although in this case the symbolism is spiritual, it is essentially the same. An entirely spiritual being like a fallen angel in this case could not be redeemed unless it possessed a physical body -- as they would not possess a physical counterpart of themselves that could 'die' so that the spiritual counterpart could live. This would not necessarily be a physical death of the body, but a death of the 'corrupted' or 'fallen' nature resident therein.

This fallen nature must first be acknowledged just as any other 'disease' must be acknowledged in order to be cured. The 'death' of the fallen nature is a death by proxy resulting from a faith-connection to the mysterious working at Calvary, wherein the second member of the Godhead became 'flesh' to serve as the final 'Passover Lamb' in order to receive the full retribution for all of the imperfect acts that all created beings with the "breath of life" have committed before an absolutely perfect Creator.

The KEY would be however to consciously APPROPRIATE this 'Work' by directly asking the Almighty for the chance to become a part of this mysterious working at Calvary, which in essence serves as the 'heart-beat' from where the universe is to be regenerated from its fallen state.

If all PHYSICAL life in the galaxy or universe originally had its origin on planet earth, then earth would have been the appropriate place for the Almighty to manifest Himself in physical form, to shed His life-blood so that the creation might be redeemed by this very Divine and absolutely pure/pristine life-essence which the Creator had loosed into His creation, as a Divine "blood transfusion" if you will.

This Divine flow was loosed into the physical universe through the uncorrupted AND incorruptible LIFE-blood of the last "Passover Lamb", which was shed and poured out into the "cradle" of life, planet earth.

More and more cultures out among the stars are beginning to realize, through ancient records that are being uncovered, that planet earth is indeed the "cradle" from whence their distant ancestors emerged, the original "cosmic gene pool", and that in a sense they are connected by an invisible umbilicus to the "mother" world, and as they begin arriving here en masse to visit the "genesis world" we Terrans or Eartheans must realize that in a sense they are also a part of this world.

The challenge will be to learn how to respect each others INDIVIDUALITY, and how to claim the FREEDOM and LIBERTY that is the inherent right of all human beings, so long as it is practiced without violating the personal space and sovereignty of our neighbors -- whether they come from realms below, above, upon or even parallel with this world... this emerald world... this garden planet... this 'divine tear' known as planet earth.

So long as an 'alien' force with ancient documented ties to planet earth 'claims territory' adjacent to this planet which has NOT YET been claimed, such as undeveloped underground areas, there should be NO problem from those living on the surface. In the same way surface dwellers should respect subterranean cultures TO THE EXTENT THAT those cultures respect them.

Being an individualist, I am a firm believer that every nation on/in earth deserves to maintain its individuality and cultural distinction SO LONG AS they do not violate the sovereignty of their neighbors. Each country should have the right to determine its own economic, political and spiritual destinies SO LONG AS they do not violate the same of other countries.

THE DULCE PROTOCOL

It goes without saying that I am totally against a one world collectivist government which cannot tolerate individuality or independence in any form. However the loss of national sovereignties are often the result of human greed, for instance international bankers loaning billions to smaller countries fully knowing that the selfish leaders of those countries will squander the wealth and fail to re-pay the loans, thus opening the way for the 'banksters' to claim that countries' national reserves, mineral rights, properties, and other national resources along with a loss of sovereignty. I would hope that the respect for sovereignty on a national basis would cascade down to the individual level also.

In addition to the above, unless their existence is being threatened by radioactive dangers or some other threat, a sub-surface culture should not interfere with the activities of surface cultures: they should not steal resources, release radioactive poisons into surface environments, or biological diseases, or mutilate animals, or abduct people against their will, or use focused electronic beams to invade the privacy of those on the surface, or interfere with the minds of surface dwellers in any way, or engage in ANY FORM OF INVASION OF OUR SOVEREIGNTY OR THE SOVEREIGNTY OF ANY OTHER NON-SURFACE COMMUNITY.

Many alien forces, especially the draconian-interventionist-collectivists who DO NOT respect individual sovereignty, have VIOLATED this universal law and as a result their territories MUST inevitably be INVADED by those cultures whom they are abusing or violating in order to preserve their national security. And it also goes without saying that the 'Dulce empire' has EARNED the WRATH of Americans due to the UNSPEAKABLE atrocities being carried out there against OUR OWN PEOPLE.

I absolutely recommend that a full-scale Congressionally-backed invasion and take-over of the Dulce base and its peripheral facilities would be FULLY JUSTIFIED, and the SOONER THE BETTER! After all, DIDN'T WE AS AMERICAN CITIZENS PAY FOR THE 'UNDERGROUND EMPIRE' WITH OUR OWN TAX DOLLARS?

Once all resistance within the Dulce facility is SMASHED and its captives are LIBERATED, and after all activities there are brought under FULL Congressional oversight, those agents operating within this facility should be tried and prosecuted by due process of law, be they human or alien, and if not executed or imprisoned they should be banished from the planet until they can PROVE that they are able to respect human individuality and freedom.

We ourselves must learn the same lesson, since it was in most cases men who violated our trust and Constitutional sovereignty as U.S. citizens -- and in fact as world citizens -- who have 'betrayed' us to these alien parasites by opening up the door for them to come in, in many cases in order to facilitate their own desires to DOMINATE their fellow human beings.

When the Dulce base is conquered and subdued, we should commence to liberate other oppressed areas within the underground network.

Let us remember however that, aside from assisting in their 'liberation', we as Americans or world citizens should not [in our retaliatory actions against invasive subterranean centers] violate the territories or sovereignty of other interior dwellers who have NOT participated in the draconian-backed abductions and attacks against the citizens of America and of the World.

THE DULCE PROTOCOL

Chapter 20

Special Forces: Defenders Of Planet Earth?

The mysterious 'insider' Commander-X related the following information in one of his numerous reports:

"...In the revised September, 1959 edition of THE EFFECTS OF ATOMIC WEAPONS, prepared for and in cooperation with the U.S. Department of Defense and The U.S. Atomic Energy Commission, under the direction of The Los Alamos Scientific Laboratory, we read about how 'complete underground placement of bases is desirable.'

On page 382: 'There are apparently no fundamental difficulties in construction and operating Underground various types of important facilities. Such facilities may be placed in a suitable existing mine or a site may be excavated for the purpose.'

In reference to the 'Delta' Force which is believed to supply security for 'Above Top Secret' projects involving 'interaction' with the aliens [greys, etc.], this government insider states:

"The DELTA Group... have been seen [within the Intelligence Support Activity] with badges which have a <u>black Triangle on a red background</u>.

"DELTA is the fourth letter of the Greek alphabet. It has the <u>form</u> of a triangle, and figures prominently in certain Masonic signs.

"EACH BASE HAS ITS OWN SYMBOL. The Dulce base symbol is a triangle with the Greek letter 'Tau' (T) within it and then the symbol is inverted, so the triangle points down.

"The Insignia of 'a triangle and three lateral lines' has been seen on Saucer [transport] Craft,' The Tri-Lateral Symbol. Other symbols mark landing sites and 'Alien' craft..."

On January 10, 1989, former Naval Petty Officer William Cooper posted the following statement on a computer network devoted to the investigation of paranormal events, which detailed still further information about the Delta forces.

Take note that the Delta's according to William Cooper, John Lear and Thomas E. Castello had played a major part in the so-called "Dulce Wars" which began in 1979:

"The following information was extracted from a rather long treatise-transcript-conversation between an individual and another who was assigned to DELTA SECURITY:

"01: Delta security has a lot to do with inter-service projects.
"02: The Trilateral insignia [alien] is valid and has been used to mark equipment.
"03: 'The whole thing is grim and won't get any better.'
"04: The Trilateral insignia has been seen on a disk at Edwards AFB, CA and Area 51 in Nevada.
"05: There is a hanger at Edwards referred to as the Delta Hanger.
"06: The Delta Hanger is on the North Base at Edwards.

"07: You need a special badge to get near it. It is a red badge with a black triangle on the face of it and personal information on the back.

"08: Disk in hanger at Edwards described as having insignia on the underside and on the top. It was about 50' in diameter, appearing like tarnished silver, about 15 to 18 feet thick. There were what looked like windows around the raised portion that were mostly described as rectangular. There was a groove around the disk about 4 feet from the edge all the way around. There was an area on the bottom that looked like vents or louvers.

"09: When people assigned to Delta would break down and cry for no apparent reason, you would never see them again.

"10: Apparently, the NRO [National Recon Organization] recruits for DELTA out of Fort Carson, Colorado.

"11: Just about everyone assigned to DELTA are orphans, have no relatives, etc.

"12: There are 'bounty hunters' connected with Dreamland.

"13: If you work at Dreamland and go on leave or are not back on time they send 'bounty hunters' after you. That's where the 'visitors' live... there is an underground facility...

"14: Area 51 is at Groom Lake in Nevada. The disks are flown there.

"15: One of the craft looked like an upside-down diamond.

"16: There is a radiation hazard apparent when some of the craft fly.

"17: No one stays at Dreamland for more than a few months.

"18: 'Everything is way out of control...'"

From his apparent though guarded vantage-point within the Intelligence Community, "Commander-X" claims to be privy to much 'deep-level' inside information.

One of the many reports that has crossed his desk involved the experience of a woman who was 'abducted' and taken over 1000 miles to the underground facility below Dulce, New Mexico:

"...One woman I have spoken with was abducted from the roof of a New York City apartment building and apparently held underground at the Dulce facility. She was taken to a cabin in the desert which was being used as a camouflaged entrance to the 'alien' base. She was eventually escorted to the laboratories to be used as a test subject, but at the last minute managed to escape thanks to the aid of one of the Nordic-type, tall aliens, who befriended her and showed her a secret way out, down an unguarded shaft.

"Back in the desert, she was rescued by members of the [Air Force] Blue Berets, and eventually flown back to Manhattan. During a de-briefing session with the military, she was warned to remain silent about her experiences. Anyone hearing such a bizarre tale would certainly think she had gone insane. It was inferred she could be committed to a mental institution at any time should she refuse to go along with the cover-up conspiracy, which she was told was being conducted 'for the sake of the country, and the sake of the world!'"

(If you believe that excuse, then I have some nice beach-front property on Mercury that you might be interested in! - Branton)

THE DULCE PROTOCOL

Chapter 21

Probing Deeper Into The Dulce 'Enigma'

The following information on subsurface anomalies and the Dulce base was compiled by researcher and explorer John Rhodes:

Legends from different parts of the globe all tell of an <u>underworld inhabited</u> by mystical beings of varied forms. I believe that the reptilian [race] still resides to this day underground. Hidden away in the dark crevices of the Earth and in the depths of the oceans. The evidence supporting this proclamation is also available through recent reports and historical documentation...

In the early 1960's, a subterranean nuclear blast occurred about 30 miles southwest of Dulce, New Mexico right off U.S. 64. This nuclear blast was conducted under the umbrella of project Plowshare, and was named Gassbuggy. It has recently been alleged that this particular subsurface nuclear blast was used to create a hollowed out chute or chimney for development of a substation for a super-secret tunnel system attached to an underground black book project base.

According to the infamous Thomas Castello -- a former Dulce base security technician -- this particular under-world city is a highly secret base operated by humans as well as reptilian aliens and their worker cast, the commonly encountered grays. It is here, apparently, that a multitude of experimentation projects are carried out. Primarily genetic experiments on kidnapped men, women, and children.

There are a myriad of other specialty science projects taking place at the Dulce base including, but not limited to:

- Atomic manipulation,
- cloning,
- studies of the human aura,
- advanced mind control applications,
- animal/human crossbreeding,
- visual and audio wiretapping,
- the list goes on...

Dulce, New Mexico is a strange place indeed. It's a sleepy little town perched upon the Archuletta Mesa, just south of the Colorado border in northern New Mexico.

Archuletta Mesa

Tourists passing through sometimes see little more life in the town other than that of a scruffy dog lazily spread out along side of the dirt road. Some claim that upon entering the town, black vehicles with heavily tinted windows tailgate them until they are outside the city limits and "heading out of Dodge"!...

THE DULCE PROTOCOL

In addition, several other sources, who wish to remain nameless, reported oddities in their work with operation 'Plowshare' during the 1960's. The project was created under the guise of the use of atomic bombs during peacetime, and forged ahead under the umbrella of "Natural Gas Exploration". In fact, several of these multi-kiloton blasts were used as a rapid way of developing huge sub-surface chambers for facility development. It is reported that the <u>technology to clean radiation</u> is available and already in use for such projects.

When I lectured on Friday, August 13th of 1993 in Las Vegas, I made public, for the first time ever, the floor plans to levels one and six of the Dulce Base. These floor plans were reproduced from the originals that were handed to Thomas Castello's friend. This friend did not previously release the floor plans because they were being used as a verification device to the claims of abductees that say they were there. To date, the originals have verified and disproved many stories circulating the field of ufology. This friend of Thomas Castello's, however, believes that it is time to begin [to] reveal the missing pieces...

The Dulce base floor plan was illustrated as per the originals by Thomas Castello and I released it... during my lecture in Las Vegas, Nevada. Its layout, when inspected carefully, appears to be extremely strategically planned.

From a vertical viewpoint, it resembles a wheel with a central hub and corridors radiating outwards like spokes. This 'hub' is the focal point of the entire base. It is surrounded by central security and extends through all levels of the base.

I believe this core to be the Achilles heel of the entire facility. It probably contains fiber optic communications and power lines. This would justify its highly guarded and central location as well as explain its vertical continuation through all levels. With all communication lines and power lines focused towards the hub, it is possible that any one level could be completely "locked down" by its own security or the security hubs from either above or below its own level. This would provide maximum control over the entire facility.

The 'spokes' or corridors radiating away from the central hub, lead to numerous other labs in five different directions. Connect the spokes and a pentagon is revealed in its design. From above, this base resembles the layout of the Pentagon in Washington D.C. complete with halls, walls and military insignias! Since we do not have the exact heading on its corridors, magnetic alignments are impossible to determine.

When viewed laterally, its appearance takes on the look of a tree with a trunk at its center and its floors extending outwards like the branches. If this is a facility of science, then one could easily say that its lateral appearance is like that of the tree of knowledge

(Note: The original Hebrew word for the tree of "knowledge" is "Dah'ath", or "cunning". It was the 'tree' where, according to Judeo-Christian accounts, the original 'serpent' convinced Eve to take part in a rebellion against the Almighty by promising her and Adam godhood. By accepting this false gospel of self-deification, so Genesis claims, Eve AND her husband who was WITH HER at the time, joined in the rebellion. Since they saw themselves as potential gods, they no longer 'needed' to depend on the Almighty as their Source, and once the flow from the SOURCE was broken the perfection that the world once knew was destroyed, as humankind -- and in fact all of nature -- began to turn 'wild'.

In light of all of this, could the DULCE BASE be the modern TREE OF KNOWLEDGE [cunning], where the seed of the SERPENT and the seed of EVE have once again met in an unholy alliance, yet in a much more sophisticated form? In THIS case the "serpent" would be the GREYS, and the "forbidden fruit" would be the OCCULT-TECHNOLOGY that is being offered BY these demon-possessed beings to humans "elite" who are intent on "playing god" over their fellow man! Could it be that the Edenic scenario NEVER ENDED, but instead HAS BEEN and WILL KEEP ON

THE DULCE PROTOCOL

REPEATING ITSELF OVER AND OVER until the "seed of Eve" once-and-for-all say "ENOUGH IS ENOUGH", and basically tell the serpent exactly where it can go!? - Branton).

Was this purposely designed this way or does it just happen to be a coincidence?

The overall design of this facility reminds one of a multi-stacked subterranean Hopi Indian Kiva. Although I believe that it's somewhat of a disservice to the Hopi to even be spoken of in association with a cave of horrors like the Dulce base, its similarity in design should not be forgotten.

As cultures around the world tend to bring their own styles of architecture with them during periods of migration, so perhaps did the advanced civilization that 'originally' built [the] Dulce Base. If the reptilian influence over man is as great as archaic documentation and myth would have one believe, then there have to be other subterranean dwellings similar to this in other locations...

(Note: The following are some additional facts and comments, concerning the late Thomas Edwin Castello, which are not mentioned elsewhere in this work. These have been 'paraphrased' from the research files of John Rhodes. - Branton):

In 1961, Castello was a young sergeant stationed at Nellis Air Force Base near Las Vegas, Nevada. His job was as a military photographer with a top secret clearance. He later transferred to West Virginia where he trained in advanced intelligence photography. He worked inside an undisclosed underground installation, and due to the nature of his new assignment his clearance was upgraded to TS-IV.

He remained with the Air Force as a photographer until 1971 at which time he was offered a job with RAND Corporation as a Security Technician, and so he moved to California where RAND had a major facility and his security clearance was upgraded to

ULTRA-3. The following year he met a woman named Cathy, they married and had a son, Eric.

In 1977 Thomas was transferred to Santa Fe, New Mexico where his pay was raised significantly and his security clearance was again upgraded... this time to ULTRA-7. His new job was as a photo security specialist in the Dulce installation, where his job specification was to maintain, align and calibrate video monitoring cameras throughout the underground complex and to escort visitors to their destinations.

Once arriving in Dulce, Thomas and several other new 'recruits' attended a mandatory meeting where they were introduced to the BIG LIE, that:

"...the subjects being used for genetic experiments were hopelessly insane and the research is for medical and humane purposes."

Beyond that, all questions were to be asked on a need to know basis. The briefing ended with severe threats of punishment for being caught talking to any of the 'insane' or engaging in conversations with others not directly involved with ones current task. Venturing outside the boundaries of ones own work area without reason was also forbidden and, most of all, discussing the existence of the joint Alien/U.S. government base to any outsider would generate severe and, if necessary, deadly repercussions.

Thomas did his job as his superiors demanded. At first his encounters with actual gray and reptilian beings in the base were exhilarating, but soon he became acutely aware that all was not what it appeared to be.

Thomas slowly began to sense that there was an underlying current of tension existing between some of the personnel and himself. Once in a while he would walk around the corner, interrupting serious discussions between coworkers and, as Thomas was a security officer, these talks would die off into a short murmur and individuals would part company.

THE DULCE PROTOCOL

One particular part of his job was to go into various areas of the base and align the security monitoring cameras when it was necessary. This afforded him the opportunity to venture out and witness things that would stagger the imagination.

Later he was to report seeing laboratories that investigated the following:

- Auraic energy fields of humans;

- Astral or spirit-body voyaging and manipulation;

- Psi studies;

- Advanced mind control analysis and application;

- Human brain memory recognition, acquisition, and transfer;

- Matter manipulation;

- Human/alien embryonic cloning;

- Rapid human body replicating by use of energy/matter transfer [complete with an individuals memory from the computer memory banks] and other scientific advances.

Once in a while Thomas would see some of the horrifying genetic creations that were housed in separate sections of the base.

These, he knew, couldn't have had anything to do with mental illness or health research. Thomas didn't want to look any further. For every time he discovered more pieces to this underground maze, it became more and more overwhelming to accept. His curious mind, however, implored him to search for the truth regardless of his own desire to turn away in horror.

One day, Thomas was approached by another employee who ushered him into a side hallway. Here he was approached by two other gentlemen that whispered the most horrifying words... the men, woman AND CHILDREN that were said to be mentally retarded were, in fact, heavily sedated victims of ABDUCTION. He warned the men that their words and actions could get them in big trouble if he were to turn them in. At this, one man told Thomas that they were all observing him and noticed that he too was 'uncomfortable' with what he was witnessing. They knew that Thomas had a conscience and they knew they had a friend.

They were right, Thomas didn't turn them into his commanders. Instead, he made the dangerous decision to quietly speak with one of the caged humans in an area nicknamed "Nightmare Hall". Through their drug induced state, he asked their name and their home town. Thomas discreetly investigated the claim of this 'insane' human during his weekends out of the facility. He discovered through his search that the person had been declared missing in their home-town after vanishing suddenly, leaving behind their traumatized families, who followed dead ends and trailed flyers.

Soon he discovered that MANY of the hundreds, perhaps thousands of men, women and children [from ALL AREAS OF THE WORLD] were actually listed as missing or unexplained disappearances. Thomas knew he was IN OVER HIS HEAD and so were several of his co-workers. All he could do, until somehow the situation changed, was to be alert and extremely guarded with his thoughts. The gray aliens' telepathic capabilities allowed them to 'read' the minds of those around them and if he revealed his intense anger, it would be all over for him and his new friends.

In 1978, tensions within the Dulce base were extremely heightened. Several security and lab technicians began to sabotage the genetic experiments. Increasingly frail nerves and paranoia finally erupted into what is commonly referred to as the Dulce Wars.

It was a literal battle between the reptilians and the humans for the CONTROL of the Dulce base. It was the reptilians more than the humans that were pushing the "Big Lie", and insisted on using humans in their experiments, AND those who did not survive the experiments [were used] as 'sources' for the liquid protein tanks which 'fed' both embryonic gray fetuses as well as full grown grays, as a source of nourishment.

THE DULCE PROTOCOL

The initial "Dulce War" conflict began on Level Three.

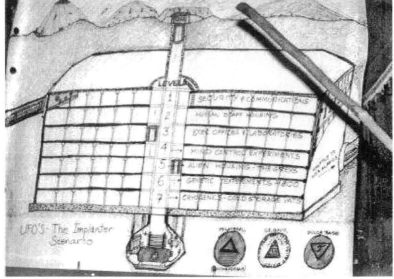

Dulce Levels and Symbols

No one is exactly sure how it started, but we do know through Thomas' account that it involved the [base] SECURITY FORCES armed with beam weapons known as "Flash Guns", machine-gun toting [U.S. Military] personnel, and the Gray alien species (who had apparently tried to turn the base security forces and U.S. Military forces against each other. - Branton).

When the smoke cleared, sixty-eight humans had been killed, twenty-two were completely vaporized and nineteen escaped via the tunnels. Seven were recaptured and twelve remain in hiding to this day. Thomas Returned to his post awaiting the planning of his own escape.

(Note: It is not known just exactly how many grays were killed in the conflict, but it is obvious that the human security personnel were far outnumbered by the aliens since literally thousands of grays worked in the lower levels of the Dulce base, according to Castello. There are indications that the 'spark' may have occurred when many of the scientists within the lower levels -- who had learned about the "Grand Deception" of the aliens and their LIES concerning the abductees -- were captured by the Reptilians and apparently confined deep within peripheral bases underneath the Ute Mountains of SE Colorado and SW Utah.

A few others apparently escaped and told those in the upper levels what was happening below. The Grays/Reptiloids could not afford to let escape the fact that they had VIOLATED the treaty with MJ-12, and in fact had been violating it ALL ALONG with NO INTENTION whatsoever to keep it. They had hoped that the humans would not become wise to their "Trojan Horse" operation until they were able to infiltrate the planet more completely.

At least 100 special forces were sent in by superiors who were ignorant of the whole picture in an effort to rescue the scientists and maintain order and control of the base, however the aliens -- who far outnumbered and out-teched the human forces -- managed to kill 66-68 of them. - Branton)

In 1979 the intense pressure that was brought upon Thomas in his job finally made him break the code of silence. He told his best friend, by a hand passed note, that he was working in a sub-surface, huge installation outside of Dulce, New Mexico.

He told his friend that he was working side by side with Gray aliens that consider themselves native Terrans and that the upside-down black triangle with the inverted gold colored T inside it was the insignia of the project.

Thomas knew that he had to leave the job for his own peace of mind, however now that he knew the truth about the abductees being held below, it would be almost impossible to live a 'normal' life. He would always be under observation and threat until the day he died. He also was aware of the fact that old age may not be his downfall. His demise could easily be expedited by certain individuals.

After one of his weekends away from the facility, he decided to Return to work. This time through one of the less guarded air shafts, unannounced and into the base by

THE DULCE PROTOCOL

way of secret passages. Once inside, he preceded to appear as if he was working his normal duties while taking charge of every thought as he passed by Grays.

During this time inside the base, he removed still photographs of the facility and treaties signed, with authentic signatures, between California Governor Ronald Reagan, several other individuals and the Grays. Thomas also managed to retrieve a 7 minute black and white surveillance video of genetic experiments, caged humans, Grays, as well as schematics of Alien devices and complex genetic formulas.

These items, he felt, were not only his chance to a seat at the bargaining table when the need arose, but also they were things that the public needed to know about.

He made copies of the films, photo's and paperwork, packed several 'packages' and instructed several different people who he trusted explicitly to bury or hide them until the right time.

He was then made aware through certain sources that his wife, Cathy, and son, Eric, had been forcibly taken from their home to an undisclosed underground facility for 'safe holding' until he decided to Return with the items. At this point, he knew that even IF he did Return everything to the Dulce commanders, that his wife and son were probably NEVER going to be the same again [if Returned at all] after being manipulated by aggressive mind control.

He also knew that he AND his family would most DEFINITELY become permanently missing due to some tragic accident. Thomas was at zero option. He quickly dissolved into a lonely life on the run. From state to state, border to border, motels to sofa's.

Always looking behind him and trying his best to look ahead...

Further notes from John Rhodes:

341

During this initial period of evasion, Thomas was able to relay quite a bit of information about what was happening behind-the-scenes and what plans were being made by the government (that is, the fascist-corporate elements within the 'Executive-Intelligence-Industrial' government such as the NSA's, MAJI and AQUARIUS agencies, which had re-established the collaboration two years following the cessation of official human interaction following the Dulce wars. - Branton) and the Grays.

Some of it has been withheld by his closest friends as a control device in order to authenticate or invalidate some abductees' stories and researcher's findings. Believe me, there are some very well-known people who make a living from selling this type of information and they have been lying through their teeth about their 'experiences'.

(Note: Are some of these false accounts given within THIS volume? I do not know, and as I stated at the beginning of this work I am not excluding ANY information source -- although I may have my own 'opinions' on certain information such as with the Phoenix Project 'research'. However, I have decided to THROW IT ALL out on the table for all to see, and will allow the future to make its own judgments. Even if one or a few of the accounts are misleading, the odds that ALL of the combined accounts within this volume are false would defy the laws of probability.

Perhaps the only way to tell for certain would be to do as the unsung hero Paul Bennewitz suggested -- that is to make a full-scale military assault on the base, conquer the aliens whether they be genetic creations or true aliens or both, and bring all activities there under full Congressional oversight. I'm sure that there will be no lack of potential military recruits for this type of assault, after all tens of thousands of young American men have in the past been sent off to die to protect CIA drug-running operations in the Golden Triangle, to give their lives for the United Nations' "New World Order", or in wars that were never meant to be won.

THE DULCE PROTOCOL

I should however in all fairness state that in the Korean and Vietnamese wars there was a very real threat in the form of Communism, and many young men bravely fought and died in the defense of freedom. However their patriotism and hopes of victory were often sabotaged by Communist sympathizing Socialist U.N. officials or by covert drug operations or other hidden agendas. In other words if we have fought wars in the past against the 'tentacles' of the beast, so-to-speak, then I see no reason why potential recruits would shy away from a battle against the 'head' of the Beast itself, especially when we consider that such a battle or war might ultimately have galactic ramifications.

One of the problems with the "Dulce Wars" was that only 100 special forces with high-level security clearances were unknowingly sent-in to a base inhabited by over 18,000 Greys. 44 of these reportedly survived the firefight -- which considering the opposition was a very good survival rate. However with the latest developments in military technology, with the current 'civilian intelligence' on the base which exists now thanks to Paul Bennewitz and others, and with the millions of American Christian Patriots who would no doubt be willing and ready to wage a HOLY WAR against the entrenched Draconian COLLECTIVIST forces on earth... the next military assault on the DULCE BASE will not be so one-sided. - Branton)

He [Thomas Castello] hopes that you find this information interesting and noteworthy. We feel that it is imperative to release more information because of the stepped-up abduction activities. If you should ever be inquisitive enough to try and do a field investigation of Dulce yourself, then you had better prepare and prepare well!... Do not treat [this] information lightly.

Thomas Castello, the former Dulce Base security technical [officer] and a personal friend of two OZ team members, may have given his life in order that some day the world may see the truth about the existence of the Dulce facility in which he worked [Thomas has not made regular visits to any of his known 'contacts' for quite some time. Some fear the worst...]

Elsewhere within the manuscript released by John Rhodes -- from which we have just quoted. -- we read the following:

"Obviously, if these snake-people or reptilians really did once live amongst the Homo Sapiens population, they have gone to extreme measures not to be revealed since they went into hiding... [However] OUR progression has been carefully monitored by the elusive reptilian race that lives within the cavernous Earth itself...

"Legends from different parts of the globe all tell of an underworld inhabited by mystical beings of varied forms. I believe that the reptilian race...still resides to this day underground, hidden away in the dark crevices of the Earth and in the depths of the oceans. The evidence supporting this proclamation is also available through recent reports and historical documentation...

If you really want to see the big show, don't look above your head, look below your feet!"

Chapter 22

Mystery-Maverick Jim McCambell Takes On the Dulce-Bennewitz Enigma

The following document [among others] originated from a U.S. Intelligence worker who has been missing for quite some time.

Concerned family members discovered this document in a locker in which the missing Intelligence officer apparently kept some of his papers. This document as well as others in his possession may have had some connection with his disappearance, although exactly what connection this might be, is uncertain.

Copies of this and other documents eventually ended up in the hands of several researchers as a result of one investigator who was approached by the family of the missing agent and given the documents. This source stated that this family was extremely disturbed not only about the disappearance but also about the nature of the documents themselves and the role they may have played in connection with the disappearance.

In the copy of the document which is quoted here, some annotations were made. These seem to have been 'corrections' on various points related in the ms. made by Paul Bennewitz himself.

These corrections will be indicated by an [*]:

"SUMMARY OF NOTES TAKEN BY JIM MCCAMPBELL CONCERNING... TELEPHONE INTERVIEWS WITH DR. PAUL F. BENNEWITZ:

"This is Jim McCampbell making a recording of a remarkable episode on July 13, 1984. It has to do with a UFO base, cattle mutilations, advanced weaponry, contact with aliens, etc.

"The episode began about a week ago when I received a little semi-annual periodical titled STIGMATA. It is number 21, the First Half of 1984. This little bulletin is prepared by Thomas Adams at P.O. Box 1994, Paris, TX 75460... (Tom Adams is the ex-husband of Christa Tilton, by the way. - Branton)

"He has a rather lengthy article. One finds point of interest on page 9 and I suppose the only way to pursue this is to read what he has here as it is fundamental to the entire story.

"Quoting:

'In May of 1980 a most interesting event occurred in northern New Mexico. An event similar in many respects to the Doraty Case. A mother and her young son were driving on a rural highway near Cimarron, New Mexico. They observed two or more craft and as Judy Doraty did, they observed a calf being abducted. Both observers were themselves abducted and taken on separate craft to what was apparently an underground installation, where the woman witnessed the mutilation of the calf.

[* Woman witnessed mutilation in the field - dead animal taken with them.] It has been alleged that she also observed a vat containing unidentified [* cattle] body parts floating in a liquid, AND ANOTHER VAT CONTAINING THE BODY OF A

THE DULCE PROTOCOL

MALE HUMAN. The woman was subjected to an examination and it has been further alleged that small metallic objects were implanted into her body as well as into her son's body. More than one source has informed us that CAT-scans have confirmed the presence of these implants.

"'Paul Bennewitz, President of his own scientific company in Albuquerque and an investigator with the Aerial Phenomena Research Organization, has been the principal investigator of the case. Interviewed in his office in April 1983, Bennewitz reports that through regressive hypnosis of the mother and child and his own follow-up investigation [including communications received via his computer terminal which ostensibly is from a UFO-related source], he was able to determine the location of the underground facility, a kilometer underground beneath the Jicarilla Apache Indian Reservation near Dulce, New Mexico. [Since 1976, one of the areas hardest-hit by mutilations coincidentally or whatever].

"'...The mother and son, by the way, were Returned back to their car that night. Since the incident, they have suffered repeated trauma and difficulties as they attempt to recover from the episode. We pass this along because the account is, of course, most crucial if true; but we are not in a position to confirm the alleged findings. Hopefully, more information regarding this incident will be aired in the near future. We can only consider such reports while continuing to seek the evidence to refute or confirm.'

"Unquote.

"That's the end of this remarkable quotation from STIGMATA.

"...I got in touch with Dr. Bennewitz by telephone and indicated that I had seen this reference to him and his work and I wanted to find out whether he was being misrepresented or whatever... It is rather mind boggling and here is the substance of that telephone conversation.

Robert K Teske

"He is a physicist and he started four years ago to determine in his own mind whether UFOs exist or do not and he has gotten much more deeply involved than he ever intended. IT HAS CAUSED HIM A GREAT DEAL OF TROUBLE FROM THE GOVERNMENT INTELLIGENCE GROUPS. He has pictures from the location. He went with a Highway Patrol Officer and they saw a UFO take off from the mesa at the location. He obtained photographs and what he calls launch ships were 330 ft. long and 130 ft. across.

The cattle rancher named Gomez and he went back to this location which is a mesa and saw a surveillance vehicle which was about 5 ft. by 10 ft., like a satellite, he said. He had been using a Polaroid camera and then got a Hausel-Bladd to produce much better pictures. He set up a monitoring station and observed that UFOs are all over the area... He has been dealing heavily with a Major Edwards [somebody] [* Security Commander] who was with Manzano Security and two [* My wife & I] of them saw four objects outside of a [nuclear] warhead storage area at a range of about 2500 feet and obtained movies of them. He now has about 6000 feet of movie footage, of which 5000 ft. is in Super Eight. THE OBJECTS HAVE THE ABILITY TO 'CLOAK,' that's the word, spells CLOAK like cloak and dagger, like cover up and he says that they can cause themselves to go invisible by a field that caused the light waves to bend around the object and that one sees the sky behind them.

"He confirmed the fact that the woman was picked up when she accidentally observed the calf being abducted. He has paid for a pathology work and medical doctor work. The pathologist is a former head of the microbiology department of New Mexico University. They have done CATscans to show that the woman and her son did in fact have implants in their bodies. [* We confirmed the woman - not her son] She has a vaginal disease like streptococci-bulbie[?] and tried many antibodies to destroy the bacteria. That it has survived off the antibodies themselves. THE ALIENS KEEP HASSLING HER. [* Still true to date].

THE DULCE PROTOCOL

"Paul kept the woman and her mother at his house and the UFOs were flying overhead constantly. THERE IS NO ESP INVOLVED, BUT IT IS JUST PLAIN PHYSICS.

"They beam down [* They send a beam down - not 'beam down']. They can communicate THROUGH THIS BEAM. She picked up their transmissions. He devised a means of communication based upon her alfbic [?] code; one is equal to 'no' and two being 'yes.' Through this code he has been able to talk to the aliens. He then computerized a system that would reject extraneous inputs. HE SAID THAT THEY CAN BE VERY THREATENING AND MALEVOLENT...

"He then told the O.S.I. OF THE AIR FORCE and he has been requested to give [* Did give] several presentations to HIGH LEVEL Air Force people in briefings on the subject, WING LEVEL Command and many others including this fellow Edwards. And he took a helicopter to the site [* No - Twice to site - 1st by OSI agent, 2nd by a Col. Carpenter]. It turned out that the WING COMMANDER, after a presentation that this fellow made, then took a helicopter to the site and made photographs.

"He says that you can see saucers on the ground. He says there is a kind of cone - a large cone and the larger vehicles come and land on top of the cone with the top of the cone fitting into a hole in the bottom. There is an elevator inside of the cone and that goes down into the mountain or ground about one kilometer. You can see the aliens running around the base getting into the vehicles and stuff.

They use small vehicles to get around that have no wheels. They are rectangular in shape and they levitate. They do not show up in color BECAUSE THEY ARE HIGHLY REFLECTIVE, but in B & W they are visible. He says that there are beam weapons that are floating in strategic locations and there is a road into the base. He obtained infra-red photos of the area from an altitude of 14,000 Ft. There is a level highway going into the area that is 36 ft. wide.

Robert K Teske

IT IS A GOVERNMENT ROAD (i.e. part of the off-limits road that goes through Colorado's Ute Reservation and then south across the border? - Branton).

One can see telemetry trailers and buildings that are five sided buildings with a dome. It is standard military procedure. There are many guard points and 'stakes' and there are launch domes that one can see. Next to the launch dome HE SAW A BLACK LIMOUSINE AND ANOTHER AT SOME DISTANCE OFF [* Apparently]. The careful measurements showed that the limousine was the same length of his Lincoln Town car. IT IS A CIA VEHICLE. ALSO THERE WAS A BLUE VAN. He has been cautioned about these limousines as they will run you off the road if you try to get into the area and in fact somebody has been killed in that manner. To the north is a launch site.

THERE ARE TWO WRECKED SHIPS THERE: they are 36 feet with wings, and one can see oxygen and hydrogen tanks. There are four cylindrical objects Socorro type -- two carrying something while flying. The whole operation is based upon a government agreement and a technology trade. We get out of it atomic ships that are operated by plutonium. The Cash-Landrum case was one of them. The doors jammed open and neutron radiation came out.

They are based at Kirtland AFB and Holloman AFB [* No - only know of one based at HAFB] and some place in Texas [possibly Ft. Hood, Texas - a guess only]. He said the government is paying the hospital bills for the Cash-Landrum victims [* OSI Input - found out later unless someone covering - not true]. Refueling of the plutonium is accomplished at Los Alamos. He had... pictures of this base back to 1948 and it has been there starting in 1948. Pictures in 1962, you can see many saucers and the base and truck... The road was 'passed off' to the local inhabitants as a lumber contract.

He has photographs [* I believe] of the firing of a beam weapon that [fires?] in two directions. [That would be necessary on a flying saucer. The reaction forces would impede the vehicle] He has computed the speeds of [the] flying saucers at 15,000 mph and indicates that THE PILOTS [* of ours] ARE FROM NSA, THE NATIONAL SECURITY AGENCY. The aliens have had atomic propulsion system for 48 years (or rather one particular 'alien' group, probably native subterranean? - Branton) and the saucers themselves operate on an electric charge basis having to do with crystal semiconductor and [* Maybe] a super lattice.

I think he said 'as you increase the voltage, the current goes down.'... At present there are six to eight vehicles, maybe up to ten over the area and sometimes up to 100. THEY CAN BE SEEN IN THE CLOUDS. They go into cumulus clouds and produce nitrogen nitride. [* I assume or speculate it is this] YOU WILL SEE BLACK SPOTS IN THE CLOUD. They eat holes in the cloud. If you can see black spots in a cloud, then you can tell that a vehicle is in there.

"He says that they come from six different cultures and in his communications (via accessing the information system of the underground base by tapping-in to their ship-to-base communications frequency using a radio-computer-video setup he developed. - Branton) [he learned that] SOME come from a binary system, possibly Zeta Reticuli and from distances up to and larger than 32 light years away.

They also [* appear to] have one to three [carrier?] ships in earth orbit at 50,000 KM altitude [* Based upon data]. He had to form the words to try to communicate and he produced a vocabulary of 627 words in a matrix form and used a computer. The Flying Saucers [* we see] are limited to operation in the atmosphere.

"Now with regard to the cattle problem, the aliens are using the DNA FROM CATTLE AND ARE MAKING HUMANOIDS. He got pictures of their video screen. SOME OF THE CREATURES ARE ANIMAL LIKE, some are near human and some are human and short with large head

(Hu-brids? It would seem that if this is the case, not all of the so-called 'hybrids' are infused with reptilian DNA, but rather cattle DNA or a wide variety of other DNA sources available in the 'Nightmare Hall' level of the base. - Branton).

They grow the embryos. After the embryos become active by a year of training presumably that is required for them to become operational. When they die, they go back into the tank. Their parts are recovered.

"In 1979 something happened and the base was closed. There was an argument over weapons and our people were chased out, more than 100 people involved. [Someplace later he indicates further details on this point] ...

(this 'may' be where the 66 -- 44 figures come from, that is 100 special forces who were sent in and forced to face literally THOUSANDS of Grays, 66 of whom fought to their deaths while 44 out of the hundred managed to escape back to the surface. - Branton)

"The base is 4000 ft. long and our helicopters are going in there all the time. When it became known that he was familiar with all this, the mutilations stopped. [* True] They are taking humanoid embryos out of this base to somewhere else. I asked if it was Albuquerque or Los Alamos, but he said he didn't know. [1/8/86 - looks like it is Albuquerque]

(Note: Subterranean bases below Albuquerque? Thomas E. Castello also stated that much of the Dulce activity was being extended into a MAJOR 'Gray' basing area below the Los Alamos region. One team of scientists who were investigating some newly-found ancient pictographs that depicted 'alien-like' scenes in or around the Santa Fe National Forest, insisted that they had seen in the early morning hours while camping in the area several dozen discs in the skies over the mountains, and shortly afterward a very large caravan of 'cattle trucks' -- which entered the area and seemed to leave hours later, after unloading their cargo.

THE DULCE PROTOCOL

This whole situation seems to 'imply' that the secret government may be 'feeding' the Grays at Los Alamos, which is apparently the largest 'nest' in North America outside of other known 'nests' near Madigan - Fort Lewis, WA; Lakeport-Hopland, Mt. Lassen & Deep Springs, CA; Area 51, NV; Dugway, UT and the Major NEXUS below DULCE, New Mexico.

This may all be part of an elaborate operation to 'appease' the aliens. The scientists stated that black helicopters, apparently having spotted their vehicles some distance away, flew over the area for some time in an effort to locate them, but apparently could not do so. They said that an almost identical scenario was repeated the following night and early in the morning. - Branton)

"He said there are still quite a few helicopters in operation. They fly at night. [* all unmarked] HE WENT UP THERE HIMSELF IN A HELICOPTER AND THE O.S.I. BRIEFED THE COPTER PILOT AND HE THOUGHT PERHAPS THE COPTER PILOT HIMSELF WAS AN UNDERCOVER MAN. They saw helicopter pads up there - Viet Nam type, with bearing markers and trees pushed off away from the location. It is such a wild area he said. He agreed to send me the coordinates of this base.

"Regarding abductions of people, they pick out medium to low IQ personnel.

(Note: They have also -- according to my information -- attempted to abduct people with higher-than-normal IQ's, with photographic memory, etc., in order to either utilize them on an unconscious basis or neutralize their intellectual capabilities if they appear to be a potential threat. - Branton)

"They are able to scope out each one [so we can do the same thing with electro-magnetic spectrum analyzers]. [* I don't know this part - word mix-up - drop]. They pick up these people and then put implants into them and then take tissue samples, including ovum from the women, sperm from the men and DNA.

"THEY CAN PROGRAM THESE PEOPLE AS SLAVES TO DO WHATEVER THEY WISH AND THEY WILL HAVE NO MEMORY OF IT. THEY [The Hard Core type] STAUNCHLY REFUSE TO BE X-RAYED OR HYPNOTICALLY REGRESSED. YOU CAN RECOGNIZE THEM BECAUSE OF THEIR EYES. HE SAYS 'PECULIAR LOOK IN THE EYES AND A FUNNY SMILE.' [* An expression]

Hynek (that is the late J. Allen Hynek, who worked for the Air Force's Project Blue Book in the early years and later became a civilian 'Ufologist'. - Branton) knows about all of this and has been in contact with Coral [Lorenzen]. He regards Hynek as a threat. [* Not really - I just think he is still a Gov. cover] At his house, he showed Hynek films and out in the back yard a flying saucer. He asked Hynek about his view with regard to abductions as to how many people might have been abducted. HYNEK, UNHESITATINGLY SAID ABOUT ONE OUT OF FORTY.

(Note: Other sources claim that more recent figures indicate this to be one out of twenty or even one out of ten Americans, since more abductees are being taken and implanted as time goes on -- most of whom are consciously unaware of the process because of hypno-electro-chemical memory suppression! - Branton)

"He said that many people come to his door to see him, just 'out of the blue' and he sees SCARS on the back of their necks. That previous old scars are easy to detect and that new ones are hard to detect. HE FEELS THAT THIS IS A SICKENING SITUATION.

"THE ALIENS HAVE GONE WILD AND USE HYPODERMICS [and notes a 'parallel four times.'] [McCampbell: I don't know what that means] [* I don't know either]. He has been paralyzed four times and has been hit 250 times by hypodermics.

THE DULCE PROTOCOL

He says they knock you cold and they do whatever they want to do and the above points have been verified medically.

"A man came to see him with a top secret document that was dated in the 50's, indicating if anybody found out about all of this they would kill them. He was asked 'doesn't that bother you?' He said 'no it didn't.'

"He said he had sent some film to Kodak and there were seven rolls. They were Ectachrome G which could not be processed locally, so they had to go to Kodak. He does all of the film work commercially so that nobody could claim that he had 'monkeyed' with the film. His films came back, but one of them -- one was plain Ectachrome, but [* Was missing for 2 months - when received] nine feet was missing and this was close-ups of UFOs that he had taken.

The missing pictures of the nine feet [* The 9 ft. didn't - others known only to me did] IN A TOP SECRET DOCUMENT THAT HE STUDIED AND THE CODE NAME IS AQUARIUS AND IT IS A PROJECT OF THE NATIONAL SECURITY AGENCY [* I was told NASA]. They are the ones that kept his film and copied it with deletions on Ectrochrome and sent it back [* I suspect].

"THERE HAVE BEEN INDIRECT THREATS BY THE AIR FORCE INTELLIGENCE AGAINST HIM.

"THE LOCATION OF THE BASE IS 2 1/2 MILES NORTH-WEST OF DULCE AND ALMOST OVERLOOKS THE TOWN. IT IS UP ON THE MESA. We discussed the similarity between everything we have been talking about here and the movie 'CLOSE ENCOUNTERS OF THE THIRD KIND'. He said he speculated that seemed to be a plan of disclosure, that is the movie. The coordinates of the location are not far off and the mountain where the actual base is looks much like the mountain in the movie.

"The next thing was -- Discussing the trade off -- all right. Here is what we got in the trade off. We got atomic technology, the atomic flying ships. Several of them, the first one wrecked on the ground and it can be seen and photographed from the air. A second one wrecked. A third one was wrecked. Apparently this last one was repaired and was the one that was in Houston -- near Houston in the Cash-Landrum case. The second items that we get out of it, are the beam weapons, the beam technology and third [* I speculate] is the thought [psionic] beam.

That is the means by which communication is accomplished. It is electrostatic in character with a magnetic component [* artifact] and it is the only way of communicating with people. They have to have the implants in order to use it. The crash occurred at the base WHEN THERE WAS A DISTURBANCE OF SOME SORT, THE ALIENS KILLED 66 OF OUR PEOPLE AND 44 GOT AWAY. [* Alien computer input - True? I do not know.].

Over an argument -- they turned on us.

"...He was familiar with what the aliens called MPS, which means manipulations per second -- no, manipulations per sequence. [An] electrostatic field that can be manipulated into many configurations and the craft can stall. In order to prevent this, the field is adjusted once every forty milliseconds. He studied the trails from UFOs and they seem to break down into a pulse rate of 62 per second. Based upon the color movie pictures, there seems to be a blast of light and spectral components and composition in there, with a Bow-Wave in front of the UFO with nitrogen showing green and oxygen showing blue, but with the saucer being invisible.

They can run into a car or airplane and this Bow-Wave will destroy them. Rockets can hit this Bow-Wave and be destroyed. They can't penetrate it. At White Sands he was shown pictures of an F-15 shooting rockets with a missile at a target and the saucers came in behind the missile, 30 ft. behind, and then flew through the explosion. He didn't know what the purpose of the demonstration was, but suspected it might be just to show how invulnerable they are. But sometimes the saucers get into trouble and they are all consumed in some kind of way.

"When he went up to Dulce in a helicopter, they landed and left some equipment there, but then when they came back the pilot was extremely nervous. Paul wanted to land on the base, but the pilot wouldn't do that. They came back to Dulce and landed at a small strip there, where they found two large Huey helicopters. The Indian [* Highway Patrolman] in charge there named Valdez went aboard one of the choppers AND THEY FOUND THEM TO BE FULL OF COMMANDOS. THEY ESTIMATED A TOTAL OF 75 COMMANDOS, fully armed with M-1 rifles [* No - M16's] and rockets [* & launchers].

"They did not have any indication of rank [* Valdez says no - not true - my mistake - I did not get that all]. They only HAD shoulder patches on and the helicopters had no identification other than numbers. The helicopters were part of a project called BLUE LIGHT and they were from Ft. Carson, Colorado [* OSI Input]. When they left they were escorted by these two large Huey helicopters. As they were flying along, in the background they saw rise up one of the advanced space technology vehicles that looked like a manta ray with a negative dihedral and projections coming down. It flew vertically past [the] two accompanying helicopters.

PAUL FEELS THAT IT IS IMPERATIVE THAT THIS INFORMATION BE RELEASED BECAUSE HE FEELS THAT IT IS UNCONSTITUTIONAL FOR THE GOVERNMENT TO BE INVOLVED IN SUCH AN ARRANGEMENT THAT INVADES THE PRIVACY OF THE INDIVIDUALS BY THE IMPLANTATION'S. HE SAID THAT 'ONCE THEY HAVE BEEN TAMPERED WITH BY THE ALIENS, THEY ARE NEVER THE SAME.' [I suppose one can easily believe that.] [Jim McCampbell comments]

So it appears that, for the privilege of collecting the biological materials in the mutilation of cattle and the abductions and the operations on board the craft, the government has allowed this to go on and even to assist for the privilege of getting the nuclear flight technology, plus also the embryos which are flown out of the base. [A rather fantastic story] [Jim McCampbell comment] Paul strikes me as being an extremely conservative, extremely knowledgeable and reliable scientist, who was intimately familiar with sophisticated laboratory equipment. His is thoroughly scientific and reliable. [Jim McCampbell evaluation]

"...I inquired about the other bases that were referred to in the 'STIGMATA' report or article. He said all that he knew [was] that one was to the south, one to the west and one to the east and he doesn't want to know anything more about it.

(Note: That is, in addition to the base north of town, there were other connected facilities west, south and east of town. In fact some sources have claimed that level 1 of the Dulce base reaches under the town of Dulce itself at a depth of some 200 to 300 feet. - Branton)

"I discussed the prospect of using the paper in the MUFON Proceedings to try to find the center of gravity for the mutilation cases from those maps that run from about 1972 to 1982 or 1983. The word gravity triggered in his mind another connection having to do with the Dept. of Interior that has a gravity dept. and they do in fact survey the United States and publish maps indicating the gravity contours. THERE IS A VERY WEAK GRAVITY at the site near Dulce.

(Note: Also another very weak gravity reading exists around Creede, Colorado, which is reportedly a northern extension from the Dulce facility. There are also southeast extensions as far away as Roswell and Carlsbad, New Mexico and an apparent southwest extension that seems to reach as far as the Superstition Mts. east of Phoenix, Arizona. These 'extensions' are not necessarily all base-complexes, but tunnels that have been excavated by aliens, secret government OR ancient cultures -- or all of the above -- via nuclear drills which eliminate waste matter by melting and cracking the rock, and pushing the molten rock as the machine moves forward into the peripheral cracks of the tunnel, where the incandescent rock cools into a super-hard glazed and water-tight lining. - Branton)

He said that the craft are very sensitive to the gravity levels and SUGGESTED THAT PERHAPS THE OTHER SITES MIGHT ALSO BE LOCATED RELATIVE TO WEAK GRAVITY.

"He indicated that the objects fly in a wobbly way. His pictures have shown that. He says 'like the rocking of a boat.' He has measured many right angle turns and also full 180 degree turns in a 20th of a second with the objects still inside the bow-wave. He has also observed and photographed the object or lights moving in a triangular pattern and square patterns.

HE SAYS HIGH POWERED RADAR CAN INTERFERE WITH THEM. I reported on the meeting that we had on Sunday afternoon and raised some of the questions that came out of that meeting. One of them was why not remove the implant? He said that this had been discussed and the lady witness finds that acceptable if she can be assured that there can be no nerve damage. He then went into great detail, which exceeds my knowledge of anatomy, in describing the location of the implants.

ONE APPEARS TO BE ADJACENT TO AND EXTERNAL TO THE CORTEX, WHICH I THINK HE INDICATED WAS AT THE BASE OF THE BRAIN. The image of the CATscan is of a very small helix, like it was joining two major nerves near the spinal column. Then on the lateral right side from the back, there is an implant of perhaps like the one above. Another is on the left side. Two others are on the forward part of the skull, which appear to be small 2 millimeter electrodes AGAINST THE RADIAL NERVE. There is a shape to these things which he indicated is like a baby bottle nipple upside down [* This shape is not the implants which **ILLEGIBLE** the skull], not the cap part, but just the nipple itself. [I raised the question of the U.S.S.R. satellites seeing this Base] He acknowledged that and also that ours can certainly see it.

He had a discussion with some photo analyst [* OSI photo analyst] who indicated that he had seen tracks up a hill and a launch location that was definitely not a rock but some kind of artificial construction. On the hazard of entering [the] area, I asked about that. He said that there is a risk if we went in on foot, but if a person tried to do that likely that the people would 'wack them.' [* I said 'zap'.

The odds are one might be accosted] But he thinks that a helicopter would be safe. But what he wants to do is to do additional aerial surveillance. Then go in with a group, the larger number of people the better.

A Highway Patrolman, a friend of his, is ready to go in at any time. He says one can't act on impulse. You have to plan out a program. He said four times he had near encounters and one was with this Major Edwards. He had received a mental communication [* No - not received - I asked them mentally - they were apparently scanning me - I don't 'receive' anything mentally.] while watching some UFOs...

"He is president of Thunder Scientific Corporation, a well known operation there, with their specialty being temperature and humidity devices. THEIR EQUIPMENT HAS BEEN ON THE SHUTTLE AND MOST OF THEIR BUSINESS IS WITH THE TOP 500 CORPORATIONS.

"His company is by Sandia on 1/2 acres and [he is] now building an additional 3500 sq. ft. building. There is another organization called Bennewitz Laboratory which is the research arm of Thunder Scientific Corporation owned 90% by the latter and operated by his three sons. They have invented a hearing device that has no moving parts that makes totally deaf people able to hear and in addition, expanding the frequency range plus 100 HZ on the high side and down to less than 10 HZ on the low frequency end.

"He said that he got involved in all this merely as a hobby and it became an obsession. He simply wanted to know what was going on and to develop instrumentation to measure data, etc. Since THE SIGNALS FROM THE UFOS <u>ARE VERY LOW FREQUENCY</u>, DOWN AROUND 200 [?] HZ and with an analyzer you just think you are looking at some noise. But I believe he said IT WAS A MEMORY SCOPE THAT WAS ABLE TO FILTER OUT THE SIGNALS INVOLVED THERE WHEREAS ORDINARY FILTERS DO NOT. They trigger signals in an on and off fashion, instead of 0 and 1 volt representing that type of communication or signal, a distinction is made between a narrow pulse and wide pulse.

Each communication is preceded by four or five pulses. HE HAD PREVIOUSLY BEEN IN TOUCH WITH THE OSI which has been verified by [the book] 'CLEAR INTENT.' But NOW HE SAYS THAT WHEN HE CALLS THEM, THEY WON'T SPEAK TO HIM SO HE IS IN A 'SHUT OUT' SITUATION. I pointed out that there were two OSI's [Office of Special Investigation] and the other is CIA [Office of Scientific Investigation]. He assured me that is was not the CIA group. He said the actual title of the group that he was dealing with was the 'Office of Secret Investigation' [or 'Intelligence'].

He says there is also a new pattern or [ILLEGIBLE] called Human Intelligence, that is they investigate the humans, that is, the government. I mentioned to him that in 'CLEAR INTENT' that it said he was under surveillance. That happens to be in error. That information comes from SOMEWHERE ELSE. But he quickly said 'I know that I am under surveillance.' They set up a site across the street from his house with computers and recorders. A girl rented the house.

He had a detective look into this and found that she was operating under an assumed name and SHE HAD NO SOCIAL SECURITY NUMBER. HE HAS PHOTOGRAPHS OF PEOPLE COMING AND GOING WITH 'NORAD' LICENSE PLATES, AIR FORCE, A.F. WEAPONS LAB.

HE THINKS NSA IS ORCHESTRATING THIS. For an entirely separate subject, he thinks [* I was told that it was by a Washington source] this whole operation,

THE UFO BASE DETAIL IS CLASSIFIED HIGHER THAN THE PRESIDENT. THAT IS, HE THINKS THE PRESIDENT DOESN'T KNOW ABOUT THIS [Not in total depth] [* True].

"He is also concerned that there are two levels of security involved. (1) Project AQUARIUS which is TOP SECRET and another (2) higher than that; where people in charge of the higher level information HAVING THESE NEW VEHICLES COULD SIMPLY TAKE OVER THE GOVERNMENT. He called the Air Force intelligence headquarters in [Washington] [* Yes - true - AF Intel.] [He didn't say Washington, but that was the idea]

The Commanding Officer was not present but he talked to a Captain who was the adjutant or executive and started talking. He said 'I know all of these facts, and this and that and what do you think about that?'

The Captain said 'JUST WRITE US A REPORT AND TELL US WHAT WE SHOULD DO.' [* About it] So he prepared a 20 page report and Edwards saw it. He forwarded it by Federal Express and also a copy to the White House in a double envelope, indicating that sensitive material was in the inner envelope. Edwards got a call from Colonel Smith [* Not Smith - Col. Don _____? Have to check files.] who was the White House Liaison to inquire who this Bennewitz fellow was. Edwards gave a positive report. The White House was extremely interested and issued orders 'TO GET ON WITH IT; TO DO SOMETHING, ASSURING EDWARDS THAT BENNEWITZ WOULD RECEIVE A LETTER WITHIN TWO WEEKS.'

(Note: This tends to confirm that TWO groups, both elected and unelected, are working simultaneously within 'government', and that each seems to have different agendas in regards to how 'government' should be run, how the alien problem should be dealt with, and how other issues should be handled. Only a small percentage of the White House executive branch and probably even a smaller percent of the Senate,

THE DULCE PROTOCOL

House of Representatives and Congress know what is going on in regards to the 'joint-interaction' projects.

The Executive branch apparently knows more than the other governmental branches because of its close ties with the Military-Intelligence-Industrial complex and because of the large number of 'appointed' rather than 'elected' officials operating within... that is, within the 'Executive' secret agencies that have been created to operate outside of presidential awareness for purposes of "plausible deniability" and which have come under the control of the Industrial elite rather than the elected Congress.

One of the reasons why the Congress and the electorate government has lost so much control over the country to the Industrial elite is because they have capitulated this authority over to the President and executive branch of government, when the President according to the U.S. Constitution should serve merely as the spokesman for the Congress, Senate, and House of Representatives. We have unconstitutionally allowed the President to have the power to appoint his own UNELECTED staff, establish Executive Orders without the consent of Congress, and create agencies that are free from Congressional oversight.

For instance Congressional overseers and investigators have been allowed to hold only a TOP SECRET security clearance, whereas many of these secret agencies like MJ12 that were created by the executive branch are classified ABOVE TOP SECRET or higher, in other words they are unelected "secret governments" operating like tape-worms within the elected government, with the potential of corrupting it from within as exemplified by the numerous black projects taking place within the Dulce base, and elsewhere.

The activities being carried out within the Dulce base have gone "out of control", and all manner of unregulated atrocities are being carried out there simply because THERE IS NO CONGRESSIONAL OVERSIGHT OF THOSE ACTIVITIES. Now that the cloning of large animals such as lambs and monkeys is a PUBLICLY KNOWN

FACT, we cannot ignore the many claims of sophisticated and unregulated cybernetic and biogenetic atrocities that have reportedly been taking place within these bases for decades. I should know, since I myself am the product of such cybernetic-biogenetic tampering -- although you might say a 'renegade' product of such black budget projects, and one who they "lost control of" along with whatever sensitive data/secrets my unconscious mind may have harbored at the time of my "defection". In regards to the problems threatening our Constitutional government, giving a U.S. President the power to create agencies which can operate with impunity far from the prying eyes of Congress and the citizens of the U.S.A. is dangerous in the extreme.

This is especially true when we consider the risk that a potential President may be the hireling of powerful corporate interests with strong media ties, and therefore able to bend public opinion in favor of the candidate of their choice while discrediting the opposition. History has shown that powerful corporate entities are more interested in making a profit -- even if it means selling out the rest of us -- than in maintaining liberty and equality.

Many of the corporate 'empires' involved with the secret government hold to the Constitution only to the degree that it serves their own self-interest. This has led America dangerously close to the edge that separates a Congressionally run DEMOCRACY from what we might refer to as a Corporate run MONARCHY, one that is ultimately controlled by unelected corporate interests rather than by elected members of Congress, the Senate, and House of Representatives. - Branton)

"Such a letter was never received. Finally, Col. Smith from the Air Force Secretary sent him a letter eventually just pursuing the 'old party line.' That said 'he should not be troubling the headquarters of the Air Force and the Executive offices of the White House with all of his stuff.'

(Note: As a result of this and other 'pressure' which came from elsewhere in the Intelligence community, nothing immediately came about, and certainly no

THE DULCE PROTOCOL

'Congressional Investigation' into the activities near Dulce, which was definitely warranted. The 'pressure' may have come from the NSA-CIA-AQUARIUS-MAJI agencies. It seems as if the alleged intelligence agent "Ufologist" William Moore played a major role in the efforts to sabotage the Dulce investigations and destroy Paul Bennewitz' reputation.

Moore was working on behalf of the 'AVIARY' -- a schizophrenic 'Alien Intelligence' Agency operating deep within the murky labyrinthine levels of the 'governmental-military-industrial' complex, an agency which is apparently carrying out the policies and agendas of the likewise schizophrenic MJ12 organization, or the policies of MJ12's superior agency MAJI -- the 'Majestic Agency for Joint Intelligence'. Depending on which 'faction' has gained the upper hand in MJ12, in the CIA, and in the AVIARY -- that is the NAVY's pro American CABAL and COM-12 agencies OR the NAZI's [er, I mean the NSA's] pro New World Order MAJI and AQUARIUS agencies -- the policies of these agencies have in the past been subject to immediate change if not absolute reversal.

As a case in point, Cattle Mutilation researcher Linda Moulton Howe was invited to Kirtland AFB in April of 1983 to visit with AFOSI agent Richard Doty. During the visit Doty showed Howe some extremely sensitive documents PROVING the existence of aliens and alien hardware now in government hands. Doty detailed a complex plan for metered public release of the entire UFO secret, and was interested in using Ms. Howe's contract with HBO -- to do a UFO / Cattle Mutilation documentary -- as a springboard for the release of such information.

Elaborate plans were made and many promises were given, however as a result of a power-struggle deep within the Intelligence community the plans for public information release were shelved and Linda Howe was left out in the cold scratching her head and wondering just what the hell the whole thing was all about. And Linda Howe has NOT been the only one to experience this bizarre type of schizophrenic activity within the Intelligence community, especially in regards to projects and plans for the 'government' to come clean on the alien agenda.

Apparently there are those patriots within government who want ALL of the facts about alien malevolence and infiltration of planet earth made public; those corporate interests who want NONE of the facts made public as they maintain their power through the suppression of truth; and those agents of the aliens themselves who want information made public SO LONG as the alien Greys are <u>presented as benevolent</u> <u>'space brothers'</u>... I would guess the latter would involve some type of propaganda meant to entice the masses themselves to accept and capitulate their will over to the Draconian Reptiloid/Grey collectivists, who have infiltrated and control certain levels of the military-intelligence-industrial complex. - Branton)

"Bennewitz showed this letter to Edwards WHO BLEW UP AND CALLED SMITH [* Col. Don. ____]. They got an answer from the Air Force that they were not interested and knew nothing about it. On another point: referencing the 'STIGMATA' article where the farmer thought that the two humanoids may have been naked. In the case with which he was dealing with -- the woman and the son, the boy upon being questioned laughed, and said 'they had no fronts or behinds.' I asked no sexual organs?, and he said yes, no organs at all.

He has received information concerning a high metabolism rate of the creatures, even birdlike. One of the witnesses, I think the woman who was being taken by the hand, said the hand of the creature was 'red hot.' And he guesses that it must have been 115 degrees F. The creatures cannot stand uncontrolled environment. THEY WEAR SUITS FOR PROTECTION AGAINST EXCESSIVE HEAT. They are fed by a formula and if they are short of that intake, they will turn green. [* Turn Grey - They are a light yellow green when healthy] The heart is on the right side and they have one lung. Elimination is through the skin. The creatures are very strong...

THE DULCE PROTOCOL

"He says that the UFOs can be detected by radar detectors and they also trigger highway patrol radar or Police radar guns. His friend Valdez, at his suggestion, was looking for water intake to the site and within about 1 1/2 miles he came upon a flying saucer at a distance of about 300 ft. THE INDIANS OWN THE AREA -- ARE QUITE SCARED AND VERY SUPERSTITIOUS AND 90% OF THEM HAVE MOVED INTO TOWN. The Chief of Police told him about an experience he had. A tribal chief had gone deer hunting on a mesa south of Dulce. Two days went by.

When he didn't Return, a search party was sent out. In the daylight on the mesa, a ship 'hopped up' from down below and came above the mesa. The guys [human] kicked the tribal chief to the ground. Then they got into the ship and disappeared. He had been hunting and had 'fell'. He had a broken leg and he was picked up by these people in the craft. They were blacks... [* No - No - the SHIP was black... black uniforms] He discussed something about some devices called sphericals that are optical in sound [* They have a sound when they move abruptly.] and apparently remotely controlled little vehicles... Spheres from 1 1/2" to 12" in diameter. (These hovering spheres have also been seen in underground bases that reach as deeply as 2 miles below Edwards Air Force Base in California. Some have referred to them as 'spybees' - Branton).

We discussed weapons used by aliens and whether or not they are used to paralyze people. Yes, they consist of a cube about 2" on a side -- called a lens hung around the neck that emits a beam. Another on the ship produces a BLUE light that he has seen. It comes from a device about 4" high and 14" long with grid black lines on it (Is Bennewitz an abductee also? - Branton). The color produced is very light blue which is like ionized oxygen. He has not sought publicity on any of this. He is only interested in getting the facts...

"I continue to get reassurance that the guy is continually on the level and what he has to say should be taken seriously... [Jim McCampbell comment.]"

Ufologist Penny Harper, in the January 1990 issue of 'WHOLE LIFE TIMES', adds an unusual postscript to the Bennewitz affair in an article in which she revealed the following:

"Paul Bennewitz -- whereabouts unknown. Paul was a scientist investigating an abduction case. A woman and her son drove down a road in the southwest, the woman witnessed aliens mutilating a calf. The aliens captured both mother and son, taking them into an underground installation."

The woman observed many frightening things, apparently much of it similar to what abductee Christa Tilton and others have witnessed, yet they - mother and son - also saw:

"...human body parts floating in a vat of amber liquid. After a horrifying ordeal, the woman and her son were taken back to their car. Bennewitz was able to determine that there is a secret 'alien' base beneath Dulce, New Mexico.

He wrote 'The Dulce Report' and sent it to the civilian UFO group called APRO [i.e. Aerial Phenomena Research Organization]. Bennewitz was then committed to the New Mexico State Hospital for the mentally ill where he was given electro-shock 'therapy.'

When he was discharged, he publicly stated that he would not have anything to do with UFOs.

He is a recluse today, but still alive, last I heard."

THE DULCE PROTOCOL

Chapter 23
Inside Intelligence On The Dulce Base

In a letter dated Sept. 1990, written by Thomas E. Castello and addressed to researcher 'Jason Bishop', the former Dulce Base technical-security officer stated:

"...The room for [the electro-magnetic] generator is nearly 200 feet diameter. This circular room covers the fifth and sixth levels [extreme westsouth wing]. Here, is the intense magnetic generator. There is a 'buffer area' made of ceramic and Latex that is four feet thick, in all directions. There [are] five entrances [plus an escape trap door on the sixth floor] on each floor. Each portal has a double door [one at the out-side of the buffer and one at the inside of the buffer].

The security is severe. Armed guards patrol constantly, and in addition to weight sensitive areas there [are] hand print and eye print stations. No one under ULTRA 5 clearance is allowed near the portals. Here, is the device that powers the transfer of atoms. No information is available to personnel with ULTRA 7 or less. [I was ULTRA 7]"

"Commander X", the mysterious and anonymous Military Intelligence officer and member of the "COMMITTE OF 12" [COM-12?] -- who has released sensitive information through Tim Beckley's New York City based UFO organization -- has stated:

"The underground...base outside of Dulce, New Mexico, is perhaps the one MOST FREQUENTLY referred to. It's existence is most widely known, including several UFO abductees who have apparently been taken there for examination and then either managed to escape or were freed just in the nick of time by friendly...forces.

"According to UFO conspiracy buff and ex-Naval Intelligence Officer Milton [William] Cooper, '...a confrontation broke out between the human scientists and the Aliens at the Dulce underground lab. The Aliens took many of our scientists hostage. Delta Forces were sent in to free them but they were no match for the Alien weapons. Sixty-six people were killed during this action. As a result we withdrew from all joint projects for at least TWO years...'

"CENTURIES AGO, SURFACE PEOPLE [some say the ILLUMINATI] entered into a pact with an 'Alien nation' HIDDEN WITHIN THE EARTH," Commander X alleges. "The U.S. [Executive] Government, in 1933 agreed to trade animals in exchange for high-tech knowledge, and to allow them to use [undisturbed] UNDERGROUND BASES, in the Western U.S.A. A special group was formed to deal with the 'Alien' beings. In the 1940's 'Alien Life Forms' [ALF's] began shifting their focus of operations, FROM CENTRAL AND SOUTH AMERICA, TO THE U.S.A.

"The CONTINENTAL DIVIDE is vital to these 'entities.' Part of this has to do with magnetics [substrata rock] and high energy states [plasma]... This area has a very high concentration of lightning activity; underground waterways and cavern systems; fields of atmospheric ions; etc."

"...From my own intelligence work within the military, I can say WITH ALL CERTAINTY that one of the main reasons the public has been kept in total darkness about the reality of UFOs and 'aliens', is that the truth of the matter actually exists TOO

THE DULCE PROTOCOL

CLOSE TO HOME TO DO ANYTHING ABOUT. How could a spokesman for the Pentagon dare admit that five or ten thousand feet underground EXISTS AN ENTIRE WORLD THAT IS 'FOREIGN' TO A BELIEF STRUCTURE WE HAVE HAD FOR CENTURIES? How could, for example, our fastest bomber be any challenge to those aerial invaders when we can only guess about the routes they take to the surface; eluding radar as they fly so low, headed back to their underground lair?

"...the 'Greys' or the 'EBEs' have established a fortress, spreading out to other parts of the U.S. via means of a vast underground tunnel system THAT HAS VIRTUALLY EXISTED BEFORE RECORDED HISTORY..."

Val Valerian, of the Washington State based 'Leading Edge Research' Group, made the following statements in one of his L.E.R. issues:

"ADDITIONAL COMMENTS ON ALIEN BASES -- There is some confusion over the subject of alien bases in the United States. There seem to be many of them, but some of them seem to stand out functionally and operationally. IT WOULD SEEM THAT THE MAIN BASE is in NEW MEXICO with small detachments [human phrase] at Dreamland and Area 51 in general. Both of those locations are used to test-fly alien craft [PROJECT GRUDGE/REDLIGHT]. The main location for the test flights appears to be Area 51. The EXCALIBUR project being developed at LOS ALAMOS is designed to try and penetrate underground facilities, since they [the grays] have entrenched themselves and no longer honor any of the dubious agreements which they have made with [certain] factions within the government.

"...Scores of underground installations hold citizens of virtually EVERY country on the planet in captivity."

Researcher William F. Hamilton revealed the following details on the Dulce base which were provided by former Dulce base security director -- who is now missing and presumed deceased -- Thomas Edwin Castello.

In his book 'COSMIC TOP SECRET' [p. 109], Hamilton writes:

"...According to Thomas, the alien androgynal breeder is capable of parthenogenesis. At Dulce, the common form of reproduction is polyembryony. Each embryo can, and does divide into 6 to 9 individual 'cunne' [pronounced cooney, i.e. siblings]. The needed nutriment for the developing cunne is supplied by the 'formula,' which usually consist of [human/animal blood] plasma, deoxyhemoglobin, albumin, lysozyme, cation, amniotic fluid and more."

Abductee Christa Tilton confirmed much of what Thomas Castello has revealed.

Christa described,

"...strange vats filled with eerie liquid...where aliens are being grown."

She stated that there were:

"Dozens of creatures in each womb. Can't count tanks, maybe scores or hundreds... womb submerged in sort of yellow liquid. Looks thicker than water. Creatures float in amber colored water. Womb is grayish..."

The creatures or embryos being bred were "not human", had bluish-grey 'resilient' skin, and possessed "three fingers" and "two toes". She confirmed that parts of human bodies may be used in the 'fluid'. She says that they used her to breed a human-like child which is being held prisoner in the underground base.

Val Valerian through one of his LEADING EDGE RESEARCH reports released the following synopsis of the so-called 'DULCE PAPERS':

THE DULCE PROTOCOL

"The Dulce papers were comprised of 25 BLACK AND WHITE PHOTOS, A VIDEO TAPE WITH NO DIALOGUE and a set of papers that included technical information of the allegedly jointly occupied [CIA-Alien] facility 1 kilometer beneath the Archuleta Mesa near Dulce, New Mexico. SEVERAL PERSONS WERE GIVEN THE ABOVE PACKAGE FOR SAFE KEEPING. Most of those given the package were shown what the package contained but were not technically oriented and knew very little about what they were looking at.

The following is written by ONE OF THESE PERSONS about what the papers contained. This person described the scenes that the video tape showed... What you see is what you get; I can't decipher what is written or drawn anymore than you can. I pass these papers on only in the interest of getting to the truth. [From] other information I have, I believe the information herein is true. I believe the facility exists and is CURRENTLY OPERATIONAL. I also believe that there are 4 ADDITIONAL FACILITIES OF THE SAME TYPE, ONE LOCATED A FEW MILES TO THE SOUTHEAST OF GROOM LAKE, NEVADA. What is the truth? Only God, MJ-12 and the aliens know for sure.

"Dulce papers: Lots of papers-documents that discuss COPPER AND MOLYBDENUM, also papers about MAGNESIUM AND POTASSIUM, BUT MOSTLY ABOUT COPPER. Lots of 'MEDICAL TERMS' that I don't understand. A sheet of paper with charts and strange diagrams. Papers that discuss ULTRA VIOLET LIGHT AND GAMMA RAYS. Papers that discuss COLOR AND BLACK AND WHITE AND HOW TO AVOID DETECTION THROUGH USE OF CERTAIN COLORS.

In addition to these papers THERE ARE ABOUT 25 PICTURES, BLACK AND WHITE, PLUS ONE VIDEO TAPE WITH NO DIALOGUE, ALL TAKEN INSIDE THE DULCE FACILITY. THESE PAPERS TELL WHAT THE ALIENS ARE AFTER AND HOW THE BLOOD [TAKEN FROM THE COWS] IS USED. Aliens seem to absorb atoms to 'eat'. ALIENS PUT HANDS 'IN BLOOD', SORT OF LIKE A

SPONGE, FOR NOURISHMENT. IT'S NOT JUST FOOD THEY WANT, THE DNA in cattle and humans is being altered.

THE 'TYPE ONE' CREATURE IS A LAB ANIMAL. 'THEY' KNOW HOW TO CHANGE THE ATOMS TO CREATE A TEMPORARY 'ALMOST HUMAN BEING'. IT IS MADE WITH ANIMAL TISSUE AND DEPENDS ON A COMPUTER TO SIMULATE MEMORY, A MEMORY THE COMPUTER HAS WITHDRAWN FROM ANOTHER HUMAN BEING. THE 'ALMOST HUMAN BEING' IS SLIGHTLY SLOW AND CLUMSY. (Several so-called "MEN IN BLACK" have been described in this manner. - Branton)

REAL HUMANS ARE USED FOR TRAINING, TO EXPERIMENT AND BREED WITH THESE 'ALMOST HUMANS'. SOME HUMANS ARE KIDNAPPED AND USED COMPLETELY [EVEN ATOMS]. SOME ARE KEPT IN LARGE TUBES, AND ARE KEPT ALIVE IN AN AMBER LIQUID.

SOME HUMANS ARE BRAINWASHED AND USED TO DISTORT THE TRUTH. CERTAIN MALE HUMANS HAVE A HIGH SPERM COUNT AND ARE KEPT ALIVE. THEIR SPERM IS USED TO ALTER THE DNA AND CREATE A NON-GENDER BEING CALLED 'TYPE TWO'.

That sperm is grown some way and altered again, put in large wombs, many destroyed, certain are altered again and then put in separate wombs.

THEY RESEMBLE 'UGLY HUMANS' WHEN GROWING BUT LOOK NORMAL WHEN FULLY GROWN WHICH TAKES ONLY A FEW MONTHS FROM FETUS SIZE. THEY HAVE A SHORT LIFE SPAN, LESS THAN A YEAR. SOME FEMALE HUMANS ARE USED FOR BREEDING. COUNTLESS WOMEN HAVE HAD A SUDDEN MISCARRIAGE AFTER ABOUT 3 MONTHS PREGNANCY. SOME NEVER KNEW THEY WERE PREGNANT.

Others remember contact some way. THE FETUS IS USED TO MIX THE DNA IN TYPES ONE AND TWO. THE ATOMIC MAKEUP IN THAT FETUS IS HALF HUMAN, HALF 'ALMOST HUMAN' AND WOULD NOT SURVIVE IN THE MOTHERS WOMB.

It is taken at 3 months and grown elsewhere."

Chapter 24

The Dulce Network – North Sector

The following account was received by Bill Cooper from a 'friend', and appeared under the title "Robert's Story". Compare this report with other accounts concerning Dulce-base extensions in northeast Arizona, southeast Utah and southwest Colorado [Four Corners Area] where "dissident scientists" are reportedly being held captive:

Robert _____ _____, a young man in his early 20's came to work at my shop as a temporary help during the 2nd week of October 1986. The first day at work, he approached me asking about my interest in the UFO phenomenon. Then he smiled, paused, and waited for my reaction. I told him that I was interested, particularly in the crash/recovery of saucers and bodies of occupants. That I was secondly interested in the rumors pertaining to an 'alien' and intelligence group alliance set up years ago.

He then told me he would reveal something to me pertaining to my second interest as mentioned above. He told me the following [condensed by me]:

He was in the military headquartered with the 4th Engineering Group at Fort Carson, Colorado. Just got out 2 months prior to the date of telling me this.

Robert K Teske

He showed me a military I.D. card from Fort Carson and another with a strange checker board design on it. He said he had a Super Top Secret clearance and worked as a laboratory assistant in southwestern Colorado associated with the Delta Group out of Fort Carson.

He witnessed cryogenic experimentation going on with human beings. This experimentation was conducted by both 'aliens' and some Super Secret intelligence group.

Some high ranking military and scientific personnel were taken down to cryogenic temperatures through a process of draining their blood and pumping a chemical mixture into the circulatory system to prevent cell destruction during the freezing and thawing periods.

The 'aliens' were the only ones who knew the mixture formula and the gradual thawing process. They at first refused to give the formula and process to the scientific team, and threatened to leave the above mentioned personnel in that cryogenic state forever unless the scientists cooperated on some certain issues.

He also told me about some 'alien' techniques concerning time travel, Dimensional travel, related to unified field physics.

After revealing these seemingly fantastic things to me over a 3 week period of time he quit the temporary job here. I finally found out that his father Robert _____ Sr. [Robert used to be Robert _____ Jr. before his father and mother divorced and he took the name of his mothers second husband, _____.] worked with me in the metal finishing department. The following was told to me by Robert _____ Sr. on Dec 16, 1986:

On the evening of Wednesday, Dec. 3, 1986, my son Robert _____ called me via the telephone [he hadn't been home for over a week]. He sounded as if he were scared to death. He said, "I have to go back to Colorado immediately". I asked why. He said, "The bounty hunters found me and told me that I had to go back with them to the base in Colorado because I know to much." I asked if there were any way he could beat them and get out of it? Robert stated, "They said there is no way out. In fact the chief bounty hunter confronted me face to face."

Evidently Robert Jr. tried to beat the bounty hunters. His alleged body was found in room #5 of the Walls Motel in Long Beach, California, with a gun in his hand and a bullet hole through his head. Drugs were found in the room, but not in his body [he was not the drug type].

The Long Beach Police Dept. investigated the case which ended very abruptly with no explanation. When I asked them why the case was closed so quickly, they snapped back, "Its none of your business". The final autopsy report stated that the death was a drug related suicide.

I was not allowed to see the body for one solid week. I would call the police, they would say the body was at the funeral parlor. The funeral parlor would say we don't have the body. This went on back and forth for that one solid week [Dec. 5th - Dec. 12th, 1986]. When I was finally allowed to view the body, I immediately could tell it was not him!! This body, alleged to be Robert _____, was about 20 Lbs heavier and about 3 to 4 inches shorter than my son. That was not Robert even though the basic facial features were his.

One very significant thing that Robert stated to me before his alleged death was, "Dad, they are coming to take me away. I will give you a code name _____ [only Robert and his father know that code name]. If you receive a letter, telephone call, or by messenger, sometime in the future [with] this code name, you will know that I am alive. They need me for my special DNA, which is why I have to go back."

Robert K Teske

Robert has special Occult Powers and has an interest in witch craft. He says all of this UFO stuff is directly related to witch craft and the occult. In February - April 1987 both Robert _____ Sr. and myself were under surveillance by what we considered an agent from the cover-up group. He went by the name of John Chunn. We finally confronted him face to face concerning all of this. Needless to say he quit work that day and never came back. Robert Sr. has been harassed several times by an individual who wanted Robert Sr. to go to the 4 corners area with him. On April 16, 1987, he said he would reunite him with his son. _____ backed out the last minute.

Later Robert Sr. was picked up by the police for no reason at all and held for one week. When he got back home he found out that his place had been ransacked.

On Nov. 9, 1987, a person riding a motorcycle and dressed like a biker approached _____, identifying himself as Lt. Leed or Reade and claimed that he had a Top Secret clearance and had access to the files pertaining to the projects that his son was still involved in. He said that he would place _____ in touch with Robert _____ and said he was working in an underground base. He said you cannot find this base on any maps or in any military directories.

Robert _____ was in the following unit. -- HHC 4th STU BU., ABN., FBG 31905v Fort Carson, Colorado.

His Command

Chapter 25

Danger Down Under - The Christa Tilton Story

The following is from an article titled "GOING UNDERGROUND", written by abductee Christa Tilton -- an attractive Blond or 'Nordic-appearing' woman who relates some remarkable contactee and abduction type experiences which she has had involving the Dulce base.

Christa was kind enough to take the time to contribute her own fascinating experiences to this work and answer several of my questions so that other abductees, like herself, might better understand their own confusing encounters with alien abductors or even underground facilities:

"Several months ago I became aware of two different cases, one in May of 1973 in which a Judy Doraty of Texas had an unusual experience in which she may have been taken to an underground facility; also an abduction case investigated by APRO and a Mr. Paul Bennewitz in which in May of 1980 a Myrna Hansen of New Mexico had a similar experience in which she was taken to some type of underground facility.

"Since I am doing the investigation into my own underground experience, I found that to be of help to me or anyone else that might have experienced anything similar, I was going to have to make myself read their transcripts. For months I would procrastinate because I suppose, subconsciously, I did not really want to relive this experience I had -- by reading about another persons' experiences. Now I am glad I did. I finally am going to reveal some of the many correlation's of all three of our cases in hopes that others will come forward with more information.

"My experience happened in July of 1987. I had about a three our 'missing time' in which later, under hypnosis, I relived the most unusual night of my life... I did not go willingly to the craft. Two small aliens dragged me by my two arms on my back to the craft after they rendered me unconscious.

The next thing I remember is waking up on a table inside some type of small craft. A 'guide' greeted me and gave me something to drink. I now believe it was a stimulant of some kind because I was not sleepy after I drank the substance. I was taken out of the craft and when I looked around I noticed I was standing on top of a hill. It was dark, but I saw a faint light near a cavern. We walked up to this area and it is then that I saw a man, dressed in a red military-type jump suit [like a pilot would wear]. My guide seemed to know this man as he greeted him as we came closer. I also noticed he wore some type of patch and was carrying an automatic weapon.

When we walked into the tunnel, I realized we were going right into the side of a large hill or mountain. There we were met with another guard in red and I then saw a computerized check-point with two cameras on each side. To my left was a large groove where a small transit vehicle carried you further inside. To my right it looked like a long hallway where there were many offices. We took the transit car and went for what seemed to be a very long time to another secured area. It was then that I was told to step onto some type of scale-like device that faced a computer screen.

I saw lights flashing and numbers computing and then a card was issued with holes punched into it. I would later realize it was used as identification inside a computer. I asked my guide where we were going and why. He didn't say too much the

THE DULCE PROTOCOL

whole time except that he was to show me some things that I need to know for future reference. He told me that we had just entered Level One of the 'facility'. I asked what kind of facility it was and he did not answer.

"This story is so very long and detailed and I hope to write more about it so I will [only] highlight some of the things that I saw... I was taken to a huge looking elevator that had no door. It was like a very large dumb-waiter. It took us down to Level Two where there were two guards in a different color jumpsuit and I had to go down a large hall and saw many offices that had computers that lined the wall. As we walked by, I noticed the lighting was strange in that I could not see a source for it. Other people walked by and never once acted like I was a stranger. I felt I was in a huge office building where there are many employees with many offices and cubicles. I then saw an extremely large area which looked like a giant factory. There were small alien-type craft parked at the sides. Some were being worked on underneath and it was then that I saw my first grey-type alien. They seemed to be doing the menial jobs and never once did they look up as we passed. There were cameras posted every where.

"Then we arrived at another elevator and went down to Level Five. It was then that I felt a sense of extreme fear and balked. My guide explained that as long as I was with him that I would not be harmed. So we got off and I saw guards posted there at the checkpoint. This time they were not friendly and were issuing orders right and left. I noticed that two of the guards seemed to be arguing about something and they kept looking over at me. I wanted to find the closest exit out of this place, but I know I had come too far for that. This time I was asked to change clothes. I was told to put on what looked to me like a hospital gown, only thank God there was a back to it! I did as I was told because I didn't want to cause any trouble.

I stepped onto this scale-like device and suddenly the screen lighted up and I heard strange tones and frequencies that made my ears hurt. What I really thought was strange is that these guards saluted the guide I was with although he was not wearing any military clothes. He was dressed in a dark green jumpsuit, but it had no insignia that

I know of. He told me to follow him down this corridor. As I passed the guard station, I noticed the humming of those cameras as they watched my every move. I was taken down another hall and it was then that I smelled this horrid smell. Contrary to Judy and Myrna's stories, I knew what I was smelling or at least I thought I knew. It smelled like formaldehyde. Because of my medical background I felt probably more comfortable with this situation because I had gone through it so many times before.

"We came to a large room and I stopped to look inside. I saw these huge large tanks with computerized gauges hooked to them and a huge arm-like device that extended from the top of some tubing down into the tanks. The tanks were about 4 feet tall so standing where I was I could not see inside them. I did notice a humming sound and it looked as if something was being stirred inside the tanks. I started to walk closer to the tanks and it was at that time that my guide grabbed my arm and pulled me roughly out into the hall. He told me that it wasn't necessary to see the contents of the tanks; that it would only complicate matters. So we went on down the hallway and then he guided my arm into a large laboratory.

"I was amazed because I had worked in [a laboratory] before and I was seeing machines that I had never seen before. It was then I turned and saw a small grey being with his back turned doing something at a counter. I heard the clinking of metal against metal. I had only heard this when I was preparing my surgical instruments for my doctor in surgery. Then my guide asked me to go and sit down on the table in the middle of the room. I told him that I wouldn't do it and he said it would be much easier if I would comply. He was not smiling and I was scared. I did not want to be left in this room with this grey alien!

"About the time I was thinking this a human man entered. He was dressed like a doctor, with a white lab coat on and the same type of badge I was issued. My guide went to greet him and they shook hands. I began shaking and I was cold. The temperature seemed awfully cold. My guide smiled at me and told me he would be waiting outside and I would only be there for a few minutes. I began to cry. I cry when I get scared. The grey alien looked at me and turned around to continue what he was doing. The doctor called for more assistance and it was then that one other grey alien came in. The next thing I knew I was very drowsy.

I knew I was being examined internally and when I lifted my head, I saw this horrid grey alien glaring at me with large black eyes. It was then I felt a stabbing pain. I screamed and then the human doctor stood next to me and rubbed something over my stomach. It was cold. The pain immediately subsided. I could not believe this was happening to me all over again. I begged for them to let me go, but they just kept on working very fast. After they were finished, I was told to get up and go into this small room and change back into my other clothes. I noticed blood, as if I had started my period. But, I continued to get dressed and when I came out I saw my guide speaking to the doctor in the corner of the room. I just stood there...helpless. I felt more alone then than I ever had in my life. I felt like a guinea pig. After we left that laboratory I was silent. I was angry at him for allowing this to happen to me 'again'. But he said it was necessary. Told me to forget.

"I see more aliens pass us in the hall. Again, it is as if I was a ghost. I asked my guide to please explain this place to me. He told me it was a very sensitive place and I would be brought back again in the next few years. I again asked where I was and he told me I could not be told for my own safety. We then got into the small transit car and it took us to the other side.

It was there that I saw the most disturbing things of all. Unlike the other two women (Myrna Hansen of New Mexico who was abducted to the Dulce base in May of 1980, and Judy Doraty of Texas who had a similar experience in May of 1973 that was investigated by APRO and Paul Bennewitz - Branton) who saw cows being mutilated, I saw what looked to me to be people of all different types standing up against the wall inside a clear casing-like chamber. I went closer and it looked 'as if' they were wax figures. I could not understand what I was seeing. I also saw animals in cages. They were alive..."

At this point the 'guide' escorted Christa to the elevator and up through the various levels, following which the transit car took her to the waiting alien craft, at which point she was Returned to her home some three hours after her abduction experience had begun.

Incidentally, Christa claims to have also experienced contacts with human-like beings from other worlds. One alien by the name of 'Maijan' who has dealt with Christa all her life has always worn an emblem of a feathered serpent, possibly symbolic of the ancient Mayan deity Quetzalcoatl. He also claims to have ancestors from the Aztec and Mayan race, as do several of the 'Telosians' inhabiting the colony under Mt. Shasta, California.

Christa Tilton admits that of the human-like Pleiadeans and Lyrans she has encountered [aside from her encounters with short and tall Greys] range from the strict non-interventionists to the imperialistic factions who believe that conquering planet earth is justified as a means to subdue their perceived enemies on or below the surface of this planet. This might imply that the 'Draconians' have, as many sources claim, maintained underground command centers beneath the surface of planet earth -- from where they direct many of their interventionist interstellar activities.

In addition to the above, Christa Tilton was kind enough to answer some questions for this present volume in regards to her own experiences.

These questions and answers follow:

INTRODUCTION BY CHRISTA: I've been investigating underground bases and Dulce -- actually underground bases all over the world -- since 1987... I've had some good experiences and I've had some bad experiences [with aliens, etc.]

QUESTION: Have you seen any people who were being held captive underground, during your abductions to Dulce and other bases?

THE DULCE PROTOCOL

ANSWER: First of all let me state [that] there is more evidence NOW to prove that a base DID indeed exist back in 1987 when I was abducted (About 8 years following the Dulce wars, after which joint-interaction ceased for a period of two years - Branton), and it was in the process of being dismantled. A lot of times the government will have underground bases for different purposes, and then will shut them down, board them up, concrete them in or whatever, and go on and built another base somewhere else. What I will tell you is this. Let me stick with the question. You asked me did I see any people being held captive during that abduction to Dulce?

I remember seeing some individuals as I was walking by. They looked as if they were in suspended animation. I went up to the clear casings that they were being held in. I put my hands on the casing and leaned towards them to see if I could get some kind of a response. I did not. I could not discern whether they were dead or alive at that point in time. They were just not moving, and I could not see whether or not there was any fluid. I think that the casings were free of any fluid in this particular case. As far as my being taken to any other bases right now, I'm not going to comment on that because I'm still researching that. There has been speculation by, and information from, an Air Force officer at KIRTLAND AIR FORCE BASE that I along with some other women and men have been, more than likely, abducted and taken to the underground research facility near Kirtland AFB. It's in the Manzano mountain range south of KIRTLAND AFB where the nuclear testing was going on at that time.

(Note: KIRTLAND AFB is the base where the 'division' within the Intelligence Community over the Dulce facility and related joint-interaction projects seems to have begun, one that initially involved Col. Doty, Col. Edwards, the Wing Commander and others, a division between the anti-Grey U.S. Navy factions in the CABAL/COM-12 -- backed by the 'Electorate' government; and their opposition, the pro-Grey NSA factions in AQUARIUS/MAJI -- backed by the 'Corporate' government. - Branton)

Q: Did any of your alien or human contacts mention the Dulce Wars?

A: No. The alien beings that I came in contact with while underground did not speak to me. The human contacts did but no, they did not mention any kind of wars going on there. So at that particular time I was not aware of any kind of a power-struggle going on. I was just taken there for a specific purpose I think, and once that was done I was rushed out of there and I don't think any kind of knowledge like that in particular would have been given to me, there wouldn't have been any reason to give it to me.

Q: What kinds of reptilians, if any, have you encountered?

A: I am almost virtually positive that... I don't believe I have come across any reptilian aliens at all. The only types that I've been associated with most of my life have been small grey aliens, the ones that I call workers. These are beings that I believe are soulless beings that are workers FOR an established alien race. They are given certain chores, certain jobs, just like we would if we worked for a large company... There are some taller Grey alien beings that I have encountered. Even though their eyes are large and dark, they don't have that 'reptilian' look. I know. I know what you're talking about and no, I really haven't encountered any of those.

(Note: Of course from many other accounts, most of the 'Greys' are reptilian BASED clones which have assimilated other genetics from insectoid or even plant-like life-forms. Outwardly they -- the clones especially -- do not normally appear obviously 'reptilian', which is likely the reason why they are most commonly used to 'interface' with planetary intelligence agencies. The "established alien race" that the Greys are working for, according to many sources, are the taller more 'reptiloid' appearing species including the "white draco" -- resident within levels six and seven, levels which Christa does not recall entering. - Branton)

Q: Do you know of any other bases that researchers may be unaware of?

THE DULCE PROTOCOL

A: That's a great question, really, because right now I'm working with two individuals from Great Britain. They're two wonderful researchers who have been associated with Timothy Good. I don't know if you've read his material, "ABOVE TOP SECRET". It's a wonderful book to get and read. Also "ALIEN LIAISON" is another one.

But yes, I am aware of many, many, many underground facilities or bases that are being used for different purposes. Most of the underground bases are being used for covert purposes or otherwise purposes involving governments who are doing certain types of testing that they consider would be safer to do underground.

And then there are the bases, one in particular north of Tucson, Arizona, where I'm almost positive I was taken to, it goes under the cover or name of "Evergreen Aviation". They have all the planes there and everything, but what I found during my ten years of research is that this is a CIA-backed or based facility. I got very, very close to the facility, I climbed over the wired fence and sneaked in with a pilot friend of mine not long ago and got some great photographs of some black helicopters. These black helicopters were unmarked. There were other types of aircraft there, and so we really believe that there are many, many bases in many states. I've heard of bases in almost every state here in the United States.

Now the two individuals that I'm doing work for or research with in Great Britain especially are researching underground bases in America and in Great Britain. I guess they contacted me because they felt like there was a tie-in or some kind of connection, and that it would be a good thing to work together and share information and see what types of facilities we can find out about. In a lot of the facilities they are doing medical testing, some are actual laboratories like Los Alamos laboratories.

They do massive amounts of covert work for Black Projects of our own government, so we're talking about installations, underground and above ground, that are doing things that we probably have no idea about. We hear rumors of course of different things that are going on. What I would venture to guess is that more than likely these rumors have been proven about 90% of the time to be true.

Q: My belief is that the Greys operate from base animal or predatory instincts in their agendas to increase their power-base and exploit other cultures, and that they will continue to do so as a collective until they are stopped by force. Some of the Greys I believe might be 'tamed' by humans so to speak, and attain a degree of emotional individuality <u>IF they can be severed from the collective HIVE mind</u>. What are your views on this?

A: I agree with you on most of that... Certainly the Greys seem to do things like a massive collective consciousness. I've noticed that they do things together, there is almost no discussion among themselves. They seem to be working on projects or on certain things that are given to them by higher-ups, or higher alien beings and/or humans. I really couldn't tell you. I have my doubts that humans would be able to 'tame' any kind of alien intelligence here on earth.

If indeed it looks like humans are working among the Greys together, that more than likely it was because of a pact or some type of a government agreement... I believe these aliens have come here for reasons, and certain individuals in the government have been given orders by their higher-ups to either give them opportunities to work alongside of these [aliens] for maybe a one-world purpose. Unless it could be shown to me to be true that the humans tamed these Greys that were working along-side with me, or on me, that would be very difficult for me to believe.

Q: Have you had encounters with any Nazi-type aliens like those described by Barney Hill, Alex Christopher, Vladimir Terziski and others, alien 'fascists' who date back to the secret Nazi flying disk experiments and who are allegedly working with the Greys and Reptiloids?

THE DULCE PROTOCOL

A: I've heard of these Nazi aliens. Of course where I first heard about them was from TAL LeVesque back in 1987. No I have never come in contact with what I would call Nazi type aliens although since most of my experiences have involved medical experimentation, genetic experimentation on me and my daughter or family, I would have to say that it reeks almost of... If you think about the medical experiments that were done on the Jews during the Holocaust, that is what I equate some of the experiments that happened to me with.

It's strange because I'm part German, I come from a family that originally came FROM Germany, so I do have some German blood in me, but I'm not leaning one way or the other and as far as being a BIGOT is concerned, I'm very, very open to all races, creeds, colors of people working together to establish a wonderful world, if that would be possible.

But anyway, no I have not encountered these Nazi types, and I've certainly heard a lot about them, I've heard they are very mean-spirited aliens, I don't know what their agenda is... Since I've not had contacts with these types I really have no reason to do any research on them, and also the same goes for the [tall] reptilians, although many, many friends and other researchers have contacted me telling their tales about reptilian alien races...

Q: What are your views of a possible CONGRESSIONALLY backed take-over of the Dulce base in the future, and what would be your views on dealing with the problem supposing the Greys don't surrender?

A: Through all of the research that I've done, and all of the proof that I've come up with the many times that I've been up there poking around with researchers and other individuals, we're almost positive now -- I don't know if you've even heard, you may have heard the rumor, or thought it was a rumor -- but I am of the belief system now that this base is or was deserted and is no longer being used by OUR government. For what reason I'm not sure. I believe a lot of it had to do with -- if there was indeed a military action there, which we have found proof of. We found some spent military cartridge shells up near where we think one of the base openings is.

We found C-Ration cans, we found different types of antennas that the government would have used for communications. These are things that have been found up in these mountainous areas. If you've ever been there you'll know what I'm talking about. These things tell me and my research partner that indeed there was some type of a military response there in the past. The areas I speak about, that my research partner who lives in the area claims were some of the openings to the base, have been concreted, cemented up. Now that's been done by somebody.

So we know that some type of government official company... we believe it was a CIA-backed organization that was there... In my Dulce papers I show an area of a ranch just north of the Archuleta mesa area (Refer to Christa's research papers on Dulce at the address given at the end of this section for current discoveries in regards to Dulce and several provocative illustrations, diagrams and photographs of the same - Branton), we've been unable to track or find the individuals who have owned this property now for many years.

What we've been told by the individuals who lived in or around the area, is that there is a landing strip on that particular property, there are large towers... I did get onto the property, and close up enough to get pictures of these bullet-proof towers that were sitting on the property.

There WERE about 20, and there are only 5 there now. We're wondering why they were taken out, and where were they taken? Anyway I've got pictures of those. These are not just fire towers. Some people try to explain them away by saying "Oh, those are just so our ranchers could go up into the towers and look for fires," and things like that. The strange part about this is that you walk up the towers and there is dark black glass... you can't look in to see, and its bullet proof. And what's strange is the opening... you are unable to get into these towers. We don't know if they were just put there for show, we don't really know exactly what they are, but we believe they were placed there for some reason.

We have no understanding of that. There have been sightings of planes, small Lear jets landing in and out of that area over the years. Nobody in the town of Dulce seems to know who owns that property... My research partner did track down someone who did own the property over 20 years ago, but after that it seemed to go into covert hands. The property also had what looked like a small wooden house. You could just walk in there, it's been evacuated and there's nothing in there. This type of facility or front for an underground base in that area would be perfect; because this area was cordoned off by what we believe at one time was an electrified fence which they said was used to keep the cattle out.

We believe that it was used for another purpose because of the signs posted all over -- NO TRESPASSING, and these were the types of signs that you would see up near AREA-51, and so we have to wonder what was going on upon that property. I don't know if you've ever seen the movie "THE ANDROMEDA STRAIN", I saw it the other day, just haven't seen it in a long time.

The underground facility that they went to [in the movie] was stationed on kind of a muck-up farm, where they went into the farm house and went into something like a tool shed, and then all of a sudden this elevator starts going down and down and down. And what they found once they went down was a massive underground biological testing facility. I have to believe that these types of facilities are all over in every state.

So then, back to the question. If there was a military takeover it already happened, and the base was closed... Again there's no proof there. Some of the Indians who live on Jicarilla Apache land, these people are very, very closed, they don't talk to outsiders. The information that I got was only from an inside source, and I can only tell you what one Jicarilla Apache Indian told his dear friend of many years there. He said that he was going up through the mountainous areas there, up through the Archuleta mesa and back into the hills, and was walking along-side of a ledge. All of a sudden he felt some dirt falling on his head.

And so of course, if you were walking around in this deserted area and you felt something fall on your head, you're immediate response would be to look up. And he did, he looked up and he said what he saw horrified him. This is a man; he's a man in his 60's. This man looked up and saw... this is what he told his friend,

"I saw a grey being with large black inky eyes staring down at me over a ledge, and it looked like a large rock had been swiveled out, was sticking out of the side of the mountain."

And he did a double-take, he looked away like someone who would rub their eyes and say, "Oh, I'm just seeing things," but then he looked back up and he saw it again.

Well this time he said he took off and he ran, he was running for his life. He was very, very frightened, scared, and what's strange is that this man is friends of the men high-up in the Jicarilla Apache tribal council, but he has kept this secret from everyone except my research partner. And he told him that when he got back he was shaking, he was very, very frightened. So THIS tells me -- and this just happened during the past couple years (this interview took place in the winter of 1996 - Branton), so this tells me that THERE ARE STILL GREY ALIENS inhabiting some part of that base.

Interesting question there that you had because if indeed there is still part of the base that's still inhabited (why would the Greys only use 'part' of the base after it had become even more secure, with the 'sealing' of many of the outer entrances? - Branton) by the Grey beings, then certainly if there is a problem there might NEED to be a Congressional-backed military take-over of that base, or they may have just left it alone, just said "let the people of Dulce worry about the aliens, we don't want to deal with them any more."

THE DULCE PROTOCOL

I don't really know what happened during the military events that they had there, I don't really know what happened, I just know that... I'm almost POSITIVE that there was some type of a confrontation!

So any way, who knows, who can say for sure? All I know is that a lot of these individuals that come up with different stories, these are individuals who are not the type of people to just come across with a tale, in fact [many of them] are not interested in UFO's, they're not interested in any of this. In fact when the subject is brought up they really just don't want to talk about it to you. It's very hard to get access into that community. I have had a lot of problems getting answers, but thank God one of my research partners, his father lives there, he's lived there all his life. And this young man was brought up there [Dulce]. He knows what happens there, he knows what all the rumors and tales are, and he knows what all the Indians have seen.

Q: Have you been taken to any other planets or spheres during your abductions?

A: Not that I know of, however I [remember] that I was taken to some type of large massive ship, it had to have been a mother ship. This thing was massive, it was miles and miles and miles long. I'm not sure exactly where I was. I received some instructions while I was there. There were "light beings" there. They looked like angelic beings, only without the wings. They were wearing long robes, and I was taken into an area where they had a podium and a teacher that came out and was teaching the people who were there. These people were human, I did not see any aliens [greys] at THAT time, so I'm not sure exactly where I was.

Q: Did you ever get to see what was inside the 'tanks'?

A: No, not during the Dulce experience. I started to walk up to the tank. It smelled very foul. It was an odor that only I can identify as being close to a sulfuric type of odor. I remember when I first went in to the medical field we were invited downtown to view an autopsy, and the formaldehyde they use there has a sickening sweet smell, its a smell that is very difficult to try and explain to somebody who has not smelled it before, but I can say that it smelled a lot like that. The officer, the military man that was with me, guiding me, would NOT allow me up to the tank to look inside. I can only speculate that there was something in there that may have been frightening to me, because he reacted very quickly to stop me. You asked if there were both breeding and feeding tanks.

I believe so, because from what I've been told by some of the other women who saw these tanks, some of them saw body parts inside. The type of tanks that I saw were used for breeding and cultivation of small alien beings. The only thing that I can describe it as is of being [like] a fake womb. A woman carries her child in her uterus, well these types of breeding tanks that you're talking about were used to cultivate the fetus' that they extract from the individuals that they abduct and take there. They extract the fetus like they have done with me MANY times, and I believe they place it in this type of a tank, a glass [looking] breeding tank.

Q: What do you think most of the hybrids feel about the position they are in?

(Note: I intended the question to mean the humanoid fetus' who have been infused with non-human, cattle, cetacean or Grey, etc. DNA and who are kept in the underground bases or on ships. However Christa took the question to mean the TERRAN-NORDIC alien hybrids like herself and her daughter who were living in OUR surface-world society. - Branton)

A: That's such a very good question and not many people ask that... I myself being a hybrid have felt that I do not fit in anywhere. I still feel like I don't "fit in" to this day. I know I don't, I know I'm different, and I don't try to tell everybody that either. I just have accepted it and go on with my life, but I can assure you that every hybrid I've spoken to has told me, has tried to explain to me the emptiness and the feelings that they feel. They feel almost like they don't belong here on earth. I certainly feel [that] I don't belong here.

Q: If the outer world gets a hold of the Dulce technology and begins using it to colonize other worlds, could this alleviate the population, economic, environmental and other problems that this planet faces? In other words take away the IMPOSED barriers that have kept us earth-bound and in essence finally let us "out of the cradle", so to speak?

The Greys for one do not wish Terrans to gain interstellar advantages and so become a threat to their own empirical agendas, and operating through various power-cults on earth they have succeeded in keeping interplanetary technology out of our hands and robbing us of our resources to finance the joint subterran and exterran projects, many of which projects and bases have been taken-over entirely by their own kind and at our expense.

Once robbed of our resources the Greys use their psychological slaves on Earth to set us against each other and then turn around and say: "Ha, you people are too violent to be allowed to have interstellar technology!" Although there have been technology exchanges, it would seem that they are either being used as a ruse by the Greys to gain access to our society so that they can impose a global electronic dictatorship, and/or it is technology that is being provided by the Federation 'Nordics' so that they can help defend planet earth for the mutual benefit of themselves and their human 'cousins' on earth.

What do you think about all of this?

A: I believe without a doubt that we have been working on projects to colonize the moon, underground, and also to colonize Mars... I've talked with scientists, I've talked with former NASA astronauts who believe without a doubt that this is what's going on. They don't feel like its anything alien, some of the astronauts say they felt like, well this is just a technology that we've developed on our own, and that certainly population is a problem that you have to think about way in advance and that humans have come to all of these conclusions themselves. I disagree, I think that it was an alien technology that was given to us (and/or recovered from "crash sites"? - Branton), and I think that we're running with it, and we've already started.

Like with the Biosphere, a lot of people think that that is just for learning about our ecology and things like that, plants, animals and all of that. I know that was a front. I know of a lot of things that went on underground there. That is also an underground facility, it's a massive facility and it's a wonderful facility. The technology there being tested was alien technology. All this will be used when they start to colonize the moon and Mars.

These are the two 'planets' right now, actually the moon not so much being a planet (some argue that the Earth-Moon system is actually a "double planet". As for other planets, it might be logical to begin with the polar regions of Venus and the equatorial regions of Mars. - Branton) but a satellite of earth, but certainly its a stepping-stone away from earth to other places, and this is what's going on, I have no doubt about it.

I've talked to too many scientists who've worked on covert or black projects for our government who have said that's exactly what we're doing... (I suppose the question I really had was is it actually OUR technology, or is it to be used ONLY by the alien-controlled "human elite" and NOT for the masses, who are instead to be "de-populated" through wars, plagues, infanticide and other genocidel eugenical methods? - Branton)

I really believe that we don't have much longer here as a people to survive on earth, the climate will be vastly changing... so we have to have the technology to go somewhere else.

THE DULCE PROTOCOL

That's what many of the aliens did themselves [long ago]. The aliens that I've dealt with, the Ones who came from the constellation of Lyra... they actually had a massive explosion on their planet (caused by invading reptilian forces from Alpha Draconis, as some contactee accounts suggest? - Branton).

They had to evacuate and migrated to the Pleiadean constellation where they knew other alien civilizations were already living. There are many different types of Pleiadean aliens, I cannot stress this enough to people who say, well there's only one Pleiadean race...

(Note: The Pleiades star cluster actually consists of over 200 stars, or those stars INCLUDING SOL which ultimately revolve around the central stars of the Pleiadean cluster, more commonly known as the "seven sisters" - Branton)

Some of 'my' people also came into our system and settled on Mars, but something happened on that planet that forced them to go underground to live.

Q: What would you consider the greatest weakness of the Greys to be?

A: I can tell you right now that the main weakness of the Greys is that they have no soul, they are soulless. Do not allow them to tell you otherwise. Some of them have been known to try to impart some type of [false] religious philosophies on people that they've abducted, and the thing is you have to realize that these aliens have their own agenda, and its not something that I feel is a positive one really.

So I have found out from dealing with them most of my life, they are soulless, they have no soul, and when it comes to my religious beliefs or background -- I'm not afraid to say it, I'm a Christian, I believe in God, I believe in one ultimate being... God, who created all, all alien beings of all kinds... all different constellations where people have COLONIZED throughout the universe... beings, animals, things we probably have no idea about.

Certainly I have to believe that the Greys are, the only way I can describe it is that they are an empty, empty case... There's nothing there other than a superior technology type of brain apparatus up in their skull area. Otherwise they are of no use to us really, they are really of no use. They are used to impart different technologies and give us information, but as far as trusting them, I do not trust them as far as I could throw them.

Q: What do you think our greatest strength as human beings is?

A: Well, our greatest strength is our belief in God... our greatest strength is [that] ability... and our only connection with each race is our connection with that one Supreme being, God. Now I do believe that God saw at some point in our history the need for someone to guide us into the positive way of living, I believe [that] Jesus was born as an example of the way that God would want us to live our lives... If we believe in Jesus Christ as the Son of God, the one and only God, then we have to believe that this is all true. I believe that He, Jesus, will be coming back... I believe in angels, I collect angels [artistic representations].

My best friend in Wisconsin sends me angel cards all the time, and I send her angel this, angel that, angel jewelry, angel statures, everything because I believe truly that angels walk among us. Believe me I have seen them, I've dealt with them, I have spoken with them (for example, her experience aboard the "mother ship".

However in THAT CASE we would have to ask if they were standing or fallen angels such as the rebel 'angels' or fallen 'light beings' that have been seen by abductees working in collaboration with Greys and Reptiloids on their starships? - Branton)...

I have had several close calls where I can only state that these angels have appeared out of just nowhere and saved my life, so I just have to believe that these are God's beings [servants]... they're wonderful.

THE DULCE PROTOCOL

(Note: Not wishing to detract from this atmosphere, however I do feel compelled to say that one should not trust any and every being that claims to be an 'angel'. For instance fallen or rebel angels can state in all sincerity that they are 'angels' and they would be correct -- however they might not tell you which 'variety' of angel they are, or which side of the angelic conflict they serve, since there are BOTH standing and fallen angels. Fortunately however, there are twice as many standing angels in this universe as there are fallen angels, although the fallen angels seem to have a particular fascination with planet earth in that the nethermost depths of this planet is apparently the realm that they have chosen to make their "last stand" or their "command headquarters" -- in alliance with the serpent races which they incarnate -- in their ancient conflict with Michael and his legions of standing angels.

The 12th chapter of Revelation is revealing in this regard, as it seems to generally convey a picture of a war in heaven between humanoids who are backed by standing angels and reptiloids who are backed by rebel angels, as well as a prophecy that the reptilian power-bases among the stars will be broken as the draconian forces retreat back to earth to make their last stand, and in so doing they from their cavernous empire will back and support a global dictatorship in a desperate effort to gain human allies for one last ditch "do or die" assault on the heavenly dominions.

The thing to remember would be to use caution, since rebel angels have the ability to appear as "angels of light" to those who they are capable of deceiving. So examine their messages as though your soul depended on it, if you do happen to encounter such a being or beings. As for the Draconians themselves, in all fairness 'individual' reptiloids are not the ultimate 'enemy', the enemy is the LUCIFERIAN COLLECTIVE under which they serve, and the same can be said for the New World Order which is prophesied in the Book of Revelation -- those who are enslaved in this system by choice or deception are not the ultimate enemy, the Luciferian SYSTEM itself is the enemy!

Something that is not often considered is the reptilian's perspective in regards to physical and spiritual survival. One of the problems is that the reptilians are intelligent and sentient enough -- thanks in part to the Luciferians who aided in destroying the original immortal status of both mankind and beasts -- to realize that when <u>they die physically, they also die spiritually</u>, due to the fact that they have no inherent 'soul'. The reptilians fully realize this, and it terrifies them to no end. One of the reasons for the 'hybrid' projects is not only to develop certain physical attributes within their race, but most importantly to give their posterity a 'soul' so that they can survive beyond the grave, hopefully in an eternity of bliss rather than one of torment.

We should not say that because a being has reptilian 'genes', they are as a result 'evil'. Evil is not genetic, but a choice one makes. Because of the fact that many of the reptilians are mere 'cells' in a Luciferian collective 'HIVE', it is not the individual reptilians that are at fault [if there is in fact such a thing as 'individual' reptilians] so much as it is the HIVE itself. The HIVE must be the target of our attacks and especially any particular power-centers or mainframes that guide the Hive. Attempts should be made by humanoids on earth and beyond to attack the Hive and break individual reptilian 'cells' free from its constraints.

Once they are free and allowed to develop emotional individuality they should be given the choice to submit unconditionally to those Andro-Pleiadean Federation humanoid societies for instance who have succeeded in taming their own base 'animal' natures. Since the reptiloids -- and especially the collective itself, lacking soul -- do not have the capability to 'TAME' their own base predatory instincts, man-KIND must do this for them [GENESIS 1:28; 3:1,14-15]. Those reptilians which will not submit to re-programming and refuse to SURRENDER to this process, should give up their right to experience a 'supervised' free agency and should as a result be subdued by FORCE... otherwise the human races throughout the galaxy or even the universe will have to live under eternal chaos -- forever plagued and tormented by races driven ONLY by base predatory instincts, because humankind had failed to take responsibility as the divinely-commissioned guardians of the creation.

THE DULCE PROTOCOL

First however we must accept that a Divine ORDER was originally established for the universe, beginning with the Almighty Creator and descending through the various angelic hierarchies, through humankind, followed by the reptiloid races that originally held a position somewhere between mankind and the beasts, and following this the lower animal kingdoms and finally the nature kingdom itself. This is the original divinely-ordered hierarchy through which divine LIFE from the SOURCE of all creation cascades down from the higher to the lower levels. If this hierarchy is broken like it was as a result of INTERVENTION by the fallen angelics, then UNITY and CONTINUITY is destroyed and CHAOS reigns.

So if one gets the sense that this volume is attacking reptilians simply because they are reptilian, then they are not looking to the deeper message. I am NOT advocating the all-out extermination of the draconian races, I am only advocating that they must of their own choice OR through force -- whichever they 'choose' -- submit to the divinely-established ORDER which was initiated from the very genesis of intelligent physical life on planet earth, and subsequently throughout the universe itself. - Branton).

The following is "A CASE SIMILAR TO THE TILTON CASE", as reported by Val Valerian in MATRIX-II, the Donavon Masters story:

"The following is what I believe to be a very real experience, which I believe ties into the experiences of Christa Tilton. Three of my friends and I were taken to what I perceived to be an underground government facility or UFO base. I say 'friends' because that is how I perceived them, although I had not met them at the time. I remember feeling as though I had been drugged, as if everything was kind of going in slow motion. We were placed on and strapped to a conveyor belt by our wrists and ankles. The conveyor was activated and as it began to move, our bodies were passed through blocks of pure intense light.

These blocks of light -- perhaps laser scanning devices -- were either green or blue in color. At each block of light there was what I perceived to be a robot controller. They also were either green or blue in color. Their color corresponded to the color of the light in front of which they stood. The robots were in human form but with no distinguishable human characteristics. Along the wall in the first room were barrels of some substance which had a very pungent odor. These barrels were stacked, one on top of the other.

"Suddenly we were on a different conveyor belt or at the end of the first one. As the belt moved around a circular console, it stopped. There were two men -- human in form and characteristics -- seated at the console. One assisted the other. One of them picked up what I thought was a razor and shaved an area on my back left side just below the waist line. I remember that the spot bled considerably. I was released and they began to do the same procedure on my friends. I remember thinking over and over -- 'What is happening to me?' He replied, 'You have just been implanted with your government control extension number.' I remember grabbing a mirror and looking at the area that bled.

The number '04' was there. In a very upset manner I turned to a woman in a uniform and exclaimed, 'You can't do this to me!' Incidentally, all of the personnel in this facility wore uniforms. I then ran back to the console where I was released. By that time my friends had also been released. I hurriedly told them what I had discovered was happening to us.

As I was speaking, the two men at the console were gathering materials hurriedly, in what seemed like an attempt to escape. In particular I remember the man that had implanted the number on me had a computer print-out list. He protected this list with his life, as my friends and I ran after him and the other man. They escaped through a set of double doors (was the drug-induced state of semi-consciousness beginning to wear off unexpectedly? - Branton). I sincerely believe that Christa Tilton was also in this facility at that time -- although I don't think this was our first meeting.

THE DULCE PROTOCOL

"I will never forget the first time I talked with Christa on the phone. It was September 20, 1987. I felt as though I was hearing the voice of an old friend, as though I had known her all my life. She later sent me a picture of herself which only solidified that feeling. When I saw that picture I had flashbacks of seeing her aboard a craft! It was a very emotional moment for me, seeing her again. Since that time a beautiful and enduring friendship of unconditional love has developed.

She is truly a flower in the garden of my life and a TRUE friend. Like Christa, I have been plagued by intense, repetitive dreams of meetings and communications with what appear to be non-human, other-worldly beings. I am also continually frustrated by my inability to learn the truth about my experiences, although Christa has been a tremendous help in my search for the truth -- proving that when people work together for a common goal, much is accomplished...

"Although Christa and myself are not alone, I suggest that there are thousands out there like ourselves, perhaps afraid to seek out help and a better understanding of their experiences because of the fear of ridicule. It is a truth that sometimes life can be very cruel because of the ignorance or lack of knowledge concerning this vast, exotic subject.

Then maybe some, like the ostrich, stick their heads in the sand because they are afraid to question their own fates."

FOR MORE INFORMATION ON CHRISTA TILTON'S EXPERIENCE AND HER ON-GOING RESEARCH INTO THE DULCE FACILITY:

Christa Tilton has compiled several hundred pages of information, documents, illustrations and photos relating to PAUL BENNEWITZ and the DULCE BASE.

Her investigations are in-depth and on-going, so if you would like to find out more about her latest research into Dulce and other underground bases, please send a self-addressed stamped envelop to:

INTEL-ADVOCATES., c/o Christa Tilton., 2163 South 78th East Avenue., Tulsa, Oklahoma 74129-2421

Chapter 26

The Dulce Caverns and Pueblo Mythology

In his article 'ALIEN INVADERS', researcher 'TAL' LeVesque reveals the following information in regards to the ancient "Evadamic-Draconian" conflict which has, for thousands of years, raged upon, within and beyond planet earth:

"The 'DRACONIAN' Group is a Confederation. They are Reptilian Humanoids, with sub-groups [The 'Serpent Race', from Sirius]...

(Note: Sirius figures prominently in reports of humanoids, and also reports of reptiloid, amphiboid and insectoid activity. In this regard the Sirius system is much like the SOL system itself. Some of these forces apparently collaborate with each other, whereas others are in conflict with the each other. - Branton)

They set up Bases inside Venus, the Earth, etc...

"AN ANCIENT CONFLICT

-- The Indians of the South-West U.S.A., have legends of tall, fair-haired Beings. They also have legends about the 'Little People'. Both are said to have 'Sky Craft' or

'Saucers'. American Indians speak of Underground Races, Surface Races and people living 'Above', in the Heavens. The Navajo legends state they once lived Underground, together with the Coyoteros and the White people, below a mountain near Silverton, Colorado. NOTE: Mt. Hesperus [meaning 'VENUS'] is sacred to them. After coming to the surface they went south and settled in the canyons of the Dinetah area, near Navaho Dam, between Aztec and Dulce, New Mexico.

(Note: Could the ancestors of the Pueblo Indians have been the one's who originally excavated the lower levels of the Dulce base and the lower tunnels which have apparently existed within the deepest levels of the base for centuries if not millennia? If so, then why did they revert to a low-technology culture once they reached the surface?. Could it be that the scientific factions of their race either established an interaction with the 'Greys' and/or left the planet altogether, leaving the rest to fend for themselves?

Hopi legends say that their ancestors were driven to the surface by another faction of their own kind who turned to practicing sorcery. Apache legends, according to Robert Morningsky, state that the "Two Hearts" or the "Children of the Lizard" drove the Pueblos to the surface after they had invaded their underground domain. Could BOTH scenarios be true? In other words, could one scientific faction have remained behind in a collaboration with the reptilians, with another faction leaving the caverns in starships and/or migrating to the surface 'world' and/or elsewhere through these ancient and massive underground systems? - Branton)

"They then set up defense sites and expanded south towards Mount Taylor and west into Arizona. Built atop high mesas were fortresses and towers consisting of three or more stories.

"The Pajaritan Pueblo Indians have a Legend that they emerged from the INNER EARTH, near the Great Sand Dunes [National Monument] in Colorado. They then traveled down the Rio Grande, setting up Pueblos. The area now known as Los Alamos, was considered evil. The home of Underworld 'Little People', from which would come the curse of 'The Gourd of Death'! -- and so it did [in the form of the nuclear bomb]. 'The Greys' ['Little People'] are 'Deros'.

"According to New Mexican Folk Myth, Montezuma was born near TAOS and trained by beings who lived in Caverns, inside Pueblo Peak. [NOTE: At near-by Blue Lake, UFOs have been seen entering and exiting the water.]

"The Aztec of Mexico, who some think originally came from here, believed that the Sun God needs Blood and sacrificed humans for its' nourishment. They killed over 20,000 people each year. Near Taos, in a Cave above the Lucero River, not far from Frijoles Canyon, is where Human sacrifices were made - some say EVEN NOW.

(Note: According to one source from Baltimore, MD., one man encountered a reptiloid being while spending the night in a cave with black rock walls near some 'springs' north of San Cristobel, not far from Taos, N.M. - Branton)

"Members of 'Secret Society' groups, in Taos, have been found beheaded. [Like Arthur Manby, who told about a secret 'AZTLAND' Hot Springs, roughly 11 miles Northwest of Taos. It is flanked by Petroglyphs on the canyon walls.] Cultists venerate the Mayan-Aztec Death God, 'Camazotz', who took the form of a WINGED CREATURE who removes the heads of his followers who displeased him. Research indicates the High Priesthood had contact with WINGED-REPTOIDS [who were known to devour humans] and the creatures were seeking various articles of commerce, possibly gold, Psycho-active [hallucinogenic] Plants, etc.

"Throughout Pueblo land, on pottery, CAVE and Kiva walls, will be found decorations representing a Feathered or horned snake [The Plumed Serpent, Quetzalcoatl]... From the Pecos Pueblo, Montezuma is said to have led his followers south and founded Tenochtitlan [Mexico City].

Robert K Teske

<u>"THE MANIPULATORS OF THE MIND</u>

-- Alien Civilizations have contacted some of the Earth's inhabitants and practiced various forms of thought control on those they have contacted. Officer Herb Schirmer, Betty and Barney Hill, and others were given post hypnotic suggestions to try and make them forget the contacts. Only through strength of character and hypnotic regression were they able to talk about their experiences.

"The 'Aliens' USE us, by reaching into our minds directly... WE SHOULD NOT RESPECT ANY GROUP WHICH USES A METHOD OF INTERFERING WITH OUR BRAINS' NORMAL ELECTRICAL PATTERNS. They use devices which produce a combination of flashing lights, pulsating sounds, ELF & E.M. Fields. It is also INSIDIOUS to put 'implants' [Brain Transceivers] into Human Beings. And WORSE, to kill them for their Blood and other nutrient substances [Vital Energy resident within their Vital Fluids].

"The 'Greys' [the short, 'Big Heads'] are mercenaries. They interface with humans in 'Secret Societies' and the [fascist] Military/Governmental Complex. An interconnected 'WEB' manipulates the surface Earth cultures... The 7'-8' tall Reptoid/Draco have been seen giving directions to the 'Greys'. The 'Reptoids' get their orders from the Elite WINGED DRACO.

(<u>Note</u>: the actual chain of command seems to begin with the rebel angels or 'poltergeists' which utilize bio-synthetic constructed physical 'forms' to operate in the physical dimension -- these 'bodies' have been recovered from crashed discs and seem to consist of a 'sponge-like' substance throughout; followed by the paraphysical 'Mantis-Insectoid' type beings and the 'Winged' and 'White' Dracos or 'Mothmen' as John Keel refers to them in his book "THE MOTHMAN PROPHECIES" - although it is not certain which of these three are superior; and then the large 'Lizard' or 'Crocodilian-like' saurian bipeds or Reptiloids; a dark large-muzzled 5 ft. tall [approx.] race that are sometimes referred to as the 'Iguanas' -- a satanic 'priest' class of human-sized reptiloids that have been seen wearing dark hooded robes and seem to be a cross between the tall Reptiloids and the smaller Grays; a race of 'frog-faced' amphiboid lizards approximately 4 feet tall; various types of 'Grays' with blue-gray, brown-gray, white-gray, green-gray, tan-gray, etc. skin as well as the 'genetically engineered' hybrid reptiloids and grays which possess insectoid and other genetic characteristics; followed by various non-hominoid reptilians such as the sea-Saurians, giant subterranean 'serpents', the so-called 'dragon-worms', etc. which have been encountered within the deeper cavern systems or in the sea and which 'seem' to be used more for 'psychic energy' channels.

All of these various alien branches collectively make up what has been referred to as the "Serpent Races". - Branton).

"THE WINGED SERPENT

-- The Reptilian/Amphibian Humanoids have been interacting with Earth for AGES. Many Contactees and Abductees repeatedly describe an Insignia of a Flying Serpent on a shoulder patch, a badge, a medallion or a helmet... NOTE: Snakes...have skeletal indications of atrophied arms and legs. There have been many transformations & metamorphosis. 'The SERPENT RACE' [like snakes] lives Underground. Yet, they can come out, in their 'Saucers' and 'FLY'...

"THE 'EL' GIANTS

-- Elite Cast 'MAN,' the 'Orion [Betelgeuse] Group', have Outpost Bases inside the planet MARS. They are also known as 'The Titans'...'The Brothers'...etc."

(Note: This 'Mars-Orion' reference is the only source we have which actually claims to identify an extraterrestrial colony of the giant 'EL' humans, Titans, Anakim, or Nephilim. The Orion star Betelgeuse is most often referred to by some contactees in reference to the 'giants'. Some of the residents of the Jovian moons claim that they previously came from or 'Returned' from Rigel and Betelgeuse, apparently after being driven from those systems by the Draconian infiltration and invasion of Orion. Although we have come across little corroborative information concerning the 'extraterrestrial' activity of this branch of the human race, there have been round-about accounts of possible interaction with the Orion constellation.

.

As for a possible subterranean presence, one source claimed that several years ago a man was let down a cable into a gigantic cavern which had been broken into by a deep 'oil' well-shaft in Texas. The man claimed to have met, within the caverns, giant 11-12 ft. tall humans -- Anakim-Nephilim? -- who claimed that the Creator and the angelic forces had ordered their civilization to remain in these caverns and to separate themselves from surface races where they might otherwise be worshipped as gods by ignorant humans because of their stature. This man was told however that this condition would last only until the day of Judgment-Purification, at which point the 'giants' would once again be allowed to Return to the surface world. This doesn't mean that the 'EL' races do not interact with other interstellar federations who are less inclined to worship them.

.

Several years ago one woman by the name of Margaret Rogers claimed to have visited the underground civilization of the 'Nepheli' deep below Mexico. They said that their name for God is 'Tamil', which was also confirmed by the Telosian 'Bonnie' or 'Sharula', whose people reportedly have considerable interaction with the 'giants'. They also told Ms. Rogers that one day man would develop interstellar craft and be so presumptuous as to approach the very throne of the Creator and invade His personal domain, and thus invoke his wrath upon the whole planet.

Could she have been referring to the 'Eternity Gate' within the Orion Nebula which lies far beyond the Orion star cluster, or to the 'New Jerusalem' Command, a virtual CITY OF LIGHT which has reportedly been seen by government astrophysicists to be emerging from the Orion Nebula vortex and is now on a direct course to Earth -- due to arrive near the end of the third 'Millennium' A.D.?

.

THE DULCE PROTOCOL

Another source has claimed that many centuries ago these human 'giants' left their underground cities and set out on a great expedition to the stars, only to Return in later centuries from their great interstellar migration or expedition. Upon Returning they RE-ESTABLISHED their ancient and vast cavern cities beneath Alaska and elsewhere -- some of which had been over-run by degenerate "animal men" from the earth's interior during their absence, who were particularly cruel to the natives on the surface. Ancient records state that the Anaks, Nepheli or Titans once dwelled in the Middle East and also the ancient Gobi region, but now live mainly in large cavernous systems deep below Alaska, Oregon, Northern California, Utah, Texas, Mexico, some of the Pacific Islands, and also other parts of the western flank of North and Central America.

.

One friend of mine informed me of a very vivid abduction-type 'dream' in which 'I' came to her and took her to a cliff in the western Rockies, somehow causing part of the cliff to open up like a door with the rock moving inward and down, and took her through an inclining tiled tunnel and to a large metallic door with a type of keyboard affair next to it. She claimed that IN this "altered state" or "alternate personality" mode 'I' used my LEFT HAND to punch-in a quick succession on the keyboard, a kind of code that opened the metallic door and we entered. Normally in my 'conscious' life -- which does NOT recall this incident other than vague subjective 'dreamlike' images and unsolicited thoughts -- I am RIGHT-HANDED. She claimed that 'I' took her inside, and we met some friendly humanoid beings about 12-14 feet tall who wore silvery uniforms which seemed to be 'ALIVE' in her words, or emanated LIFE-energy.

.

During another experience she claims 'I' had taken her to large underground chambers below the Salt Lake valley where I was directing some kind of operation and instructing humans from the surface, who were also experiencing a 'double' existence in this 'other' world. My impressions are that although this collective-based alternate identity was originally psychotically-induced by the Greys during past abduction experiences [as they have done with NUMEROUS abductees], this alternate 'self' was to a CERTAIN degree re-programmed by more friendly alien forces and became involved with various humanoid cultures within the "inner earth" who are making a common defense against the Reptilian invasion of their native territories. Aside from the obvious 'angelic' influences that have guided my life, the interaction that more benevolent beings have apparently had with my 'alter-ego' would help to explain the steady flood of "inspiration" which has resulted in the manifestation of this current project.

.

So I am certainly NOT the ultimate SOURCE or mastermind behind these Nexus/Dulce files, but merely a willing [and sometimes semi-willing] 'vessel' for other SOURCES you might say, who have continually inspired me and led me towards a 'mother lode' of information which would otherwise defy the laws of probability or synchronicity. These 'sources', based on my own personal perceptions, would include humanoid Giants, Hu-brids, Sasquatch, Dwarfs, Extraterrestrials, Aghartians, deep level surface Military Agencies who are against the Draconian agenda, and what might be considered 'faerian-type' people of an ethereal quality yet no less 'human' than us. Should it sound strange that there are also 'people' dwelling within this planet who are ALSO against Draconian collectivism and who value freedom and liberty as [hopefully] most of us do?

.

There IS INDEED a war going on right under our feet that is just as intense as anything that might have been conceived by your average science-fiction or fantasy author. If this sounds unusual, then consider that an entire 'lost world' existing throughout the crust of this planet -- which has for ages remained separated from the often superstitious residents of the surface -- would tend to develop a state of HIGH-STRANGENESS, at least from OUR perspective. The outer world would probably seem as 'alien' to them as their world seems to us.

The separation and distinction between these two 'worlds' -- aside from the fact that it is usually only the most powerful secret societies who have access to BOTH worlds -- is often augmented by the fact that most of those throughout history who have encountered the outskirts of this 'lost world' often reacted with fear of the unknown when they encountered something strange and unusual in connection with these portals, and normally wanted nothing more to do with them, interpreting the experiences according to their own frame of reference... and the reality of this other world below would surface in a more diluted form through legends, myths, folklore and such. If, as I am convinced, many abductees are living similar nocturnal "double lives" with interventionist or non-interventionist aliens, or both, we might look no farther than our own unconscious minds in order to find the "aliens". In fact, from one perspective the following might be true: "We have found the aliens, and they are us!" - Branton)

TAL continues:

"'The ELs' will engage 'The DRACO' in battle around this Planet. Most will die. REVELATION 12:7: 'Now war arose in Heaven, Michael and his Angels fighting against the Dragon and his Angels...'

"The Elite Corporate/Military/Governmental Complex of this country, and its' connection to One-World control cliques, are currently in negotiation with the Draco. They have threatened 'Fail-Safe', if the Draco [the Serpent Race] and their minions [The Greys and their human Agents] do not stop exploitation of the Earth. In other words, an Elite Control Group who have moved most of their chosen race to Underground Cities on the Moon & MARS, are willing to launch 'Super-Dirty' Nuclear Weapons [from Deep Sub-City Bases, manned by patriotic 'mind controlled' orphans] to poison this entire Planet and kill everyone, so that NO ONE can have the Jewel EARTH ['The Divine Tear']...

(Take note of the references made by contactee Alex Collier and others to the effect that some of the elite Military-Industrial Alternative-3 bases on the Moon and Mars were sabotaged by the Draco in 1985, and that the Draco are currently targeting the Alternative-2 underground bases below the surface of the earth. This would tend to polarize the "secret government" factions even more... those who, once in alliance with the reptilian collective, are now opposing the Draco-Orion collectivist forces. These are those who had not succumbed to the absolute psychological control of the draconian collective -- or have not been 'infected' by 'collectivitis' you might say -- when the

Dracos made their move and took possession of many of the former joint-operational bases.

Unless the leaders of this Military-Industrial underground come clean with Congress and the patriotic citizens of the United States of America and ask for their assistance AND open up their "Underground Empire" for ALL Americans, and not just the fraternal 'elite', then these people will find themselves in a VERY difficult situation -- trying to keep Draconian infiltrators at bay on the one hand and attempting to appease the wrath of an awakening giant in the form of freedom-loving Americans on the other. Americans who will begin DEMANDING access to the underground network which THEY paid for via taxes and other collective economic losses. - Branton)

"THE SECRET OF 'V'... The following is a list of those Organizations which repeatedly advertised on NBC during the first 19 'V' Programs [a weekly, hour T.V. Series]. Advertising support came from 'GENERAL ELECTRIC' [who happens to own NBC and has worked on the Government/Alien 'Saucer' Projects]... 'U.S. ARMY RECRUITING COMMAND'... 'AT&T'... 'EASTMAN KODAK'... 'UNION CARBIDE'... 'CHRYSLER CORP.'... 'MARS, INC.'... 'WARNER-LAMBERT'... 'FORD',... 'SEARS ROEBUCK & CO.'... 'McDONALDS'... 'ZALE CORP.'... 'KELLOGGS'...

(Note: For years it was impossible to buy a video set of the 'V' series. As of the beginning of 1995, the 'V' series was released on video and became available through major video outlets! - Branton)

"The 'Reptoids' are Returning to Earth! The INVADERS are here. We must convince a disbelieving World that the nightmare has already begun. Their Purpose: to make Earth their World. It is not over for the Human Race. 'Freedom Fighters' join together...for the sake of ALL of US..."

Chapter 27

Dulce and the Secret Files of A U.S. Intelligence Worker

The following information was released by Jefferson Souza, a contactee who has had repeated encounters with the Vega Lyrans, who according to Souza are similar in appearance to the "dark skinned Orientals" of India. Souza also claims contacts with Scandinavian-appearing humans from Iumma or Wolf 424 [the 'Ummo' people].

Both cultures utilize a huge 'Federation' base located within a vast system of caverns deep beneath the Death Valley - Panamint Mts. region of California. In fact, several federation groups utilize the base according to Souza, which contains whole areas specifically conditioned with the various gravitational, atmospheric and environmental conditions necessary to meet the needs of the various Federation visitors and dignitaries.

The Paihute Indians of the southwest USA claim that a Greek or Egyptian-like race first colonized the massive caverns within the Panamint Mts. thousands of years ago [one source claims the base was established around 2500 B.C., which is incidentally about 600 years following the beginnings of the rise of Egyptian intellectual culture] when Death Valley was part of an inland sea connected to the Pacific Ocean.

When the sea dried up these people -- who were described as wearing flowing robes draped over one shoulder, head-bands holding back their long dark hair, and bronze-golden skin -- out of necessity began to develop their collective knowledge and intellect and soon afterwards began to construct "silvery flying canoes".

At first these flying machines possessed wings, were relatively small, and flew with a dipping movement and a loud 'whirring' noise. As time passed the ships became wingless, grew larger in size, and flew ever more smoothly and silently.

Eventually these people, the HAV-MUSUVS moved their civilization into still deeper caverns which they had discovered farther underground, and commenced to explore the nearby planets and eventually other star systems as their own technological explosion began to refine every aspect of their society.

These Hav-musuvs have apparently had interplanetary or interstellar travel for 3000-4000 years since they first developed their flying machines. Could they have been one of the many native-Terran "ancient astronaut" civilizations which apparently had colonized Lyra and other systems? The story of the Panamints was related by a Navaho Indian by the name of Oga-Make, who in turn heard it from an old Paihute medicine man.

What about Souza's reference to the Vegans, who are similar in appearance to East Indians? I believe that India is a major key to understanding our planet's lost history. The ancient Vedic texts speak of flying ships called "Vimanas" as well as nuclear technology which was utilized by the ancients there. Hinduism itself arrived in India as a result of the Pre-Nordic 'Aryan' invasion from the North [the Gobi region?].

Some researchers insist that the Mayas AND Egyptians were originally navigators from India, possibly explaining the similarity in architecture and their advances in medicine, astronomy, mathematics, and so on. Swiss Ethno-archaeologist Yves Naud also quotes from ancient Indian texts which state that the leaders of ancient

THE DULCE PROTOCOL

India later collaborated with secretive Grecian intellectual societies in the development of aerial ships.

So then, the "Hav-musuvs" may have been representatives of any one of these cultures [Nordic-Aryans, East-Indians, Egyptians, Mayas, and Greeks] or a combination of cultures. However one thing is certain, only a VERY SMALL portion of the true history of planet earth, as of this writing, <u>can be found in the standard historical textbooks</u>.

Jefferson Souza claims that the following revelations are from the personal notes and scientific diaries of a scientist who was commissioned by the U.S. Government over a period of several years to visit all crash sites, interrogate captured Alien Life Forms and analyze all data gathered from that endeavor. Eventually this person was discovered to have kept and maintained personal notes on his discoveries and was therefore scheduled for termination [not just "job termination"!]... which he narrowly escaped.

Following 33 years of investigations, he went in to hiding in 1990:

[THE] BLUE PLANET PROJECT:

ALIEN TECHNICAL RESEARCH - 25 WESTCHESTER CAMP; OFFICE OF CENTRAL RESEARCH # 3

    - ALIEN LIFE FORMS. CODE: ARAMIS III - ADR3-24SM

    - SECTION: THE DULCE BASE. CODE: J.B.III

The following material comes from people who know the Dulce underground base exists. They are people who worked in the labs; abductees taken to the base; people who assisted in the construction; intelligence personnel, [NSA, CIA; etc.] and some specific UFO inner Earth researchers. **This information is meant for those who are seriously interested in the Dulce base. For your own protection, be advised to "Use Caution" while investigating this complex.** An ongoing investigation made by J.B. III, [Code: SR24.3B7]...

Robert K Teske

(<u>Note</u>: The author is no doubt quoting from some of the writings of a researcher and friend of yours truly, who has been at the very center of the Dulce investigations and has met with Thomas Castello personally. J.B. III would be "Jason Bishop III" - Branton)

Who's PLANET IS THIS? - These specific Aliens [Grays, Reptiloids] consider themselves Native Terrans. They are an Ancient race, descendants of a reptilian humanoid species... They are untrustworthy manipulator mercenary agents from another Extra-Terrestrial culture, "The Draco's" who are Returning to Earth -- which was their ancient outpost before the coming of the original Uni-Terrestrials -- to try to use it as a staging area, which is not easy at all because it causes all the other one hundred seventy [170] different Alien species to want their share of the Metagene secrets

(<u>Note</u>: These 170 are in most cases various sub-species of the humanoid and reptiloid root species, although various other trans-dimensional species are also visiting earth, like the 'Insectoids', etc. This also includes various humanoid and reptiloid species who are the products of genetic integration with various bizarre 'animal' life forms. The meta-gene <u>is an inbred gene within humans on Terra</u> resulting from the mixture of various cultures upon the "mother" world or "genesis" world, a genetic anomaly which can produce extraordinary characteristics and abilities in individuals, allowing them to accomplish what would be considered by many ET's to be extraordinary physical and psychic feats. - Branton)

But, these Alien cultures are in conflict over whose agenda will be followed for this planet. All the while mind control is being used to keep humans in place, artificially of course, especially since the forties. The Dulce complex is a joint U.S.[?] Government and Alien base. It was not the first one built with the Aliens, and others are located in Colorado, Nevada, Arizona, Alaska, etc...

The NAVAJO DAM is a main source for conventional electrical power, with the second source in ELVADA [which is also an underground entrance to the Dulce base].

THE DULCE PROTOCOL

NOTE: If RAND is the mother of "Think Tanks", then the "Ford Foundation" must be considered the Father. Rand's secrecy is not confined to reports, but on occasion extends to conferences and meetings.

On page #645 of the Project Rand, proceedings of the Deep Underground Construction Symposium of March 1959, we read:

"Just as airplanes, ships and automobiles have given man mastery of the surface of the Earth, tunnel boring machines will give him access to the subterranean world."

(Note: The September 1983 issue of OMNI, page 80, has a color drawing of "The Subterrene", the Los Alamos Nuclear powered tunnel machine, that burrows through the rock, deep underground, by heating whatever stone it encounters into molten rock [Magma], which cools after the Subterrene machine has moved on. The result is a tunnel with a smooth, glazed lining. These underground tubes are used by electro-magnetically powered sub-shuttle vehicles, which can travel at great speeds. They connect the so-called "Hidden Empire" sub-city complexes. Also, the top secret project code-named "NOAH'S ARK" used the tube shuttles in connection with a system of over one hundred [100] bunkers and "bolt holes", which have been established at various places on Earth (including beneath nearly every military base and many Airports in North America. - Branton).

They built the same type of subterranean tunnels at the ultra-top-secret Moon and Mars bases as well. Many of these underground cities are complete with streets, sidewalks, lakes, small electrical cars, buildings, offices and shopping malls...

Deep sections of the [Dulce] complex connect to natural cavern systems. A person who worked at the Base [CR-24/ZM 35-File IV], who had an "Ultra 7-B" clearance reports the following:

"There may be <u>more than seven levels</u>, but I only know of seven. Most of the Aliens are on levels 5, 6, and 7. Alien housing is on level five [5]."

<u>TRANSAMERICAN UNDERGROUND SUB-SHUTTLE SYSTE</u> [T.A.U.S.S.]: OVERT AND COVERT RESEARCH WITHIN DULCE -- As U.S. Energy Secretary, John Herrington named the Lawrence Berkeley Laboratory and New Mexico's Los Alamos National Laboratory to house new advanced genetic research centers as part of a project to decipher the Human Genome. The Genome holds the genetically coded instructions that guide the transformation of a single cell, a fertilized egg, into a biological being

(<u>Note</u>: Contactee Alex Collier claims that the reptiloid species of Alpha Draconis and Rigel Orion, although involved in short-term mind-control projects, are also interested in long term genetic-control, that is introducing genetic information into a conquered race in order to keep succeeding generations subjected to the Draconian elite by sabotaging certain genetic strengths - Branton).

"The Human Genome Project may well have the greatest direct impact on humanity of any scientific initiative before us today", said David Shirley, Director of the Berkeley Laboratory.

Covertly, this research has been going on for years, at Dulce labs. Level # 6 at Dulce is privately called "Night Mare Hall", it holds the Genetic Labs. Reports from workers [CR-24/ZM 52-Files VII], who have seen bizarre experimentation, are as follows:

"I have seen multi-legged humans that look half-human, half-octopus. Also reptilian-humans, and furry creatures that have hands like humans and cry like a baby, it mimics human words, and also huge mixture of lizards [and] humans in cages."

THE DULCE PROTOCOL

There are fish, seals, birds and mice that can barely be considered those species. There are several cages and vats of winged humanoids, grotesque bat-like creatures about three and a half to seven feet tall. Gargoyle-like beings and Draco-Reptoids.

Level # 7 is the worse, row after row of several humans and humanoids [hundreds, perhaps thousands] in cold storage. Here too are embryo storage and storage vats of humanoids, in various stages of development...

NOTES:

1.- Human and animal abductions, for their blood and other parts, slowed in the mid-1980's when the Livermore Berkeley Labs began production of artificial blood for Dulce and its sister complexes.

2.- About the confrontation, Human and Alien at Dulce, eighty-two [82] people were killed between scientists and the National Recon Group (apparently 66 from special forces and 16 scientists!? - Branton), the DELTA GROUP, which is responsible for security of all Alien connected projects. Also, there were hundreds of other wounded people and one hundred thirty two [132] dead Aliens...

The Dulce facility is the most well-known place where this [joint-interaction] activity occurs, although there are at least another twenty six [26] bases within the United States that have similar facilities...

In the book "ETS AND UFOS -- THEY NEED US, WE DON'T NEED THEM," was an original idea for one title, but not my personal choice, by Virgin 'Posty' Armstrong. He reports how his friends Bob and Sharon stopped for the night in Dulce and went out to dinner, they overhead some local residents openly and voice-fully discussing Extra-Terrestrial abductions of the townspeople for purposes of experimentation.

Robert K Teske

The ETs were taking unwilling human guinea pigs from the general populace of Dulce and implanting devices in their heads and bodies. The townspeople were frightened and angry but didn't feel they had any recourse since the ETs had our Government's knowledge and approval [CODE: SR-24/AK.5]...

Several Dulce residents are not naturally from this area, single people and even couples with children, have just come to the town of Dulce since 1948. Generations of frozen agents occupied in suspect positions... work in a gas station, drugstore, bar, restaurant, etc. They're there to listen and report anything which violates their limit of security. Always in the town of Dulce, you never know who is who!...

The Dulce Base is run by a Board:

- The Chairman of the Board is John Herrington
- Jim Baker of Tennessee is the NSA/CIA link to Dulce
- House speaker Jim Wright of Dallas Texas, the Nation's third highest office, is the Treasurer at Dulce

There is currently a power struggle going on, as Rep. William Thomas, R-California, put it, "Part of Jim Wright's problem is he fails to understand what's equitable and fair. It's the arrogance of power." Even among his fellow Democrats, many find Wright to be uncomfortable, Wright's operating style leaves him vulnerable.

Most meetings of the Dulce Boards are held in Denver, Colorado and Taos, New Mexico. Former New Mexico Senator Harrison Schmitt -- publicly known as "Last Man on the Moon" -- has full knowledge of Dulce. He was one of seven astronauts to tour the base. In 1979, he held an "Animal Mutilation" conference in Albuquerque, New Mexico. This was used to locate researchers and determine what they had learned about the links between the 'Mute' operations and the Alien/Government deals.

THE DULCE PROTOCOL

Senator Brian of Nevada knows about the "Ultra Secrets at Dreamland" and Dulce. So do many others in the Government, "This is what the UFO researchers are up against," SO BE CAREFUL! They have killed to keep this information secret, and by reading this document, you now know more than they want you to know!... After all, a FASCIST group, within this country, had John Kennedy assassinated and got away with it. Look to the links within the larger umbrella, the 'Web' of a fascist totalitarian Secret Police State, within the Pentagon; JCS; DIA; Division Five of the FBI; DISC/DIS and CIA.

Other information contained in the BLUE PLANET PROJECT manuscript includes information on various secret government projects, including the following:

THE 'MAJI' [Majestic Agency for Joint Intelligence] PROJECTS:

- SIGMA -- Initial project involved with attempts to establish communication with alien intelligence.
- PLATO -- Responsible for establishing Diplomatic Relations with the Aliens. This project secured a formal treaty, illegal under the U.S. Constitution, with the alien Grays.
- AQUARIUS -- Concerned with investigating the history of alien presence on earth and interaction with human beings. An outgrowth of this project is a huge Thesaurus-like document called the YELLOW BOOK describing aliens, their history in regards to humanity, and technology.

(Note: Some believe that the YELLOW BOOK is filled with alien propaganda meant to make government agents vulnerable to alien psychological manipulation... for instance this would include the deception that humanity is a genetic creation placed on this planet by the reptilians, and so on... and the potential results of such propaganda, for instance: that since they are our 'creators' we have absolutely no defense against them and might as well try to negotiate with them and attempt to appease our 'creators' by giving them what they want. - Branton)

- **GARNET** -- A project responsible for control of all information and documents regarding the Alien subjects and accountability of their information and documents.

- **PLUTO** -- A project responsible for evaluating all UFO and IAC [Identified Alien Craft] information pertaining to Space technology.

- **POUNCE** -- A project that was formed to recover all downed and/or crashed craft and Aliens, and provide cover stories and operations to mask the true endeavors whenever necessary, i.e. such as cover stories of crashed 'experimental' Aircraft, Construction, Mining activities, etc.

- **NRO** -- National Reconnaissance Organization, based at Fort Carson, Colorado. Responsible via DELTA FORCES for security on all Alien or Alien Spacecraft and underground base projects.

- **DELTA** -- The special arm of the NRO which is especially trained and tasked with SECURITY of all MAJIC projects [MAJI or MAJIC oversee MJ-12]. Also code-named "MEN IN BLACK", the Delta Forces are trained to provide Alien tasked projects and LUNA base security.

- **BLUE TEAM** -- The first project responsible for reaction and/or recovery of downed and/or crashed Alien craft and/or Aliens. This was a U.S. Air Force Material Command project. Also synonymous with ALPHA team crash/retrieval projects.

- **SIGN** -- The second project responsible for collection of Intelligence and determining whether Alien presence constituted a threat to the U.S. National Security. SIGN absorbed the BLUE TEAM projects. This was a U.S. Air Force and CIA project.

THE DULCE PROTOCOL

- **REDLIGHT** -- The project involving the test-flying and back-engineering of recovered Alien craft at AREA 51 - Groom Lake - Dreamland, Nevada. UFO sightings of craft accompanied by Black unmarked Helicopters are project Redlight assets.

- **SNOWBIRD** -- Established as a cover for project Redlight. This project is activated from time to time when it is necessary to provide cover stories for Redlight operations, etc., by releasing information on advanced conventional military aircraft which are used to explain 'unexplained' UFO sightings.

- **BLUE BOOK** -- A U.S. Air Force, UFO, and Alien Intelligence collection and disinformation project. This project was terminated and its collected information and duties were absorbed by Project AQUARIUS. A classified report named "GRUDGE/BLUE BOOK, REPORT No. 13" is the only significant information derived from the project and, other than information from second hand sources, is unavailable to the public. Reports No. 1-12 and No. 14 ARE available to the public. The Grudge/Blue Book Report No. 13 mentions that many military government personnel AND CIVILIANS have been terminated [murdered without due process of law] when they had attempted to reveal the alien interaction with the SECRET government.

SOME OF MAJI'S SECRET WEAPONS AGAINST THE ALIENS INCLUDE:

- **GABRIEL** -- A project to develop HIGH Frequency-pulsed sound generating weapons that would be effective against alien crafts and beam weapons. The project also involves working with high frequency microwaves.

- **JOSHUA** -- The development of LOW Frequency-pulsed sound generating weapons. This weapon was developed and assembled at Ling Tempco Vaught in Anaheim, California. It was described as being able to totally level any man-made structure from a distance of two miles. It was tested at the White Sands Proving Grounds, and developed between 1975 and 1978. It is a long horn-shaped device connected to a computer and amplifiers. The project also involves low frequency and microwave projection.

- **EXCALIBUR** -- This is a weapon designed to destroy alien underground bases [developed and funded mostly by intelligence branches connected with the U.S. Navy and SDI projects who have rejected any further interaction with the Greys after they turned on 'us' during the Groom massacre and the Dulce wars. Some patriotic elements of MJ12 and the MIC --Military-Industrial Complex--support this agenda of resistance, whereas other elements tied-in with the 'corporate imperialists' of the international banking community support continued collaboration for purposes of acquiring further mind-control technology for their 'New World Order'].

Excalibur is a missile capable of penetrating 1,000 meters of Tufa/Hard packed soil, such as is found in New Mexico, with no operational damage resulting. The missile's apogee is not to exceed 30,000 feet Above Ground Level [AGL] and impact must not deviate in excess of 50 meters from designated target. The device carries a one to ten Megaton Nuclear Warhead. The secret for a self contained missile 'drill' [a vertical shaft over 1,000 meters deep] consists in an energosintetizer macrowave deflector in the "Missile Warhead".

MAJIC has five other major weapons to be used against the Aliens, however little if any information on these is available.

THE DULCE PROTOCOL

Also from the same report we find the following information on Reptiloid alien forms:

- Average Height: Male - 2.0 Meters; Female - 1.4 Meters
- Average Weight: M - 200 Kilos; F - 100 Kilos
- Body Temperature: M - Ambient Temperature; F - Ambient Temperature
- Pulse/Respiration: M - 40/10; F - 40/10
- Blood Pressure: M - 80/50; F - 80/50
- Life Expectancy: M - 60 Earth Years; F - 23 Earth Years

Cold-blooded like all reptiles, the Reptiloid is found to flourish in a warm, tropical clime [normally artificial... big caves].

With imperfect respiration providing just enough oxygen to supply tissues and maintain the processing of food and combustion, their temperature can be raised only a few degrees above the ambient [this suggests that 'heat' weapons, like flame-throwers and so on, may prove to be nearly immediately effective and fatal to this species under battle conditions].

The reproductive system is ovouniparous, with eggs hatching in the oviduct prior to birth. The underdeveloped Reptiloid [for faster activities, physical activities] cerebellums results in a slowness and simpler city of movement. The Reptiloid eye is composed of thousands of microscopic facets, each facet with its own independent protective lid. The eye is almost never closed entirely during waking hours; rather, sections of the organ are shut down in conjunction with the dominant light source. The reptiloids survived 'hidden' inside the Earth [within] Big Caves Underground.

Information on the Insectoids:

- Average Height [Master Race]: Male - 1.6 Meters; Female - 1.2 Meters
- Average Height [Servant Race]: M - 1.0 Meters; F - 1.0 Meters
- Average Weight [Master Race]: M - 70 Kilos; F - 40 Kilos
- Average Weight [Servant Race]: M - 35 Kilos; F - 35 Kilos
- Body Temperature: M - 110/2; F - 110/2
- Life Expectancy: M - 130 Earth Years; F - 130 Earth Years

(Note: are the current attempts to create a genetic reptilian-insectoid hybrid race, like those genetically mutated species reportedly existing in Bellatrix Orion, a result of the Reptiloids' desire to increase their life-span? - Branton)

The Insectoid retina is composed entirely of tone-sensitive rods, and is incapable of discrimination between different wavelengths of light. Therefore, the addition of 'color' to the Insectoids vision is accomplished by the dual antennae which, in addition to being auditory receptors, are made up of a complex network of wavelength-sensitive cones. Owing to the highly directional nature of the antenna, the corona of vision is perceived by the subject in the tones of grey.

Because of this correlation of four independent light-receptive organs, Insectoid vision can be correctly termed 'Quadroscopic', resulting in relatively superior depth perception. Insectoid auditory capabilities are highly developed, and Insectoids are capable of distinguishing from among a wider range of audio frequencies than is normal for humanoids.

Because of the mono-directional antennae, Insectoids (most of which have been observed in the form of giant mantis, locust or grasshopper type entities - Branton) usually listen with their head tilted slightly downward. They also have a limited exoskeleton.

More alien races mentioned in the secret report:

THE DULCE PROTOCOL

1. Type A: Rigelian, Rigel, or the Gray

2. Type B: 2-Reticulae, Z-Reticulae 1, or Grey

3. Type C: 2-Reticulae, Z-Reticulae 2, or Grey

4. Type D: Orion, Pleiades, or Nordic

5. Type E: Barnard's Star, the Orange

Information on the Rigelian Reptilian Grays:

LUNA-1 is the Rigelian base on the far side of the Moon. It includes a base, a mining operation using very large machines, and very large Alien Crafts or carrier ships. WAVENEST is the Rigelian base in the Atlantic Ocean, and includes an underwater Alien base, mining and big cigar-shaped crafts.

Rigelians made contacts with certain members of the MILITARY-INDUSTRIAL ['Corporate' or 'Secret' government] complex from 1947-1971... The 'government' thought that the Grays meant us no harm, but in 1982 and 1988 the picture that emerged was exactly the opposite. The story now is one of great deception at several levels. The Grays 'Trojan Horse' style manipulation and lying involved MJ-12/MAJIC Forces (The CURRENT agreements with the Grays within the NSA-connected levels of the Military-Industrial Complex, some sources have implied, continue as a result of the large level of alien infiltration and mind-control that exists throughout certain levels of the Intelligence Community - Branton).

The inner core of the CIA/NSA is deeply controlled by the Grays... Working under the instructions of the aliens from Rigel, the CIA and former[?] Nazi scientists have developed and deployed malignant strains of bacteria and viruses, including AIDS, in order to exterminate 'undesirable' elements of the human population.

Information on the Nordic races:

- Average Height: Male - 2.0 Meters; Female - 1.7 Meters

- Average Weight: M - 90 Kilos; F - 70 Kilos
- Body Temperature: M - 98.6 degrees Fahrenheit; F - 98.6 degrees Fahrenheit
- Pulse/Respiration: M - 72.5/16; F - 72.5/21
- Blood Pressure: M - 120/80; F - 80/50
- Life Expectancy: M - 60 Earth Years; F - 23 Earth Years

(Note: According to other sources, this low life expectancy is probably greatly exaggerated. - Branton)

Information on the Orange:

- Average Height: Male - 1.7 Meters; Female - 2.0 Meters
- Average Weight: M - 70 Kilos; F - 50 Kilos
- Body Temperature: M - 91 degrees Fahrenheit; F - 91 degrees Fahrenheit
- Pulse/Respiration: M - 242/61; F - 242/61
- Blood Pressure: M - 80/40; F - 80/40

(Note: The Orange are reportedly humanoids with red, stalky hair and in some cases may have been genetically tampered with and imputed with various levels of reptilian genetics, making them a quasi-hybrid race although apparently mostly 'human' in many cases. Unlike the reptilians however they have external reproductive organs and are apparently capable of mating with other 'humanoid' races. They come from the Barnard's Star system. On certain rare occasions they have been seen with facial hair, beards, etc. Apparently some strains of the Orange hybrids are more 'humanoid' than are others. - Branton):

We will close this section by quoting from one more installment of the BLUE PLANET PROJECT:

THE DULCE PROTOCOL

THE METAGENE FACTOR: The Metagene is a biological variant lying dormant in select members of the human race [especially on planet earth], until an instant of extraordinary physical and emotional over-stress activates it. (Apparently a latent self-preservation 'gene' capable of producing seemingly 'superhuman' abilities in earth humans during times of extreme stress or crisis. - Branton)

That's an energochemical, in response to adverse stimuli. A chromosomal combustion takes place, as the Metagene takes the source of biostress, be it chemical, radioactivity, or what ever and turns the potential energoresponse into a catalyst for genetic change. The main focus of the catalyst power is a gland in the middle of the human brain called the PINEAL gland, and the nutrient for increasing the Pineal's action is the adrenaline. The Metagene factor gives the ability of Psionic Power [for better or worse].

The main interest of the Aliens, especially the Grays, is to understand and control the Metagene for their own race. They try to do this using Biological Experiments to make Hybrids from both humans and aliens. They believe perhaps the MEN FROM PLANET EARTH ARE THE DEADLIEST CREATURES IN THE UNIVERSE. Because ONLY on Earth people are apparently capable of generating the Metagene Factor, which means Natural Psionics ability, "Real Power"

(Note: Power for good OR evil, you might say. One of the reasons that humans on earth are being controlled/harnessed as is the case with the Nazi-NSA-Military-Industrial space forces, or DENIED advanced interplanetary technology as in the case of those who have NOT been brought under their control, is simply because the aliens -- especially the malevolents -- are terrified that if a FREE non-collectivist human society from earth gets a foothold in space, then they/we would pose a deadly threat to their alien agendas of conquest and manipulation throughout the galaxy. This is why they are INTENT on taming or harnessing the Metagene factor as they have done with the fascist forces based in Antarctica via massive mind control, so that these forces can be channeled as 'human shields' or 'warriors' to fight their battles in space against interstellar cultures who would otherwise resist the activities of the draconian collective.

We must DEMAND from the Military-Industrial complex which has been built with OUR tax dollars -- and which is being deeply influenced by alien/fascist forces -- that they CEASE from selling-us-out, and share their interplanetary technology with the rest of us, so that we as a whole can access the stars rather than just a core of super-wealthy and alien-controlled 'elite'.

If we as a Constitutional Republic [and Congress] rightfully take overt control of whatever space projects have and are being financed BY OUR TAX DOLLARS, then the open space policy and public conscience itself will prevent these space forces from engaging in any unjustified military actions against peaceful worlds that would defy the foundational ethics of the U.S. Constitution on the one hand; or will prevent us from allying ourselves with any exploitative and manipulative alien force on the other hand. - Branton).

The principle races in the Universe are psychologically the same. The pure cold logic is a normal order to most important races. Basic sameness makes for predictability and security, the enemy one knows, are the ones you can guard against. This is not the case with [unpredictable] mankind.

While most are uniformly human, some [many more, apparently, than anyone had dreamed] possess a latent tendency towards super humanity, Natural Psionic Abilities. That in itself could prove dangerous for any idea of Alien domination on Earth.

(Note: for instance, some Terrans have the ability to 'scan' the UPF or universal psionic field with their super-conscious minds via projecting and focusing their 'magnetic' body at various levels on a conscious or unconscious basis, and any subjective 'danger' that is detected through this process is converted to consciousness via 'intuition'. This might be compared with 'remote viewing', which is simply the human brains' ability to 'tune-in-to' and 'ride' the Universal Psionic Field or the 'Flowline' like a biochemical radio receiver scanning the psionic 'air' waves -- and psionic-waves ARE a tangible energy-form that can be measured just as radio waves can.

The electro-magneto-gravitic 'grid' of any planet, and supposedly the EMG fields which connect the planets and stars at a subtle level, serve as the energy 'web' in which thought forms are trapped and contained. Humans are multi-dimensional beings and therefore have the ability to perceive the vast 'reservoirs' of thought forms within these interstellar grids on an intuitive level, for instance when they are dreaming.

During the dream-state the brain operates on a lower frequency -- and what we might call psionic LONG waves are produced which can reach out and connect with others 'long' waves on the same frequency, or connect with the psionic field itself and observe the 'psychic atmosphere' resident within any certain area through tapping-in to the reservoir of 'thought forms' there. This would explain why people often have 'vivid' dreams near high energy grid areas, simply because these areas tend to 'trap' more thought form, psionic or psychic energy residue than do other areas.

Also astral, human or animal life forms which have become 'trapped' within these psionic energy grids by encountering powerful EMG zones like that which exists in the Bermuda Triangle area -- essentially having entered into or become part of a "world of thought forms", a dimension density where events and objects are more 'fluid' than they are in the 3rd dimension -- might be contacted, for better OR worse, while in the 'dream' state. Not ALL of the 'beings' or even 'dreamscapes' that one encounters within the dream-state are the exclusive products of ones own subconscious mind. - Branton)

By coupling mankind's inherent belligerence with the fact of the Metagene affect, each human is unique and Earth becomes a spawning ground for an unpredictable super-race, "if we have the chance". Others have already demonstrated an awareness of Man's Potential [throughout] human history.

This is because the Aliens are here to try to CONTROL Earthlings before WE dominate THEM, and they want our most important secret: THE METAGENE FACTOR, which is the Aliens' only hope.

Chapter 28

"The Organization"

Inside The Collaboration

The following information comes from an article written by researcher William Hamilton, titled MAGICAL CAVERNS, which was in turn based upon Hamilton's book ALIEN MAGIC:

The first case of subterranean abduction that I investigated occurred in 1988. I never reached a firm conclusion regarding the information that resulted from this investigation, but did receive corroborating reports from other abductees. The incident occurred in the Rosamond area of the Antelope Valley in California up on the sides of the Tehachapi Mountains.

The Tehachapi Mountains rise on the north side of the valley. There is a saddle in the mountains and a secret Northrop electromagnetic testing facility is in the area just below the saddle. The Northrop facility has been dubbed the "Ant-hill" or the "Black Hole" by some of the locals who refer to it as a multileveled underground facility.

Ray and Nancy worked at the Northrop B-2 assembly factory in Palmdale. Ray is a Native American. Ray was an aircraft inspector and worked swing shift. One June night he decided to take a midnight ride with Nancy up to the cut in the Tahachapi mountains. This cut appears as an inclined whitish mark on the side of the foothills. It actually marks the site of a road that winds up around the mountains.

On the backside is an entrance to an artificial plateau that had been blasted out of the rocks. Ray parked his truck on this plateau. They got out to look at the stars and the city lights of Lancaster and Palmdale in the valley far below. While looking at the stars, Nancy noticed that some of them were moving around and brought it to Ray's attention.

Ray got his flashlight out of the truck and started signaling the lights. At some point, Nancy noticed a bright basketball-sized orb hovering just above a nearby knoll. They both walked closer to get a better look at the orb. Ray thought it had just risen out of some invisible opening in the ground. It seemed to be flashing and sparkling. Some sort of line dangled from its underside. It rose a little higher and Nancy tried to speak to it, having an intuitive feeling that some intelligence has guided the orb to that plateau for their benefit.

As they watched this strange phenomenon around one o'clock in the morning, they next observed the morning dawn light over the far distant eastern hills. Something had just snatched four hours of time out of their lives. The orb was gone. They were terrified and drove quickly home. The next day, they felt a vibration going through their apartment. When they went outdoors, they saw two orbs hovering above their apartment. This scared them badly.

I took Ray and Nancy to a local hypnotist and she regressed Ray. Nancy refused to be regressed, expressing fear over what she might discover about those four hours of missing time. Ray was an excellent subject. When in trance, with little prompting, he fell backwards nearly to the floor before we caught him. The regression brought out some amazing revelations. Ray and Nancy had been abducted and taken underground!

THE DULCE PROTOCOL

Under hypnosis he kept mentioning the Kern River to the north. "There is an area near the Tehachapi Mountains called the Kern River Project. The upper river is being used by the government for hydro-electric power to power an underground facility at Tehachapi Ranch [actually, the Tejon Ranch]. The mountain next to the power facility is being hollowed out...there is mud all around and it's so obvious, but apparently people aren't looking.

All the power is being used for the Ranch, which is the site of underground 'skunk works' where highly technical aircraft, spacecraft and all kinds of stuff are being dealt with. It is a huge underground base, probably close to the size of the one under 29 Palms Marine Base. It has huge hangers and very large elevators as well as technical laboratories. There is a whole city under there, large passageways...the whole valley is full of tunnels. You can drive from one end to the other underground.

You can drive from Palmdale, site of the Northrop, Lockheed and 'black project' areas, to California City...all underground. There are tunnels all the way to George AFB. Aliens apparently have ACCESS...they've been seen all over the place. The [corporate] government LETS them do whatever they want.

They're probing the human brain, trying to find our WEAKNESSES and learning how to CONTROL us (like they've apparently 'learned' to 'control' the secret [corporate] government elite who in turn control these underground military-industrial networks and who have in essence turned these facilities over to the aliens, whether out of fear of retaliation, out of some type of global control agreement, or just plain mind control? - Branton). They dissect humans...can't describe the dissections because they are not humane. Really morbid. The 'government' knows it...they just turn their heads.

Some people in the government want to STOP this but they don't know HOW to stop it."

(Note: As so many "in the know" have already said, the entire "alien-interaction" scenario is completely "out of control", which I would guess means that WE are NO LONGER in control of the situation. In other words the "framework" which was created as a result of the alien-interaction projects when most of the human collaborators believed that the "aliens" were benevolent, is STILL in place, even after "we" lost control of the situation.

Since the aliens now have CONTROL of much of the INFRASTRUCTURE that grew out of the early interaction projects, the control-structure or "establishment" itself WILL NOT and CAN NOT do anything about the situation. It is up to those on earth who are NOT bound by security RESTRICTIONS, or fraternal secret society OATHS, or in the case of humanoid "visitors" those who are not bound by non-interference DIRECTIVES -- such as the many Nordic-Terran HYBRIDS who have according to Michael Wolf and others been LEGALLY born into this society.

In other words it is those AND ONLY THOSE who are FREE from and operating OUTSIDE OF 'THE SYSTEM' who have the power to change the situation for the better. - Branton)

Ray was disconcerted that Greys had Nancy strapped to a table in this facility. He could see instruments all around. During hypnosis he would freeze up when recalling this scene. He yelled and became very emotional. He was convinced they would rape her and violate her, yet he was helpless to prevent it.

He and Nancy also felt they had contact with a benevolent race of aliens who had observed their capture [by the Greys]. After a few months, Ray and Nancy announced to me that they wanted little more to do with reporting further events. They felt exposed and monitored and feared retribution if they continued talking. They last told me they intended to go to Bible classes to find refuge from this enormous EVIL that encroached upon their lives.

THE DULCE PROTOCOL

Many witnesses have observed unusual phenomenon over the Tejon Ranch. One night on March 3, 1991 Pearl Schultz and Aric Leavitt sighted five or six UFOs moving in pairs at various speeds and sometimes switching directions over the Tehachapi Mountains. Each had a pulsating light that alternated from bright white to heavy red. Mrs. Schultz noticed orange and yellow colors. Some of the UFOs seemed to come from the saddle area.

A man named Stan saw a bright flash of orange light which seemed to have a cigar-shape. He saw this from Avenue I looking northwest over the Tehachapi's.

Three witnesses went up to the plateau near the Anthill on January 31, 1991. They saw a green-glowing disk take-off from this facility without any apparent acceleration and climb at a 45 degree angle to the south. They also heard a tone when they sighted the object. When traveling back down the road [170th Street West], they saw two <u>black vans and two black helicopters</u>.

In the morning dawn, a pilot was flying out of Fox Field on Avenue G headed for Merced. His flight path would take him over the Tehachapi's. When passing over the saddle where the Anthill is located on February 23, 1991, he observed four white rectangular objects hovering over the facility. He described them as being four times the size of a typical highway billboard. They were each separated by about 200 yards. Another observer, who was called on the phone, drove his car out to the highway and observed these same objects before they winked out! (cloaked? - Branton)

One local man who has property on 170th Street West reported seeing the ground open up like a missile silo within the fenced parameter surrounding the Northrop installation. He saw a flying saucer emerge from this 'silo' and take off. He also claimed that someone from Edwards had come to talk to him about his story and told him to shut up. I further found out that the man's name is Chuck and he was a contractor who worked on the underground tunnels in the Anthill facility.

He said the tunnels have round doorways with panels that have red and green lights for ID and entry. There are no doors covering these doorways, but some kind of field is projected from cylinders embedded in the door wall. Tiny globes hovered in the tunnels and followed Chuck and his crew around. He thought they were being used by the Air Force as sensors. But where did the Air Force get the technology to levitate these orbs?

Joe told me a lot of stories. He attended many of my UFOrum meetings in Lancaster. He claims to have had a close encounter and missing time when traveling a road through the south side of Edwards AFB one night. Joe was in construction and held clearances for working in military operation areas. He said that he had worked on an underground tunnel project below Haystack Butte on the Eastern boundary of Edwards near the NASA Rocket Test Site. He also claimed that he saw orbs roving around these tunnels.

He painted numbers inside a box located on a stripe that ran horizontally midway along the tunnel walls. I asked him how far this tunnel ran below the earth's surface. He said that he and fellow employees used to count as the elevator descended to the tunnel level. From the count and from the elevator speed, I estimated that the tunnel must have been around 3,000 feet deep.

One time he saw a door open to a room in one of these tunnels and he could see a very tall alien standing next to two men in white lab coats. He thought this alien was all of nine feet tall. He claims that he saw two grey aliens inside a hangar at China Lake one day when he went back inside the hanger after finishing his work to retrieve a tool that he had left behind. Joe was always telling me fantastic stories, yet he seemed very sincere. I never knew whether to believe him.

One day Joe told me about two old school buddies he had run across. They both held jobs in underground facilities and had worked at the Anthill, he said. They would work underground for two weeks at a stint. They lived in condos when working underground. These condos were also built into the underground facility. The government even picked up the tab on one guy's alimony.

One was known as a computer genius. He said that he had seen both grey AND reptilian life forms in various underground facilities. One of the underground projects was Project Startalk. The work involved lasers. The informer, a guy named Paul, said that he worked in a big underground building [350 feet across]. Project Startalk utilized a powerful laser which strikes a mirror and is sent into space. The laser is modulated with a signal and acts as a beacon to bring in UFOs.

Apparently, the beacon is directed at friendly forces from other systems. He also worked at the Douglas facility near Llano. He once saw a saucer land and go into an underground hanger. Inside the underground building is a huge computer complex. The workers wear white clothing and white socks [no shoes]. The computers use an alien symbolic language. Manuals indicate codes that can be entered. There is a large lexon plastic screen in this complex that displays various star systems and galaxies.

A wax pencil is used to indicate targets for the laser. The technology used is so far advanced that it is beyond known engineering technology. The laser is also capable of INTERDIMENSIONAL communication. (Hyperspace or subspace communication? It would HAVE to be so, since laser-light modulated in third dimensional beams would take at least 3 years to reach the nearest star. - Branton) Security workers accompany all workers, even to the bathroom.

Phones are tapped, even worker's home phones. It took Paul and Gopher [the second guy] two years to get a security clearance.

(Note: If the Military-Industrial establishment or the 'corporate' government is involved with the alien interaction as it would seem to be, then the electorate government does not have entire control of the situation... those who control these corporate structures do! Or those whose motivation is to increase their wealth and power even if it means making "business deals" with malevolent alien forces. Their motivation would NOT necessarily be to govern the American citizen's nor uphold and defend the Constitution of the United States! As they say, the lust for money is the root of ALL evil. - Branton)

Gopher also worked at the Anthill as a computer specialist.

He has also worked at Lockheed's Helendale facility and at the Nevada Test Site. Gopher says that we are working with aliens and alien technology and it scares the hell out of him. He gets paid well. He makes $145 thousand a year and the 'government' pays his alimony. He says he has also worked at SECTION D, better known as the DULCE facility. He has seen reptoids and Greys in these underground facilities. He doesn't have a life of his own. He worked with white-skinned reptoids (probably the "white Draco" that Thomas Castello spoke of - Branton).

He has also seem members of the Orange race. HE HAS NOT SEEN ANY BENEFIT TO HUMANITY. He is trying to find out what is going to happen. He is worried about what the future holds. He foresees an ALIEN WAR. He has a good lifestyle underground. Besides the condo, he has swimming pools, saunas, and a gym at his disposal. He works 14 to 16 days on a shift. He is not allowed to leave the country and must obtain permission to leave the state. He says the main control center in the valley is at Haystack Butte.

A tunnel runs from Haystack Butte to the Anthill. Gopher believes there are benevolent aliens and says he saw one once. They are from a Federation. The one he saw was human looking, a tall blond [Nordic] that wore a white jump suit and had a green coat over it. He believes that we are trying to enlist the aid of such friendly beings. This is a very similar scenario to what I received in the letter from a veteran.

My friend's stepson obtained a job in an underground facility at Los Alamos. He says there is a tube shuttle that runs from that underground facility to SECTION D. He worked on Level I which RUNS UNDER MAIN STREET [in Dulce]. One block from the PAN AM building is the old high school, now used as an engineering facility by HAKEN HANGAR [Originally ZIA Corp].

INSIDE THE FACILITY IS AN ELEVATOR THAT DESCENDS TO THE COMPUTER ROOM. From the computer room a side tunnel intersects the main tunnel transit tube that runs from Los Alamos to Albuquerque. These levels are protected by PROFORCE Security.

At deeper, more secure levels exist automatic devices that kill intruders. A security guard accidentally tripped an alarm and was killed by one of these. These tunnels are a minor part of a VAST network of such tunnels. One other thing mentioned by this source is an underground city which housed a population of thousands who occupied CONDOS. Many of these people lived permanently underground. Some of the advanced technological research going on involves genetic labs using laser fusion.

The budget for the SURFACE facility [alone] is OVER A BILLION DOLLARS A YEAR, but the underground research projects get MANY TIMES THIS AMOUNT.

(How much of this comes from our hard-earned tax dollars? Is the American economy and our wealth literally "going down the tubes"? - Branton)

Pam and I were introduced to an abductee named Diane a few years ago. Diane lives over in the Apple Valley area. She had ongoing alien encounters since she was a child. As she grew older, she started experiencing abductions by humans that took her to underground facilities. One of these underground facilities she believed was located at China Lake Naval Weapons test center (just west of the Panamint Range and Death Valley - Branton).

She was taken down to lower levels in an elevator.

Her description of this elevator matched the description given by a man named Thomas of an elevator in use at the Dulce facility. Thomas' description of this and other details were never published [at the time] so that we could check out corroborating eyewitness reports. Evidently these elevators have an unusual shape and operate on magnetic forces in the elevator shaft rather than using cable systems to run the elevator up and down the shaft.

Diane also reports that she was taken on a tour of one part of the facility by a man in a white coat. He showed her humans that had been biologically altered. These humans were housed in cages set about a foot above the floor. She also saw altered animals. Her story was just as bizarre as Thomas' story of Level 7 at Dulce.

The story of an underground base on the Jicarilla Apache Indian reservation first came to light around 1980 when Albuquerque physicist Paul Bennewitz reported the crash of an alien ship on the slopes of Archuleta Mountain. Paul wrote a letter to Senator Pete Domenici and Paul Gilman in Washington D.C.

This letter was accompanied by a report. He said, "Atomic ship originally outlined in my report... copy to you... several years ago had crashed approximately two miles northwest of Dulce, NM near Archuleta Peak on Archuleta Mesa". He believed there was a concern because gamma and neutron radiation could be emitted from the crash site if there had been a nuclear meltdown. Paul's THUNDER SCIENTIFIC CORPORATION manufactured various detection instruments.

In his PROJECT BETA report, Bennewitz stated that humanoid aliens had a base near Archuleta Mesa and that he had established direct computer communication with aliens at the base. He did not believe the aliens to be trustworthy. Paul became paranoid about the government, the aliens, and admitted abductees whom he believed were being controlled by the aliens.

THE DULCE PROTOCOL

At a MUFON conference held in Las Vegas in 1989, featured speaker Bill Moore made the statement that Paul Bennewitz was fed disinformation by intelligence agents, that he contributed to this effort, and the WHOLE STORY concerning the Dulce facility was constructed around these bits of disinformation that were fed to Paul (or was it a case of "reverse disinformation" in the same vein as "reverse psychology"? - Branton).

However, testimony from Walter Baumgartner and state police officer Gabe Valdez indicates otherwise. According to them, they had SEEN video images of aliens that Paul had made contact with using his special equipment (that is, a video-radio link utilizing a hexadecimal code with computer printout which he used to 'interrogated' the alien's collective intelligence via ship-to-base communication frequencies - Branton).

These aliens would send messages that would output on Paul's computer printer. Some of the sentence structure was disjointed. Were intelligence agents taking extreme measure by hoaxing computer communications with Paul? For what purpose? Apparently Bennewitz was using special transmitter coils to send and receive electromagnetic signals to and from the alien base.

Then along came Thomas. Thomas E. Castello was born in Glen Ellan, Illinois on April 23, 1941. Thomas was the man who released the Dulce papers. His good friend, Ann West (pseudonym - true name on file.- Branton), tells his story -- as Thomas has not been heard from since 1991.

Thomas had a passion for antique cars, any antique car, but especially Packards, and especially the big-nosed cars of the forties and early fifties. A lot of his spare time was spent modifying his 1949 Packard, and he needed special parts. His friends told him about an older man in town that had a machine shop that could rebuild antique cars. This old man was Ed West, Ann's father. He found Ed easy to talk to, not just about cars, but anything. The two spent endless hours discussing cars, planes, and the space program. Tom and Ed found they were both fascinated with flying saucers.

After a few months, Ed introduced Tom to "THE ORGANIZATION", a group that did deep research on flying saucers and contactees. Tom completed INITIATION into the group and was soon on several assignments.

At that time in 1961, Tom was in the Air Force, stationed at Nellis AFB [near] Las Vegas. He was schooled in photography, and had received a top secret clearance. He was given the opportunity of receiving additional training in Virginia. There, he had his first experience of working in an underground base. When he left that facility, his top secret clearance was upgraded to TS-IV.

His duties as an Air Force sergeant included photographing a runway exercise in Florida. He would meet with Ann during his off-duty time in Orlando. Tom was pleased to discover that Ann drove a classic 1950 Packard straight-eight with a beautiful swan as a hood ornament.

The next year, 1963, Ann moved to Las Vegas to be near her folks.

When she was in Florida, she had a close encounter with a glowing flying saucer and was actually taken on board. The haunting dreams and memories of this incident bothered Ann. Tom introduced HER to "The Organization". After a few visits, Ann became initiated into the group and started certain assignments. She and Tom began to collect books, articles, and magazines about UFOs. They would spend nights doing research.

Over the years, Tom became like a brother to Ann. His parents were killed in a car accident so he adopted Ann's parents into his heart.

Tom stayed in high security photography for seven years, then left the Air Force in 1971. He began working for RAND Corp. in California as a security technician. Within a year, his clearance was upgraded to ULTRA-3.

THE DULCE PROTOCOL

Tom met Cathy in 1972 and got married. In November, 1974, Cathy gave birth to Eric Scott Castello. They moved to Santa Fe, New Mexico in 1977. Tom had been transferred and his clearance upgraded to ULTRA-7. He found his new position financially rewarding, but more stressful. He told Ann that he worked in an underground facility that had incredible security, for the photography department.

His job touched on all aspects of photography from large format cameras to mini cameras. It was his responsibility to check, align, and calibrate all the security video cameras, from the doors to exit tunnels. His position required that he be armed at all times. It was also his job to escort visitors to certain areas of the base. This facility came to be known as the Dulce Base. When Tom finally left his job, he had earned the security rank of Major.

Tom and Cathy, and TAL and Mary LeVesque, all lived in Santa Fe, New Mexico in 1979 when Ann went to visit them. Tom seemed more intense than usual. He said that he wished that he could talk to Ann about his concerns, but his high security clearance prevented him from saying much. The day Ann left New Mexico, Tom pressed a folded piece of paper into her hand and whispered quietly, "don't let anyone see this."

She slipped it into her pocket. That night, alone at a motel in Durango, she opened the paper. There were three things on its yellow page: a sketch of an alien; an inverted triangle; and the name Dulce. She stared at the mysterious drawing and tried to figure out what it all meant. The alien in the drawing had a large head, big black eyes, no nose and no hair. The triangle was shaded black. After looking at it, she flushed the paper down the toilet. That night, she had nightmares about aliens.

The next morning, over coffee, she was looking at a map for a route back to Las Vegas when she noticed the name of a small town near the New Mexico state line called 'Dulce.' Were there aliens in Dulce? What was Tom trying to tell her? Then she remembered where she had seen the black triangle before. The symbol was on a hat on Tom's coffee table. It was burnt orange with a black inverted triangle with gold bands cutting it in three sections.

(Note: It is interesting that this three-level triangle is inverted, when we consider that some 'Nordic' groups use an UPRIGHT triangle with three horizontal lines through it as their emblem. Some 'Christian' sources have reported 'visions' of the 'New Jerusalem' city mentioned in the book of Revelation, as being a vast city of LIGHT and of pyramidal shape and in three levels. This 'city of light' has been reportedly observed -- using super-powerful telescopes -- to be emerging from the 'nebula' far beyond the Orion cluster, and it is said to be on a direct course to earth.

This is reportedly the supreme headquarters of the angelic forces and the Triune Godhead under whom they serve, according to these Christian sources. This description would coincide with the Nordic emblem of an upright three-level triangle or pyramid, in that these humanoids would no doubt be aware of this Divine center of angelic activity IF our elite scientists are, and the fact that an INVERTED or upside-down three-level triangle is associated with the Dulce base might denote a direct Luciferian connection. This is especially interesting if the reports are true which state that the Dulce base has its counterparts within the 4th and 5th densities or dimensions of that particular point in time-space. - Branton)

She decided to drive through Dulce looking for something suspicious, but found nothing. She went back to Durango and drove to Cortez. She fell in love with it, and moved to Colorado.

Early in December of that year, Tom paid Ann a surprise visit. He told her that he had walked out on his job some months ago after a major dispute broke out between security workers and a military group. Tom said that the security force used "flash guns," but the military group was armed with machine guns.

THE DULCE PROTOCOL

(Although an apparent human/alien security force may have possessed flash guns and the military force machine guns -- this does not necessarily mean that a weapons dispute was the SOLE 'trigger' of the conflict - Branton).

He said it was like a war with screaming and panic in all the tunnels. A lot of people died in the conflict. He wondered what story the government would use to cover-up the deaths. In February, 1980, the media reported a prison riot near Los Alamos and that many prisoners died. Was this the cover-up?

Tom admitted that he was in trouble. He went back to the base and took photos, papers, and other items. He had entered and left through a ventilation shaft inside an ICE CAVE. After leaving the cave, he Returned to a prepared box, put everything in the box, and buried it. He went back to his car, but security was waiting for him. They questioned him about his purpose for being there, but allowed him to leave. He was on his way to Colorado Springs, and now he was "on the run."

He asked Ann to have faith in him and that he was still the same man she had always known as a friend.

The next day, after he had left, three men from O.S.I. showed up and questioned Ann about Tom's whereabouts. On four other visits in December other men questioned her and she told them she knew nothing about where he had gone. In January, the CIA came to her door. They insisted that she was withholding information.

Ann had been in a car accident in 1978 and had recurring headaches. In January, 1980 she checked into a hospital in Farmington, New Mexico. She went in for an angiogram, but woke up to find that she had had a stroke. She had to re-learn everything again. At that time the OSI and CIA stopped bothering her.

It was June of 1982 before she heard from Thomas again. He called from her dad's house. They talked for hours. He had been running for his life and had been in twenty states and four countries. He showed her medical papers and scientific diagrams, but Ann could not make sense of it all. Tom told her that the 'government' had a treaty with an alien nation and that aliens had been on [under] this earth for countless centuries. He showed Ann pages of alien written material and translated papers. It was horrifying.

He told her that Cathy and Eric had been KIDNAPPED and were being' held CAPTIVE in a subterranean base. He needed a safe place to hide all the original papers that he took from the Dulce Base and other things of a substantial nature to prove the alien conspiracy. Tom and Ann buried the box of material on a mountain. Years have changed the terrain, and Ann has not been able to relocate the exact burial site.

Sound like a tall tale? Many think it is. Ann had photos of Thomas and details of his life in her files. TAL met with him once. He is a real person. He answered some of my questions by mail. He fully believes what he says and has answered the questions when he knows the answers. Some of this information has been published in hopes of eliciting further witness testimony. So far, I only know of three others who claim they have been to this underground facility. One man is known to a friend of mine and was trained as a nuclear physicist.

The Dulce Facility is a seven-level underground research base, run by the D.O.E. [Dept. Of Energy] (As is the Nevada Test Site - Branton) and connected to the Los Alamos labs. Level I has garages, street maintenance equipment, photo labs, hydroponic gardens to grow fresh vegetables, fruits, legumes, etc., human housing, a mess hall, VIP housing, a kitchen, and a security vehicles garage.

Each of the levels has color-coded electric cars that are used for short-distance transport. Level 6 houses the infamous "Nightmare Hall"; a security arsenal; a military arsenal; military security; and a generator/impulsor. The generator is 200 feet in diameter, and has a two-level Electromagnetic impulse device that can create a perfect clone [duplicate or replicate] of a person.

THE DULCE PROTOCOL

Science-Fiction? Abductees have described being taken to similar facilities.

There is no proof unless someone can find the box. If it is there!

(Or unless one succeeds in discovering one of the entrances to the base, although there would no doubt be risks if one were to attempt entrance to the base without full-scale military backup. - Branton).

However, these stories have prompted researchers, including myself, to find documented evidence of underground facilities, and we have found plenty. That such an underground EMPIRE exists in almost total secrecy is absolutely amazing.

Few question its existence, its purpose, or the tremendous expenditure of monies that must have gone into the design, construction, maintenance, and operations of these facilities...

Chapter 29

"They Live": Chameleons In Our Midst!?

John A. Keel, in his book 'OUR HAUNTED PLANET', gives an interesting introduction to the reality of an alien race that has taken careful measures to remain hidden from the mass consciousness of those dwelling on the surface of planet earth -- or those ignorant 'human cattle' whom they are intent on manipulating and exploiting from their secret hiding places above, below and even amongst the inhabitants of planet earth:

"...The parahuman Serpent People of the past are still among us. They were probably worshipped by the builders of Stonehenge and the forgotten ridge-making cultures of South America.

"...In some parts of the world the Serpent People successfully posed as gods and imitated the techniques of the super-intelligence [God]. This led to the formation of pagan religions centered around human sacrifices. The conflict, so far as man himself was concerned, became one of religions and races. Whole civilizations based upon the worship of these false gods rose and fell in Asia, Africa, and South America. The battleground had been chosen, and the mode of conflict had been decided upon.

"The human race would supply the pawns. The mode of control was complicated as usual. Human beings were largely free of direct control. Each individual HAD TO CONSCIOUSLY COMMIT HIMSELF TO ONE OF THE OPPOSING FORCES...

"The main battle was for what was to become known as the human soul.

"Once an individual had committed himself, he opened a door so that an indefinable something could actually enter his body and exercise some control over his subconscious mind.

"...the Serpent People or OMEGA Group, attacked man in various ways, trying to rid the planet of him. But the super-intelligence was still able to look over man... God worked out new ways of communication and control, always in conflict with the Serpent People."

In relation to these 'Serpent People' -- who some claim are now living among us and have been doing so for a very long time -- the anonymous Intelligence officer and planetary patriot 'Commander X' released details of an incident which may well have come right out of a John Carpenter movie, if not for the fact that the Commander himself, from his own high-security position within the Intelligence Community, is convinced of its potential reality:

"...Another story comes from a private stationed on the surface at Dulce. He soon realized something mighty 'odd' was going on around there, but it took a while to put his finger on it.

"'One morning last September, I was working on a routine job when another of the young enlistees, a mechanic, came in with a small rush job he wanted welded at once. He had the print and proceeded to show me exactly what he wanted. We are both bending over the bench in front of the welder when I happened to look directly into his face.

THE DULCE PROTOCOL

It seemed to suddenly become covered with a semi-transparent film or cloud. His features faded and in their place appeared a 'thing' with bulging eyes, no hair and SCALES for skin. I stood and looked at it for about 20 seconds. WHATEVER IT WAS stood and looked at me without moving.

Then the strange face seemed to fade away, and at the same time recede into the ordinary face of the young man underneath. The dissipation of the imposed face lasted or took about five seconds before it was completely gone and I was standing there weak, my mouth open and staring at the young man who had come in with the rush order.

The young 'man' did not seem to be conscious of the elapsed time when I had observed all this but went right on talking about the job as if nothing had happened.

"'This is hard to take but I assure you it was still harder for me. No one can realize a jolt you could get from seeing anything like this until they have experienced it for themselves. It was several days before I had myself convinced that maybe after all what I had seen was real and that I was not suffering from illusions and the beginning of insanity. Days passed before I saw this particular phenomena again. The next time was later at night at the guard house near the front gate, on the way to work. I had purchased some small items and on arriving I went around to the guard house with my slip to retrieve my package.

There was only one guard on duty. I handed him the check and he began to look at the package, taking his time. I waited a minute, then happened to look directly at him again. His face began to change. Again a face of a strange creature was imposed. You could see through the imposed face for a few seconds and then it became the only one visible [solidified is the word] and again about 20 seconds duration.

Again five seconds for dissipation and the guard started to move normally again, found my package and gravely handed it to me and I walked out without a word being said.'"

Since coming across this report from the 'Commander', I made an effort to see if there were any other similar accounts that might confirm the existence of 'Chameleons' or alien 'infiltrators' working on the surface of planet earth in an apparent attempt to pass themselves off as human beings and blend-in with our society, for whatever nefarious agenda they might be serving.

Some of the reports of quasi-human infiltrators spoke of the "Men In Black" who have terrorized UFO witnesses. Although many of the 'MIB' who have been reported were obviously humans working for some obscure surface, other-planetary or subterranean intelligence agency AS WELL AS others that appeared to be either cyborgs, clones or even paraphysical manifestations, there was a branch of the so-called MIB which betrayed definite reptilian characteristics.

These in essence were reptilian humanoids with a full-blown -- although at times not-too-convincing -- 'reconstructive surgery' job, apparently intended to allow them to operate in human society undetected.

Some of the early 'infiltrators' betrayed themselves with their 'plastic' or artificial appearance, whereas in more recent years the 'disguise' has become far more sophisticated with the advent of molecular shape-shifting occult-technology, techno-hypnotic transmitters, and portable laser-hologram technology [according to one source], and therefore harder to detect. However there ARE ways...

Researcher George Andrews, in his book EXTRATERRESTRIAL FRIENDS AND FOES [ILLUMINET PRESS., P.O. Box 2808., Lilburn, GA 30226] quotes a statement made by Valdomar Valerian, director of LEADING EDGE RESEARCH:

THE DULCE PROTOCOL

"...A friend of mine and four of his friends experimented with crystalline structures a year or two ago (mid-1980's - Branton), and they figured out how to cut them along certain planes so they could actually see the aura or energy field around people. That's when they discovered that <u>all people aren't 'people'</u>, or the people they thought they were. It appears that some E.T. humanoids <u>have a dark blue ovoid aura</u>.

(<u>Note</u>: Aura cameras developed by Chuck Shramek -- yes, the same Chuck Shramek of the 'Hale-Bopp Companion' controversy -- and others clearly show the 7 multi-colored 'chakra' points of the human soul/spirit matrix. Presumably since reptilians <u>have NO soul</u>, they would have NO multicolored auric field. - Branton).

It so happens that all the people they checked that met this criteria also wore dark glasses and made every attempt to act like they really wanted nothing to do with people in general.

"They followed one of these people out into the desert where he evidently had a trailer. After waiting until dusk, they made a pretense of needing help and knocked on the door. After a short while, the light went on and the man came to the door. He looked normal, EXCEPT THAT HIS PUPILS WERE VERTICAL SLITS INSTEAD OF CIRCLES. It works. The only trouble is that it costs $2,000 to put a pair of those glasses together..."

Several areas across the Western U.S. where surface and/or underground military installations exist have reportedly produced similar 'Chameleon' sightings.

There seems to be a trend which involves the infiltration of the NSA-CIA and the subsequent 'replacement' of agency personnel, and in turn Military-Industrial personnel, by alien life forms not loyal to planet earth nor to the human race in general.

These reports are very similar to other reports that made the rounds within 'fringe' research groups during the early 1980's concerning the reported 'assimilation' of high-ranking Communist officials and scientists by serpent-like humanoids, reptilian beings that were reputedly revived out of suspended animation from a frozen city that was discovered under the northern Siberian ice fields. The was referred to as the "Siberian Affair". Are their really 'tares' living among the 'wheat' as all these reports suggest?

Aside from Dulce, New Mexico and the Nevada Test Site, other areas where these "chameleon" sightings have taken place include Deep Springs, CA where these alien "impostors" have allegedly been sighted; and Dugway, Utah where one woman by the name of Barbara who worked as a hair stylist claimed she saw one of the HIGH RANKING MILITARY OFFICIALS transform temporarily into an entity with 'reptilian' features.

Another source at Dugway who worked in an auto shop claimed that he saw a similar phenomenon while changing the tires on the car of one Dugway military official. Remember that Dugway works closely with Area 51, which is just to the west and across the state border. It is interesting that there are claims that the joint CIA-alien activity within the 'Dreamland' underground complexes of Nevada have and are being extended to the underground facilities below the St. George and Dugway areas of Utah, among other sites.

Another 'sighting' of these impostors occurred just south of the mid-point of an old toll road that ran between Hopland and Lakeport, California. The sighting involved large black automobiles that would leave and enter a dead-end road in the area. When investigated, the tire tracks ran right up and under a large boulder at the base of a cliff and seemingly disappeared beneath it, and since the roads were fenced on one side and a steep hill existed on the other, it is unlikely that the large automobiles were able to turn around.

This same area, especially one particular mountain there, is known as a very unusual place. 'Bottomless' caves with stone stairwells have been reported. Government vehicles and personnel have 'disappeared' without a trace on the road. An 'atmosphere of fear' is said to exist in an area approximately 30 miles in diameter. Also there have been a lot of unexplained deaths among the settlers in the area. Apparently this area is the site of a large underground center of 'alien' activity. This activity was taking place back in the 1930's, long before the so-called ALIEN "Men In Black" started getting any major attention from Ufologists in America.

The Dulce enigma [and the "chameleons"] have not only infiltrated Utah, Nevada and California, but seems to have stretched its tentacles all the way up to the Pacific northwest. One area of particular interest is the Madigan Military Hospital south of Seattle, Washington near FORT LEWIS... which has been investigated by Val Valerian.

In June of 1992 Valerian released the following article, titled "ALIEN INFILTRATION OF THE MILITARY MEDICAL SYSTEM: MADIGAN HOSPITAL IN WASHINGTON", in his LEADING EDGE newsletter:

"About a year ago, we ran into SEVERAL PEOPLE who stated that they 'had heard' that 'REPTILIAN HUMANOIDS WERE WORKING AT A U.S. ARMY HOSPITAL' NEAR FORT LEWIS, WASHINGTON. At that point, these statements were simply filed away in 'rumor' status, pending the arrival of something more substantial. Descriptions of the nature of and appearance of alien humanoid forms that could be termed 'REPTILIAN' vary widely.

REPTILIAN HUMANOIDS HAVE BEEN DESCRIBED IN ITALY AS LOOKING VERY LIZARD-LIKE, EVEN WITH TAILS. Pictures showing some of these entities were published in an ITALIAN magazine and eventually ended up in the United States in 'The Leading Edge'. Logic would seem to tell us that if alien humanoids were in fact in 'collusion' with military medical personnel at a hospital, they would not in fact have the appearance of anything other than humans, or be close enough to humans to blend in.

Robert K Teske

About a month ago, the nature of synchronicity brought me to an espresso bar, where I chanced to engage a lady in her early 50's in some small conversation about an entirely unrelated matter. She had been a nurse for some twenty years, and sixteen of those twenty years had been spent working for the U.S. Army. She retired from the service and was now job hunting in the local area. She was very professional, and seemed to know a lot about the nursing field.

Gradually, her conversation got around to a 'very unusual place', Madigan Military Hospital, which is located on Route 5 south of Seattle. She had applied for work at the hospital and noticed that it was indeed a hospital unlike any she had ever seen before. Madigan is a brand new $150 million dollar facility, built about a year or so ago. From her description, there are small R2D2-type robots that shuttle prescriptions between floors, all the equipment is prototype 'one-of-a-kind', like laser x-rays and a lot of equipment that was extremely high tech. It was not this alone which peaked my interest, but a comment she made later.

She made the statement that when she entered a specific lab in the hospital, she noticed that all the personnel were extremely absorbed in their work -- nothing too uncommon about that. But then she stated that she had the thought that some of the equipment looked quite 'alien', AND TWO MEN WHO LOOKED EXACTLY ALIKE TURNED AND LOOKED AT HER IN RESPONSE TO HER THOUGHT.

She said that THE EYES OF THESE TWO MEN WERE QUITE PENETRATING AND THAT THEY BOTH MOVED IN UNISON. That got my interest. She then stated that during the tour of the facility, the individual who was escorting her said that the top floor of the hospital AND TWO OF THE SUB-BASEMENT FLOORS were Top Secret R&D areas and were off limits to BOTH military and civilian personnel. That really got my attention.

THE DULCE PROTOCOL

"Subsequently, I ran into a cable repairman who was installing cable TV in a nearby town, and decided on a hunch to mention to him about the strange nature of Madigan. The hunch paid off. He said he had been involved in the installation of fiber optic networks between the floors of the hospital when it was in its construction stage, and that there was a three foot space in between the floors where the optics ran.

"Since these observations were the result of her [the nurse's] preliminary interview, I talked to her about the idea of getting more information, since she would be going back at least one more time. She agreed to make some tapes of her observations.

The transcript of these tapes is as follows:

"'VISIT TO MADIGAN HOSPITAL -- The entrance to Madigan hospital is off of Interstate 5 past Olympia, Washington. The exit is marked as 'Madigan Hospital, Camp Murray Exit'. As you enter the area the hospital sits to the right -- a massive white structure. As you enter the parking lot, there is a pond and sunken area that runs through a bridge which connects the 'medical mall' area to a three story building that serves as the main core of the hospital, where the services like x-ray, nuclear medicine and other services are performed.

"'The three story complex is connected to an eight-story tower dubbed 'the nursing tower.' The tower has a floor that is closed off, and I could find no access to it.

"'I entered the front of the hospital, and the lobby was very typical, but not typical of a hospital of this size. I then went to the information desk and was greeted by an 'oriental' Specialist 4th Class, who was seated. He seemed very low key and laid back. I was directed to Human Resources.

"'As I walked through the corridors, I noticed how beautiful and calm I was beginning to feel. The colors are very soft and conducive to feeling mellow (a 'tranquilized' atmosphere designed to negate any apprehensions? - Branton).

Robert K Teske

"'The military personnel WERE VERY SLOW-MOVING [which has NOT been my experience in the past, having served five years as an Army nurse], and LOW KEY. I went to the Human Resources and asked about an application, and was directed to a Master Sergeant -- director of personnel.

"'Having been a medical technologist for the better part of 25 years, the equipment I saw at the hospital was far beyond anything I have ever seen. I was shown an area where there was a long room with computer banks on both sides where both civilian and military personnel were working. Before entering the room, I was asked to stand in front of the door, where I was scanned by some beam-like light. I was told that my thermal pattern was being recorded in order to permit my entry to the room.

"'Off this room was another room where procedures were conducted on patients, and I noticed that a patient walked over and climbed on an exam table. The procedure they were doing always requires that the patient must be sedated, HOWEVER I NOTICED THAT THE PHYSICIAN LEANED OVER THE PATIENT AND TOUCHED THE PATIENT IN THE CENTER OF THE FOREHEAD WITH 'HIS' INDEX AND MIDDLE FINGER OF ONE HAND. IMMEDIATELY, THE PATIENT FELL INTO A STATE OF SEDATION AND THE PROCEDURE WAS STARTED.

What kind of doctor can touch a patient in that way and sedate him?

"'I looked around at the other personnel in the room at this time. There were two, a Private First Class and a Specialist 4th Class at opposite ends of the room from where I was standing. BOTH OF THESE MEN WERE THE SAME SIZE, HAD THE SAME SKIN COLOR, AND MOVED IN A VERY DELIBERATE MANNER.

I was talking with the Sergeant and happened to say something to myself very softly while having the thought how strange these people seemed. BOTH OTHER MEN TURNED AND LOOKED AT ME ALMOST AS IF TO STARE AT ME. I GOT THIS

THE DULCE PROTOCOL

STRANGE FEELING. I had heard before from a friend whose brother had made the uncharacteristic comment that 'ALIENS WORKED AT MADIGAN'.

'ALL' THE PEOPLE IN THE ROOM AND THE MILITARY PERSONNEL IN GENERAL THAT I HAD SEEN IN THE HOSPITAL SEEMED TO MOVE VERY VERY SLOWLY, ALMOST IN SLOW MOTION. I left the area and went back to the Sergeant's office.

"'A month later, I returned to Madigan with a friend to see, without telling her anything of my experience, if she saw and felt the same things I did. She is very sensitive to variations in electromagnetic fields, and eventually had a headache and became nauseated. There are many other things about this place. Between the floors there are spaces where small robots move to deliver supplies to all the wards and other areas in the hospital, according to the Sergeant. I was told that there is no reason for personnel to go into these areas -- that the robots do all that. I did see one of the robot devices. It looked like the R2D2 character on 'star wars'.

"'My friend and I entered through what is known as the clinic mall. This area houses the outpatient clinic. THERE WERE VERY FEW PEOPLE THERE FOR SUCH A LARGE CLINIC. We were told that THERE ARE THREE FLOORS BENEATH THE HOSPITAL and one floor above that are off limits to ALL PERSONNEL, MILITARY AND CIVILIAN, and that these areas were classified Top Secret and were research and development [R&D] areas.

THERE ARE VERY UNUSUAL ANTENNAS ON TOP OF THE HOSPITAL. The three-story main service area has a complex on top of it THAT APPEARS TO HAVE NO ENTRANCE AND NO WINDOWS. Judging from the way the hospital is built, there are a lot of 'DEAD AREAS' that comprise spaces THAT CANNOT BE ACCESSED FROM THE MAIN SERVICE AREA.

"'The personal feeling we both got being in the hospital WAS THAT WE STARTED TO FEEL VERY DRAINED, AND WE BOTH EXPERIENCED GETTING A DULL HEADACHE. It wasn't until we had driven SEVERAL MILES from the facility that we started to feel better.'"

I came across yet another report suggesting that reptiloid entities were infiltrating our military-industrial complex, however the exact source of this particular story was not confirmed and therefore should be taken as is.

The report stated that sometime during the 1980's a Secretary working in the Pentagon noticed a high-ranking Pentagon 'official' who had apparently lost a contact lens.

The eye from where the lens fell out <u>was NOT human</u>, but instead contained a vertically-slit pupil. No one working at the Pentagon seemed to know where the official worked although they had apparently assumed that he was supposed to be there in some capacity or another. The Secretary however informed her superiors of the strange incident, and immediately Security Personnel approached the 'officer' who apparently was not aware of his missing contact lens. The 'man' did not make any major attempts to resist.

When the apartment of this 'official' was searched, copies of several sensitive documents on the "Star Wars" or "Strategic Defense Initiative" program were discovered. Apparently the entity had been stealing the documents and transmitting their contents to some point beyond the planet. Rumor had it that the entity was physically examined and it was discovered that <u>its internal organs were NOT human</u>.

In reference to the Draconian interest in our planetary defense net, I pass on the following information from British Ufologist Timothy Good, who described the unfortunate fate of several experts who assisted in the development of the STAR WARS defense system. Apparently, they were either eliminated by those they worked for so that they would not reveal what they knew, or someone or something 'else' that was not pleased with the ultimate products of their efforts was responsible for their tragic deaths.

Certainly, all of these scientists dying at once cannot be explained in coincidental terms, whatever the case:

"...Reports of suspicious deaths, darkly and deeply linked to UFO's, persist, however, and continue to cause speculation. Word comes from Gordon Creighton, editor of the informative FLYING SAUCER REVIEW, who notes a possible deathly tie-in with the U.S. 'Star Wars' program. He wrote to me in Nov. 1988 as follows:

"'...here in Britain 22 scientists have reportedly either taken their own lives or died in very strange or mysterious circumstances. And it seems that most... were engaged in British work on behalf of, or related to the U.S. 'Star Wars' program. The British government, it seems, was trying to hush it up. But press statements here say that the U.S. government had put our government on the spot and demanded a full inquiry. So, quite clearly, it is either the Russians or THEM...'

"As many researchers have surmised, 'Star Wars', ostensibly conceived as a defensive system against Russian missile attack, may have had from it's beginning a 'defensive' UFO connection. Whatever the case, a 'mock test' in September, 1988, of an earth-shattering warhead -- much like 'Star Wars' in reverse -- was conducted at the Tonopah Test Range in Nevada. Announced as a proposed super-weapon designed to destroy 'Russian' underground command centers dug in solid rock down to 1,000 [feet], some UFO analysts believe that the real target is not Russian but another adversary deep down in cavernous installations IN NEVADA AND NEW MEXICO.

(Hopefully this weapon will only be used only against those underground bases where no human captive presence exists. In those bases where humans captives ARE present, which is probably the reality in the greater majority of the bases, a full-scale 'ground assault' should be considered instead. - Branton)

Robert K Teske

"According to the Pentagon, the proposed earth-penetrating warhead is 'urgently needed'. According to rumor-mills, an alien race -- the 'grays' -- in their fortified underground laboratories, are genetically experimenting with the human race. Even more ominous, rumors say that their intransigence today may lead to new perils tomorrow."

In reference to the "Chameleons" and CERTAIN elements of the so-called "Men In Black" phenomena, I cannot help but include the following account from Brazil which apparently puts everything in perspective. The following excerpts were taken from a report by Brazilian researcher Antonio Huneeus, titled: "THE 'CHUPAS' -- UFO HORROR STORIES FROM BRAZIL".

Mr. Huneeus describes the following incident that was investigated by APEX [Association of Extraterrestrial Investigations] in Sao Paulo, one of the best known UFO groups in Brazil, founded by Dr. Max Berezowsky:

"...The affair began near Vitoria, the capitol of [the] state of Espiritu Santo north of Rio state, where there are beaches rich in mineral contents. It happened either in late 1979 or early 1980, [Osni] Schwarz wasn't sure, when he told the story in 1986...

"A youngster called Aeromar sold beverages at the beach, where one day he encountered three men dressed with suits and tie -- highly unusual clothing for the beach, especially in Brazil -- who approached him and said they wanted to talk to him. Aeromar became scared, thinking they were perhaps policemen who wanted to implicate him in a drug case, so he avoided the beach for a few days. As he Returned home after dropping off his girlfriend one night, he saw a car with the same three men inside. He ran to the house, but suddenly he couldn't hear well. His mother took him to the hospital where he was not cured, although about a month later he suddenly could hear well again.

THE DULCE PROTOCOL

"Aeromar moved to Rio, finding work at a bakery in a shift between 4 and 11 PM. One night, as he was crossing one of the many TUNNELS that link the Rio bays, he saw two of the MIB's walking in his direction. The youngster ran in the opposite direction, only to find the third MIB waiting at a bus stop. He escaped and went back to the bakery, where he told his boss that the Vitoria police were chasing him. The boss accompanied him to the nearest police station to make a complaint, which he did, but he was not believed. The boss then convinced him that he should perhaps move to Sao Paulo, a bigger city where it may be easier to go unnoticed.

"So Aeromar moved to Sao Paulo, finding work in an electrical company and sharing a room with another man. He also became friends with a vendor of beverages from Vitoria who had a stand near a movie theater. While hanging out there one night, a car stopped right in front of the stand and the door opened.

"Even through he didn't want to go, Aeromar LOST HIS WILL and entered the car. The door closed and he found inside -- not surprisingly -- the three same men whom he had been dodging for months. They drove for a while, leaving the city and entering a wooded area.

"The car stopped and they all walked up to a big UFO surrounded by some sort of luminous ring and hovering above the ground. The men walked underneath the craft, which emitted a ray of light and they suddenly were inside. Still drained of any willpower, Aeromar walked to a chair and sat down. From the arms of the chair appeared handles that secured his wrists.

An iron bar then pressed his forehead backwards while another gadget fastened his neck. Up to here the men were always dressed with suits, but at this point an incredible transformation took place: the MIB'S HEAD RIPPED OPENED INTO A HEART SHAPE AND THE SKIN BECAME GREEN AND SCALED LIKE A REPTILIAN. Take into account that while the popular image of the MIB was well known 14 years ago, the idea of reptilian abductors was then not in vogue as nowadays.

"Be that as it may, the UFOnauts proceeded to interrogate and tell him things that were going to happen both to him and the earth. To make the story even more 'Hollywoodesque', a door in the room opened at one point and Aeromar was able to peek at HUMAN CORPSES HANGING BY THEIR FEET FROM HOOKS. The man naturally became traumatized, remembering only that his straps were loosened. Everything went blank after that...

"Aeromar's conscious recollection places him next back at the theater, but several hours later since there was no traffic in the streets. He returned to his room in panic and began to tell the story to his roommate. A strange force PUSHED HIS BODY, however, throwing it AGAINST THE WALL in front of him, as he remembered the aliens had told him that he shouldn't speak about the experience or he would suffer. Aeromar cried for a while, not knowing what to do.

A few days later, his friend contacted the Globo TV network, which was working on a UFO documentary. Globo, in turn, passed the tip to Dr. Max Berezowsky. Aeromar and his roommate went to APEX on a very busy day when the office was full of people. They told the whole story to Dr. Berezowsky and a few assistants, Osni Schwarz among them.

"Berezowsky attempted to do hypnotic regression with the witness, but there was too much interference in the office and Aeromar was in total panic.

He was saying that 'they' were going to take him on the next Thursday and that a UFO was going to land in a Sao Paulo neighborhood on Tuesday night. A crowd of people, in fact, went that night to the supposed landing site but nothing happened. Although Dr. Berezowsky was in touch with Aeromar, HE VANISHED A FEW DAYS LATER AND NOBODY EVER SAW HIM AGAIN.

THE DULCE PROTOCOL

I wrote down at the end of my notes on this affair, 'the whole case is like a UFO horror movie.'"

Chapter 30

Confessions of an FBI "X-File" Agent

The following is from a secret report released by an FBI special agent code-named JORDON, who has been involved with the intrigues taking place near Dulce, New Mexico and Area 51 [Dreamland] Nevada.

Among his fellow colleagues within the FBI, Jordon was often referred to as "The X-File Man". 'Jordon' claims to be an abductee whose birth in 1962 was genetically engineered by "tall greys" that had apparently altered the genetic codes within the ovum of his human mother -- who was also an abductee -- and infused the genetic coding of the ovum with certain specific genetic characteristics taken from another female abductee for some undetermined purpose.

Although his life was being severely manipulated by the aliens, agents of the Department of the Navy apparently stepped-in to counter some of the machinations which the aliens were carrying out, using abductees like 'Jordon' as pawns in a vast game of cosmic chess.

With the permission of the agent himself, the following is reproduced from Mia Adams' book "THE EXCYLES" [Escelta Publishing, Ft. Lauderdale, Florida -- 1995].

Incidentally, the author uses the British spelling of Grey -- with an 'e' -- rather than the American spelling of Gray -- with an 'a' -- just in case the reader has wondered which is the 'correct' spelling... they are both 'correct':

The account I am about to give is based on my experiences and the personal investigation I have conducted over the past several months. I cannot, and in a few instances I am specifically prevented from, revealing where and when I acquired all of the information I will present. I will state that on two occasions I deliberately violated secure areas and on one occasion participated in a rather unorthodox field interrogation in order to obtain data. I also deliberately involved several innocent parties who, unfortunately, may become subject to penalties which should rightfully only be mine.

I have lied and have done so knowingly and repeatedly in order to elicit information and in order to cause governmental entities to react to moves they only thought I was making. I freely admit that I am guilty of abusing the power of my office and my credentials. I do not apologize for this, but I may soon become subject to the administrative or legal consequences of these actions. So be it. At the risk of appearing melodramatic, more dire consequences may also follow. I can only state that, if resistance is within my power, I will not go quietly.

I am taking the precaution of disseminating this account [both on paper and on disks] to several individuals solely and exclusively as a means of forestalling the desirability of attempting to silence me entirely. It is my belief that revenge would not be the goal of those opposed to my efforts, but, rather, the prevention of the leakage of information...

As a copy of this report is now in your hands, I urge you to make numerous additional copies and to place these copies in several locations to avert efforts at recovering all of them. Let me be very clear: If my opponents are able to recover all the copies of my report, then they will inevitably turn to the matter of muzzling me as the only remaining threat to security they face...

I am firmly convinced that I was abducted by non-human sentient beings at the age of six [SECTION DELETED] and that my newly surfaced [Thanks to Dr. -- NAME DELETED] recollections regarding this incident are reliable and real. These beings strongly resembled the Grey 'Breeders' I will describe below, but, as I remember no 'Workers,' I cannot be entirely sure of what these beings represented. However, I have incontrovertible evidence that the aliens who abducted me as a child have maintained an interest, if not an influence in my life. This evidence has already been provided to those who could make best use of it...

The Department of the Navy [DON] is a relatively SMALL clandestine agency within the United States Government which is staffed primarily by individuals ostensibly recruited and trained by other elements of the Federal Government.

It is funded and supported by the National Security Agency and is also augmented by very tightly compartmentalized elements of the armed forces [I believe that BLUE LIGHT is the original code name for the U.S. Army's EBE-related unit, which was allegedly converted into the now famous counter-terrorist DELTA FORCE] and other governmental organizations. [Approximately one third of headquarters DIVISION FIVE of the FBI is actually a front for DON, with at least several dozen HQ special agents devoted to these matters.]

Despite its name, the "Department of the Navy" has <u>very LITTLE to do with the actual United States Navy</u>. Its existence is known only by an extremely limited number of individuals and its actual mission is known by an even smaller number.

The Department of the Navy's purpose is to direct extraordinary unique activities in relation to extraterrestrial biological entities [EBEs] and alien technologies with the primary missions of combating alien operations which are hostile to the national security of the United States, gathering and exploiting alien technologies, and the containment of premature disclosure of information regarding the presence and intentions of the EBEs.

Ironically, while NASA supposedly suspects or knows that there are alien artifacts on the Moon and is suppressing data on this subject [This was only mentioned to me as an aside], NASA has no official role in dealing with EBEs. This is not to say, however, that NASA, like the rest of the overt government is not penetrated by some DON personnel. Furthermore, the DON has had some interaction with NASA personnel who accidentally became aware of too much. I was also told that an overt NASA effort to detect non-human civilizations was doomed to failure, but I was not told why...

The Greys are divided into quasi-sentient asexual WORKERS who are, on average, four feet tall, AND dominant BREEDERS who have large eyes and are, on average, almost six feet tall. Both types of Greys have four fingers on each hand. This alliance emerged from the successful recovery of several apparently crashed Grey craft and the subsequent establishment of relations with this species. This relationship is, for the time being, clandestine by the choice of both parties and involves a very limited and gradual sharing of information and technology by the Greys.

(Note: This would seem to contradict the earlier statement that the DON is interested in defending our National Security from malevolent alien species. However we must understand that initially the decision of MJ12 to establish contact with the Greys was partly motivated by National Security concerns, for instance the desire for advanced weapons, the establishment a 'treaty' with the Greys in order to appease any intent on their part to take control, all the while studying them and their weaknesses. In reality, it seems as if some of the Intelligence agencies were attempting to do to the Greys what they have done to other cultures, including our own.

That is, USE the treaties as a WEAPON against the Greys to infiltrate their operational structure and find out their weaknesses and exploit their technology at the

THE DULCE PROTOCOL

same time. According to contactees, most of the human cultures who have been taken-over in the past as a result of 'Trojan Horse' treaties with the Greys were sincerely blinded by the Greys' feigned platitudes of benevolence and friendship. The much more cynical and untrusting Intelligence Agencies of planet earth who were no strangers to war and betrayal, although hoping for the best, were at the same time preparing for the worst once the 'treaties' were established. In the end, the choice of the Greys to play their hand and match wits with the Intelligence Agencies of planet earth -- whose cunning and expertise in manipulation are notorious -- may ultimately be their downfall.

Nevertheless these agencies on earth are playing a high-risk game. In their bid to gain 'galactic intelligence' and technological parity with the Greys they run the high risk of having many of their own agents fall under the psychological control of the Greys. In other words while reaching one hand out in feigned friendship towards the Greys, the other hand is busy developing technological weaponry with the hope of potentially exploiting, conquering or destroying them just "in case" they turned on us. We must admit that there are various different motives in dealing with the Greys. The 'elite' globalists of course NEED the Greys' mind-control technology to assist in the implementation of their planetary dictatorship.

Others want nothing to do with the Greys, but desire only their technology. In a strange twist of irony the military alliance, and subsequent resistance, to the Greys may work for the eventual good of the planet. The reason for this is the fact that in their attempt to infiltrate and subvert our planet, the Greys made some grave underestimation's. One of the major 'mistakes' they made -- probably out of fear of reprisals, resulting from the growing knowledge within intelligence agencies of the blatant betrayals of the 'treaties' -- was to jump the gun and attempt a planetary takeover before they were ready for it. They discovered that their methods which have succeeded on other worlds did not work quite as well on planet earth.

When the 'takeover' came about, they were only able to 'conquer' a large segment of the underground 'world', whereas their attempts to use their human agents on the surface to take control of the 'world above' by precipitating a full totalitarian coup in America was STRONGLY resisted. Because of this resistance they could achieve no better than a stalemate.

Now it is a tooth-and-nail battle between <u>freedom-loving sovereigntist</u> humans above and <u>freedom-hating collectivist</u> reptilians below for control of the minds of the leaders of the Military-Industrial Complex which operates both above and below the surface of the planet. Whichever 'side' comes out in control of the M.I.C. will possess BOTH 'worlds'. The aliens are running scared because in 1989 their secret, the 'Enigma', came crashing through the surface and out into the open when Robert Lazar had the guts to come clean about what was happening at Area-51.

Once he stood up to 'the Beast', others joined him in his crusade,

- John Lear
- William Cooper
- Don Ecker
- Paul Bennewitz
- Christa Tilton
- Val Valerian
- Phil Schneider
- Thomas Castello
- Jason Bishop
- Norio Hayakawa
- Bill Hamilton
- Agent 'Yellowfruit'
- John Rhodes
- Michael Lindemann
- Michael Corbin
- Commander 'X'

THE DULCE PROTOCOL

- Jim McCampbell
- Robert Morningsky
- Colonel Steve Wilson
- Bill English
- Jefferson Souza
- Yours Truly, etc. etc.
- **"Ditto" for "Me Too"**

I cannot name all of the names here as <u>the list grows every day</u>.

Although many of these may have some heated personality and philosophical differences among themselves, they nevertheless have the same thing in common -- each of them possessed a different 'piece' of the overall 'puzzle' on the human-alien interaction. Once the 'dam' broke so-to-speak, what had previously been a situation that was 'out-of-control' in respect to the U.S. Government, became a situation that became 'out-of-control' for the Greys. Expect some rather desperate attempts by the Greys in the future to resolve the situation and take back CONTROL.

As I said, they are running out of time and they are running scared and desperate beings do desperate things. Will they simply concede defeat and leave this planet, or do they consider planet earth and its resources to be the KEY to the continued survival of their empire? I personally get the feeling that the infernal 'leaders' of the reptilian collective or hive have already invested too much in this planet to leave so easily. This means that a resolution of the situation will be up to US, and hopefully more than a little Divine Intervention.

With this in mind, one might better understand the seemingly schizophrenic actions of the DON, CIA, NSA, MJ12 and other agencies which are being influenced and contested by basically three different groups with different agendas:

- those intent on maintaining TRUE National Security
- those intent on selling-out the U.S. for personal gain
- and those in the middle who are just obeying orders and essentially don't know where they stand

Several sources claim that the U.S. Navy structure has been infiltrated to some extent by fascist elements operating deep within the CIA and NSA in an effort to use its organizational structure to serve their unconstitutional agendas, in most cases without the knowledge of most Navy personnel themselves. Through misrepresentation of their motives and intentions, these infiltrators have succeeded in gaining support from Navy personnel for their clandestine activities using the false facade of "Patriotism" or "National Security", when in reality many of the joint NSA-Alien projects have in reality SUBVERTED the National Security of the U.S.A. - Branton)

Several underground and underwater facilities [at least one underwater facility is off the Florida coast and has a terrestrial access point in south Miami... I and my unseen cohorts have already provided the address to several individuals] have been established to support these [joint operational] activities and to provide a suitable habitat for the EBEs involved.

Parenthetically, the multiple protective shelter [MPS] ICBM basing scheme proposed in the early 1980s was actually a <u>cover for the construction of 4,600 EBE related bunkers</u>; this scheme was politically untenable and had to be abandoned, but would have allowed for a tremendous expansion of alien activity in the United States. There is presently an on-going competition for influence if not outright domination, over the earth and its life forms between the Greys and another species commonly identified as 'Reptilians' or 'Lizards'.

THE DULCE PROTOCOL

(Note: It is interesting that several other sources claim that the Orion Greys are willfully working WITH and on behalf OF the Draconian 'Lizards' or Reptiloids. Is the 'suggested' animosity between the Greys and Reptiloids a ruse to keep the government in a state of confusion, i.e.. to pressure them to make alliances with the Greys to fight the Reptiloids, or vise versa in order to ensure complete governmental submission to one or the other 'sides' of a SINGLE alien collective power-structure? - Branton)

It is supposedly known that this species ominously refers to itself as 'Earthlings'. I was shown extremely clear photographs of examples of this species. Reptilians appeared human sized, had three toes on each foot, and had notably large mouths [muzzles?] with prominent teeth. This competition has resulted in the destruction of several craft both within and without the earth's atmosphere and has prompted the development of certain aspects of the United States' Strategic Nuclear Forces as well as the Strategic Defense Initiative [SDI].

The DON [Department of the Navy] conducts extensive surveillance and monitoring of individuals who are unknowingly part of an on-going program of manipulation of the human gene pool by competing non-human alliances.

This manipulation was initially undertaken by the reptilian species, apparently to direct certain human traits in ways favorable to this species. In addition reptilian efforts have apparently focused on the United States and, to a lesser extent, its allies due to the United States' leading ECONOMIC and MILITARY (or Military-Industrial - Branton) role worldwide.

Study has determined that the Reptilian efforts in this area amount to long-term genetic sabotage. The reptilians have also been responsible for livestock mutilations and some human abductions for other negative purposes.

Strangely, there is some historical connection between the Reptilians and the Development of nuclear energy, but this was only hinted at by my sources.

(Note: It is interesting that many of the nuclear scientists had ties with the Bavarian Illuminati... the 'bomb' was developed at Los Alamos, beneath which some believe exists the MAJOR concentration of Reptiloids/Greys -- those which commute underground to work in the lower Dulce base 90 miles away -- in North America... and also there is an ancient Hopi prophecy about the Greys and the part they would play in the creation of the "gourd of death". Did they want to provoke an inevitable nuclear conflict that they hoped would destroy all human life on planet earth?

The fact that the greys interacted with the scientists of the Manhattan Project is evidenced by a personal friend of mine whose father was one such scientist. She has experienced numerous abductions throughout the years and claims to be a part of an alien program involving genetic manipulation. She DID show me some unusual scale-like skin on her legs, a condition that I have not seen on any other person. - Branton).

However, the Grey abductions of human subjects have been aimed primarily at the creation of a particularly hardy elite hybrid species which would be initially capable of forming the leading elements of Grey society as well as serving a similar role in human society.

(Note: Since the Reptiloids/Greys have basically failed in producing an actual "cross-breed" capable of reproducing itself, they may instead opt for the development of a 'race' of genetically-altered humans or implanted clones -- patched-in to the collective -- who have been fused with some degree of reptilian DNA and RNA, and once this has been accomplished transfer an individual and/or collective alien intelligence matrix into these genetically altered 'hosts' as they HAVE been known to do in some cases.

There is some question as to whether the original 'soul' of the individual is removed OR suppressed when this occurs, both may be possibilities, and one would probably need an aura detection device capable of 'seeing' the multi-colored 'soul-chakras' in order to determine whether that 'human' has a soul or not. Nevertheless this would be one manner in which an alien force could infiltrate a human society. In other cases humans may be manipulated WHILE IN an altered state of mind while at the same time living a conscious life separate from and unaware of the induced alternate personality.

I have encountered several cases, including 'my own', involving abductees who are living "double lives". In these cases an alien 'sleeper' or 'walk-in' intelligence-matrix has apparently been electronically IMPLANTED in these people via miniature artificial intelligence implants that are programmed with alien thought patterns and attached to the major nerve-centers of the brain.

Recently there has been some progress in mainstream science in regards to programming computers with human thought patterns, 'growing' human brain tissue in a laboratory for use in 'organic computers, or direct mind-machine communication as is being developed for advanced jet pilots. The 'implant' in such cases house an individual or collective alien personality that is activated when the conscious identity is asleep. In this manner an alien 'parasite', whether malevolent, neutral or in very rare cases well-intentioned, may operate through the body of the host without the host being fully aware of just how his or her unconscious existence is being used or manipulated, for whatever purposes the aliens choose.

As for the 'hybrids' that have been developed by the Greys, another problem with producing a ACTUAL hybrid is that humans have 'souls' whereas Greys do not, therefore the 'hybrid' must fall to one side or the other -- soullish human or soulless reptilian, regardless of what the genetic physical makeup of the "physical shell" may be. I prefer to use the term hu-brids to denote the hybrids who have been born with a soul-matrix and re-brids to denote those that have not. - Branton).

The hybrids would also be able to survive destructive ecological changes that the Greys believe will take place on earth in the near future.

The hybrids I saw had the appearance of human children with unusually large heads and eyes as well as fine, sparse hair. Earlier, and unsatisfactory, efforts supposedly resulted in a more fetus-like appearance on the part of these hybrids. All hybrids thus far produced are sterile and unable to reproduce. However, all hybrids have well-developed digestive systems.

The implantation of bio-electronic (?) devices in proximity to the central nervous systems of abductees has been utilized by the Greys for several complementary purposes, but the most important reason is in order to have a more reliable means of MIND CONTROL at a distance. Such control is necessary in order to facilitate follow-up abductions and in order to prevent male subjects from having voluntary sterilization's.

The DON has taken a very active, and largely successful, role in countering reptilian genetic sabotage. However, it is tasked with taking no role other than observation of Grey abductions, to the extent permitted by this group. This fact results in morale and control problems within this organization

(Note: That is, they are to work to prevent alien sabotage of the human race, yet not interfere or try to prevent abductions that they know are occurring or going to occur. It's like MacArthur's forces in Korea. They were told by their U.N. superiors to keep the peace in South Korea and defend it from Northern Communist aggression, yet not attempt to destroy the main supply depots in the North from where the attacks were originating! As with the Korean conflict, the problem with the Greys would seem to be a "no-win" situation.

No wonder there has been "morale and control problems" within the organization, and this may explain why an inner core within Navy Intelligence has formed around agencies like the 'CABAL' and 'COM-12', which are made up of patriots who are fed up with all of the waffling and compromise -- and outright betrayal of our nation and our planet by unelected corporate collaborators working within the Executive branch of government -- and want to take DIRECT action against the Greys. - Branton).

These morale problems have benefited me on more than one occasion and I strongly believe that governmental collusion in these activities is UNCONSTITUTIONAL.

The Greys, like the Reptilians, routinely attempt to erase the abduction related memories of those they abduct.

One of the most exotic elements of Grey technology exploited by the DON involves the deliberate regulation of human brain activity including telepathic communication, and propulsive technologies which include temporal and, for lack of a better term, "Trans-Dimensional" facets. Grey bio-technologies are, paradoxically, fundamentally primitive, but have some extremely advanced facets.

Particularly significant is an ability to manufacture synthetic biological-mechanical (?) entities. I wonder if the so-called "Men In Black", if they exist, are examples of these sorts of beings.

The conditioning of human brain [temporal lobe] activity through electromagnetic and advanced medical techniques is used by the DON in two primary ways. The most obvious is in the elimination of undesirable memories from the minds of accidental witnesses to Grey abductions; in this case somewhat less reliable electromagnetic means must normally be utilized. The second, but actually more important use for this form of advanced mind control is in the elimination of undesirable memories in the minds of DON personnel and other knowing participants in governmental activities relating to EBEs.

This latter form of hypnosis is normally done through more reliable medical or chemical means and is utilized for two reasons. The first reason is actually in the interests of the mental health of certain individuals unable to successfully cope with the unique psychic environment surrounding EBE activities. The second reason to utilize voluntary mind control on government personnel is to delete information from the minds of these individuals which could be exploited by either terrestrial or extraterrestrial forces.

DON field agents are therefore often referred to as "Zombies" and their units as "Zombie Squads". Voluntary erasures are far more reliable than those IMPOSED upon the subject, especially if they have a surgical component.

However, neither technique is absolutely reliable and, therefore, all 'erasures' also include elements of disinformation implanted in the mind of the target [agent] which would tend to render any recalled accounts contradictory or otherwise unreliable. Zombies are also programmed against allowing themselves to by hypnotically regressed or otherwise medically examined by unauthorized personnel.

[This is particularly important as most of these agents have implants placed in their bodies by the Greys to supposedly monitor DON compliance with mutual agreements.]

(Note: The above is in reference to those agencies which integrate both CIA and NAVY Intelligence. According to an agent code-named 'Panda', "the Navy has been manipulated via the intelligence community," especially by the CIA-NSA which has attempted to take full control of all military-intelligence and bring it under the control of those human and alien influences who are running the collaboration projects. - Branton)

Morale among DON agents is particularly impaired by the obvious deterioration of mental and emotional function among these individuals as a result of these psychic interventions. The Department of Defense has been a primary beneficiary of alien derived technologies which have been disseminated in a largely covert manner. In other

THE DULCE PROTOCOL

words, even the military engineering units and defense contractors involved have been unaware of the actual source of key breakthrough technologies supplied to them.

Although some alien technologies have been adopted [specifically in the hypersonic "#####" Stealth and "####### #######" Reconnaissance programs] and some anti-gravity drive extraterrestrial craft are now being actually duplicated [I was shown one hovering almost silently in a hanger at a sub-site of the Nellis Air Force Base and can state that rumors regarding such craft were accurate], the most significant alien technologies being acquired are supposedly in the field of computing.

These technologies have provided the United States with a secret, and therefore largely theoretical, technological superiority over all other nations. I will also mention that I was flown aboard a helicopter of a design I had never before seen which was not only unbelievably quiet, but could also 'cloak' itself from being seen by the naked eye during the hours of darkness using a system which was referred to as "###".

There is also an ongoing program of gradual societal conditioning to ACCEPT the existence and influence of EBEs in Earth's history.

(Does this include obvious FALLACIES that have been spread among intelligence agencies and abductees by the Greys, such as their claim that they originally genetically 'created' the human race and placed them on planet Earth? - Branton).

This is being undertaken by the DON on a worldwide basis in order to prevent cultural disintegration in the event of an uncontrollable catastrophic leak of intelligence regarding the aliens and also in order to allow for a more orderly eventual unveiling of the truth to the general public.

The Greys have themselves promulgated a desire to overtly reveal themselves to human society by the turn of the century (...of course passing themselves off as the "good guys", however at this point in time when the overall malevolent activities of the grays are being exposed -- especially in network TV programs like DARK SKIES -- this would take an incredible feat of psychological engineering to accomplish. - Branton).

Accordingly, the DON (CIA-NSA elements within the DON, that is - Branton) currently has plans to eventually stage a "first contact" event similar to that depicted in the film CLOSE ENCOUNTERS OF THE THIRD KIND so as to prevent any immediate disclosure of the fact that first contact actually took place fifty years ago [mid-1940's]. This is only PART of a classical psychological warfare program directed AT the American people by their own government without appropriate authority.

There is also a DON effort in progress to fully identify other alien entities which have had an impact on this planet. Specifically, there is an EBE species known as that of the 'Birdmen' which is believed to be somehow reptilian related (variously known among sources as the Mothmen, Ciakars, Winged Draco, Pterodactoids or Pteroids - Branton).

There is also an alien species which has been colloquially identified as the 'babies' for their somewhat neonatal appearance [These might be some sort of hybrid humanoid].

The interspecies rivalry currently in progress involves elements of what can only be termed espionage. In other words, both sides have utilized tactics and strategies usually associated with covert intelligence agencies. The most striking tactic employed by the Reptilians is that of the "false flag" which involves the portrayal of hostile Reptilian actions as being those of more benign species.

This particular technique has been focused on the United States Government on several occasions and, in one instance that was recounted to me, resulted in the killing of numerous Grays by United States military forces.

THE DULCE PROTOCOL

The dissemination of disinformation is also a favored technique. The Utilization of mind control techniques by both sides makes this particular espionage game a difficult one to comprehend or master...

As they say, "THE TRUTH IS OUT THERE," but can we recognize it when we see it?

Chapter 33

Phil Schneider VS. The New World Order

[The following article was downloaded from the INTERNET...]

Underground Bases: A Lecture by Phil Schneider: May 1995

Phil Schneider, a very brave man, recently lost his life due to what appeared to be a military-style execution in January 1996. He was found dead in his apartment with piano wire still wrapped around his neck. According to some sources, he had been brutally tortured repeated before being killed. Phil Schneider was an ex-government engineer who was involved in building underground bases. He was one of three people to survive the 1979 fire fight between the large Greys and U.S. intelligence and military forces at Dulce underground base. (Actually, one of several firefights, according to other sources. A man by the name of L. Anderson of Denver has informed this writer that the survivors of the Dulce wars were taken and placed together in groups of three and told that they were the only survivors of the conflict. Apparently this was done to maintain more control over these personnel and prevent potential leaks of information. - Branton)

Robert K Teske

In May 1995, Phil Schneider did a lecture on what he had discovered. Seven months later he was tortured and killed by those for whom he had previously worked. This man's final acts should not go unnoticed.

#

"It is because of the horrendous structure of the federal government that I feel directly imperiled *not* to tell anybody about this material. How long I will be able to do this is anybody's guess. However, I would like to mention that this talk is going to be broken up into four main topics. Each of these topics will have some bearing on what you people are involved in, whether you are patriots or not.

"I want you to know that these United States are a beautiful place. I have gone to more than 70 countries, and I cannot remember any country that has the beauty, as well as the magnificence of its people, like these United States.

"To give you an overview of basically what I am, I started off and went through engineering school. Half of my school was in that field, and I built up a reputation for being a geological engineer, as well as a structural engineer with both military and aerospace applications. I have helped build two main bases in the United States that have some significance as far as what is called the New World Order. The first base is the one at Dulce, New Mexico. I was involved in 1979 in a firefight with alien humanoids, and I was one of the survivors. I'm probably the only talking survivor you will ever hear. Two other survivors are under close guard. I am the only one left that knows the detailed files of the entire operation. Sixty-six secret service agents, FBI, Black Berets and the like, died in that firefight. I was there.

"Number one, part of what I am going to tell you is going to be very shocking. Part of what I am going to tell you is probably going to be very unbelievable, though, instead of putting your glasses on, I'm going to ask you to put your 'scepticals' on. But please, feel free to do your own homework. I know the Freedom of Information Act isn't much to go on, but it's the best we've got. The local law library is a good place to look for Congressional Records. So, if one continues to do their homework, then one can be standing vigilant in regard to their country.

THE DULCE PROTOCOL

::: Deep Underground Military Bases and the Black Budget :::

"I love the country I am living in, more than I love my life, but I would not be standing before you now, risking my life, if I did not believe it was so. The first part of this talk is going to concern deep underground military bases and the black budget. The Black Budget is a secretive budget that garners 25% of the gross national product of the United States. The Black Budget currently consumes $1.25 trillion per [2] years. At least this amount is used in black programs, like those concerned with deep underground military bases. Presently, there are 129 deep underground military bases in the United States.

"They have been building these 129 bases day and night, unceasingly, since the early 1940's. Some of them were built even earlier than that. These bases are basically large cities underground connected by high-speed magneto-leviton trains that have speeds up to Mach 2. Several books have been written about this activity. Al Bielek has my only copy of one of them. Richard Souder, a Ph.D architect, has risked his life by talking about this. He worked with a number of government agencies on deep underground military bases. In around where you live, in Idaho, there are 11 of them.

"The average depth of these bases is over a mile, and they again are basically whole cities underground. They all are between 2.66 and 4.25 cubic miles in size. They have laser drilling machines that can drill a tunnel seven miles long in one day. The Black Projects sidestep the authority of CONGRESS, which as we know is illegal. Right now, the New World Order is depending on these bases. If I had known at the time I was working on them that the NWO was involved, I would not have done it. I was lied to rather extensively.

::: Development of Military Technology, Implied German Interest in Hyperspacial Technology, and More :::

"Basically, as far as technology is concerned, for every calendar year that transpires, military technology increases about 44.5 years [compared with the increase rate of 'conventional' technology]. This is why it is easy to understand that back in 1943 they were able to create, through the use of vacuum tube technology, a ship that could literally disappear from one place and appear in another place. My father, Otto Oscar Schneider, fought on both sides of the war. He was originally a U-boat captain, and was captured and repatriated in the United States. He was involved with different kinds of concerns, such as the A-bomb, the H-bomb and the Philadelphia Experiment. He invented a high-speed camera that took pictures of the first atomic (Hydrogen or H-Bomb - Branton) tests at Bikini Island on July 12, 1946. I have original photographs of that test, and the photos also show UFO's fleeing the bomb site at a high rate of speed. Bikini Island at the time was infested with them, especially under the water, and the natives had problems with their animals being mutilated. At that time, General MacArthur felt that the next war would be with aliens from other worlds.

"Anyway, my father laid the groundwork with theoreticians about the Philadelphia experiment, as well as other experiments. What does that have to do with me? Nothing, other than the fact that he was my father. I don't agree with what he did on the other side, but I think he had a lot of guts in coming here. He was hated in Germany. There was a $1 million reward, payable in gold, to anyone who killed him. Obviously, they didn't succeed. Anyway, back to our topic -- deep underground bases.

::: The Fire Fight at Dulce Base :::

"Back in 1954, under the Eisenhower administration, the 'federal' government decided to circumvent the Constitution of the United States and form a treaty with alien entities. It was called the 1954 Greada Treaty, which basically made the agreement that the aliens involved could take a few cows and test their implanting techniques on a few human beings, but that they had to give details about the people involved. Slowly, the aliens altered the bargain until they decided they wouldn't abide by it at all. Back in 1979, this was the reality, and the fire-fight at Dulce occurred quite by accident. I was involved in building an ADDITION to the deep underground military base at Dulce, which is probably the deepest base. It goes down seven levels and over 2.5 miles deep. At that particular time, we had drilled four distinct holes in the desert, and we were going to link them together and blow out large sections at a time. My job was to go down the holes and check the rock samples, and recommend the explosive to deal with the particular rock. As I was headed down there, we found ourselves amidst a large cavern that was full of outer-space (or "inner-space"? - Branton) aliens, otherwise known as large Greys. I shot two of them. At that time, there were 30 people down there. About 40 more came down after this started, and all of them got killed. We had surprised a whole underground base of existing aliens. Later, we found out that they had been living on [in] our planet for a long time... This could explain a lot of what is behind the theory of ancient astronauts.

(Note: This report seems to reveal a limited 'perspective' on the overall 'Dulce war' conflicts based on the experience of one individual. It appears, however, as if there was much more involved in the overall scenario than what Phil Schneider describes. For instance from Phil's description, it appears as if his team broke-in to the base 'accidentally'. It could be that IN RESPONSE to the captured scientists mentioned by Thomas Edwin Castello and others, the Special Forces and Intel agents intentionally attempted to break-in to the underground alien bases through a "back door" so-to-speak, yet Schneider may have not been aware of this part. Other reports would suggest that the conflict was more complex than this, and involved more than one firefight. According to other sources, the "Dulce Wars" involved AT LEAST a hundred highly-trained Special Forces. - Branton)

"Anyway, I got shot in the chest with one of their weapons, which was a box on their body that blew a hole in me and gave me a nasty dose of cobalt radiation. I have had cancer because of that.

"I didn't get really interested in UFO technology until I started work at Area 51, north of Las Vegas. After about two years recuperating after the 1979 incident, I went back to work for

Morrison and Knudson, EG&G and other companies. At Area 51, they were testing all kinds of peculiar spacecraft. How many people here are familiar with Bob Lazar's story? He was a physicist working at Area 51 trying to decipher the propulsion factor in some of these craft.

::: Schneider's Worries about Government Factions, Railroad Cars and Shackle Contracts :::

Robert K Teske

"Now, I am very worried about the activity of the 'federal' government. They have lied to the public, stonewalled senators, and have refused to tell the truth in regard to alien matters. I can go on and on. I can tell you that I am rather disgruntled. Recently, I knew someone who lived near where I live in Portland, Oregon. He worked at Gunderson Steel Fabrication, where they make railroad cars. Now, I knew this fellow for the better part of 30 years, and he was kind of a quiet type. He came in to see me one day, excited, and he told me "they're building prisoner cars." He was nervous. Gunderson, he said, had a contract with the federal government to build 107,200 full length railroad cars, each with 143 pairs of shackles. There are 11 sub-contractors in this giant project. Supposedly, Gunderson got over 2 billion dollars for the contract. Bethlehem Steel and other steel outfits are involved. He showed me one of the cars in the rail yards in North Portland. He was right. If you multiply 107,200 times 143 times 11, you come up with about 15,000,000. This is probably the number of people who disagree with the federal government. No more can you vote any of these people out of office. Our present structure of government is 'technocracy', not democracy, and it is a form of feudalism.

(Note: I would venture to say that it is more like a techno-monarchy, since several of the U.S. presidents have been placed in office with Rockefeller financial and media backing, suggesting that these same presidential hirelings were inclined to favor certain Rockefeller and in turn International banking agendas. Techno-Monarchy would constitute those parts of the Military-Industrial Complex or M.I.C. that are largely influenced by Rockefeller interests. According to various sources, the German immigrant Rockefellers are not the "top of the ladder" for the world conspiracy. True, they 'control' much of the eco-political system in the UNITED STATES of America, however they are following the agenda of the Bilderberger cult: the 13 Wicca Masons, 13 Black Nobility, and 13 Maltese Jesuits who have joined together UNDER the covering of the Bavarian Illuminati -- which in turn is the modern manifestation of the joint human-alien 'serpent cult' which seems to have had its origins within the ancient underground Masonic systems of Egypt, a cult or collaboration that was brought to Bavaria by the early Germanic Trade Guilds during the height of the so-called 'Holy Roman' [German] Empire - Branton).

THE DULCE PROTOCOL

It [this 'technocracy'] has nothing to do with the republic of the United States. These people are god-less, and have legislated out prayer in public schools. You can get fined up to $100,000 and two years in prison for praying in school. I believe we can do better. I also believe that the federal government is running the gambit of enslaving the people of the United States. I am not a very good speaker, but I'll keep shooting my mouth off until somebody puts a bullet in me, because it's worth it to talk to a group like this about these atrocities.

::: America's Black Program Contractors :::

"There are other problems. I have some interesting 1993 figures. There are 29 prototype stealth aircraft presently. The budget from the U.S. Congress five-year plan for these is $245.6 million. You couldn't buy the spare parts for these black programs for that amount. So, we've been lied to. The black budget is roughly $1.3 trillion every two years. A trillion is a thousand billion. A trillion dollars weighs 11 tons. The U.S. Congress never sees the books involved with this clandestine pot of gold. Contractors of [these] programs: EG&G, Westinghouse, McDonnell Douglas, Morrison-Knudson, Wackenhut Security Systems, Boeing Aerospace, Lorimar Aerospace, Aerospacial in France, Mitsubishi Industries, Rider Trucks, Bechtel, *I.G. Farben*, plus a host of hundreds more. Is this what we are supposed to be living up to as freedom-loving people? I don't believe so.

::: Star Wars and Apparent Alien Threat :::

"Still, 68% of the military budget is directly or indirectly affected by the black budget. Star Wars relies heavily upon stealth weaponry. By the way, none of the stealth program would have been available if we had not taken apart crashed alien disks. None of it. Some of you might ask what the "space shuttle" is "shuttling". Large ingots of special metals that are milled in space and cannot be produced on the surface of the earth. They need the near vacuum of outer space to produce them. We are not even being told anything close to the truth. I believe our government officials have SOLD us down the drain -- lock, stock and barrel. Up until several weeks ago, I was employed by the U.S. government with a Ryolite-38 clearance factor -- one of the highest in the world. I believe the Star Wars program is there solely to act as a buffer to prevent alien attack -- it has nothing to do with the "cold war", which was only a ploy to garner money from all the people -- for what? The whole lie was planned and executed for the last 75 years.

::: Stealth Aircraft Technology Use by U.S. Agencies and the United Nations :::

"Here's another piece of information for you folks. The Drug Enforcement Administration and the ATF rely on stealth tactical weaponry for as much as 40% of their operations budget. This in 1993, and the figures have gone up considerably since. The United Nations used American stealth aircraft for over 28% of its collective worldwide operations from 1990 to 1992, according to the Center for Strategic Studies and UN Report 3092.

::: The Guardians of Stealth and Delta Force Origins of the Bosnia Conflict :::

"The Guardians of Stealth: There are at least three distinct classifications of police that guard our most well-kept secrets. Number one, the Military Joint Tactical Force [MJTF], sometimes called the Delta Force or Black Berets, is a MULTI-NATIONAL tactical force primarily used to guard the various stealth aircraft worldwide. By the way, there were 172 stealth aircraft built.

Ten crashed, so there were at last count about 162. Bill Clinton signed them away about six weeks ago TO THE UNITED NATIONS. There have been indications that the Delta Force was sent over to Bosnia during the last days of the Bush administration as a covert sniper force, and that they started taking pot shots at each side of the controversy, in order to actually START the Bosnia conflict that would be used by succeeding administrations for political purposes.

::: Thoughts on the Bombings in the United States :::

"I was hired not too long ago to do a report on the World Trade Center bombing. I was hired because I know about the 90 some-odd varieties of chemical explosives. I looked at the pictures taken right after the blast. The concrete was puddled and melted. The steel and the rebar was literally extruded up to six feet longer than its original length. There is only one weapon that can do that -- a small nuclear weapon. That's a construction-type nuclear device. Obviously, when they say that it was a nitrate explosive that did the damage, they're lying 100%, folks. The people they have in custody probably didn't do the crime. As a matter of fact, I have reason to believe that the same group held in custody did do other crimes, such as killing a Jewish rabbi in New York. However, I want to further mention that with the last explosion in Oklahoma City, they are saying that it was a nitrate or fertilizer bomb that did it.

"First, they came out and said it was a 1,000 pound fertilizer bomb. Then, it was 1,500. Then 2,000 pounds. Now its 20,000. You CAN'T put 20,000 pounds of fertilizer in a Rider Truck. Now, I've never mixed explosives, per se. I know the chemical structure and the application of construction explosives. My reputation was based on it. I helped hollow out more than 13 deep underground military bases in the United States. I worked on the MALTA project, in West Germany, in Spain and in Italy. I can tell you from experience that a nitrate explosion would not have hardly shattered the windows of the federal building in Oklahoma City. It would have killed a few people and knocked part of the facing off the building, but it would never have done that kind of damage. I believe I have been lied to, and I am not taking it any longer, so I'm telling you that you've been lied to.

(Allow me to interject at this point five items relating to the Oklahoma City bombing and/or the role Oklahoma City and FEMA plays in a possible United Nations - New World Order agenda. - Branton)

#1 - From the WWW-INTERNET Page: THE EYE OF THE EAGLE SPEAKS:

...An evil element of the U.S. government's CIA, known as the "Committee of Ten," admittedly blew up the Federal Building in Oklahoma City. The blame was put on Timothy McVeigh [a "throw-away/patsy" like Lee Harvey Oswald]. The children were murdered to procure sympathy, money, power, and control over the American people, and the "Constitution-loving" people known as patriots are BLAMED [proof: see Internet, also Associated Press Investigation -- Call EDT Short-wave Channel 12160, satellite Galaxy 6,5-G2 transponder 14]. Two CIA agents, James Black and Ron Jackson, admit to Boswell they were part of the "Committee of Ten" who blew up the Oklahoma

City Federal Building on April 29, 1995. They gave sworn affidavits to U.S. Justice Department officials [out of guilt for the dead children?]. They are in hiding until the case comes to court.

On the Dan Gregory Radio Talk Show WPBR 1540, Florida, Ted Gunderson, retired FBI Regional Director -- Mr. Gunderson tells how TWO explosions occurred, and that the bomb used was called a barometric bomb, or "daisy cutter." The fertilizer bomb was also a smoke screen. The ATF Office was the blast target -- and ALL 17 ATF EMPLOYEES DID NOT SHOW UP FOR WORK that morning. Call CNN News for a transcript of CNN News correspondent's Gary Tuchman's May 29, 1995, CNN News interview with Edye Smith, a mother who lost two children. She wanted to know if government employees had advance warning of the blast because her two little boys, Chase [3 years] and Colton [2 years], had none. "We [all the mothers who lost children] are being TOLD to keep our mouths shut, not talk about it, don't ask those questions."

#2 - "The Phoenix Project" is an Ashtar Collective outlet, although they do carry 'conventional' conspiracy-related news releases. Before quoting from "The Phoenix Project" paper I would like to make some comments on the "Ashtar" alliance which backs this organization and its intervention in the affairs of planet earth. It is the policy of the channeled 'Ashtar' sources to expose certain conspiracy-related information, however in most cases the blame for these conspiracies are laid on 'Jewish Zionism'. When you understand the conflict between 'Jewish' and the Ashtar-backed 'Bavarian' secret societies you may further understand this animosity. True, because Zionism is a political force they do have some connection with the Masonic element of the 'conspiracy', the B'nai Brith and so on, as do ALL religious movements who stray into areas of Masonic-economic-political manipulation [which constitutes most of the major denominations by the way, considering the massive Scottish Rite infiltration of the major denominational structures] However 'Jewish Masonry' is NOT the dominant Masonic faction, that place is reserved for the Jesuit's 'Scottish Rite' and the Black Nobility's Rite of the 'Illuminati'. So then, some elements of 'Jewish Masonry' may be 'cooperating' with the New World Order agenda, but they are ultimately subservient to the racist power cults of BAVARIA. This is why the Zionist Rothschilds were UNABLE TO PREVENT the slaughter of over 6 million Jews in the Holocaust, because the Jewish Masons were NOT the dominant force. The Rothschilds' supposed economic collaborators in America, the Germanic-racist Rockefellers, were pressured into serving and carrying out the RACIST-EUGENIC policies of their cultic superiors in Bavaria, in order to be allowed to maintain their economic stranglehold on America. Following World War II, the Rockefellers recieved a flood of Nazi War criminals into their fold, giving them refuge and immunity within their massive corporate network.

The Jewish Masons, such as the Rothschilds, were only a PART of a THIRD [Wicca Masonic] element of the global power network, competing with the other two-thirds working within the Black Nobility and the Maltese Jesuit lodges. That is, until all three agreed to work together under the 'Bilderberger' organization in order to implement the NWO and then decide later just who would dominate it. Just why the Rothschild Wicca-Masons would agree to become a part of the Bilderberger cult is uncertain. Perhaps they were not fully aware of the part that the Jesuit-Rockefeller elements played in the Nazi Holocaust, or the actual extent of the influx of Nazi war criminals into the Rockefeller empire following the war? A more likely explanation would be a combination of the following: Some of the Zionists who collaborated with the Rockefellers were not fully aware of the racist Anti-Jewish elements involved; some of the 'Jewish Masons' just didn't care and were in essence willing to sell out their own kind in exchange for POWER; also the Jesuit's Scottish Rite had succeeded in Infiltrating Jewish [and York Rite British] Masonry to the point where its assimilation into the Bavarian-controlled NWO Bilderberger cult would be ensured.

In fact there is some reason to believe that the Bavarians [and aliens?] were using the Wicca Masons, Black Nobility and Maltese Jesuit as HIGH-LEVEL Machiavellian 'arms' to create political, economic and religious conflict in the world. In other words the lower levels of these three formerly 'competitive' global power cults would be individuals who were devoted to the idea that THEIR respective lodge[s] should be in control of the New World Order and were therefore to engage in fraternal warfare with the 'others', the Jesuits against the Masons and vice versa for example. On an other-planetary level it could be the Sirian-backed Masons vs. the Rigelian backed Jesuits. The Sirian humanoids

Robert K Teske

and the Rigelian reptiloids, being formerly at odds, were now being brought together by the Aldebaran-backed Ashtarian collectivists and their 'New Galactic Order' agenda. Planet earth is NOT the only place where 'Machievellian/Hegalian' political agendas have been carried out. On earth the Aldebaran collective in turn backs their 'Bavarian Black Nobility' allies and repeats the same thesis-antithesis-synthesis scenario on earth between the Masons and Jesuits, eventually merging them into a power structure that is ultimately controlled [on earth] by the Bavarian black Gnostic 'serpent' cult from it's secret hideaways below Gizeh, Egypt; Pine Gap, Australia; Dulce, New Mexico, etc. This power-center would in turn have placed its agents within the Jesuit, Nobility and Masonic 'arms' in order to manipulate these three power-groups towards their own ends. For instance, even though lower-level initiates of these three lodges would favor their own lodge over the others, the CONTROLLING ELITE of all three elements would never-the-less be agents of the Bavarian 'Babylonian Serpent Cult' itself. Certain members of the Black Nobility families would sell out to the cult and turn these families in whatever direction the cult dictated; high-ranking Scottish Rite members of the Wicca Mason faction would likewise be serving the Bavarian agenda via the Illuminati; and the high-ranking Jesuits themselves would in turn be serving the Bavarian elite, since Germany was after all the headquarters of the [Un]Holy Roman Empire and NOT Rome, which capitulated its center-of-power over to Germany following the decline of the earlier Roman Empire.

This is one 'perspective' from which this can all be viewed, although it is certainly not the only perspective.

According to contactee Israel Norkin however, the Ashtar or Astarte alien collective -- which has a large following in Aldebaran and other systems and which played an integral part in the ancient Sirian-Orion conflict over ancient Egypt -- is a subterran/exterran alliance, a virtual 'collective group mind', that has since been infiltrated by the 'Unholy Six' Empires of Orion. If this is true, then this does not necessarily mean that ALL of the members of the 'Ashtar collective' are working for UH6, especially when more recent contactee accounts have stated that a civil war has been taking place in Sirius. This 'war' has apparently been waged because the 'infiltrated'

502

faction of the collective that has been infiltrated and commandeered by the Orionite forces, has in turn broken free from the remaining segment of the collective. This remaining segment has since established close ties with Pleiadean non-interventionists. Actually, IF they hold true to the non-interventionist policies, one would think that this remaining element of the 'alliance' would give up the collectivist agenda altogether, and adopt the sovereigntist philosophy which teaches the respect for personal sovereignty from a planetary down to an individual level. Since a collective, hive or group mind tends to KILL human individuality and sovereignty, such an existence would seem to be ever at odds with non-interventionism.

Just as non-interventionists believe in planetary sovereignty, which is a more 'cosmic' manifestation of the same principles which appear in the American 'Bill of Rights' in respect to personal sovereignty, we must realize that just as with America, the non-interventionists have not "arrived" at the perfect fulfillment of their philosophy any more than the 'American dream' has become a full reality. Since this universe is imperfect and subject to human agency, it is a continuous struggle to FIGHT to defend liberty, freedom and sovereignty whether on an inter-planetary or an inter personal level. So even though we must continue to fight and struggle to maintain planetary, national or personal sovereignty in a universe where it is continually being threatened by parasitical-interventionist-imperialistic forces, the non-interventionist charters of the 'Federation' and the Constitutional charters of 'America' are nevertheless GOALS for us to work towards.

With this foundation laid then, the following are excerpts from CONTACT: THE PHOENIX PROJECT, June 20, 1995:

"I happened to mention that I had heard, very early after the Oklahoma City bombing, some mention of there being an 18-story underground associated with that building, including five floors of underground parking garage space. This tantalizing bit of news came about because some network TV interviewer was discussing the bomb pattern with, I think, the building's original designer or architect.

"But I never heard it mentioned again, in all the days of further reporting, as the enormous magnitude of that tragedy continued to unfold, amidst spin doctoring of the most dazzling intensity (that is, anti-militia and anti-patriot 'spin-doctoring'. - Branton)

"As happens in such cases of instant news sanitation, one begins to question if one EVER REALLY heard what one was SURE of just a week or so earlier. After all, you would think such information couldn't easily be hidden so well.

"So, in that 5/30/95 Front Page editorial I asked if anyone else out there had heard about this interesting and apparently 'neglected' feature of the Oklahoma City federal building. After all, longtime CONTACT readers are well aware of all the diabolical, tunnel-interconnected, secret underground facilities around the country. Thus, even the mere possibility of a major UNDERGROUND aspect to the structure beings a whole new provocative array of dimensions into this already bizarre picture called the 'official' Oklahoma City blast story. For instance, the 'rumors' about serious Fed-incriminating Waco evidence being stored at that Oklahoma City site take on new life if an underground connection is genuine (for instance, there were reports that some agents IGNORED wounded children and employees among the ruins and went instead straight into the rubble to 'rescue' the boxes of secret implicating documents deeper within the building. Or did they remove these documents only to be destroyed at a later time, so that 'they' could claim that all of this 'evidence' had been destroyed in the blast? - Branton).

"On 6/7/95 we received an interesting, excited telephone call at the CONTACT offices from someone who had read my editorial and could confirm having heard EARLY news reports which were not only similar to what I had heard, but made what I heard sound like last week's used coffee grounds. Rick Martin took the call and, after hearing the news, asked this person to take a deep, calming breath and then put their thoughts down on paper.

"Let me quote from that letter, received at the CONTACT offices on 6/15/95. This is from E.B.W., writing from the Pacific Northwest State of Washington.

"[QUOTING] I watched the Oklahoma bombing RIGHT AFTER it happened. I had the TV on and all of a sudden it switched to this scene where a bombing had just taken place. At first, I did not pay much attention; I was busy doing something else. I would listen in every once in a while. The anchorwoman, or reporter, from the local TV station, was running around, babbling excitedly. At least once, that I remember, all people were asked to leave the scene and it showed everybody running like mad. They HAD FOUND ADDITIONAL BOMBS, or bomb, and the detonation squad was called in to defuse it.

"During all this commotion, running and reporting, the lady reporter kept talking about the UNDERGROUND TUNNELS, which had been blown open. She kept referring to the HUGE UNDERGROUND TUNNELS and there may be people trapped in there. I heard her refer to the UNDERGROUND TUNNELS at least about 6 to 7 times during the period I watched. I'm not quite sure how long that was. Maybe 1 to 2 hours.

"A lady friend of mine called me and wanted to know if I had seen the FIREMAN ON THE SCENE, who went in front of the camera, totally freaked, wide-eyed and scared, who talked about HUGE UNDERGROUND TUNNELS, where ENORMOUS SUPPLIES OF ARMS WERE STORED. He said he saw MISSILES, TANKS, ETC., ETC. I don't remember what else he saw. But HE WAS TOTALLY FREAKED OUT. He looked like he had seen a ghost. Hope this helps.

P.S. Please don't use my name. I will try to get my friend to write down what she knows.[END OF QUOTING]"

An 18-level underground base? CIA involvement? A huge military arsenal? Unless I'm mistaken, could this be ONE of the NEW WORLD ORDER underground bases mentioned by Phil Schneider? If so, then if or when an attempted UNITED NATIONS crack-down on American Patriots, AND/OR a possible European NEW WORLD ORDER invasion of American soil occurs... could such an invasion come not only from the air, ground and sea, but from BELOW as well? Take note that Oklahoma City is supposed to be one of the 'biggie' NWO transfer points when things get rolling, or so the 'Commu-Nazi's' running the New World Order plot hope. There are some who believe that the U.N. - N.W.O. forces are attempting to precipitate internal civil crisis' in America as a pretext to bringing in multi-national U.N. "peace-keeping" forces to restore "order", that is, the "New World" type of "Order". If there is too much resistance, then a possible U.N.-backed invasion by U.N. member countries -- many of whom despise America anyway thanks to the likes of the CIA -- will be initiated to help these "peace-keepers". I recently read a news-story where the entire Iranian parliament collectively shouted "Death to America", and from what I've heard that wasn't the first time another countries' leadership declared their hatred for the USA and their desire to see it [and Israel] destroyed... and we can include several Communist dictators as well. The Iranian reaction may have been partly due to the CIA's intervention in their affairs, however I think the main reason is that the USA is one of Israel's strongest allies. I would suggest that we remember that Israel is the oldest continuous culture on earth -- predating the Chinese culture by 500 years; it is one of the smallest cultures whereas numbers are concerned; has fought more enemies who have sought its destruction than possibly any other nation on earth; and has against ALL possible odds survived to this day as a single people. I would suggest that we DO NOT cease from an alliance with the Jews. Whether one considers Israel as having 'God' or 'good-fortune' on their side, history nevertheless has shown that those cultures that have opposed Israel have a strange] way of disappearing from the face of the earth.

As for a possible New World Order takeover, some skeptics -- in spite of the lessons that should have been learned from World War II -- claim that conditions could never reach such a point. However what if the following report has any truth to it?

#3 - Keep in mind that the following incident ties-together the UNITED NATIONS - NEW WORLD ORDER scenario [which is obviously intent on destroying the American Independence movement which is the last MAJOR obstacle to World Government], the OKLAHOMA CITY AREA, and multi-national U.N.-backed military forces now training on American soil. The following information comes from a source which has investigated actual UNITED NATIONS preparations, IN THE UNITED STATES, to deal with any resistance to a 'New World Order' dictatorship.

Take note that FEMA is a major New World Order front with SEVERAL extensive operational underground bases which, like underground Trojan horses, exist beneath strategic locations throughout the United States:

THE DULCE PROTOCOL

"'FINCEN' CONFIRMED PRE-DEPLOYMENT LOCATIONS: south and east-central California; west-central Montana; north Texas; west-central Wisconsin; north-east Illinois; south-east Michigan; central Indiana; south-west Ohio; north New York; south Delaware; south Maryland; north-east Virginia. North-east North Carolina; central, south Florida.

"ALL FINCEN EQUIPMENT IS BLACK, FINCIN UNIFORMS, HELICOPTERS, ETC. FINCEN ARE FOREIGN MILITARY AND SECRET POLICE BROUGHT INTO THE UNITED STATES FOR DEPLOYMENT AGAINST THE U.S. CITIZENS. MOST IDENTIFIED FINCEN UNITS ARE AT COMPANY STRENGTH (160+). SOME ARE AS LARGE AS BRIGADE STRENGTH (2600+)

"FINCEN'S MISSION IS:

"A) House to house search and seizure of property and arms.

"B) Separation and categorization of men, women and children as prisoners in large numbers.

"C) Transfer to detention facilities of aforementioned prisoners.

"CONFIRMED MJTF [Multi-Jurisdictional Task Force] POLICE LOCATIONS: north-west Washington; central, south California; south-west, south-east, north Wyoming; north, north-west, south-west Nebraska; north Texas; south-east Missouri; west-central, south-east Wisconsin; north-east Illinois; central, south-east Michigan; central Indiana; north-central Kentucky; south, south-west Ohio; north, south-east New York; south-central North Carolina; west-central Georgia; south-east Florida; central(?) Alaska.

"'THE MJTF IS THE VELVET GLOVE ON THE IRON FIST' -- MOTTO ON THE COVER PAGE OF THE MJTF GUIDELINES AND AUTHORIZING LEGISLATION.

"The MJTF Police is made up of:

"1) MILITARY - Converts those National Guard Units that are not banned by the president, into a National Police Force.

"2) Converts all surviving local and state police to national police.

"3) Converts street gangs into law enforcement units for house to house searches [L.A., Chicago, and New York are in the process now]

"MJTF POLICE MISSION:

"1) House to house search and seizure of property and firearms.

"2) Separation and categorization of men, women and children as prisoners in large numbers.

"3) Transfer to and the operation of detention camps in the U.S. [43+ Camps]

"UNITED NATIONS COMBAT GROUPS CONFIRMED LOCATIONS: east-central, south California; north-west, west, south-west Montana; south Arizona; north Texas; east Michigan; north, south-east New York; north New Jersey; north-west, north-central, north-east North Carolina; west-central Georgia.

"UNITED NATIONS BATTLE GROUPS ENTRANCE TO UNITED STATES PASSED UNDER PRESIDENTIAL EXECUTIVE ORDERS SIGNED 11 NOVEMBER 1990 (Note: There are those who are convinced that WITH the Assassination of President John F. Kennedy a 'coup d'état' took place within the Executive branch of American government via Internationalist groups who are determined to destroy the U.S. Constitution, and that the 'presidents' who were manipulated into office since that time -- mostly C.F.R., T.L.C. and BILDEBERGER members -- have signed numerous un-constitutional 'executive orders' designed to pave the way for world dictatorship. If this is the case, then Americans have the CONSTITUTIONAL RIGHT to resist this FOREIGN U.N. - N.W.O. government, a right which is also laid down in the DECLARATION OF INDEPENDENCE. As for the Kennedy assassination itself, and those behind it, Louisiana District Attorney James Garrison in an interview with Playboy magazine made the following statement in regards to Lee Harvey Oswald: "...Our office has positively

THE DULCE PROTOCOL

identified a number of his associates as neo-Nazis. Oswald would have been more at home with Mein Kampf than Das Kapital." - Branton)

"DETENTION FACILITIES AUTHORIZED THROUGH FEMA AND AUGMENTED BY DOD BUDGET AMENDMENT PASSED WITH 1991 FISCAL BUDGET:

"North, south-west, south-east Wyoming; north-west, north-east, south Nebraska; north, central (?) Texas; central Wisconsin; central, south-west, south, south-east Michigan; north-east, west-central, south Indiana; north-west, north-east, central, south Ohio; west, north, east New York.

"A) Each site can detain between 32,000 to 44,000 people min.

"B) It is indicated that the Texas and Alaskan sites may be much larger and more heavily armed.

"C) For the areas west of the Mississippi, OKLAHOMA CITY is the central processing point for detainees and can handle up to 100,000 people at a time.

"D) The Eastern processing center is not yet identified at this time.

"DETENTION FACILITIES -- 23 FEMA Authorized and stationed; 20 DOD [Department of Defense] Budget authorized and stationed -- 43 TOTAL.

Note: In Red China an untold number of people are suffering in Communist 'Laogai' camps as slave laborers; in Soviet Russia it was the 'Gulag' camps. In Nazi Germany the 'Concentration' camps were not only used as slave camps, but also as extermination camps to carry out the genocidal plans of American Corporate and European Militant 'Nazis'. The enemy of SOVEREIGNTISM is COLLECTISM, which is also known as "Socialism". Socialism comes in many forms: Global Socialism [Communism]; National Socialism [Fascism]; and Corporate Socialism [Technocracy]. All three movements are ultimately controlled by the same Luciferian cults of Bavaria who backed Vladimir Lenin, Adolph Hitler, and John D. Rockefeller, and who are descended from the very same cults which ruled the [Un]Holy Roman Empire during the

Dark Ages [see Revelation chapter 17]. I have only one thing to say concerning these plans for confinement camps here in America, and I'm sure that most of our Jewish-American citizens who share this country with us -- ALL of us whose ancestors came from all parts of the world and from all different cultures in order to be free from tyranny -- will agree with me whole-heartedly when I share their battle-cry: "NEVER AGAIN!!!"

#4 - The following is from the Patriot Archives ftp site at: ftp://tezcat.com/patriot

If you have any other files you'd like to contribute, e-mail them to alex@spiral.org.

:::

The Federal Emergency Management Agency

:::

Although an excellent article, the January 1995 edition of 'Monitoring Times' magazine published only a tiny portion of what FEMA has been tasked by Executive Order to perform. FEMA was brought into existence by E.O. [That is, by Presidents like those who replaced or came after JFK!!! -- many of whose campaigns were financed by the Rockefellers and promoted by Rockefeller-backed media agencies -- Presidents who have the power to appoint their own unelected staff, create Executive Orders at a whim, and establish secret military-industrial-intelligence agencies that are NOT subject to Congressional oversight!]

All the frequencies I have for FEMA follow my comments here:

Federal Emergency Management Agency [F.E.M.A.] [and other emergency agencies]:

F.E.M.A. [Federal Emergency Management Agency] has been 'authorized' for the past 15 years by Presidential Executive Orders to confiscate ALL PROPERTY from the American People, separate families in the current 43 internment camps [already built and operational by the way, 5 of which are located in Georgia. The largest can confine somewhere on the order of 100,000 American citizens], called relocation camps by the 'government', for assignment to work camps; declares martial law and TOTALLY OVER-RIDES the U.S. Constitution. Presidential Executive Orders that are related or control this are given at the end of this. Two of the state prisons here in Georgia are currently empty, although manned by a minimal number of staff, have been setup and intentionally unpopulated by prisoners just to support this political policy.

Concentration [internment] Camps. An Executive Order signed by then President BUSH in 1989 authorized the Federal Emergency Management Agency [F.E.M.A.] to build 43 primary camps [having a capacity of 35,000 to 45,000 prisoners EACH] and also authorized hundreds of secondary facilities. It is interesting to note that several of these facilities can accommodate 100,000 prisoners. These facilities have been completed and many are already manned but as yet contain no prisoners. [Remember all the TALK of over-crowded prisons that exist...]. In south Georgia there are several state prisons that except for a few guards, are completely devoid of prisoners.

Under F.E.M.A., the Executive Orders which are already written and is the current law of the land, calls for the COMPLETE suspension of the United States Constitution, all rights and liberties, as they are currently known. The following executive orders, which are in the Federal Register located in Washington DC for anyone to request copies of, call for the suspension of all civil rights and liberties and for extraordinary measures to be taken in, as most of the orders state, "any national security emergency situation that might confront the government." When F.E.M.A. is implemented, the following executive orders will be immediately enforced:

E.O. 12148 - FEMA national security emergency, such as: national disaster, social unrest, insurrection, OR national financial crisis.

E.O. 10995 - "... provides for the seizure of ALL communications media in the United States."

E.O. 10997 - "... provides for the seizure of ALL electric power, petroleum, gas, fuels and minerals, both public and private."

E.O. 10998 - "... provides for the seizure of ALL food supplies and resources, public and private, and ALL farms, lands, and equipment."

E.O. 10999 - "... provides for the seizure of ALL means of transportation, including PERSONAL cars, trucks or vehicles of any kind and TOTAL CONTROL over all highways, seaports, and waterways."

E.O. 11000 - "... provides for the SEIZURE OF ALL AMERICAN PEOPLE for work forces under federal supervision, including SPLITTING UP OF FAMILIES if the government has to."

E.O. 11001 - "... provides for government seizure of ALL health, education and welfare functions."

E.O. 11002 - "... designates the postmaster general to operate a national REGISTRATION of all persons." [Under this order, you would report to your local post office to be separated and assigned to a new area. Here is where families would be separated].

E.O. 11003 - "... provides for the government to take over ALL airports and aircraft, commercial, public and PRIVATE."

E.O. 11004 - "... provides for the Housing and Finance Authority to relocate communities, designate areas to be abandoned and establish new locations for populations."

E.O. 11005 - "... provides for the government to TAKE OVER railroads, inland waterways, and public storage facilities."

E.O. 11051 - "... the office of Emergency Planning [has] complete authorization to put the above orders into effect in time of increased international tension or economic or financial crisis."

(What about an 'engineered' financial crisis, which in turn would most likely lead to 'social unrest'? This all depends on the decision of the current President. But then we must ask, just how legal is the U.S. Presidency anyway? MANY within the Continental

THE DULCE PROTOCOL

Congress, fearing the rise of Monarchy, had originally opposed the establishment of a Chief Executive position such as the one that General George Washington was elected to. They were assured however that those who followed Washington would have his example of integrity to base their own presidencies on. I have a suggestion: do away with the U.S. Presidency and the entire Executive Branch of government altogether -- especially now that it is, according to many sources, under the control of unelected Military-Industrialists since the coup of 1963 -- and give back control of the government to the CONGRESS as it was in the beginning. Congress by majority vote CAN do away with the Executive position if they choose to do so - Branton)

All of the above executive orders were combined by President NIXON (I rest my case - Branton) into **Executive Order 11490**, which allows all of this to take place if a national emergency is declared by the President. The burning and insurrection in Los Angeles in the case of Rodney King could have executed [and partially did execute] these Executive Orders.

Executive Order 12919: "National Defense Industrial Resources Preparedness" signed by CLINTON June 3, 1994, delegates authorities, responsibilities and allocations of F.E.M.A.'s Executive Orders [last entry] for the confiscation of ALL PROPERTY from the American people, and their re-location and assignment to 'labor' camps. The Executive Order also supersedes or revokes eleven (11) previous Executive Orders [from 1939 through 1991] and amends Executive Order 10789 and 11790. This executive order is A DECLARATION OF WAR AGAINST THE AMERICAN PEOPLE by the [Secret] Government of the United States in concert with the UNITED NATIONS.

Operation Dragnet. Janet Reno can implement this operation upon receiving one call from the President. Arrest warrants will be issued via computer to round-up over 1 MILLION PATRIOTIC AMERICANS who may 'resist' the NEW WORLD ORDER. Americans who are not 'politically correct.' Specifically mentioned are CHRISTIANS or those who read the Bible. Concentration/internment camps have already been built to accommodate these American prisoners. See above paragraph as these internment camps have been setup and are run by F.E.M.A.

Robert K Teske

(Note: In reference to Christians, just where should they/we stand in regards to defending America? Should Christians take up arms if necessary? Apparently the Founding fathers of the American Republic believed so, so long as it was in order to DEFEND their country, their women and children... and NOT in order to engage in offensive warfare for the sake of conquering and exploiting others, which to me would be "living by the sword" or you could say "making a living" by the sword. This could be exemplified by the Germans who initiated unprovoked invasions of their neighbors to meet their economic needs during World Wars I and II. One might ask, what about all the Orthodox Jews and Greek Orthodox Christians who went to their deaths like lambs to the slaughter without resisting during World War II? Why didn't they fight more zealously to defend themselves? That is a hard question and one that I don't have an answer for. All I can say is that from my study of the Old and New Testaments, I find no passage that forbids us from defending ourselves from aggressors -- at least in a national sense, however we ARE forbidden to become aggressors ourselves or engage in conflicts which are offensive rather than defensive oriented. The offensive attacks against the native Americans for instance, resulting from the Anglo invasion of North America, can NOT be justified through scripture, and such policies and mistreatment of the native Americans, the continuous betrayal of treaties, and the stealing of their God-given land in the past have or will doubtless have an adverse affect on America's destiny UNLESS reparations are made to the native peoples -- for instance a restoration of historical territories. Perhaps the Greys felt justified in repeatedly violating our government's secret 'treaties' with them because 'we' had done the exact same thing to the native Americans? Perhaps we DESERVED the abuses that the Greys and their Bavarian collaborators have inflicted upon us? Perhaps our nation's destiny will be largely determined by how we treat the native Americans from here on out, whether or not we begin to honor ALL of the treaties that 'we' had made and broken in the past? Could it be? On the other hand, if OFFENSIVE warfare is forbidden by God, then DEFENSIVE warfare against a foreign invasion of American soil or an internal threat to our freedoms as they are guaranteed in the Bill of Rights WOULD from my perspective be justified. In Psalm 125:3 we read how the rule of the wicked is a DIRECT VIOLATION of the will of God: "...For the wicked shall not rule the godly, lest the godly be forced to do wrong." A perfect example

514

would be the Lutherans of Germany who all-too-often capitulated to the Nazi's and their 'state church', in spite of the fact that most of the Nazi leaders were themselves backed by Luciferian cults which the Christians should have resisted. Instead, many of these backslidden Christians in Germany grudgingly supported the atrocities of their Nazi leaders, and by default the extermination by the millions of Jewish men, women and children. Why could Martin Luther himself stand alone against hundreds of pompous religious hypocrites at the council of worms in Germany and boldly accuse them of parasitical blasphemy and idolatry to their face, yet many of his Protestant followers -- not detracting from those few brave souls who DID resist -- gave-in right and left to the Nazi Satanists, and in some cases even contributed to the atrocities of World Wars I and II? In short then, Christianity does not teach that one SHOULD take up the sword, and it does not teach that one SHOULD NOT take up the sword in a defensive capacity. It all depends on one's own personal choice and faith. There is a warning however that those who do take up the sword should consider the possibility that they might die in battle. Then again one might die by NOT taking up the sword if they are captured and placed in death camp. It all comes down to ones personal choice, based on the prevailing circumstances. It is written that the "meek shall inherit the earth". This does not mean the "weak", since the actual meaning of "meek" is literally "a stallion in restraint" or someone who shows self-control over their passions. Logically those who run out onto the battlefield "to die for their country" in a blaze of suicidal zeal and vainglory will probably do just that. Those on the other hand who are cautious and wise and fight with the motive of "defending their family" will not be so careless with their lives, since they are the provider of their family as well as its defender. If they are dead then they can no longer provide nor defend. - Branton)

Operation Rolling Thunder. Reno and Benson have mentioned this operation which comprises county-wide sweeps of house to house, dynamic entry, search and seizures for all guns and food stockpiles by B.A.T.F., state national guard, active duty soldiers, as well as local police. This function is also run and coordinated through F.E.M.A.

Public Law 100-690 banned almost ALL RELIGIOUS GATHERINGS [not yet enforced..]. (Note: When and if this is enforced, this will be a blatant defecation upon the BILL OF RIGHTS, and in this event every true American is allowed -- and in fact it will be his and her Patriotic DUTY -- to implement the clause within the DECLARATION OF INDEPENDENCE to OVERTHROW such an alien, foreign or domestic tyranny-structure which has infested the governing body of America. - Branton); grants no-knock search and seizures without a search warrant; expands the drug laws to include EVERY American. This will generally be the prelude, or in addition to, a F.E.M.A. operation and contingency plan implementation.

The Omnibus Crime Bill of 1990. Ensures confiscation of all private property via money laundering, environmental violations of the Clean Water and Air Act, and extends as far as child abuse. This act also coordinates activities through F.E.M.A. and the Department of the Army, Commanding General, U.S. Forces Command, Fort McPherson, GA which is the executive and implementing agency upon initiation of many of these acts. The responsible agency within U.S. Army Forces Command was what used to be known as the Deputy Chief of Staff for Operations, Plans Division [DCSOPS, Plans], which was changed several years ago to J-3 after the Headquarters became a joint headquarters. They keep on file copies of all F.E.M.A. Emergency Management Operation Plans, including those plans developed by the Army to support the F.E.M.A. plan to eliminate the U.S. Constitution upon implementation. According to current plans, the Constitution will be 'temporarily' discontinued and shelved until the real or perceived and declared 'threat' has been neutralized (ask yourself -- who or what is the REAL threat that needs to be 'neutralized'? - Branton). But once 'shelved,' as with almost every other action of the Government, it STAYS shelved.

The Crime Bill of 1994. Banning of all military weapons which are necessary to the formation of a militia [when needed], denies other military equipment to the people's militia units (that's OK... the average American gun owner can legally acquire this 'equipment' from off the DEAD BODIES of FEMA-backed or related domestic/foreign Gestapo forces when they break-in-to our homes to steal our personal property or try to take us and our families prisoner without due process of law. - Branton), prelude to confiscating ALL guns in the hands of private citizens, DESTROYS the 1st Amendment, and makes virtually every American an outlaw. See above comments concerning the house-to-house search. The agency responsible for the actual implementation and search is the Department of the Army in concert with local and state police, including F.E.M.A., FBI, BATF, and other Federal Agencies.

SECRET UNDERGROUND BASES. There have been documented over 60 secret, VIRTUAL CITIES, UNDERGROUND, built by the government, Federal Reserve Bank Owners (such as the 'Rockefellers', etc. - Branton), and high ranking members of the Committee of 300 [some of these underground areas can be seen in Kansas City, Missouri and Kansas City, Kansas]. In additional, there exist underground Satellite Tracking Facilities which have the ability to punch your 911 address into the computer and a satellite can within seconds bring a camera to bear on your property to the point that those monitoring can read a license number on an automobile in your driveway. These facilities have as of Oct. 1, 1994, been turned over to the [foreign power of the] UNITED NATIONS. (Note: Forget the license plate, according to Norio Hayakawa, this satellite technology is now so sophisticated that they can CLEARLY read every word on your driver's LICENSE, supposing it were in view of the satellite. - Branton)

#5 - HAS IT ALREADY BEGUN? U.S. MILITARY OFFICERS -- SHACKLED BY U.N. FORCES

A report from SEVENTH WEEK MAGAZINE states that U.S. Military Officers were observed gagged, cuffed, and shackled to their seats aboard a white U.N. 747 en-route to the Federal Transfer Center near OKLAHOMA CITY! Part of this report follows:

"At a survival/preparation seminar in S.E. Oklahoma, on 3/25/95, an attendee interrupted one speaker, and stated that a neighbor, who apparently serves as a reserve crew member aboard one of the all white, unmarked, United Nations B-747 aircraft [which are assigned to FEMA, Black Operations, i.e. U.N. / N.W.O and hubbed at the Federal (prisoner) Transfer Center or FTC at WILL ROGERS AIRPORT], had been dead-heading back to Oklahoma City on the flight. He descended from the flight deck to see what the "prisoner cargo" consisted of, however, not only did he see the normal armed, black uniformed guards, and a load of bound humans, but he saw several U.S. Military officers, in full uniform, gagged, and shackled to their seats! They were in the front of the cabin, and from their visages, he discerned that they were violently angry at their situation. No doubt!

"At this point I guess you might think this is a joke? Nope, because in April 1993, and July 1994, an ex-Army intelligence analyst postulated THIS EXACT SCENARIO would happen! He also stated, in the 94 interview, 'they' were going to use white 747's to fly 'detained' [kidnapped] conservative, etc., etc., 'political' prisoners around the U.S., via the TFC, to the NOW-existing, 130 FEMA "RESISTER/DISSIDENT" DETENTION CAMPS. The above operation, among many others in this overall incredible takeover conspiracy, INCLUDES EARLY-ON LEADERSHIP KIDNAPPING, PERFORMED BY FOREIGN [ASIAN] CREWS NOW HIDDEN IN THE U.S. [on 'closed' U.S. bases] (UNDER closed military bases? - Branton), using the 3,000 choppers provided TO THE U.N. under the auspices of the 1989 "Open Skies Treaty," signed by good ole New World Order Sultan George Bush; a member of the Skull and Bones Secret Society, and the Trilateral Commission. The Treaty allows for the aerial observation of the U.S. [and, yes, your house -- if you have been tagged for observation, along with your phone being tapped], No Questions Asked! The majority of the recent BLACK CHOPPER sorties have nothing to do with lawful military/police department operations, but are presently locating, and setting up for seizure, people/guns, who will not take the 'mark' of the coming One World Government/Order! So PREPARE accordingly!"

(With the preceding confirmation of his claims, we now return to the Phil Schneider lecture. - Branton):

::: The Truth Behind the Republican Contract With America :::

"I don't perceive at this time that we have too much more than six months of life left in this country, at the present rate. We are the laughing stock of the world, because we are being hood-winked by so many evil people that are running this country. I think we can do better. I think the people over 45 are seriously worried about their future. I'm going to run some scary scenarios by you. The Contract With America. It contains the same terminology that Adolph Hitler used to subvert Germany in 1931. I believe we can do better. The Contract With America (or is it the "Contract ON America"? - Branton) is a last ditch effort by our federal government to tear away the Constitution and the Bill of Rights.

::: Some Statistics on the Black Helicopter Presence :::

"The black helicopters. There are over 64,000 black helicopters in the United States. For every hour that goes by, there is one being built. Is this the proper use of our money? What does the federal government need 64,000 tactical helicopters for, if they are not trying to enslave us. I doubt if the entire military needs 64,000 worldwide. I doubt if the entire world needs that many. There is 157 F-117A stealth aircraft loaded with LIDAR and computer-enhanced imaging radar. They can see you walking from room to room when they fly over your house. They see objects in the house from the air with a variation limit of 1 inch to 30,000 miles. That's how accurate that is. Now, I worked in the federal government for a long time, and I know exactly how they handle their business.

::: Government Earthquake Device, AIDS as a Bioweapon based on Alien Excretions :::

"The federal government has now invented an earthquake device. I am a geologist, and I know what I am talking about. With the Kobe earthquake in Japan, there was no pulsewave as in a normal earthquake. None. In 1989, there was an earthquake in San Francisco. There was no pulse wave with that one either. It is a Tesla device that is being used for evil purposes. The black budget programs have subverted science as we know it. Look at AIDs, invented by the National Ordinance Laboratory in Chicago, Illinois in 1972 (and passed to the United Nations - World Health Organization via the military Biogenetics facility at Ft. Detrick, Maryland to be injected into Small Pox vaccines in Africa and Hepatitus-2 vaccines in America, according to Drs. William Campbell Douglas, Alan Cantwell, Jr. and Dr. Robert Strecker - Branton). It was a biological weapon to be used against the people of the United States. The reason I know this is that I have seen the documentation by the Office of Strategic Services, which by the way is still in operation to this day, through the CDC in Atlanta. They used the glandular excretions of animals, humans and alien humanoids to create the virus. (according to the above mentioned Drs., part of the production of the virus involved the splicing of the Bovine Leukemia and Sheep Visna viruses in cancered human-tissue cultures. - Branton). These alien humanoids the government is hobnobbing with are the worst news. There is absolutely no defense against their germs -- none. They are a biological weapon of terrible consequence. Every alien [Gray] on the planet needs to be isolated.

"Saddam Hussein killed 3.5 MILLION Kurdish people with a similar biological weapon. Do we, the people of this planet, deserve this? No, we don't, but we are not doing anything about it. Every moment we waste, we are doing other people on the planet a disservice. Right now, I am dying of cancer that I contracted because of my work for the federal government. I might live six months. I might not. I will tell you one thing. If I keep speaking out like I am, maybe God will give me the life to talk my head off. I will break every law that it takes to talk my head off. ELEVEN of my best friends in the last 22 years have been MURDERED. Eight of the murders were called 'suicides.' Before I went to talk in Las Vegas, I drove a friend down to Joshua Tree, near 29 Palms. I drove into the mountains in order to get to Needles, California, and I was followed by two government E-350 vans with G-14 plates, each with a couple of occupants, one of which had an Uzi. I knew exactly who they were. I have spoken 19 times and have probably reached 45,000 people. Well, I got ahead of them and came to a stop in the middle of the road. They both went on either side of me and down a ravine. Is this what its going to take? I cut up my security card and sent it back to the government, and told them if I was threatened, and I have been, that I was going to upload 140,000 pages of documentation to the internet about [secret] government structure and the whole plan. I have already begun that task.

"Thank you very much."

End of May 1995 Lecture

THE DULCE PROTOCOL

* * * *

[Following is yet another article downloaded from the Internet with reference to Phil Schneider. Although not written by Schneider himself, the following is an interview with a woman who was aquatinted with the late underground base technician. Although many of the joint CIA-Alien bases have no 'obvious' or overt surface presence or facilities -- for instance Deep Springs, CA; Mercury, NV; Page, AZ; Dulce, NM -- OTHER underground facilities involved with the joint Bavarian-Alien New World Order agenda, aside from those existing below most of the active and 'deactivated' military bases, DO include surface facilities, and some of these for some strange reason are located directly below major Air Port terminals. For instance there is a large underground FEMA base below the Salt Lake City airport; another apparently exists at the Oklahoma City airport which serves as a joint FEMA - UNITED NATIONS "New World Order" detention/transfer center; however the most unusual 'Airport' of this nature seems to be the newer Denver International Airport, as described in the following interview]:

Leading Edge Research: The KSEO 4/26/96 Interview with Alex Christopher. Extract from Leading Edge International Research Journal #92. The KSEO 4/26/96 Interview with Alex Christopher, Author of "Pandora's Box" and "Pandora's Box II". Transcript 6/1/96 by Leading Edge Research Group. Legend: DA [Dave Alan, Host] AC: [Alex Christopher] C: [Caller]

DA: My special guest tonight is Alex Christopher, author of "Pandora's Box", an expose of the British instigation through Washington D.C. over the last 200 years (or more precisely, British-based Masonry, and most notably Scottish Rite Masonry which has long-since infiltrated British and American Masonry. - Branton). You thought you were free? This stuff has been going on forever. The idea was to make us perceive we were "free and independent"... She has a lot of information here, and we are going to have to have her back again for more. I talked to her last night. Just a fascinating individual. She is going to talk about the Montauk Project and extraterrestrial influences, and more. So, Alex, where do you start?

AC: Somebody told me one time, start in the middle and go from there. If you want to, pick a subject and we'll start from there.

DA: Last night we talked about a few things. We talked about the Denver airport last night and what is really going on down there, and we talked a bit about the Montauk project and Al Bielek, and then we skipped around a bit about some of the things in Pandora's Box. You mentioned that the Queen of England has been buying up a lot of property in Colorado under a pseudonym. Why don't we start on the subject of the British. (Note: according to former British Intelligence agent Dr. John Coleman, the London-based Wicca Mason lodges are one-third of the overall global conspiracy. The other two thirds are the Black Nobility banking families who claim direct descent from the early Roman emperors, and also the Maltese Jesuits or the Jesuit - Knights of Malta network. All three networks each have 13 representatives within the Bilderberg organization, which is a cover for the Bavarian Illuminati, suggestive that Bavaria itself has orchestrated a "marriage of convenience" between these three formerly competitive global control groups. - Branton)

AC: All right. The information, primarily, that is in "Pandora's Box" covers how the major corporations, railroad and banking concerns in this country were set up through a 'trust' that was originally known as the Virginia Company... The deal was that everything would remain under English control, or subservient to it, and that brings us right up to today, because we are still looking at everything falling under that 'trust' system going back to the Crown of England. It is mind boggling to think that everyone in this country has been led to believe that the people in the United States had won independence from England, when in fact they never did.

DA: Well, look at President Bush, wherein two years ago he went to England and was knighted by the Queen. Where is that coming from? Is it that he was a faithful servant? (Bush is allegedly a high-level Mason, and a member of the neo-Masonic Skull & Bones lodge. - Branton)

AC: You bet. All of them are doing the bidding, and it goes back to their secret societies and the establishment of the New World Order, which all leads back to the house of Windsor. There has been in this country for a long time a grooming process whereby people carry on the bidding of the Crown of England. (I did incidentally have somewhat of a confirmation of this when a friend told me that an American judge confided to her that the judicial system in America is now based after the monarchical judicial court systems of England. - Branton). That is one of the things the system involving the Rhodes Scholars was set up to achieve. Cecil Rhodes set it up to groom people for this task, to carry the United States into the New World Order. It appears, from what I have been able to find out, that the Crown of England has had this very skillfully planned for hundreds of years, and it could be possible that they have been privy to information that not many of us have been [privy to] for a long long time, about the chaos involving Earth changes that are coming. It is my understanding that England is not going to make it through the changes, so they set up a whole new Empire over here. That goes back to some of the things we discussed before, about lands being bought up in Colorado.

(Note: With the fascination Britons have with time-travel, "DR. WHO" and so-on, is it possible that British intelligence could have gained a glimpse into the future and 'seen' what was coming? The Britons have British Columbia, Canada as their possession - - if they are so desperate and convinced that their nation will not survive the 'changes', then why not move the British Empire to B.C. rather than risk offending Americans by opening old wounds that date back to the revolutionary war, and losing their World War I and World War II allies in the process? Just as in America, it is not the general CITIZENS of Britain who pose a threat to freedom, it is the so-called 'elite', the Rockefellers of America and the Rothschilds of Britain who would and have SOLD-OUT their own peoples for personal gain and god-like domination over the lower classes. The Americans and Britons who fought and died together on the battlefields of World War I and II did not realize that the Rothschild-Rockefeller monarchies were the one's who had betrayed them by helping to CREATE the 'monster' that they were fighting in both world wars for the sole purpose of gaining even greater wealth and power. In the end it all came down to base human greed! America has strayed a long ways from the ideals established by the founders of the U.S. Constitution. And, needless to say, Britain has strayed a long ways from the ideals established by the legendary King Arthur whose greatness came from his ability to make all of his knights equals amidst the 'round-table' rather than succumb to vainglory and the temptation of establishing himself as some kind of human deity. Whether the legend of King Arthur was based on fact or not, the IDEALS themselves are nether-the-less real and true. - Branton).

DA: Yes, the area is of a pretty high altitude, where it will be safe.

AC: Yes. Plus, all the symbolism that is apparent in the layout of the new Denver airport says that it is "a control center for world control". There is a lot of "secret society" symbology at the airport. We started researching all of this to find out what it all means. It's all very scary. A gentlemen by the name of Al Bielek, who has been involved in some very unusual government projects in the past, told me that "the Denver area is where the establishment of the Western sector of the New World Order will be in the United States". Little bits and pieces keep coming to me, confirming things I have not had confirmed before.

DA: Do you know of John Coleman?

AC: The Committee of 300?

DA: Yes. What's your take on that?

AC: I think his information is fantastic. If he had had the information that I put in "Pandora's Box" when I put that together, it would have blown his mind. But, as far as I know from my standpoint, both sets of material go hand in hand, right down the line.

DA: Some of these things about the background of the British invasion, taking over the land over here while they let us think that we are running this country. How they had a bone to pick with the Czar of Russia years ago, how they have pushed the socialist revolution....like they say, the sun never sets on British soil. About some of these things on the airport in Denver. Would you mind discussing some of those things again?

AC: Well, the first thing that got my attention at the airport was the 'capstone' that I saw in a photograph, that had a Masonic symbol on it. So, I really wanted to go to the airport and see that, because I thought it was very unusual.

DA: The capstone?

THE DULCE PROTOCOL

AC: The capstone, or the dedication stone, for the Denver airport has a Masonic symbol on it. A whole group of us went out to the airport to see some friends off and see this capstone, which also has a time capsule imbedded inside it. It sits at the south eastern side of the terminal which, by the way, is called "The Great Hall", which is what Masons refer to as their meeting hall. And, on this thing it mentions "the New World Airport Commission". I have never heard of that, have you?

DA: Never.

AC: It has a Masonic symbol on it, and it also has very unusual geometric designs. It depicts an arm rising up out of it that curves at a 45 degree angle. It also has a thing that looks like a keypad on it. This capstone structure is made of carved granite and stainless steel, and it is very fancy.. This little keypad area at the end of the arm has an out-of-place unfinished wooden block sitting on it. The gentleman that was with me on the first trip out to the airport has since died. They say he committed suicide, but everything else tells me that this is not possible. No one can double-tie a catheter behind his own neck and strangle himself. I just don't think that is possible. But, his name was Phil Schneider, and he started blowing the whistle on all this stuff going on in the underground bases that he had helped build for years and years. He worked on the underground bases at Area 51 and Dulce, New Mexico, as well as several other places. Schneider told me that this keypad-looking area looked like a form of techno-geometry that is "alien-oriented", and that it had something to do with a "directional system", whatever that meant, that functioned as a homing beacon to bring ships right into the "Great Hall".

In the same general area on this capstone, there are some most unusual designs on the floor that are all Masonic in nature, which lead right back to the "Black Sun" [Editor Note: According to Al Bielek, Schneider's father was a U-boat captain during the Nazi regime who was also on the Eldridge in 1943 in a medical capacity], which goes back to Nazi symbology. See, the "secret societies" are supposedly into Sun worship. The Nazi's were into "Black Sun" worship, which connects with the idea of Saturn. Saturn and Satanism kind of go hand-in-hand. (Note: The "Black Sun" also refers to the massive black hole at the center of our galaxy. In regards to "unusual designs on the floor", one source claims that the base of the Hoover Dam near Las Vegas, not far from Area 51, contains "wild inlays" of occultic and Masonic zodiacal symbolism. Reports stated that as the cliffs were being blasted open to make way for the dam, huge caverns were penetrated. Could these have connections with the underground network? Another unusual dam is the Glen Canyon dam near Page, Arizona which could conceivably provide hydroelectric power to a base that allegedly lies below the area and ties the Dulce and Area 51 bases together subterraneally. - Branton) Then, we have this system of murals at the airport that are the most grotesque things you've ever seen.

DA: What's on the murals?

AC: I say that they are about what they plan to do to us, and the world as a whole, not what has happened or some fantasy. One of them that is very unusual has three caskets with dead people in them...

DA: That's part of the ritual connected with the Skull & Bones Club.

Yes. There are evidently three groups of people that they would like to see dead. The first casket has what the artist told me was a Jewish-American child, a little girl, and she has the 'star' on her clothes and a little Bible and a locket... (this may be a depiction of both Judeo & Christian believers, both of whom have historically been the target of the 'inquisitions' of some of the more occultic secret societies of Europe, such as the Thule-backed inquisition against the Jews and the Jesuit-backed inquisition against the Protestants. - Branton)

DA: Jewish lineage is passed through the female...

AC: Yes. Well, all these caskets depict women who are dead. Then, in the center casket there is depicted a Native American woman, and the last casket has a black woman in it. Now, normally I would not have thought too much about these murals if I had not done a lot of research. Even in the government documents I have run across gene-splicing discussions on how they would like to "splice out specific races", and also whoever these people are do not like the Jewish people. This is just one of the murals, and these murals are huge. This same mural depicts the destruction of a city and the forest, and there is a little girl holding a Mayan tablet that speaks of the destruction of civilization. There is a mural that depicts this 'thing' standing over a city that looks like a green "Darth Vader", with a sword, that has destroyed the city. This character is huge, and there is a road depicted with women walking holding dead babies. This same mural extends over to another mural which depicts all of the children of the world taking the weapons from each country on earth and giving them to a central figure which is a GERMAN boy who has this iron fist and anvil in his hand that is totally out of proportion to the child's body, beating the swords into plowshares. I thought, well, this is very odd depicting a German child doing this. What all this symbology on the airport murals seems to convey is that not only do we have a secret society behind this, but that it is a German [Bavarian] secret society behind this, working in the vicinity of this New World Control Center.

DA: It is interesting when you consider Operation Paperclip wherein all these Nazi's were brought to the United States to be groomed, financed, and basically brought back into power.

(Note: That is, by the Rockefeller cartel who supplied Nazi Germany with the oil and materials necessary to keep their war machine operating. Rockefeller-connected OIL companies include EXXON, ARCO, ZAPATA, etc. It is alleged that these corporations initially took in and gave refuge to some 3000 Nazi SS war criminals by providing them with immunity, new identities, and positions within the Bavarian-backed Rockefeller corporate empire and within the CIA -- with the help of Bavarian agents like Allen Dulles, Otto Scorzeny, Reinhard Gehlen and later Vice President Nelson Rockefeller. These were then used as a covert force to destroy American independence and make America subject to a Bavarian-backed New World Order. Remember even through the Bilderbergers consist of a "marriage of convenience" between Londonese Wicca Masons, Basilian Black Nobility and Roman Maltese Jesuits... the supreme controllers of the Bildeberger cult itself are the secret black gnostic cults of Bavaria whose 'Cult of the Serpent' -- or Illuminati -- can be traced back to Egypt and ultimately to Babylon itself. These Rockefeller-Nazi projects reportedly continued through at least 1975 during which period many thousands more "underground Nazis" were brought into America from Europe and also, if we are to believe some reports, from the secret German "New Berlin" base under the mountains of Neu Schwabenland, Antarctica that was established during World War II via Nazi-occupied South Africa. Is Neu Schwabenland the REAL power behind the joint Bavarian-Alien New World Order Agenda? The fact that British and American Masons would be pulled into a Bavarian-backed New World Order conspiracy run by anti-British Nazi's and anti-Masonic Jesuits -- in spite of the animosities of World Wars I and II -- would seem contradictory to the extreme. However NOT if we consider the fact that Roman Jesuits had secretly created the Scottish Rite of Masonry at the Jesuit college of Clermont in France and also the Bavarian Illuminati via the Jesuit Adam Weishaupt. Both the Illuminati and Scottish Rite worked together to INFILTRATE Masonry and subdue the traditional Judeo-Christian York Rite. The Masonic elitists in Great Britain and America would have as a result of this infiltration become subject to the influences of the Scottish Rite dominated 33rd degree -- falsely believing that 'Masonry' was still the enemy of the 'Jesuits', as in earlier times the conflict between the two was notorious. They might have been deceived into believing that 'British Masonry' would come out on top of the New World Order when in fact Rome and Bavaria, the two power-centers of the old [Un]Holy Roman Empire, had the REAL control. But blinded by their own delusions of grandeur and world domination, the British elite failed to see how their Masonic lodges were being infiltrated and manipulated by their sworn enemies. Some of the elite might have been oblivious to the ins-and-outs of Masonry altogether, being conscious only of their own greed. - Branton)

AC: Well, I know they're here, because I have seen them [Germans] alongside the Americans in the more sensitive areas of the airport. But, these paintings are most disturbing and very unusual. When I first tried to contact the artist and talk to him about these murals, he told me that he was given guidelines on what to paint and put in the murals. When I showed up in his studio, I asked to see the guidelines for the last two murals he was working on, he suddenly went "brain dead" and said "of course, there are no guidelines." It took myself and two other people over eight months to figure out all the symbology that is embodied in these murals. It turned out that some of these are 'trigger' pictures, containing symbology designed to trigger altered personalities of people that have been groomed in MKULTRA type programs for specific tasks that they have been trained to do in terms of something connected with Satanic rituals and mind control. I had one woman that called me out of the blue one night, and she was really disturbed about some information. She told me many different things that later turned out to be known MKULTRA triggers. Also, almost every aspect of these murals contains symbols relating back to secret societies. When you get the overall view of what they are talking about in these things, it is very very scary. It goes back to the Bio-diversity Treaty, getting rid of specific races of people, taking over the world and mind control.

There is one picture in which every plant turns out to be mind-altering or poisonous, and all the animals are Masonic symbols used in literature in every country in the world. It took a very long time to track all this stuff down and figure out what they're trying to say. The one way they tell stories is in pictures. It's right there in our face when you go into the airport. Most people look at them and say, "those are crazy-looking pictures, what are they doing in this airport?"

DA: Now, you mentioned that underneath this airport it goes down many levels.

AC: Yes.

DA: Does the fact that all these underground levels are there have something to do with why it took so long for this airport to open?

AC: Well, the gentleman that I was dealing with, Phil Schneider, said that during the last year of construction they were connecting the underground airport system to the deep underground base. He told me that there was at least an eight-level deep underground base there, and that there was a 4.5 square mile underground city and an 88.5 square-mile base underneath the airport. It is very unusual that they would allot a 50 square-mile area on the surface at which to locate an airport in the middle of nowhere unless they really planned to use it for something very unusual later. There is a 10-mile, 4-line highway out to this airport, and there is nothing out there in between the airport and Denver. Not even a service station, at least in September 1995. The people in Denver are really upset with the fact that this airport went in the way it did.

There was this fellow who wrote a book in which he made the statement that they had a copy of an audio tape on which a Denver city official was talking with people from the CIA, and that he was paid 1.5 million dollars to allow the 'airport' to be built, no matter what it took. It appears that there was a lot more interest in getting the airport built from just officials in the Denver area. They plan on using this facility for something else other than just landing planes.

DA: So, this guy got you down there to take a look at the underground?

AC: Well, he was invited to go along on the trip. I had a friend that actually got us down into the active area in the underground. It's very interesting down there. The baggage equipment area is very unusual. All the old luggage equipment that wouldn't work right doesn't look much different than the stuff that is working today.

DA: You were telling me that there are huge concrete corridors with sprinklers all along the ceiling. What are these sprinkler heads doing in a concrete bunker, pray tell? (Presumably concrete will not 'burn' if there is a potential fire, so is it possible that something other than 'water' is meant to be expelled from these sprinklers which are located "all along" the ceiling? - Branton)

AC: Well, this is the same question we asked. These shafts are huge and run along adjacent to the tramline on both sides. So, there are two of these huge shafts large enough to fit a two-lane highway in there. There are very FEW openings into and out of the tram shaft, but at the end of them, going out into this 50 square miles of acreage is a huge steel door that would facilitate the entrance of a great big truck. It could be used for almost anything, but what is so unusual about it is that about EVERY FIVE OR SIX FEET on the ceiling, across almost the full width of the area, there is a pipe with three or four sprinkler heads. This goes on for the FULL length of the thing, "which must be close to a mile". There are two of these shafts, and I got a picture in the mail the other day which was very unusual that was taken by someone on board the tram in the shaft. The picture appeared to actually show ghost-like figures on it. It was a mother and a baby wrapped in a blanket. When you are down in that concrete shaft, both times I got nauseated. There are some very unusual vibrations down there (from other 'time dimensions'? - Branton). Now, the tunnel shaft that the tram comes in on could connect up with an underground tunnel coming in from five buildings that were built and buried. There was already a 40 foot diameter tunnel there when construction started. Those five buildings they built 3 1/2 years ago, and suddenly they said "oops, these are in the wrong place", and buried them, along with a very high-tech runway that is buried under about four inches of dirt. It seems insane that they would build a very technical building complex with interlocking tunnels and a tunnel going back to the tram tunnel at the concourse, and then state that they built it in the "wrong place" and cover it up with dirt. I don't believe that people are that stupid.

DA: No. Projects like that are strategically planned, and they just don't go and do that.

AC: Some of these five buildings are 150 feet tall. There is one 78 feet tall, and one that is 126 feet tall. They are all in that range. From this complex there is a shaft that runs to concourse "C". When they started this project, as I said, there was also a huge 40 foot diameter shaft brought in there from somewhere that was off-limits to the work crews. It was there when the project was started. And, everybody that worked on these projects....there were five different contractors, and the people on each contracted crew did not interact with the other ones. When the project was done, everyone was fired and sent away.

DA: You would think that during this massive construction they would not be able to keep this stuff secret.

AC: I think a lot of the people saw things that disturbed them so much that they would not talk about it. I know several people who worked on the project that managed to find their way down into the depths, probably close to the deep underground base, and saw things that scared them so badly they won't talk about it. I interviewed a few of the former employees on these construction crews that worked out there on these buildings that ended up buried, and they are afraid to talk. They say that everybody is real nervous about it, and they decided to tell some of the secrets that they knew, but they don't want anybody to know who they are. So, I can tell you that it is a very unusual and spooky type of place, and if you are a sensitive person you get nauseated as soon as you enter the perimeter of the airport. Especially when you go down underground. You become very nauseated a nervous. There is also so much electromagnetic flux in the area that if you get out on the open ground around the airport, you will 'buzz'.

DA: Where is this flux field coming from? What do you think the purpose of this is?

AC: I think that its coming from some kind of underground electrical system, because where we were there were no power lines, and the whole place was just buzzing with this free energy floating around. Very unusual. In addition, there are areas in the underground that have chain-link fences with the barbed wire tops pointed inward, like they were there to keep people in, not keep people out. All these areas are there, acres of it, and none of it is in active use. There are many terraced areas that go down. One area in particular is forbidden to go into unless you are wearing a biological protective suit. They say there is some kind of "unidentified biological fungus" in that area that attacks people's lungs.

DA: Hmmm. Some kind of way to hide something that is in this area?

AC: Well, we think that area is one that leads to deeper levels underground at the airport. But, it is surrounded by a chain-link fence and you can't get in there. We think this is the area that one of the electricians kind of stumbled into that went down about six levels below the fourth level, and ran into some really weird stuff. He won't talk about any of it now.

DA: Real weird stuff.

AC: Also, at the airport there are what look like miniature nuclear reactor cooling towers, and I don't understand why they are there. When people asked, the reply is that they are part of the ventilation and exhaust system. Ventilation and exhaust from where?

DA: What do you think its for?

AC: I think it is all hooked up to the deep underground.

THE DULCE PROTOCOL

DA: They say that this place looks like some underground "holding area"...somewhat like a cattle lot....a place that could hold thousands of people. The gates, fences....

AC: The luggage transport vehicles move on a full-sized double-lane highway, and along this highway are chain-linked areas that could be used for holding areas. I don't understand why they built this the way they did, unless they planned to use it for something like that in the future.

DA: So what could all this be for?

AC: If Phil is right, and all this hooks up to the deep underground base that he was offered the plans to build back in 1979, and that what this other man TOLD me in private [is] that there is a lot of human SLAVE LABOR in these deep underground bases being used by these aliens, and that a lot of this slave labor is children. HE SAID that when the children reach the point that they are unable to work any more, they are slaughtered on the spot and consumed.

DA: Consumed by who?

AC: Aliens. Again, this is not from me, but from a man that gave his life to get this information out. He worked down there for close to 20 years, and he knew everything that was going on.

DA: Hmmm. Who do these aliens eat?

AC: They specifically like young human children, that haven't been contaminated like adults. Well, there is a gentleman out giving a lot of information from a source he gets it from, and he says that there is an incredible number of children snatched in this country.

DA: Over 200,000 each year.

AC: And that these children are the main entree for dinner.

(Note: Many will read this and scoff in utter disbelief at such a claim. This is all well and fine, and even Phil Schneider warns us to put on our 'skepticals' when investigating claims and to investigate them so that they can be definitively proven one way or the other, as all claims of an extraordinary nature should be. So, I would suggest that Congress by-pass the EXECUTIVE branch of government -- which has sold-out to the Intelligence-Military-Industrial Complex, a branch that was originally intended by the founders of the Republic to be the 'servants' of CONGRESS, the SENATE and the PEOPLE -- and undertake a full-scale investigation of this and other underground bases, even if this calls for full-scale Congress-backed military mobilization. The excuse for such an undertaking could for instance be to investigate claims of unethical use of U.S. tax dollars, violations of Federal Medical Regulations in regards to genetic research, failure to pay property taxes on underground facilities used by non-elected officials, harboring of "illegal aliens", bribery and treason, illegal cattle rustling in regards to the Dulce and other bases, possible kidnapping and human rights abuses against children, and so on... - Branton)

DA: How many Draconians are down there?

AC: I have heard the figure of 150,000 just in the New York area.

DA: Underneath New York?

AC: Yes. In some kind of underground base there.

DA: Interesting. Now, you've seen pictures of these things?

AC: I have seen them face to face.

DA: You have?

AC: Yes. From some information that has been put out by a group or team that also works in these underground bases that is trying to get information out to people that love this country, THERE IS A WAR THAT IS GOING ON UNDER OUT FEET, AND ABOVE OUR HEADS, that the public doesn't know anything about, and its between these ALIEN forces and the HUMANS that are trying to fight them.

THE DULCE PROTOCOL

DA: What other types have you seen?

AC: The ones that I have seen are the big-eyed Greys and the Reptilians.

DA: What do these Reptilians look like?

AC: There are three different types.

DA: Can you tell us how you happened to come into contact with them?

AC: When I lived in Florida in Panama City, at that particular time the Gulf Breeze sightings were going on, and the area was virtually a hotbed for strange events. I had neighbors that were into watching UFOs and getting information about them. One night about 2:30 am, my neighbor called me and was absolutely frantic, and wanted me to come over there. I ran over there and went in the front door, and she and her boyfriend, who is a commercial airline pilot, were in the living room scared out of their wits. I looked over at her, and her eyeballs are rolling back in her head and she was passing out and sliding down the wall. Her boyfriend was trying to tell me what was going on, and I was feeling this incredible energy that felt like it was trying to penetrate my head. So, I grabbed both of them and pulled them both outside, where we stood for a while and talked...

DA: Some people would say that this is a case of demon possession...

AC: Oh, no. There was radiation in the room. The next day all of her plants were dead. So, there was a massive amount of energy focused on that room. Anyway, after about an hour had passed, we had discussed what went on and decided to go back into the house. They had both been in bed and were pulled out of their bed during the night. All they remember is a flash of light in their faces and the next thing they know they're both scared to death. But, when we went back into the house, I noticed that the man had a small palm-print on his side with fingers that must have been 10 inches long, with claw marks on the end that were burned into his side. The next day, that area was so swollen that he could not touch it. I have video pictures of these things on his side. The prints were there from someone bending down from behind him and pulling him out of bed.

They had been making love, and 'somebody' lifted him off of her and left these burns there.

Anyway, they were both totally flipped out. I finally got them calmed down enough to let me go home. I went home and went to bed. The next thing I know, I woke up and there is this 'thing' standing over my bed. He had wrap-around yellow eyes with snake pupils, and pointed ears and a grin that wrapped around his head. He had a silvery suit on, and this scared the living daylights out of me. I threw the covers over my head and started screaming....I mean, here is this thing with a Cheshire-cat grin and these funky glowing eyes...this is too much. I have seen that kind of being on more than one occasion.

DA: What else can you say about it?

AC: Well, he had a hooked nose and he was [humanoid] looking, other than the eyes, and had kind of grayish skin. Later on in 1991, I was working in a building in a large city, and I had taken a break about 6:00, and the next thing I knew it was 10:30 at night, and I thought I had taken a short break. I started remembering that I was taken aboard a ship, through four floors of an office building, and through a roof. There on the ship is were I encountered 'GERMANS' AND 'AMERICANS' WORKING TOGETHER, and also the GREY ALIENS, and then we were taken to some other kind of facility and there I saw the REPTILIANS again ... the one's I call the "baby Godzilla's", that have the short teeth and yellow slanted eyes, and who look like a VELOCI-RAPTOR, kind of.

DA: So, why would these people pick on you?

AC: Well, I found one common denominator in the abduction, and it keeps on being repeated over and over again. I deal with lots of people who have been abducted, and the one common denominator seems to be the blood line, and its the blood line that goes back to ancient Indian or Native American blood lines.

DA: Are these people looking for genetic material?

AC: Well, I don't know if it is a very ancient blood line that they want to try and stop, or what the reasoning is. I know that I was asked some questions, like how I was

536

capable of doing some of the psychic things I was doing at the time. But, it is very unusual to find anybody that remotely thinks they have been taken that doesn't have the Indian blood line, somewhere.

DA: Now, after that experience, what happened after that? What were some of the other times you saw some of these beings?

AC: Well, at that facility I saw the almond-eyed Greys, but the thing that sticks in my mind are the beings that look like reptiles, or the veloci-raptors. They are the cruelest beings you could ever imagine, and they even smell hideous. There were a couple of very unusual areas down there where I was taken which looked like cold storage lockers, where these things were in hibernation tubes, and that is about all I remember, other than seeing some black helicopters and little round-wing disk type aircraft. At that point, the memory seems to be cut off and I can't tap through to anything else. They're there, folks.

DA: Maybe I'll open up some phone lines, and maybe we'll talk about Al Bielek and some things you discussed with him. Are you open to that?

AC: Sure.

Caller (C): On those ships where the Germans and Americans were, did they have any kind of an insignia on their uniforms?

AC: Yes, they did. I have been told that the organization is called "The Black League" (possibly the "Black Monks" within the NSA who reportedly interact directly with aliens? - Branton); by people that might know. A blue triangle with a red-eyed black dragon, with a circle around it. It was very unusual. There's another woman that has written a book about an encounter she had in Fort Walden. I met her some years back, and we were taking about things we've seen. She also talked about this strange insignia. She and I both sat down a drew what we saw, and they were virtually carbon copies of each other. (Note: Winged serpent symbols have been observed by several abductees, including policeman Herbert Schirmer who reported the insignia on the uniforms of the reptilian-eyed grays that had abducted him. - Branton)

Robert K Teske

In the book "Cosmic Conflict", the author talks about the ancient city that was uncovered by the Germans before World War II, and tells about their effort to revive some frozen humans they found in this underground city, and that the true humans couldn't be revived, but the ones that could be revived were in fact reptilians in disguise, and the reptilians have the capability to do shape-shifting and create a [laser] holographic image so when you look at them you see a human, but under that there is no human there. It's like a "deja vu" of the movie "They Live". (Note: An early newsletter called THE CRYSTAL BALL published information along this line, which stated that the Soviets had during the investigation of a meteor crash uncovered a buried city in Siberia where they discovered the frozen bodies of both humans -- who could NOT be revived, and human-appearing reptilians -- who WERE revived from the frozen state. Allegedly the reptilians re-animated and killed the Soviet scientists and through some type of psychic osmosis drained their minds and assimilated their memories and features through a molecular shape-shifting type process. John Carpenter, who directed THEY LIVE, also directed an earlier movie called THE THING which was based somewhat on a similar theme. The alien 'impostors' then called for backup and more scientists came out and were 'replaced', and these eventually returned to Russia and began to infiltrate the Communist government. Although such claims may seem preposterous, it is nevertheless interesting how numerous 'preposterous' claims as this contain identical 'reptilian' themes. Aside from the instinctive and basic racial fear in humans of things 'reptilian', could this re-occurring theme be more than mere coincidence? - Branton) Cathy O'Brien, who wrote "Trance-Formation in America", revealed that George Bush projected a hologram that he was a reptilian .... real crazy stuff, but if this technology that they possess is there, why couldn't a race do something like that ... these 'people' that are working with our government?

C: I believe that, but I do believe that these are demons that manifest themselves as alien beings, and that this has been going on for a long time...

DA: Demons? Who are demons?

C: Fallen angels.

538

THE DULCE PROTOCOL

DA: The reptilians look like that anyway. All the scriptures around the planet talk about serpent beings, (or in the case of Judeo-Christian scriptures like Genesis chapter 3 and Revelation chapter 12, serpent beings possessed by 'demons' or through which demons are able to or allowed to 'incarnate'. - Branton) what do you think, Alex?

AC: Well, I think that's pretty much what the bottom line is. Also, they talk about the rapture...

DA: It could be like an alien 'thanksgiving'.

AC: These people that have done all this research and are part of the underground government are telling that the humans on this planet have been at war with these reptilian aliens for thousands of years. At one point, things got so hot on the planet, like it is now, aliens took on this holographic image and infiltrated the human race in order to take it over and undermine it, just like this New World Order is doing right now. They're saying that the same thing happened to civilization on Earth before, and that the humans before actually had the capability for interplanetary travel, and that it was so bad here with the reptilians that they had to leave... What they are also saying is that these beings that are human-looking that are visiting our planet, at this time, trying to inform people what is going on, and guide them, are actually OUR ANCESTORS THAT ESCAPED FROM EARTH before, when it was under reptilian domination.

DA: What is your take on these crop circles?

AC: Oh, the crop circles that are the real ones are a type of geometric language containing some kind of information. There was one that was a Mandelbrot fractal. How do you fake that? They say that there are a lot of crop circles going on in the United States, and that the government shuts the information off (or destroys the crop circles before the public can find them, others claim. - Branton) about their occurrence.

DA: Canada and Australia as well.

C: It seems that we are having an increase in these encounters and sightings.

AC: Things are escalating at an incredible rate. I think a lot of these movies in the media are trying to get us softened up for what they plan to unleash on us.

C: So, in just a matter of years, they plan to bring it out and bring people to that airport?

AC: You know, Reagan said more than once that the only thing that would bring people together would be some kind of "outside force".

DA: Exactly, I remember that. He said that several times.

AC: I went to South Florida a couple of weeks ago and interviewed a man who had done research for 30 years, and oddly enough, he tapped into some of the same information I had, in that our government has had round-winged, saucer-type technology, high mach speed aircraft since the 1920's, and that in 1952 they had over 500 of these aircraft hidden in secret bases. Now, if they had that in 1952, considering that military technology grows by 44 years for every year that goes by, what do you imagine they have now, 44 years later, after technology has advanced the equivalent of 1,936 years?

C: About two or three months ago, I went to do a business transaction with a fellow I have known for about two or three years, and one of his relatives had just died -- we were pretty close, and we got into a deep conversation about stuff, and he told me he worked in an underground military base in Colorado. I asked him what he did there, and he said that if he told me he'd have to kill me. I told him I didn't want to know. I was really shocked, and didn't know what to think of it, and then I heard this program. I want to know what your guest thinks about the Iron Mountain report the government did in the 1960's, and if that ties into the Nazis and the Americans [CIA] working together. Also, this would also explain George Washington's vision where this country was invaded from the East by a foreign power, and then when all hope seemed lost, the angels of God would come down and the nation would be saved. Anyway, I never could understand why angels of God would come down and fight with men to save a puny little country that has been around for only 200 years, but in this scenario, there seems to be some explanation here.

AC: Yes, the Iron Mountain report. The guy that claims to be the author of it now claims that it was nothing more than a joke, but for a joke, it seems to be following the time line to the hilt, so I think it was something that made its way out and they are trying to cover that up. Everything that was in that report is happening in great detail right now.

C: Do these reptilians bleed if they get shot?

DA: Has anybody ever killed one?

AC: Phil Schneider did. He killed several of them. When he was involved in cutting some tunnels at Dulce, he was lowered down a shaft and ended up in a nest of these things. He and some of his team were in there, and some of the Delta Force came in. They had a shootout with these aliens, and he killed a couple of them before they got a round off and shot him with some sort of laser weapon. He used to pull his shirt up and show me where they darned near blew a hole in his chest with whatever kind of laser weapon they were using.

DA: So they can be killed, then?

AC: Yes, if you have the drop on them. They die just like everyone else. They consist of mass just like we do.

C: It is interesting that high officials in the Clinton administration, like Cisneros, were deeply involved with the construction of this airport. Also, Pat Shroeder. All of a sudden, she's leaving office. It's like a lot of people who have been involved with this airport are leaving town. Also, there is a fellow by the name of Rodney Stitch, who writes about the total corruption in the Denver area. Does this tie in with what you were talking about?

AC: Well, he is the one that wrote the book "Defrauding America". He said that they had a tape of a CIA agent paying off the mayor of Denver to get the airport built. There is just so much corruption. They are selling the good American people out. We have some of our own people selling the rest of population out for a few pieces of gold.

DA: What about Al Bielek and how what he is saying may relate to this?

AC: I met Al about a year ago.

DA: Who is Al Bielek?

AC: He claims to be one of the ones who jumped overboard off the Eldridge when it went into hyperspace during the Philadelphia Experiment. He actually traveled forward in time, and asked the people that he encountered there what happened in his future. At that time, he was given the information about the New World Order and that Denver was the location for the NWO Western Sector, and that Atlanta was supposed to be the control center for the Eastern Sector. Can it be that the fact that the Olympics is supposed to be in Atlanta is part of a scenario? All the highways in Atlanta have high-security monitoring cameras just like those seen in some of the underground areas at the Denver airport. These monitors are all over the interstate highway and on many of the streets in Atlanta. Last week, I was talking to a fellow who was actually working on the Olympic project, in terms of the main stadium, and he said that they're gearing up for the possibility of terrorist acts. Do they know something we don't know?

(Note: As for 'Denver' being the center of a New World Order control system in the west, we should realize that the future is not fully SET. It IS subject to change. There are, according to contactees, different 'parallel realities' that exist. The 3rd dimensional or 3rd density reality is the 'foundation' upon which all others exist. Other realities exist in 4th, 5th and other 'densities' wherein objects and events are somewhat more 'fluid' than in 3rd dimensional reality. Many who claim to have traveled in time state that while doing so they were out-of-phase somewhat with the people within the other time-zones. They could observe them yet were 'invisible' or in a phased-out state, in essence unable to 'interfere' to the point of changing 3rd dimensional past events. Others, involved in the Montauk project for instance, state that the 'futures' that they observed were of a quasi-reality or semi-dreamlike nature, as if 'future' reality was like wet clay that had not yet 'set' and solidified into a CONCRETE reality. So if this is the case, then Denver does NOT necessarily have to be a New World Order control center, even though the 'thought forms', or what you might call 'reality blueprints', ARE being created by the secret government and are in the process of 'solidifying' as the future gets closer. However, ANY thought form can be destroyed and replaced BEFORE it solidifies into 3rd density concrete reality. Those living within the 3rd density event-flow have the POWER to determine the outcome of events through their connection to the eternal NOW, just as a large river has first priority over the smaller tributaries in determining the course of a river bed. So then we are living in an eternal NOW which is continually in the process of being converted from a FLUID thought form state and into CONCRETE material form state. Once 'set', an event cannot be undone. However if there is even a minimal amount of malleability left to the event, then that event can potentially be turned... for better or worse. - Branton)

DA: Maybe they want to go ahead and perpetrate something again. One thing after another. It's all part of their scenario. Let's take a call.

C: Yes, I would like to thank you and your guest for coming forward with this information. And, as unbelievable as it is for the audience, I personally have had first-hand experience with some of this stuff. Not so much with the reptilians, but when you talk about this technology base that the government is working with, my own encounters with this technology were basically terrifying, in that I didn't know what was going on. I got indoctrinated into some type of mind control program that was perpetrated on me. I was in the wrong place at the wrong time. It's amazing to me that this stuff is going on, and I know that it is frustrating to get people to wake up to this. I am a little nervous here. It runs a little deeper than just on a physical level of threat. I think a lot of this stuff is not just about suppressing our minds and will to resist the government. It's about getting our minds to the point to where we're so "droned down" that we have no chance of reconnecting with the source. I think this whole thing has to do with us on a soul level.

AC: That's right. That's what it's all about. It's the last great adventure to control the space between our ears and to eventually take over our souls. I also think that a lot of the people who have sold us out and are involved in this have no idea what the BIG picture is, because it is all so compartmentalized. This is a very demonic scenario that is going on here.

C: That is why I will spend the rest of my days trying to bring this to people's attention. My take on it is that if you don't make the cut when all of this comes to a climax, and they do achieve that ultimate control, your chances of reconnecting are delayed indefinitely.

AC: Well, you know, we have some beings that are waiting for people to ask, en masse, for help, and they are there, and they will help, but we have to ask for help, because they honor free will.

C: My previous experience was pretty nightmarish, but I did get through this, and my perspective on God is a gift.

DA: Alex, how do we get a hold of your book, "Pandora's Box"?

AC: You can write to PANDORA'S BOX, 2663 Valleydale Road, Suite 126, Birmingham, Alabama 35224. "Pandora's Box - Volume One" is $50 [$80 Overseas], and "Pandora's Box - Volume Two" is $35 [$65 Overseas]. The book called "The Cosmic Conflict" is $40 [$75 Overseas]. These are big books, with lots of information.

DA: Well, Alex, thank you for being here, and we'll have you back here again.

* * * *

TODD J. VS. THE GRAY EMPIRE:

(Recently a friend of mine related an unusual experience involving an abduction to an underground system southeast of Denver. I personally believe that his experience supports Alex Christopher's claim of a vast underground network under the D.I.A. area. This individual, Todd J., has experienced abductions by the Grays ever since he was a child. In later years he and a friend by the name of Mike traveled to Nevada to investigate Area 51, and while there witnessed an unusual orange object in the sky that they could not identify through conventional means. While staying in a motel room on the way back from their experience, Todd had the following experience - Branton):

"...I opened my eyes and saw someone standing beside the bed. A faint blue light surrounded the personage which appeared to be a gray colored 'man' with a big head and large black almond-shaped eyes. It reached out and GRABBED my hand and all of a sudden the room changed into some type of a laboratory with strange computers and screens. The alien spoke to me, and I sensed he was trying to 'show' affection towards me. He called me The chosen One. I expressed I have had it with you guys, I told you before to leave me alone, you are not good and can not make me believe you are good. The being explained that I was chosen as a Prophet and he spelled out on a paper a new name for me. I read the name and it said Enoch. I told him that God may have chosen me but not you, and not in this manner. You can not deceive me, I know what you are and what you are doing, and you have no right to take me from my bed at night against my will. The being replied, 'You do not realize what you are saying, we are also creations of God and are good. We shall show ourselves to the world soon and then you must decide what to do'. I got angry and commanded the alien in the name of Jesus Christ to take me back. All of a sudden the strange room was filled with a bright white light and I was taken into it. The next morning I awoke with a slight headache and a nose-bleed...

"Here is an experience I had with the underground...

"The most unusual abduction I have had so far occurred in May of 1993. I remember first being inside a UFO high above the earth, not remembering how I got there. I was standing on a circular silver pad with two grays beside me -- it reminded me of the teleporter room you see on Star Trek. I could not move and I noticed my hands were bound by some sort of metallic device. I saw the front of the room turn into a type of window and we were looking down over the earth, but I could not see any stars. The gray at the control panel was moving its hands back and forth but there did not seem to be any dials on the panels just holes and places to put their hands. The larger gray beside me held up his arms and we flew down to the earth at a great speed. We then appeared to be flying over a city, which reminded me of Denver. We flew south-east to a deserted area with some mounds and the ground opened up and the entire craft went down into the earth. We rapidly went through some type of tunnel and then finally came to a stop.

"A door opened to the left of us and a strange light poured into the craft. I noticed that above the door were some strange glyphs - like some form of altered Egyptian. I could move my legs and the larger gray directed me outside the craft with two smaller grays. We were in a very barren place full of dirt -- the sky appeared unusually orange and gray as if it was some type of artificial light. I saw a building with the initials MJ upon it and was greeted by three peculiar looking men dressed in black. The men told me that they were MJ 1, 2 and 3. I at that time did not know what it stood for. I was then turned about and taken down a cavern entrance until we came to some very huge ancient looking doors. The grays waved their arms and the doors opened.

"Inside was one of the most beautiful places I ever had seen. It was an underground city paved with marble and gold. There was abundant plant life and lots of water. I saw many people walking about dressed in white robes and they were all busy doing something. I was taken into a palace type building and we came to a throne.

"The throne turned around towards me and I was face to face with a strange looking man. It appeared to be half human -- half alien. It was quite huge, and was clothed in a crimson robe. Its eyes were large and black but had pupils. It had almost full lips and a nose. It wore a crown of some sort.

"It then spoke to me telepathically. 'Greetings Todd, The chosen one, we have awaited your arrival.' I inquired 'The chosen one? Chosen for what?' It explained that they had chosen me to join their people and that I was a prophet to lead them. They would give me great powers -- every power I had ever dreamed of -- I could fly, I could tell the future, I could heal the sick and travel through time. I got angry and said 'I am a servant of Jesus Christ and the only power I need is the priesthood of God. If I was meant to have the things of which you speak then God would show them to me in his due time. Now I ask for you to let me go -- you have no right to do this to me.' The being then said that God had made them also and that God had sent them to tell me these things. This made me even more upset, because it seemed they would have told me that in the first place if they were really from God. Instead they did not mention that until I said I was a servant of God. So I commanded them in the name of Jesus Christ to let me free. In which the being tapped the metal bands on my wrists and they flowed like mercury into the shape of a ball into his hand. He then bowed his head and told us to depart.

"The two small grays took us back to the entrance. I looked around one last time and the people were looking at me with confused faces and a bit of interest in me. Who ever they were I had a desire to HELP them and to know what they were doing here. But

THE DULCE PROTOCOL

I wanted to leave and as we were walking away back toward the cavern entrance one of the grays asked me if I was sure I was making the right decision. I affirmed I knew I was. I asked it if it knew Jesus Christ, and it seemed to be AFRAID of the word and affirmed he did NOT know him. I got angry and picked up the gray and threw it against a wall until it collapsed. I was about to try and turn back to the PEOPLE when I felt a buzz on my neck and everything went black. When I came to I was back in my bed..."

Todd's anger was apparently sparked as a result of the smaller Grey saying it did not know Jesus Christ / God when the large being had implied that they DID, and that they were operating under His orders. It would seem that deception was used here. This anger may also have been a response on Todd's part to years of violation by the Grays of his free agency. Some believe, and I tend to agree, that the Greys have to have some kind of 'open door' to manipulate a person's life. It may not necessarily be an 'invitation', but a 'crack' in the psyche that the Greys could exploit in order to get a person to open themselves up to their influence. The Greys are apparently determined to look for ANY loophole. The individual abductees themselves might be encouraged into capitulating their will over to the Greys through alien deception and trickery. However the 'open door' might also be -- as in the case of a child -- a result of a 'foothold' the aliens have established in the minds of a parent, a religious leader, or political leader in whom the child trusts... someone who HAS surrendered parts of their body, mind or spirit to the alien influence. For instance a parent might buy the lie that the Greys are benevolent 'space brothers', a religious leader could accept the lie that they are 'angelic beings', a politician might see them as an other-planetary political force that must be appeased and negotiated with at all costs, and so on. From these people, the influence might 'trickle down' to the children under their care. This would explain why generational abductions seem to be occurring in many families over many generations.

We must remember that alone however, a typical Gray is not nearly as intelligent as a human being. Their overall intelligence comes from the alien group or collective mind, since they operate as part of a 'hive' type of mentality. Some believe that this group-mind is, in turn, controlled by invisible entities associated with the fallen angelic factions which have since ancient times been incarnating through the reptilian races for the purpose of using these entities as physical 'channels' through which they are able to carry out their purposes in the physical domain. This may explain why the Grays have knowingly and blatantly lied to abductees and attacked traditional spiritual belief systems by making such claims as the following: "We genetically created the human race" [the result, we must acknowledge them as our 'gods']; or, "We created Jesus Christ" [this is interesting, especially when we consider that Jesus of Nazareth verbally blasted and condemned the 'serpent' race as being in league with Satanic forces, on more than one occasion]; and in the case of Todd's experience... that he was a "Chosen One". Thousands of abductees have been told that they are the supreme spokesperson for the aliens on earth, or specially chosen for some mission. In other words they gain their followers the same way Adolph Hitler did -- by stroking their egos: "YOU ARE THE MASTER RACE," etc., etc., ad nauseum. And it would seem that in the same way that many 'religious' leaders claim to be the SOLE spokesman for God on earth -- these contactees, abductees or mediums consider themselves to be the sole voice of the aliens. I would suggest that you do not respect any HUMAN who claims to be the 'sole spokesman' of God, not unless they are able to back up their claims by living a perfectly FLAWLESS life. All of this has contributed to the overall division and animosity which exists among various UFO research groups. Playing on human ego's is apparently a time-tested and very effective way for the Grays to gain the trust and cooperation of humans on, within or beyond the planet earth.

Following are additional experiences that were related by Todd J, beginning with an incident that occurred while he was still a child. While looking through UFO books in a school library in Sunbury, Pennsylvania, Todd experienced a disturbing flashback:

"...I came across a drawing of an alien made by a little boy who said he saw one in his back yard. It was the exact same thing I saw in [a] dream when I was little, it shocked me so much that I immediately closed the book and left the library. "Then it started to happen, at night I would always have a strange feeling of being watched while I slept. Sometimes the FEAR became so intense that I couldn't sleep, which would result in me sleeping-in the following morning and skipping school. Then the weird stuff started. I began to wake up at night and see balls of light floating around in the darkness and I couldn't move, so I just closed my eyes. Then one night I got up to go to the bathroom and for some reason I felt I needed to go look in my brother's room. When I looked in I saw that face in the window, the big black eyes, the round head and slanted chin. It freaked me out because we lived in a two story house. I ran to my room and hid under the blankets.

"The following nights I would pray about it and asked God to protect me. Then as I laid in bed after everyone was asleep I started to hear buzzing from outside the window. An extreme fear came over me and I couldn't move and I couldn't yell for my parents. An eerie green light started to fill my bedroom from outside and then I would somehow just wake up the next morning not remembering anything after the green light. I would usually have a severe headache, a sore throat, or feel extremely tired and drained of all my energy.

"After about three or four nights of this I knew it would probably happen again, and it did. This time I prepared myself... When the green light entered the room, my body was paralyzed. I tried to call upon Heavenly Father to cast it out of my room but I could not speak, my jaw was really tight. So I prayed in my head when all of a sudden I saw that the wood-grain on my bedroom door appeared to be forming into the face of man with a beard and long hair. I thought it was Jesus Christ. Then a bright white light came from above me and chased the green light away. As soon as this happened I had control of my body and I immediately pulled the covers over my head, I had no idea that God would actually do such a great thing. I then heard a voice which was so calm and loving saying to me 'You are safe now Todd, you may go back to sleep.' And I peeked through the blankets and saw a man in white clothes standing beside my bed. I was still a little frightened but I felt peace and that the terror was over...for now.

"...It was the Thanksgiving of 1992, my grandmother and uncle had come up for Thanksgiving dinner and to spend the day with us. During the day my grandmother started talking to me about aliens for some reason and I started telling her of the things I had seen when I was little.

"Then that night I remember being awaken by a noise, I first noticed that my computer monitor was reflecting a bright green light and then my whole room was filled with a bright green light. My first thought was, 'Oh no, they're back!' Then I again was paralyzed as it had happened to me when I was twelve. I was looking out my bedroom window and I stared face to face with a gray alien. There were two more behind him. I tried to yell but again my jaw was tight and my tongue was stiff. It just looked at me with those scary big black eyes liked it looked into my soul. I felt evil and fear, I am surprised I did not release my bowels! Then the light consumed me and I was drawn out of my bed into the light. While this was happening I was praying in my head and all of a sudden I was walking down the street in front of my house with an angel.

"This angel was a magnificent looking man. He was about seven feet tall and the bright white light around him was as pure as freshly fallen snow and it radiated about the entire front yard like a morning sunrise. His face was gentle and happy and his eyes looked at me lovingly. His whole countenance was just amazing beyond description.

"He placed his hand upon my shoulder and pointed toward the house. I looked over to my bedroom window and saw the three beings still at my window hovering above the ground in a bright green beam of light which seemed to be coming from nowhere. The angel stayed by my side and protected me. I tried to cast the small gray aliens away with my priesthood but they were still there (Todd at this time was a member of the Mormon religion, and tried to respond to these 'evil' creatures according to how he had been 'taught'. - Branton). I was so angry, the things that had made my life miserable since I was a child now there within my view, and I saw how weak they were, how small. And I thought 'These beings are so small, yet their power is enough to stop me in my tracks.'

"But this time I was FREE, this time I could harm them and I did. I ran to one and grabbed it by the neck and started to strangle it. I could feel its spine coming through the back of its neck as it let out a horrible screeching noise.

"They were not very tall, only about four feet high -- but they hovered in this light up to my height until they were next to my face. Their skin was like a reptile's, cold and leathery. Their damn eyes got to me the most... big black liquid eyes, just two holes for a nose and barely a mouth, just a slit. Their bodies were not very proportional as ours are. Their arms hung down a little past their knees, and their heads seemed too large for their neck to support it.

"The angel just stood by as I went into a rampage and killed all three of them. They were so fragile. The angel smiled as if I had done the right thing. And we then proceeded to lay the dead bodies on the lawn. I watched the green light fade away and saw no light except the brilliant radiance of the angel's. The angel knelt down at the bodies which seemed to be changing from gray into a sick yellowish color. I watched as the angel opened his robes and unsheathed a golden sword and began to cut away the tops of the beings' heads and their brains came out in an upper and lower section.

"The angel arose and spoke, 'Behold, they are nothing to us. They are nothing but creatures of evil.' Then a blue light or conduit from the sky actually transported them into small balls of light and took them away. So I have no evidence that I actually killed them. We, the angel and I then entered the house, and in the kitchen were three more aliens. One came up to me with a long shiny metal rod that seemed to have a laser beam coming out it. The alien stuck it in the left side of my neck and it stung really bad and then I could not move, so the angel touched me and I could move again. I then immediately punched the alien square in the face breaking its neck and killing it instantly. The other two stood by looking at their fallen comrade -- their moves were very quick and their heads rotated almost as fast as a lizard. The angel held up his arms and spoke. 'In the name of Jesus Christ I command you to depart.' Then both the creatures immediately fell to the floor and these gray aliens were again taken up into a beam of light in the same manner as before.

"Then the angel covered my eyes and then uncovered my eyes. I was all of a sudden on top of a large mountain looking down over a large valley FILLED with aliens and strange looking humans and their spacecraft. Then I saw hundreds of people dressed in white walking on the mountain with us as if they had come to watch. And then a voice from heaven said 'Behold, these evil ones have perverted the ways of the Lord and deceived many and fornicated with my children. They shall have no place in my kingdom nor in this world to come.' Then a FIRE came down from the sky and CONSUMED all the beings and all the strange human[oids] and all the UFOs and nothing was left. The angel then spoke saying I had seen enough and he again placed his hand over my eyes. I awoke from my bed and it was morning.

"Later in that year even in the same month I noticed a scar in the shape of a circle that I never had before. I couldn't recall how it got there but one day when my mom asked me how it got there I had a flashback of when the alien stuck that silver rod in my neck. Now I had proof that I've seen them!

"On this SAME NIGHT of November 22, 1992, there was a UFO crash on Long Island, New York which was supposedly shot down by the government with a plasma cannon. I have seen the pictures of the small gray alien captured at the crash site and it was exactly the same type that abducted me."

Note: All of this brings to mind the controversy over the 'material' aspects of UFO encounters vs. the 'supernatural' aspects. It would seem from the above, as well as from other sources, that the 'Greys' for instance are both physical as well as supernatural beings... or rather malevolent spirit-entities utilizing or possessing physical alien 'bodies'. In a sense you could say that the same holds true about humans themselves: we are physical-soular-spiritual beings, we possess 'blood plasma' which contains both physical AND spiritual essence -- which may be why the Greys are so interested in human 'blood' by the way.

Although traditional 'Greys' have a strong collective mentality in addition to a [gross] spiritual and physical nature, they have no 'soul'. Since supernatural forces play a major part in alien operations against humans on earth, humans must develop their SPIRITUAL defenses as well as their intellectual and physical defenses, since the Greys attack on all three levels of our beings through what might be described as a form of Psychotronic techno-sorcery.

One must be careful not to open oneself to their influences however. There is a growing number of quantum physicists who are beginning to realize that there is a 'spiritual' side to science. At the lowest sub-atomic levels the physical laws of 'logic' seem to break down into what might be referred to as 'etheric' or 'spiritual' laws that do not necessarily apply to physical laws, or what many spacefaring cultures refer to as 'Divine Geometrics' or the 'laws of spirit' at work behind the 'laws of physics'. So it is difficult to find where the electromagnetic realm ends and the etheric realm begins. This is the very basis of the OCCULT TECHNOLOGY that is being developed within the Dulce base, it is SUPERNATURAL TECHNOLOGY, a deadly form of Techno-Sorcery. This who attempt to resist the Greys will soon discover that the conflict they have become involved with is not just a spiritual one, and not just a physical one, but a warfare that is in fact a FUSION of material and spiritual realities.

Most people do not realize that our modern 'science' has largely developed from the occult-sciences of the past, or the 'Alchemists'. So who can say exactly where science ends and the supernatural begins? Apparently at least with much of the UFO phenomena, the exact distinction may be very hard to find. Does this mean that technology and the supernatural are 'evil'? Not necessarily, for the physical 'forces' of the universe and the supernatural 'forces' of the universe can be used by our physical and spiritual natures respectively for either good or evil. Being that we are of a spiritual-psychic-physical nature, we as humans possess abilities that we can not begin to understand. In this cosmic battle there are no 'neutral' forces. In other words we can NOT utilize these spiritual-psychic-physical abilities in a 'neutral' way or believe that we are in ultimate control of these abilities ourselves, since there are intelligence's which are so powerful in this universe that to them we appear as mere 'pawns' who can be manipulated for their own use. The important thing is not for the pawn to 'realize its own pawnhood', but for each of us to consider which 'player' has our best interests at heart. I definitely believe that one of the 'players' is much more benevolent than anything we can imagine, and the other is far more malevolent than anything we can conceive. I believe that we must DECIDE which side of the cosmic battle we will serve, and this all comes back to the old fundamental reality that we have known all along: will we commit our spiritual-psychic-physical abilities to 'God' [good] or to the 'Devil' [evil]? To the Almighty, who desires to establish a universe of perfect harmony, order, truth and love; or to the collective rebel angels and their alien 'puppets' who desire only to devour and consume everything around them like the 'spiritual black holes' that they are?

Robert K Teske

There are more and more reports coming my way, like the one that appears above, which strongly suggest that in spite of the physical and tangible aspects of many of the aliens [Greys, Reptiloids, etc.], the true powers that must be contested are the motivating supernatural entities which possess and incarnate many if not most of these soulless 'aliens', simply because at some point in the past these 'aliens' themselves submitted to the complete control of these supernatural beings. They rejected the universal law of respecting the Divinely-established sovereignty of other beings, whether on an inter-planetary, inter-national or inter-personal basis. In violating the sovereignty of others they themselves lost their own personal sovereignty, liberty or independence. They chose to ally themselves with members of a collective 'hive' mind which assured them that it was right to violate the sovereignty of other beings, and that it was logical for the 'collective' to assimilate all things under its control even if the individuality of those assimilated was all but destroyed. So in joining with a force which advocated the conquest of other 'sovereignties', they in turn forfeited their own.

Will our human race be the next race to be 'assimilated' by these astral parasites and the corrupted physical alien races under their control? I believe the decision is entirely and individually up to us.

Chapter 34

A Closing Message To The People Of Earth -- From An Agent Of The Federation

I've thought about an eloquent way to end this volume with a flourish of cosmic wisdom that would bring the entire contents of this work into perspective and balance, an ending that would be worthy of all of those brave truth-seekers who have so generously contributed to this project.

Having failed to do this, I will gladly give this opportunity to one who should know, more than anyone else, just exactly what we as a planet are going through in our struggle for freedom from interventionist oppression.

The following appeared in Val Valerian's MATRIX II work, and although I've made some interjections throughout, I would ask that you pay special attention to the words of a certain 'Nordic', born among the stars, who can fully sympathize with our plight here on earth.

But first, some words of introduction from Val Valerian:

THE GRAYS, THE NORDICS, AND INTERSTELLAR CONFLICT:

The first type [of Gray] is the short gray humanoids with the large heads, which resemble embryos and average about four and a half feet in height. They are from a solar system that revolves around Rigel. Rigel is a double bluish-white star on the left foot of Orion...

It is this type of humanoid that is performing most of the animal mutilations and human mutilations, which has made a secret deal with our government, and which was in contact with Hitler [Nazis]. They derive nourishment from the glandular secretions and the enzymes they extract from the animals they mutilate, which they absorb through their pores. Our 'government' permits such activities partially because of its acute fear of these beings, and partially because it is under the delusion that they will give us technical information enabling us to attain military superiority over the Russians in exchange for our permitting the mutilations and abductions.

The Stealth Bomber and Star Wars technologies are being obtained from them. However, our government does not appear to realize that when it comes to the crunch the technology they are transmitting will not work as it is supposed to (Note: More advanced technologies have been obtained via crash-retrievals, an aspect that the aliens may have underestimated. - Branton). It is not in their interest to give us decisive military superiority over the Russians, or vice versa. It is in their interest to keep us in a state of unresolved conflict with each other, the old game of divide and conquer...

Working under the instructions of the humanoids from Rigel, CIA and former NAZI scientists have developed and deployed malignant strains of bacteria and viruses, including AIDS. The rationale from the fascist point of view is to exterminate portions of the population considered to be undesirable. The rationale from the Rigelian point of view is to decimate the human population to such an extent that the survivors would accept [not resist] open control by the Rigelians...

The humanoids that have been nick-named 'Swedes' are on the average between six and six and a half feet tall. They [some] are from a solar system that revolves around Procyon, a binary yellow-white and yellow star system that rises before Sirius in Canis Minor [in the body of the Lesser Dog], about 11.4 light years from Earth. They are from the fourth planet in orbit around the Procyon double star system. The tall blond humanoids from Procyon and the short gray humanoids from Rigel have been enemies for thousands of years.

The tall Blonds from Procyon have a benign attitude toward humanity, except for their strong disapproval of our inhumanity to each other. This strong disapproval is further intensified by our government having made a secret alliance with their hereditary enemies, in order to obtain even more destructive weapons systems than those already in existence. Our 'government' is not interested in negotiating with the Procyonians, as they would not provide us with weapon systems...

Their motivation for breeding with humans is to tune-up the frequency of our species, in order to help us to help ourselves. Their concern is for the well-being of all forms of life, not just humanity. The entire biosphere will benefit if we fulfill our positive potential, instead of self-destructing our planet's biosphere in the process.

It would be a mistake to count on them to clean up the mess we have made of our polluted planet, or to bring peace by dismantling our nuclear weapons. It is up to us to solve the problems that we have ourselves created...

In order to extricate ourselves from the covert alliance the CIA (and their Nazi SS predecessors. - Branton) had made with Rigel, without our knowledge or consent, we must first regain control of our government...

Valerian then quotes the following words of one Procyonese star-traveler by the name of KHYLA, who revealed the following to an un-named earth woman with whom he had established contact:

"...Tyrants have been defeated many times on many planets, in countless solar systems and galaxies. How strange it is that as soon as one tyrant of any species is thought to be banished forever another always, but ALWAYS, takes his place. The idealistic revolutionaries who defeated King George III in America went on to oppress the Indians and Blacks. Many of those who fought most courageously against the Axis powers of fascism later became fascists themselves, as is demonstrated by the present plight of the Palestinians, Afghans, Chileans and Nicaraguans. Yes, you must try to regain control of your government, but if so much as one individual involved in this process has not first gained control of his or her selfhood, it will be for naught. One can never defeat or gain control of anything but oneself. Those destined to ouste the Rigelians must always keep track of the state of their selfhood, and learn first to defeat within themselves the essence of that which is tyranny. Through this type of awareness, they will know when to and when not to act. Through understanding a hostile entity to be but one of the ineffable countless facades, it loses its power over you. Through the ability to wisely perceive a hostile entity, you may gain control of it. In overcoming the Rigelians, one must take great precautions not to become oneself the enemy."

Or, as the old Chinese proverb says:

"BEWARE WHEN FIGHTING A DRAGON THAT YOU DO NOT BECOME ONE!"

Khyla, the Procyon Intelligence agent, continues:

"If you were a highly advanced culture about to invade a relatively primitive culture, you would not do it with a flourish of ships showing up in the heavens, and take the risk of being fired upon. That's the type of warfare less evolved mortals would get into. You would begin by creating intense confusion, with only inferences of your presence, inferences which cause controversial disagreement (Note: It is interesting that the major Intelligence projects designed to discredit UFO witnesses and cause confusion and contention among -- and infiltration of -- various UFO research organizations have been traced back to the Nazified NSA-CIA, which in turn maintains, as this is being written, continued ties with the Grays. - Branton).

"You would go to the most secret and powerful organizations within the society. In the case of the United States, you would infiltrate the CIA, and through the use of techniques unknown to them, you would take over some of the key people in their innermost core group. You would proceed in the same fashion to take over key members of the KGB. You would also create great dissension among the public at large, some individuals and groups insisting that they have seen UFOs, others insisting with equal vehemence that such a thing is not possible, and that they are either liars or deluded.

"You would involve the planet's two major nations in an on-going idiotic philosophical dispute, keeping them constantly at each other's throats over such questions as whether Thomas Jefferson was greater than Karl Marx or vice-versa (that is, whether 'Capitalist' tyranny or 'Communist' tyranny is worse than the other. By the way, don't confuse Communism with Communalism, and don't confuse Capitalism with Democracy. Communalism and Democracy are sovereigntist movements that respect the personal rights and freedoms of others. So-called unrestrained Communism and Capitalism are co-dependent collectivist evils. Capitalist tyranny created Communist tyranny, and Communist tyranny justifies its existence as a force to fight Capitalist tyranny. Insane world we live in, is it not? - Branton). You would keep them continuously occupied with quarreling like two adolescent boys trying to prove their masculinity over who has which piece of territory, whether one has the right to invade Afghanistan or the other has the right to invade Nicaragua, persistently exchanging threats and insults like a couple of macho teen-agers, while arguing whether one should dismantle one type of nuclear warhead, or the other should dismantle another type of nuclear warhead. As you watched all this, you would sit back and you would laugh, if you had the capacity to laugh...

"You would occasionally let your ships be seen by some of the ordinary citizens, so that the elite governmental groups would become involved in attempts to keep them quiet, clumsily squelching attempts to make information about UFO activity public. This would result in the mass population losing confidence in the veracity of their elected officials. There would be constant arguments between the authorities and the public as to whether or not the persistently reported phenomena genuinely existed, thereby setting the population and the government at each other's throats. You would have already set the two major super-powers at each other's throats. By subtly causing economic turmoil, you would set the "Haves" and the "Have Nots" at each other's throats. In all possible ways, you would plant the seeds of massive discontent.

Robert K Teske

"After you had manipulated the population to the point where your covert control over it was complete, you might decide to go overt, and let a few ships land in public. But you would not go from covert to overt until you were sure of the totality of your control...

Those who have experienced UFO sightings or ET close encounters will constantly be at odds with the government, which will continue to retaliate by stigmatizing them as liars or deluded... The impoverished will become even more impoverished, and more filled to overflowing with explosively righteous anger. The wealthy will cling even more greedily to the wealth that they already have, creating a social atmosphere of sheer desperation and complete confusion. To add to that, there will be series after series of 'natural' disasters, some genuinely natural, some human-induced through aberrant scientific activities such as underground nuclear testing, others deliberately induced by the Grays through the (Scalar-type? - Branton) technology they are in possession of. When approximately three-quarters of the planet's population has been eliminated in this fashion, the Grays can then make an overt appearance as saviors from the skies, distributing food and medicine to the survivors. As the survivors line up to receive their quotas of food and medicine, implants will be inserted, supposedly to aid in further food distribution, actually to guarantee complete Gray control with no possibility of rebellion (Note: Electronic chip implants have already been developed. These operate on bodily temperature changes and it is interesting that the part of the body which experiences the greatest ranges of temperature change are the forehead and the hands, which is interesting when compared to the prophecies in the 13th chapter of the book of Revelation. These chips will not only serve to control individuals, but will also be able to track their every movement by satellite. One individual who worked on such a chip stated that the implant would decay after a certain period of time, at which point a poisonous virus would be released into the bloodstream of those who had received it, eventually killing the person and effecting a type of automatic "population control" for the electronically-controlled society. - Branton). From the point of view of the Grays, terrestrial humanity will have been reduced to manageable numbers and to eternal submission.

THE DULCE PROTOCOL

"Humanity is not about to be invaded. Humanity is not in the middle of an invasion. Humanity has been invaded! The invasion has taken place, and is NEARLY in its final stages. Great invasions do not happen with thundering smoke and nuclear weaponry. That is the mark of an immature society. Great invasions happen in secrecy.

"You throw a crumb out here and there. You bribe the U.S. government with a few tidbits -- a Stealth bomber, a Star Wars system. You encourage the government to think that the UFO researchers indeed threaten the security of this great secret they have. You tempt and tease the Soviet Union with a laser system far finer than any their own scientists could think of. And you always keep that subtle inference just on the borderline of consciousness that the elusive will-of-the-wisps termed UFOs may in fact exist, yet you persistently repress this borderline perception, and make it seem so insane that there is a social stigma attached to declaring one's conviction that the phenomena are in fact real.

"While all this confusion is going on, the Grays are gradually changing you over. The inner core of the CIA is deeply controlled by the Grays. The CIA see the Grays as a path to greater scientific achievement, as a way of overpowering the Soviet enemy (Note: since the overt breakup of the Soviet Union, the Grays may provoke a new "Cold War" with another Superpower, possibly China? It has also been suggested that the 'Bavarians' engineered the dissolution of the Soviet Empire because at the time their agenda called for a merger of the East and West into a Bavarian-backed New World Order. In other words for this to occur Russia had to become less 'Communist' and America had to become less 'Capitalist' so that they could both merge somewhere within the realm of "Democratic Socialism", with more than a little 'help' from the UNO or United Nations Organization. - Branton). Surprisingly enough, the obtuse collective mentality type that makes up the bulk of the CIA also makes up the bulk of the more fanatical Star People, those who babble and mush and gush so endlessly. All those who have to cleave to or be fused with some form of group mentality (most notably, the 'Ashtar' collective, much of which according to contactee Israel Norkin has been infiltrated and taken over by the "Unholy Six" star systems of Orion - Branton) leave themselves wide open. They have already been taken over. There is a large and ever-growing cult of contactees who think of the Grays as liberators, sincerely believing them to be heavenly Star Brothers who have come to help humanity (Note: One common brand of 'intellectual defecation' that the Grays have been spewing forth through their human 'channels' is that the Grays are really the "good guys", and that they have been 'conquered' and exploited by the taller Reptiloids and therefore are working with the secret government in an attempt to throw off the yoke of their oppressors. Any one who is at all familiar with 'Gray' mentality should know that they are WILLFULLY working WITH the taller Reptiloids, and that they are reprobate LIARS who have no conscience whatever when it comes to using multi-leveled deceptions to get their way. Unfortunately many metaphysical-minded "gray huggers" are accepting these lies and others like them. Other lies that have originated from the Grays include: * We are the genetic creations of the Grays, so we must submit to our 'creators'; * Jesus Christ was a genetic creation of the Grays -- interesting, in that Jesus blasted the serpent race in more than one instance; * The Grays are a superior race -- they may be superior intellectually, however they have no internal or eternal soul-matrix as do humans, and so from a spiritual perspective they are inferior, in essence being little more than 'predators with brains'. - Branton).

"The reason the awful little Grays mutilate animals is the stuff that they eat. They eat pulverized hormonic secretions, what you would call subtle essences. They live on the stuff of life. There is something deathlike about their species. They always bring about the death of animation, the death of individuality.

"How to I know? I am a Blond from Procyon. We were a culture that could travel through time (that is, phase through various time-space dimensions or densities where the 'flow' of time and 'frequency' space are different from the time-space dimensions of the 3rd dimension. - Branton), but also lived on a planetary sphere. And the little Grays, our insidious little 'friends', did to us exactly what they are doing now to you. This is what happened to our planet.

"Having come in war, but having been unable to obtain any decisive victory, the Grays expressed the desire to make peace. We had not wanted to fight with the 'survivors' of the Rigelian Great War to begin with, and gladly accepted their offer. As time went by, they said they wished to normalize relations and be our friends. We were in doubt as to whether it would be safe to trust them, and debated the issue for a long time before finally deciding that we should trust them...

"The Grays began to visit us, first a few as ambassadors, then as specialists in various domains where their expertise could be useful to us, as participants in different programs that developed which involved mutual collaboration, and finally as 'tourists'. What had begun as a trickle became a flood, as they came in ever-increasing numbers, slowly but surely infiltrating our society at all levels, penetrating even the most secret of our elite power groups...

"Just as on your planet they began by unobtrusively gaining control over key members of the CIA and KGB through techniques unknown to them, such as hypnosis... so on Procyon through the same techniques, whose existence we were not aware of either, from the start they established a kind of telepathic hypnotic control over our leaders. Over our leaders and over almost all of us, because it was as if we were under a spell that was leading us to our doom, as if we were being programmed by a type of ritual black magic that we did not realize existed.

"Just as a few of the original tall Blonds clandestinely left Rigel when the Great War was about to break out, so did a few of the original tall Blonds clandestinely leave Procyon and escaped into the corridors of time just before the Grays completed the slow undermining that culminated in their sudden take-over of Procyon. Those who stayed behind came under the total domination of the Grays.

"The Blonds you see on the same ships as the Grays, working with them, are hybrids, or they are clones. One way to distinguish the clones is that they look alike. The real Blonds have distinct facial feature differences, and do not look alike. The clones have thick necks and coarsely muscular bodies. They do not have the ability to teleport or to travel interdimensionally. They can be contacted by telepathy, but are unable to send. They can be given orders telepathically. They are zombie-like flesh robots. You can tell that they are of low intelligence by looking into their eyes.

"The real Blonds are also muscular, but have slender necks and agile bodies. Their eyes are alert and of high intelligence. Physically they are almost identical to humans, the main difference being that by human standards their blood circulatory system is under-developed, while their lymphatic system is over-developed. This gives them stronger immune systems than terrestrial humans.

"The hybrids are in an intermediate state between the real Blonds and the clones.

"After what has happened to Procyon, NO TRUE BLOND would collaborate voluntarily with the Grays. The Grays have taken some prisoners of war, who have no choice in the matter, and are forced to work with them in order to survive, with the hope of escaping. There are also a few Blonds who have become degenerate renegades, space pirates and mercenaries who sell their services to the highest bidder. But many of us remain free, and continue the fight to the finish with the life-form that has become our hereditary enemy. We choose to remain in exile in the corridors of time, where they can not reach us, rather than to live under the domination of the insidious Grays. It is dangerous for us to venture forth from the corridors of time, but occasionally we do so for a hit-and-run strike, similar in nature to a cosmic version of terrestrial guerrilla warfare.

"We must periodically enter a substantial physical form for a period of repose, or to breed progeny, in order to continue to survive, but otherwise we constantly travel the vast corridors of time. That is why we may appear to fade in and out like holographic images to human perception. What I have come here to communicate, if only to one or two people or a small group, is that what is now in the process of happening to your culture, also happened to ours. It is the same fate our own culture suffered. And the Blonds you see with the Grays are either hybrids, clones, or prisoners of war. Because no true Blond who got out untouched, unscathed, uncrossed with those Grays would ever be with them. He or she would prefer to be in a state of non-existence.

"Besides the Blonds and the Grays, ships from many other space cultures are watching planet Earth at this time with extreme interest. Scientists from other space cultures are studying what is going on here during this decisive period of your history. If your elected representatives had not so stupidly made a deal with the only aliens willing to provide them with weapons systems, with the short-sighted goal of overpowering the

THE DULCE PROTOCOL

Russians, the Grays would not have achieved their present dominance, and you would now be exchanging ambassadors with a wide variety of space cultures.

"What I want to get across to you is that the ultimate evil, which underlies all the negativity in the cosmos, finds expression in that masked form of psychological complacency which leads an individual to adhere to a group philosophy rather than to think things through for oneself! Those who feel safe and comfortable in no matter what belief system merely because many others adhere to it, who get together and form an arrogant self-righteous group convinced it has a monopoly on the truth, and those who are ready to persecute, kill or stifle anyone who challenges that group's philosophy, have formed an alliance with the ultimate evil, whether they know it or not. It is the self-righteousness and implacability of certain elite power groups like the CIA and the KGB, certain organized religions, and certain so-called lunatic fringe groups such as some of the more fanatical Star People, which are so objectionable...

"I have seen civilizations rise and fall, begin again only to die again, over and over and over. It isn't only a problem of this planet. It's a problem that must be faced by all civilizations in the course of their development, no matter where they may be located in the cosmos. Everyone wants that slightly larger piece of the pie than their neighbor for themselves, and eventually this tendency always culminates in choking them. Sooner or later this will be the undoing of the Grays as well, thereby enabling us to return in triumph from our exile in the corridors of time. The Grays do not see and are incapable of understanding their own fundamental error: that the very weakness they seize upon in humanity is their own inherent weakness, the blind spot that inevitably seals their doom...

"The only way to victory is through the strength of your consciousness. When genetic or other manipulations are being performed on abductees, the Grays expect them to cringe in fear, and derive a second-hand high from the intensity of the emotions expressed. If instead of cringing in fear, an abductee can put his or her mind elsewhere, focusing attention on dynamic protective imagery of a religious or mystical nature, it decreases the gratification that the Grays are getting from their second-hand high, and it confuses them. Center the consciousness on something so different from what they expect that it puzzles them.

Robert K Teske

(Note: In most cases the image of an empty red or crimson CROSS seems to be especially debilitating to the Grays. For instance the legendary soldier-saint, St. George, reputedly wore a shield with a red cross emblazoned on a white background. Whether one believes that the dragon slayers existed or not, the legend itself claims that the Christian dragon-slayers of Europe more-or-less marked the end of the dragon race's infestation of the old world. One such legend concerned the city of Silene, Libya which had been plagued by a draconian beast for a long period of time. The king of the city had offered up sheep and livestock in an effort to appease the beast. However the time came when all the livestock had been used up, and this was when human sacrifices were chosen, by lot, to appease the fearsome beast. One day the lot fell on the king's own daughter, and the grieved king, honoring his word, allowed her to be taken and tied to the post outside of the city gates. As the beast was about to pounce upon the princess, so the story goes, Saint George appeared in shining silver armor and -- before the beast knew what was happening -- the soldier-saint had pierced it through with his lance and rescued the princess, who later became his wife. Whether or not such legends have any basis in reality, the story nevertheless symbolizes the unconscious animosity between 'Saints' and 'Serpents'. If we are to believe the legends, then this was only one of the many 'vermin' -- as they were referred to in those ancient times -- which St. George had vanquished during his life, and although not the only dragon-slayer of legend, he was perhaps the most renowned. - Branton)...

"The only reason the Grays have such a degree of dominance over you is because your elected officials stupidly made clandestine agreements with them, binding you to them in an exclusive alliance that is respected by other space races, allowing them to install themselves in underground bases impregnable to your weaponry, a situation you must now find a way to extricate yourselves from (Note: In that the Grays have repeatedly violated these treaties, they should legally be considered null and void. In fact since the Executive branch of U.S. government was taken over by a fascist CIA coup d'état in 1963 at the time of the John F. Kennedy assassination -- AS WERE the governments of several other countries throughout the world where CIA backed military coups resulted in the establishment of fascist puppet dictatorships -- should we not consider the Executive branch of government which made the 'treaties' with the Greys, to be null and void as well? It certainly was not Congress who authorized such 'treaties'. - Branton)

"In antiquity this planet was divided into sectors between four different groups: Blonds, Grays, large lizard-like beings [now connected with] the Capella system, and beings [now connected with] the Arcturus system. These groups still consider themselves to be the owners of this planet. They do not recognize the human claim to ownership. However, some of us do recognize human rights, as well as the rights of other life-forms...

"The Grays are having problems not only within their own ranks, but also on other planets they have colonized. As a species they are afflicted with severe, perhaps terminal, health problems (a weakness that can and should be exploited. - Branton). They have substantial captive populations of Blond, human and other prisoners of war, eager to join a revolt at the slightest opportunity...

"One must be rational in attempting to fight back, and understand the proper way to proceed. Your own consciousness is the most potent weapon that is available to you at the present time. The most effective way to fight the Grays is to change the level of your consciousness from linear thinking to multi-dimensional awareness. Your secret weapon, your ace in the hole, is that you are not hive-minded collective thinkers, though many of you do fall into that category by conforming to conventional group-patterns, and are therefore easily controlled by the Grays. It is your INDIVIDUALITY which is your best weapon, because it is the one weapon you have that the Grays do not have. The major weakness of the Grays, their area of vulnerability, their Achilles heel, is their inability to think as individuals. They are an extremely telepathic high-tech society, but as individuals they are not creative thinkers. They take orders well, but they do not conceptualize well. They have the technology to throw your planet out of orbit, but there is one key ability that you have and they do not have: the ability to hold in mind imagery that inspires an individual to realize his or her direct personal connection to the source of ALL THAT IS, which is the ineffable Godhead, no matter what name you may call it. That is your key to victory..."

AND FINALLY, A MESSAGE FROM THE HYBRID COUNCIL -- THE 'REAL' INSPIRATION BEHIND THIS VOLUME:

It would be a grave error to give myself full credit for this volume, as I can state for absolute fact that most of the work on this volume was carried out by 'others' who -- operating through my unconscious mind -- inspired me intuitively with the information, and led me to the sources and documentation, which were necessary for the completion of this book, which I consider a major challenge especially in spite of my own personal shortcomings.

This "backup team", you might say, consists of a number of so-called 'hybrids' or 'hu-brids' who have broken free from the draconian collective and established their own resistance movement based mainly within the underground systems of this planet -- at least in the case of those 'family members' or 'relatives' of mine 'beyond' this world who have inspired me with this work. Although they dwell within the cavernous recesses of this planet, they nevertheless interact with other worlds within the 'Federation' who oppose the activities of the Draconian-Orion-Reticulan 'collectivists'. They are constantly working to establish freedom and truth here on [and under] planet earth.

Since the hybrids/hubrids 'communicate' with me on the intuitive level rather than through audible or visual communication, I will attempt to 'translate' their often strong impressions into 'words' and convey what I believe they would have the readers to know and understand about themselves and their feelings towards us.

So here then is what I strongly feel, and believe, that these wonderful 'people' would 'say' to us:

Greetings friends;

Or should we say brothers and sisters? For indeed we are your brothers, your sisters, and your children! Many of those who have had encounters with the 'Greys' will understand exactly what we mean.

We are the children of your 'seed', and although our DNA has been altered we nevertheless possess souls, and this makes us just as 'human' as you.

THE DULCE PROTOCOL

Unlike our erstwhile masters who are lacking what you call 'soul', many of us 'hybrids' -- realizing our foundational humanity -- began to develop emotional individuality.

There are apparently several reasons why the Greys began the 'hybrid' projects. Some projects were to breed stronger beings to serve their collective empire, others to breed 'Greys' with human characteristics and specialized psionic abilities who could be used to understand humans on their own level and who could in turn teach the Greys how to more easily manipulate humans on various levels.

The Grey collective apparently did not take into account that there would be -- by the Grace of God -- so much resistance among our kind to their plans. You see, they could not fully understand the concept of individuality, compassion and loyalty to one's own kind.

We speak of the 'collective' here and not of the individual 'Greys', for when it comes down to it, there are no individuals among the reptilian collective... all serve as individual 'cells' within a vast organism -- the collective intellect or 'Hive' you might say.

But those of us who have developed free-agency and have broken free from the 'Hive' HAVE developed human individuality. It is a long and difficult process to 'wean' ourselves entirely from the collectivist mindset that many of us were born into. We maintain a limited degree of collectivity; however have established what you might refer to as a 'firewall' between our society and that of the draconian 'hive' itself. This is largely for the sake of other Hubrids who are joining us from time to time, and is necessary for the process of 'deprogramming' them from a mentality of collectivism and the continual development of their individuality.

We cannot say that it is the 'individual' Greys and Reptiloids who are the source of the 'evils' which are committed against humans throughout the universe by the 'Draconian collective'... for as we have stated, there are no 'individuals' within the collective itself, save for the malevolent beings who are its ultimate masters. Those supernatural beings who control the draconian collective ARE the sources of the evils -- the Greys and Reptiloids are merely the 'tools'. This is true in most cases except in the context that many of the rebel beings who you call 'fallen angels' have been incarnating through the soulless reptilian races since very ancient times.

Although we must see things as they really are, we realize that many of these supernatural beings have corrupted themselves to the point where there is no more hope for them to return to the good side, having annihilated any and all goodness within them. However we would like to believe and hope that some of these rebel beings regret their present state and the part they played in the ancient rebellions against the Almighty One. We would like to believe that one of the underlying motives for the reptiloids/greys and their breeding a race like ours would be for the purpose of raising up a race genetically akin to their own kind, yet not their own kind, who could understand where both the human and reptilian species are coming from.

Could it be that a faint spark of individuality and concern within the legions who compose the collective somehow influenced the 'hybrid' projects, could it be that somewhere deep within the collective there existed and exists a desire to break free into individual consciousness and in so doing break free from those supernatural tyrants who control the collective with a supernatural iron fist?

Could it be that these intelligence's within the collective saw that the 'logical' thing to do would be for the Greys and their collective to work in harmony with the universe rather than against it? For the sake of their own survival? After all, they ARE 'logical' beings, and many of the directives that have come down from the central command of the collective have contradicted 'logic' and contributed to a kind of pervasive confusion and even self-contradicting schizophrenia if not insanity within the collective.

Being that these intelligence's did not have the power to develop individual consciousness of their own initiative in the face of the overwhelming tide of the collective and its twisted leaders, they understood that if they did succeed in breeding offspring that possessed natural individuality and emotionalism then these offspring might in turn break free from the collective, and once having broken free, help others of their kind who do not possess the self-motivation to do so. Once these were 'tamed' and 'deprogrammed' and placed in an environment where free-agency could develop, these 'aliens' could then be given a choice to decide which side they will serve -- whether they will remain with us or return to the collective and lose their individuality in the process.

Knowing full well the dangers of a 'collective' system where no individual expression is allowed, we have come to develop a deep and abiding respect for the sacredness of free agency, even to the point of allowing other beings to 'choose' to destroy themselves if they are fully intent on doing so. We have also come to deeply respect the non-interference directives of our dear friends of the Federation worlds.

Ours is a continual struggle, and we are not too proud to say that our ultimate victory or defeat depends largely on YOU.

Every time YOU give-in to the will of the draconian collective, every time you believe one of the lies of a 'Grey' that is under the control of the 'Hive', every time you trade a little piece of you're soul for the supposed 'benefits' that the collective will tell you are yours IF you serve them... every time you do this you weaken yourselves and capitulate you're power to the enemy. In so doing, you make our struggle all the more desperate.

On the other hand every time you CHALLENGE the claims of the collective and expose their lies and refuse to allow them to manipulate you into their agendas, then you strengthen us in the process. Remember that we are truly YOUR CHILDREN, because the majority of us within the 'resistance' are more human than beast [reptilian, insectilian or what have you]. Those genetic hybrids that do not possess a soul are rare among us because they find it very difficult to comprehend those individual virtues which come naturally [or should come naturally] to those possessing a human soul-chakra matrix and a 'conscience'.

Above and beyond anything else, we would ask that you PRAY to our ultimate Creator -- as best you understand the concept of 'God'. Ask the all-knowing and all-loving one to be merciful. Plead for us -- your brothers and sisters and children who live within, parallel to, and out among the stars, beyond this planet earth. Please PRAY for us and also for the many others of our kind and your kind who are presently the captives of the soulless entities serving the collective. Since physical and intellectual defenses are not sufficient, being that we are also battling supernatural evils, we NEED the Divine Intervention of God and his holy 'standing' angels. Since the draconian collective attacks you and also us on the physical, psychic and spiritual levels -- we cannot neglect the spiritual aspects of this conflict.

With this, we of the Hybrid council wish you all the best. May we -- all of us -- do all that we can to bring about a future that will be everything we had hoped for, and MORE. To our 'parents' out there. You know who you are. Those of us who have separated ourselves from the controllers and also those who still remain in their grasp... we send you our LOVE and our HUGS!!! We remember and cherish every hug and warm touch that you have given us during those times in the night when you have been brought to us. Those times, whether you remember them consciously or not, when you have shared with us your feelings, your love, and in some cases your fears, and have shown us what being human is really all about. We want to say, WE LOVE YOU!!! Pray for us as we pray for you.

Until that time when we can all meet together as one, in TRUE freedom and peace, may the Almighty SOURCE of all LIFE protect and bless you all!

THE DULCE PROTOCOL

MARTYRS OF THE UNDERGROUND RESISTANCE

By B. Alan Walton

PHIL SCHNEIDER- Phil was hired by the Secret government as an explosives and excavation engineer for the underground bases of the New World Order, at one point having been involved in one of the many firefights between human and alien forces within the Dulce, Mew Mexico base complex.

After exposing---during a series of lectures--the alien infiltration of over 120 New World Order bases (such as the Dulce base in New Mexico, the Groom Lake Base (Area 51) in Nevada and one beneath the new Denver International Airport (to be used as a transfer center to underground concentration camps in times of chaos), and in addition to revealing a conspiracy to fit rail boxcars with literally millions of shackles, Phil Schneider was murdered, set up to make it look like a suicide. Who was responsible? Agents of the secret government. Even though there was evidence of foul play---having been strangled to death by piano wire---the "official" conclusion was "suicide".

THOMAS E CASTELLO- Castello was a security guard in the underground mega-base beneath Dulce, New Mexico. After he and other "employees" of the organization had learned of the existence of vast underground "concentration" camps and "cryogenic" facilities in the deeper levels where thousands upon thousands of "abductees" from this and other worlds were being held (tortured, used for genetic experiments or as sources for the "liquid protein vats" which feed the winged white Dracos, the tall green

Dracos, and the short gray Dracos), Castello---after many of the human and alien members of the "resistance" had died or disappeared in the "Dulce Wars"--decided to defect.

He left the base with damning evidence of illegal treaties with alien forces (the three types of dracs mentioned above, the Germanic "Aryans", the reptilian-human-synthetic tribreds, known as "The Orange:, and others . ..), some of them signed by Reagan and other U.S. presidents who made their secret "covenant with death" to turn over the planet to the Draco collective in exchange for certain favors for the Masonic elite.

When Castello arrived home, a "government" van (secret alien-corporate-military-executive government" that is not the representative "congressional" government) was waiting for him, with agents who informed him that his wife and son had been abducted and would not be returned unless Castello turned over the artifacts that he removed form the base.

Castello escaped, never seeing his family again, being a fugitive for several years, until at last report from his co-researcher, Jason Bishop, he was 'rumored' to have died in Costa Rica.

STACY BORLAND- Borland, a researcher who inspired John Grace (AKA Val Valerian) on his path which led to the establishment of the Leading Edge Research Group, had also been working with employees of Reynolds Electric Corp., who has exposed the fact---over the Billy Goodman Radio Talk Show---that several of their co-workers were being held captive in an underground base below the Mercury Test site in Nevada, after having stumbled across a conspiracy involving an alien (reptilian) takeover of U.S. underground installations.

This was also confirmed by a former Wackenhut employee, Michael Riconosciuto, who implied that the entire underground system, linking Nellis AFB, on the outskirts of Las Vegas, with Edwards AFB in California, was no longer under human control, and that many who had learned too much either turned up missing or dead, just like the 5 test site employees whose chopper was shot down as they were trying to leave the base with an aircraft packed with damning evidence on antigravity, genetic and underground base atrocities.

Borland was attempting to expose this conspiracy and help the "Mercury workers" in their desperate struggle. Shortly afterwards, Stacy and her brother were murdered in a "gangland style" slaying in Las Vegas.

DANNY CASSOLARO - Cassolaro was in the process of writing a book on "The Octopus", a multi-leveled conspiracy of corporate-military control, much of the technocracy for which is being developed at Area 51. The Wackenhut Security Agency, owned and controlled by retired CIA and NSA fascists, is used as a parameter security force to augment the internal Delta Force security for several alien-infiltrated underground bases. Wackenhut and other tentacles of "The Octopus" was to be heavily implicated in the Cassolaro expose, in large part due to former Wackenhut employee and source for inside dirt on the "Inslaw" scandal, Michael Riconosciuto, who was himself convicted and sent to a federal prison on what he claimed were falsified drug charges.

Cassolaro was found murdered in his home, and his research papers and manuscript for his book were nowhere to be found.

JIM KEITH - Keith was an outspoken exposer of the multi-leveled conspiracy involving underground bases, black helicopters, New World Order plans, illegal industrial-military treaties with ETS, aerospace antigravity secrets preserved by deadly force, kidnapping and genetic engineering, experiments which take place "in the black" (in that the alien-corporate monopolies operate under industrial security clearance levels so deep that even congressional regulators cannot access and oversee them), It is a matter of aerospace, petrochemical, and banking monopolies placing those whom they wish into the executive, senatorial, and judicial branches of government...considering themselves to be above the law while imposing the fullness of the letter of the law upon those whom they perceive to be competition to their military-industrial fraternity.

Jim Keith entered a hospital after suffering minor cuts from tripping. He never emerged alive. Many find the events surrounding this death to be highly suspicious, and suspect that foul play was involved.

Robert K Teske

J.R.- This "martyr' is different from others in that this true identity is unknown, save for the initials "J.R." as given in a letter to Paul Shockley in which he describes other nameless martyrs connected with an underground facility near Salt Lake City, Utah.

J.R. was not the first to describe this underground base. For instance, Irvarene Davis of West Valley City, Utah (an abductee herself_ was told by a son-in-;law of hers---who worked in the police department---that he was familiar with a case where a murdered insisted that he had been instructed by "underground" beings to kill a certain person.

Another son-in-law (or the same one?) By the name of Peter, along with her son, Robert, worked as security guards at the crossroads Plaza in downtown Salt Lake City, just one block south of the Mormon Temple. Peter and Robert had learned that when Crossroads Cinemas were being excavated, an ancient tunnel was uncovered, and a worker went in to investigate, but never returned.

Other Salt Lakers have confirmed this account. Todd Jumper of Eaglenet learned of yet another incident where another worker entered the tunnel (behind the right-hand theater in the Crossroads Cinemas?) And while exploring the labyrinthine dungeons below was "attacked" by a a lizard or serpent man." He barely escaped with his life intact, and once the story started making the rounds, the "Feds" came in and reportedly sealed the passage to this real-life dungeon's and dragon's realm.

Peter and Robert themselves claim to have penetrated the underground levels to the 3rd sub-level beneath Crossroads, but turned back, fearful to continue when they came to a door behind which they noticed a strange green Luminescence. In another penetration, Robert and an unnamed friend entered the city's strange system through a manhole and adjacent to the Mall, and made their way down to the 3rd sub-level and, following a tunnel, came to a door that opened into a 300 ft. Long room where they saw men in suits carrying Uzi machine guns. They retraced their steps and made their way down to the 5th sub-level where they emerged into a large cavern in which they saw human-sized yet, 3-toed footprints in the dust, a seemingly bottomless shaft, and a tunnel large enough to drive a semi through strung with lights and leading off in a southerly direction.

JR revealed that one man had reported on a cavern entrance that he knew of in southern Utah which led to this underground "world", where he found remains of a lost Troglodytic race and ancient artifacts including some sort of crystal-based weapons.

This nameless man was murdered in the process of having his secret beat out of him by mob-types (who have reportedly used these ancient caverns of Pennsylvania, Arkansas, Nevada, etc.., to carry out their furtive practices, which according to Richard Shaver is where the term "mob-underworld" had its origin. And with the industrial-Masonic Palladium connections to some levels of the Mafia, we might imagine that organized crime was also in cahoots with subterranean alien influences long before the Illuminati's treaties of 1933 and onward.

JR. spoke of yet another nameless martyr who was a high-up official in the Mormon Church, and who worked in the Granite Mountain "vault" in little Cottonwood Canyon's north slope (first switchback...although two other switchbacks farther up the canyon lead to another access point used by the military and CIA).

This man, as well as other "vault" workers, were aware of a tunnel that led from the depths of the vault into the heart of the mountain, yet they were forbidden access to this tunnel by "U.S. Government: officials who told the vault workers that it was their patriotic duty to keep silent regarding what lay beyond the tunnel. However, on certain occasions, he and other workers observed "gray" aliens with big dark eyes peering from the darkness of the passage as if to observe their activities.

One day, this church official's curiosity got the best of him and he followed the restricted tunnel until he eventually emerged into a huge cavern filled with all kinds of activity, and construction projects were going on everywhere throughout the cavern system which honeycombed the mountains in a seemingly endless network. Amidst of all this, was the sound of the steady drone of machinery. He walked into one "building" and saw humans and fray aliens working at benches on electronic (mind control, etc..) Equipment.

Two military guards apprehended him and took him back outside, and with a DEATH THREAT warned him not to talk about what he had seen. However J.R. stated that something may have happened to this informant, and this prompted him to expose the story to Paul Shockley and others.

J.R. had also learned that, just as with the Dulce base (to the SE) and the Groom Lake Base (to the SW), thousands of men, women and children have been abducted into the underground labs of Utah, to be used to satisfy the perverted sexual addictions of the 33+ Masons or to become the victims of alien experimentation, or worse . . .

The "word" is that a massive cavern system (like described by Betty Andreasson, after having been taken there by the gray alien "Guazgaa") lies beneath Utah's Great Basin, with underground branches reaching into all surrounding states.

An underground sea-lake large enough to be moved by tidal forces fees several underground rivers that run below Nevada and California and eventually emerge into the oceans depths through the continental slope (Kokoweef River, for instance). A large number of human colonists, descended from ancient surface dwellers, once lived in relative security in their underground forming communities until the Dracos, Reptiloids, and Grays moving northward form south and Central America invaded from the South and Central America invaded from the south. Thirty-third (33+) Masons, Jesuits and Nazis who were based in re-animated "Atlantean" strongholds below the east coast, (underneath New York's Church of St.. John, the Divine; Boston's First Church of Roxbury; and the Masonic "House of the Temple" in Washington D.C.) Who were/are in collaboration with the Reptilians, invaded from the East and took control of the underground colonies at about the same time that World War II was raging above. Many of the survivors of this underground war were left at the mercy of the merciless cult of the serpent which has sought to control the world below just as they have the world above. This is why you will find that all terminals or passages between the two worlds are controlled by one form of Masonry or another.

Richard Shaver and others (some say successfully, others unsuccessfully - having come under the psychic influence of the "insiders" who pushed them to extremism, resulting in discredit in the minds of some, or over - fanaticism in the eyes of others) tried to interpret the "surface echoes" of these subterraneous events in the best ways that they knew how, during the height of the "Shaver Mystery" which filled the pages of AMAZING STORIES (science fiction/science fact) magazine for half a decade following WW2, and which gave rise to other publications like FATE, FLYING SAUCERS, SEARCH, HIDDEN WORLD and numerous other UFO organizations which were rooted in the Richard Shaver - Ray Palmer - Kenneth Arnold alliance.

Many in fact consider Ray Palmer to be the father of Ufology, however Palmer himself was inspired by Shavers claims of physical and psychic encounters with both friendly (Tero) and unfriendly (Dero) traglodytic races who were descended from the survivors of Mu and Atlantis, and who were/are at war with each other both under the earth and out in space... Nothing further has been heard from the mysterious "J.R.".

John F. Kennedy - A professed Air Force intelligence agent who did not wish to be named has stated that in early 1963 John F. Kennedy had met with MJ12 member Gordon Gray and told him emphatically that he would "dismember" the CIA (which was jointly founded by the Bavarian Illuminist Allan Dulles and the Nazi S.S. General Reinhardt Gehlen) if they did not cease dealing in international drug traffic to finance their "joint" military - industrial - alien underground base projects.

Later that year John Kennedy lay dead in Dallas Texas (on the 33rd parallel) on Nov. (or 11-22 which equals 33), in a triangulated Masonic style slaying, and fasocialist coup d'état of the U.S. executive government.

Louisiana District Attorney (see the Kevin Costner movie "JFK") James Garrison accused the CIA agent Clay Shaw and his military-industrial collaborator Fred L. Crisman of complicity in the assassination. Crisman just happened to have been a "witness" of the infamous Maurey Island UFO incident near Tacoma, Washington where several donut-shaped antigravity craft (allegedly the product of Nazi-based military industrial technology) had been observed dumping metallic "slag" over the harbor.

Ray Palmer had commissioned Kenneth Arnold to investigate the incident. A conversation he had with an Air Force officer was bugged, and Arnold himself barely escaped a deadly crash near that time when his private plane mysteriously stalled. Arnold incidentally was the first to coin the media phrase "flying saucers" following his own sighting of a formation of crescent - shaped flying discs near Mt.. Ranier, Washington. One reporter investigating the Maurey Island incident died mysteriously, two Army G-2 pilots carrying slag samples to Wright - Patterson AFB in Ohio died when their plane crashed, and strange agents were seen apparently involved in "damage control" following the incident, at the heart of which we find the M.I. agent Crisman, who would turn up almost 15 years later in connection to the JFK assassination. Crisman also was an avid supporter of Nazism by the way.

Shaw, Crisman and others were not convicted largely due the fact that David Ferry, Garrison's star witness, was killed only a few days before the trial was to begin.

Writer John A. Keel revealed some strange UFO type incidents surrounding the JFK assassination, for instance the sighting of unusual "long haired" men in Dealey Plaza (this was before the Beatles brought the "long hair" fad to America), an Oswald look - alike who was seen at a shooting range near Dallas with a rifle that shot at balls of fire at the target, others who heard "voices" in their heads about the death of JFK prior to the actual event, and so on.

According to Jeraldo Rivera, nearly 300 premature deaths of witnesses to the assassination have occurred in the intervening years, deaths which defy the laws of statistics and probability.

In spite of his known marital indiscretions John F. Kennedy (being only human) may nevertheless have been the most notorious of all of the martyrs of the "underground resistance".

RON RUMMELL- "Sometimes people who write controversial books die before the book is released. In early August, 1993, Ron Rummell, also known as Creston, was found dead in a Portland, Oregon park. He had been shot through the mouth and was supposedly holding a gun in his hands. The police called it a suicide and cremated the body the next day without an autopsy and without notifying relatives. He published 'Alien Digest' and was close friends with people who publish 'Revelations of

Awareness.'...On (June 2, 1995) , Fox TV discussed this death because he was writing about the supposed suicide and accidental death of over 30 British scientists working on top secret projects in the British defense industry. These projects included mind control, star wars, and the implantation of devices n the brain without the recipient being aware of this. In some of these 'suicides' the victims were found with their hands and feet bound. While the U.S. press has otherwise refused to cover this story, the British press has had broad coverage.... If the country (U.S.) one day learns how many people have been murdered by the secret government there will be a great shock."

Guradas, "Treason the New World Order." Chapter XVIII, "Murder As a Political Act." Cassandra Press. 1996.

(Note: More details on the above may be accessed via profusion.com. using key search phrases such as: "Phil Schneider Shackles"; "Thomas Castello Dulce"; "Stacy Borland Mercury"; "Danny Cassolaro Wackenhut"; Jim Keith conspiracy"; Granite Mountain aliens"; John Kennedy UFO"; and "Branton" + casualties of a cosmic war" (or) "battles beneath the earth".)

15303001R10310

Made in the USA
Charleston, SC
28 October 2012